T0366231

Utilizing and Managing Commerce and Services Online

Mehdi Khosrow-Pour
Information Resources Management Association, USA

A volume in the Advances in
Electronic Commerce (AEC)
Book Series

Acquisition Editor:	Kristin Klinger
Senior Managing Editor:	Jennifer Neidig
Managing Editor:	Sara Reed
Assistant Managing Editor:	Sharon Berger
Development Editor:	Kristin Roth
Copy Editor:	Holly Powell
Typesetter:	Amanda Appicello
Cover Design:	Lisa Tosheff

Published in the United States of America by
      CyberTech Publishing (an imprint of IGI Global)
      701 E. Chocolate Avenue
      Hershey PA 17033
      Tel: 717-533-8845
      Fax: 717-533-8661
      E-mail: cust@igi-global.com
      Web site: http://www.igi-global.com

Library of Congress Cataloging-in-Publication Data

Utilizing and managing commerce and services online / Mehdi Khosrow-Pour, editor.
    p. cm.
  Summary: "This book provides comprehensive coverage and understanding of the social, cultural, organizational, and cognitive impacts of e-commerce technologies and advances in organizations around the world. E-commerce strategic management, leadership, organizational behavior, development, and employee ethical issues are only a few of the challenges presented in this all-inclusive work"--Provided by publisher.
  Includes bibliographical references and index.
  ISBN 978-1-59140-932-2 (hardcover) -- ISBN 978-1-59140-933-0 (softcover) -- ISBN 978-1-59140-934-9 (ebook) 1. Electronic commerce--Management. 2. Electronic commerce--Technological innovations. 3. Electronic commerce--Computer network resources. 4. Internet. I. Khosrowpour, Mehdi, 1951-
  HF5548.32U85 2007
  658.8'72--dc22
                       2006032166

This book is published in the IGI Global book series Advances in Electronic Commerce (AEC) Book Series (ISSN: 1935-2921; eISSN: 1935-293X)

British Cataloguing in Publication Data
A Cataloguing in Publication record for this book is available from the British Library.

Advances in Electronic Commerce (AEC) Book Series

Mehdi Khosrow-Pour (Information Resources Management Association, USA)

ISSN: 1935-2921
EISSN: 1935-293X

MISSION

The impact of information technology on commerce is a dynamic and perpetually evolving field of research, most notably as electronic approaches for business transactions shift to the Internet and other telecommunication networks. Given the rapid advancements in the field, research addressing e-commerce and its related areas needs an outlet to reach its audience.

The **Advances in Electronic Commerce (AEC)** series provides comprehensive coverage and understanding of the social, cultural, organizational, and cognitive impacts of e-commerce technologies. The series provides accounts from both the consumer perspective and the organization perspective. AEC aims to expand the body of knowledge regarding e-commerce technologies and applications, thus assisting researchers and practitioners to develop more effective systems.

COVERAGE

- Commerce strategy
- Digital economy
- Electronic banking
- Mobile commerce
- Online marketplaces
- Social media & e-commerce
- Virtual marketplaces
- Virtual storefronts
- Web commerce

IGI Global is currently accepting manuscripts for publication within this series. To submit a proposal for a volume in this series, please contact our Acquisition Editors at Acquisitions@igi-global.com or visit: http://www.igi-global.com/publish/.

Titles in this Series

For a list of additional titles in this series, please visit: www.igi-global.com

Virtual Worlds and E-Commerce Technologies and Applications for Building Customer Relationships
Barbara Ciaramitaro (Ferris State University, USA)
Business Science Reference • copyright 2011 • 399pp • H/C (ISBN: 9781616928087) • US $180.00 (our price)

Consumer Behavior, Organizational Development, and Electronic Commerce Emerging Issues for Advancing Modern Socioeconomies
Mehdi Khosrow-Pour (Information Resources Management Association, USA)
Information Science Reference • copyright 2009 • 410pp • H/C (ISBN: 9781605661261) • US $195.00 (our price)

Outsourcing and Offshoring of Professional Services Business Optimization in a Global Economy
Amar Gupta (University of Arizona, USA)
Information Science Reference • copyright 2008 • 438pp • H/C (ISBN: 9781599049724) • US $180.00 (our price)

Commerce in Space Infrastructures, Technologies, and Applications
Phillip Olla (Madonna University, USA)
Information Science Reference • copyright 2008 • 400pp • H/C (ISBN: 9781599046242) • US $180.00 (our price)

E-Commerce in Regional Small to Medium Enterprises
Robert MacGregor (University of Wollongong, Australia) and Lejla Vrazalic (University of Wollongong in Dubai, UAE)
Idea Group Publishing • copyright 2007 • 428pp • H/C (ISBN: 9781599041230) • US $99.95 (our price)

www.igi-global.com

701 E. Chocolate Ave., Hershey, PA 17033
Order online at www.igi-global.com or call 717-533-8845 x100
To place a standing order for titles released in this series,
contact: cust@igi-global.com
Mon-Fri 8:00 am - 5:00 pm (est) or fax 24 hours a day 717-533-8661

Utilizing and Managing Commerce and Services Online

Table of Contents

Preface

In the time of ceaseless technological reform, e-commerce has materialized as an indispensable element for contemporary educators, researchers, and professionals. In order to remain the vanguard of the information era, a source of the latest research regarding e-commerce, e-business, and e-government has emerged to provide the most recent discoveries, advancements, and implementations. *Utilizing and Managing Commerce and Services Online*, part of the *Advances in Electronic Commerce Series*, uncovers the rewarding prospects associated with the adaptation of e-technologies for business, academic circles, and global organizations, while exposing the most effective strategies in employing them worldwide.

Chapter I, *Managing Online Customer Service Operations,* by David Barnes, Royal Holloway, University of London (UK) and Matthew Hinton, Open University Business School (UK), investigates the implications of moving customer service operations online. Many organizations believe that e-business can provide opportunities to improve customer service operations by enabling them to get closer to the customer and enhance the customer contact experience. However, use of the Internet fundamentally changes the nature of a customer's interaction with an organization, as the customer interacts with a computer screen rather than a human being. The online customer service encounter within the business processes of ordering and delivering was investigated in eight companies. It was concluded that an enhanced experience was only likely if the emotional aspects of customer service are considered alongside the functional.

Chapter II, *Firm Value Effects of Web Site Redesign,* by Raquel Benbunan-Fich, Baruch College, CUNY (USA) and Eliezer M. Fich, Drexel University (USA) uses the event study methodology on a sample of Web site redesigns from 1995 to 1999 to investigate the types of commercial organizations that announce changes to their Web presence and to study whether such redesign initiatives affect the value of publicly traded firms. Our findings indicate that, on average, refining a Web presence does not produce significant firm valuation adjustments. However, cross-sectional analyses reveal that Web site redesign increases firm value in service companies.

Chapter III, *Jurisdiction in B2C E-Commerce Dispute within the European Union,* by Ong Chin Eang, Monash University (Malaysia), discusses how e-commerce jurisdiction has always been an issue because e-commerce exists in a borderless environment, and this e-environment diminishes the importance of physical location and locality. The current jurisdictions by the European Commission (EC) within the European Union (EU), The E-Commerce Directive—Country of Origin and Rome II are still in the drafting process. These legislations are not the total solution. This paper reviews the issue of current jurisdiction, whether there is a need to call for a single jurisdiction, and what complications arise when seeking redress in this borderless e-environment. This paper also raises important issues that relate to the gaps and loopholes that exist in Country of Origin and Rome II.

Chapter IV, *Failures of B2C Retailing: A Services Industry View,* by Anil Pandya, Northeastern Illinois University (USA) and Nikhilesh Dholakia, University of Rhode Island (USA), discusses how conceptualizing B2C businesses as an innovative class of technology-infused services yield insights into the factors that may lead to success or failure of such businesses. Drawing from services' marketing literature and recent thinking on Internet service metrics, this paper presents a framework for analyzing B2C businesses.

Chapter V, *Inducing Online Trust in E-Commerce: Empirical Investigations on Web Design Factors,* by Ye Diana Wang, George Mason University (USA) and Henry H. Emurian, University of Maryland, Baltimore County (UMBC) (USA), describes how two studies were undertaken to investigate interface design features that might impact customers' trust in an e-commerce vendor's Web site. In a first quantitative survey study, experienced Internet users rated 14 features of a synthetic e-commerce interface for their trust-inducing effectiveness. Users' reports from interviews generally supported the importance of socially rich Web sites in promoting online trust, and they deepened our understanding of the functionalities and suitability of various communication media for the adoption of virtual re-embedding strategies. The complementary outcomes from both quantitative and qualitative sources of information are anticipated to contribute to future applications and research in e-commerce interface design considerations affecting online trust.

Chapter VI, *Public Perception—A Newspaper Medium Perspective: E-Commerce in Australian Manufacturing (Revisited),* by Jing Gao, University of South Australia (Australia), describes how major Australian newspapers were examined for public discussions about e-commerce in manufacturing industries. The political-legal, economic, social, and technological (PEST) framework was used as a lens to subdivide issues, problems, and opportunities identified in the academic e-commerce literature. This lens was then used to examine 103 newspaper articles identified using the keywords "Australian manufacturing" and "e-commerce" in what was believed to be all the major Australian newspapers. It was found that some articles merely report vendors' promises of potential cost savings while overlooking the need for investment in technology, training, and maintenance costs, while other discussions focused on "users as victims" issues such as security and privacy. In-depth issues such as reliability, communication protocols, bandwidth availability, and integration problems were overlooked. In particular, the problem of business strategies was ignored.

Chapter VII, *Netrepreneur Simulation—The Development of Realism in Virtual E-Entrepreneurship Learning,* by Salim Jiwa, The Manchester Metropolitan University (UK) and Dawn Lavelle and Arjun Rose, University of the Arts London (UK), reviews the pedagogic requirements of entrepreneurial education within one specific context of e-commerce. Netrepreneur simulates the initial start-up phases of e-business creation and, through the modeling and electronic simulation of the e-commerce environment, it aims to create a holistic understanding of the entrepreneurial process as well as encouraging participants to learn by doing. This paper documents the underpinning objectives of design conceptualization and the integration of the real and virtual worlds within system development. The latter section of the paper reports on the user survey responses to Netrepreneur, which demonstrates a strong sense of presence experienced by participants. The sense of presence experienced by learners in a virtual environment can be considered to be a key feature in ensuring the efficacy of learning and the following transfer of knowledge and skills from the learning context to the "real world."

Chapter VIII, *Conceptualizing Failed B2C Dotcoms as Innovation Failures,* by Anil M. Pandya, Northeastern Illinois University (USA) and Nikhilesh Dholakia, University of Rhode Island (USA), covers how the 1998 to 2003 "dotcom bust," had many Internet-based Business-to-Consumer (B2C) companies failing to fulfill their initial and alluring promises. Concepts derived from the investigation of product and services innovation failures can provide a valuable strategic market framework to understand why so many dotcom B2C ventures crashed so fast. Early B2C ventures represented an entirely new class of technology-driven services. These B2C dotcoms sought to inform, promote, sell, and deliver consumer items in radically unfamiliar ways. In doing so, many B2C firms did not follow time-tested business precepts. In particular, the failed B2C firms did not realize they were marketing innovative services. Our framework uses the continuum of need-solution context in conjunction with the notion that seller/buyer perceptions about the scope of innovations are not necessarily concordant. Matched or "concordant" perceptions lead to success, and mismatched or "discordant" perceptions often breed failures. Using short cases and historical data, this chapter illustrates the explanatory power of the framework.

Chapter IX, *Implementation of Privacy Protection Policies: An Empirical Per-spective,* by Noushin Ashrafi and Jean-Pierre Kuilboer, University of Massachusetts (USA), attempts to examine privacy issues in the context of fair information practices and how they are perceived and practiced by the top 500 interactive companies in the United States. Our results confirm that most companies ask for consumer trust by claiming benevolence. However, they fall short when it comes to costly implementations of comprehensive privacy protection policies.

Chapter X, *Design Considerations in the Development of an Online Course in E-Business,* by Wing Lam, U21 Global (Singapore), describes how U21 Global (U21G), an e-university formed by a consortium of traditional brick-and-mortar universities, approached the design of MBA650, its online course in e-business. MBA650 is a core course in U21G's MBA program. Gagne's theory, a pedagogical framework taken from the literature, is used to frame and explain the rationale for the design of MBA650. Gagne's theory identifies a number of instructional events including the identification of learning objectives, presentation of content, provision of learner guidance, feedback, and performance assessment. An evaluation of MBA650 based on student feedback is presented. Finally, several key design considerations in the development of e-business courses are discussed, such as including attention-to-learning outcomes, the student audience, syllabus, key messages, theory versus practice, team working, and the use of case studies.

Chapter XI, *E-Recruiting System Development and Architecture,* by In Lee, Western Illinois University (USA), proposes six categories of e-recruiting sources and presents the architecture of the next-generation, holistic e-recruiting system. This architecture consists of eight distinct yet interrelated subsystems: (1) applicant tracking management subsystem; (2) job requisition management subsystem; (3) job agent management subsystem; (4) prescreening/self-assessment management subsystem; (5) e-recruiting performance analysis subsystem; (6) candidate relationship management subsystem; (7) workflow management subsystem; and (8) database management subsystem.

Chapter XII, *Lessons Learned from EDI and Its Impact on Institutional Trust in Electronic Marketplaces,* by Pauline Ratnasingam, Central Missouri State University (USA), David Gefen, Drexel University (USA) and Paul A. Pavlou, University of California, Riverside (USA), examines the role of institutional trust, which has been viewed as a key facilitator of electronic marketplaces (Pavlou, Tan, & Gefen, 2003). In doing so, we draw upon the principles of research on traditional EDI via Value-Added Networks to develop a set of theory-driven, institutional trust-building, facilitating conditions, namely IT connectivity, standards, security and, uniform product descriptions. This study has implications for (1) the nature and role of institutional trust in e-marketplaces, (2) the strategic design of trust-building mechanisms in e-marketplaces, and (3) an extension of the literature on institutional trust.

Chapter XIII, *Digital Watermarking and Its Impact on Intellectual Property Limitation for the Digital Age,* by Tino Jahnke and Juergen Seitz, University of Cooperative Education Heidenheim (Germany), gives an overview about the basic ideas of watermarking, application for e-business, problems, and limitations. Digital media like audio and video images and other multimedia documents can be protected against copyright infringements with invisible, integrated patterns. Such methods based on steganography and digital watermarking techniques. Most watermarks are inserted as a plain-bit or adjusted digital signal using a key-based embedding algorithm. The embedded information is hidden (in low-value bits or least significant bits of picture pixels, frequency, or other value domains) and linked inseparably with the source data structure. For the optimal watermarking application a trade-off between competing criteria like robustness, nonperceptibility, nondetectability, and security have to be made. Most watermarking algorithms are not resistant against all attacks, and even friendly attacks like file and data modifications can destroy the watermark very easily.

Chapter XIV, *Framework for User Perception of Effective E-Tail Web Sites,* by Sang M. Lee, University of Nebraska–Lincoln (USA), Pairin Katerattanakul, Western Michigan University (USA) and Soongoo Hong, Dong-A University (Korea), presents the development of an empirically validated framework for users' perception of effective Web sites for retail e-commerce (Etail). In particular, we attempted to answer the main research questions: What are the major designs determining Etail Web site effectiveness? How do these designs support Web users' objectives in using the Web? Based on the concept of "fitness for use" and the reasons that consumers use the Web, we proposed that "effective designs for Etail Web sites should support Web customers for their: information search, pleasure, and business transactions." Then, data were collected from a survey on 427 potential Web customers. An exploratory analysis was conducted to refine the proposed framework and to provide structure of the constructs in the framework to be validated by a following confirmatory analysis.

Chapter XV, *E-Commerce Education in China: Driving Forces, Status, and Strategies,* by Xianfeng Zhang and Qi Li, Xi'an Jiaotong University (China) and Zhangxi Lin, Texas Tech University (USA), investigates whether the education system in China well accords with the market demand and the status of e-commerce programs in China, so as to seek for the strategies for China to cope with the challenges from the global e-commerce empowered by fast updated information technologies. First, we construct a four-layer conceptual model to describe the relevant factors influencing e-commerce and e-commerce education. We then present the status of China's e-commerce education in different educational categories. Although we find that current problems in China's e-commerce education can be resorted in quantity and quality aspects, it is generally on the right track. Finally, we propose several main strategies for promoting the development of e-commerce education, in which the education system reformation is of the top priority and the government will play a critical role.

The prevalence and magnitude of e-commerce continues to accelerate, and its developing importance in the information age persists. The utilization of e-technologies has secured itself as a front-runner for adoption by all competitive modern organizations, researchers, and educators. The foremost contributors to information technology will find that the *Advanced Topics in Electronic Commerce* series provides the mechanism essential for adaptation and insight into the growing e-commerce field. As an exemplary compilation of the most recently discovered tools associated with e-commerce, e-business, and e-government, *Utilizing and Managing Commerce and*

Services Online serves as a pertinent resource for the most up-to-date examination of e-technologies and their rapidly intensifying function in the technological era of today.

Mehdi Khosrow-Pour, D.B.A.
Editor-in-Chief
Utilizing and Managing Commerce and Services Online
Advances in Electronic Commerce Series

References

Pavlou, P. A., Tan, Y. H., & Gefen, D. (2003). The transitional role of institutional trust in online inter-organizational relationships. *Hawaii Information Systems Science Conference.*

Chapter I

Managing Online Customer Service Operations

David Barnes, Royal Holloway, University of London, UK

Matthew Hinton, Open University of Business School, UK

Abstract

This chapter investigates the implications of moving customer service operations online. Many organizations believe that e-business can provide opportunities to improve customer service operations by enabling them to get closer to the customer and enhance the customer contact experience. However, use of the Internet fundamentally changes the nature of a customer's interaction with an organization, as the customer interacts with a computer screen rather than a human being. The online customer service encounter within the business processes of ordering and delivering was investigated in eight companies. It was concluded that an enhanced experience was only likely if the emotional aspects of customer service are considered alongside the functional.

Introduction

As marketplaces have become more global and customers more demanding, many companies have realized the importance of improving customer service (Ngash, Ryan, & Igbari, 2003). It has become increasingly difficult for any business in a developed economy, whether a manufacturer or a service provider, to compete on cost alone. A sustainable competitive advantage is only likely to result from strategies of differentiation—offering a product or service package that is perceived by customers to add value, and/or focus—targeting a specific market segment that the organization is well placed to serve (Porter, 1980, 1985). The ability to offer an enhanced level of customer service could play an indispensable part of such strategies (Kardaras & Papathanassiou, 2000; Talley & Axelroth, 2001). Companies have increasingly moved many aspects of their customer service online—seeking to take advantage of the almost limitless connectivity, between both organizations and individuals that the Internet and its associated information and communications technologies (ICTs) of e-business can offer. Company Web sites have now become an important medium through which organizations and their customers can interact (Piccoli, Brohman, Watson, & Parasuraman, 2004). Zeithaml (2002) points out that "Companies are using the web to enhance communications with customers, to sell more products and services through an alternative channel, and to reduce the costs of interacting with customers" (p.135). Similarly, Voss (2003 p.88) argues that "the advent of e-commerce has led to a rethink of the nature of customer service" as organizations can enhance their customer service operations by enabling them to get closer to the customer enhancing the organization-customer contact experience.

The ICTs of e-business are becoming ubiquitous due to their low cost and widespread availability. As such, their use seems unlikely to afford a competitive advantage of itself. As Porter (2001) argues, the Internet is "an enabling technology—a powerful set of tools that can be used, wisely or unwisely, in almost any industry and as part of any strategy" (p.64). The challenge for organizations of all kinds, is how best to utilize Internet-based ICTs within their operations in order to enhance their customer service operations.

This chapter reports on research that investigated the impact of e-business on customer service operations in eight companies that are using e-business in their ordering and delivery processes. The research takes an operations management perspective, examining the customer service encounter from the service deliverer's point of view. The chapter opens by reviewing relevant literature to identify key aspects of the customer service encounter that can provide a basis for the analysis of these online operations. The results from the case studies are then reported and discussed. General conclusions are drawn about the likelihood of enhancing customer service through the use of e-business, the barriers to so doing, and what needs to be done to ensure that these processes can better serve customers. The chapter closes by pointing the way to future research.

Literature

The widespread availability and subsequent adoption of the Internet for commercial use is generally referred to as e-business. Although there are a number of different definitions of e-business, its essence is captured by Poon and Swatman (1999), who argue that e-business is "the sharing of business information, maintaining business relationships and conducting business transactions by means of Internet-based technology." E-business transactions can occur between an organization and its customers, suppliers, and intermediaries in the supply chain. (NB Unlike some authors [e.g., Chaffey, 2002], we do not seek to distinguish between e-commerce and e-business and use the terms more or less interchangeably.)

The academic discipline of operations management views organizational activity as a series of business processes that transform resource input into outputs of goods and/or services within an operating system—for producing physical goods or delivering services (Slack, Chambers, & Johnston, 2001). Operations management literature typically distinguishes between two elements of the operations system: (1) structure—the physical aspects, especially the nature, extent, and scope of its technology; and (2) infrastructure—the way in which the operations system is managed (Hayes & Wheelwright, 1984). In customer service operations, it is the customer who is transformed; the service delivery system changes the customer's physical and/or psychological state. Service operations management writers characterize customer service operations as a series of contacts between the customer and the service delivery system (Johnston, 1987; Shostack, 1984). Great emphasis is placed on the design and management of those points in the delivery system in which the customer interacts directly with the service deliverer—often termed *moments of truth*. Existing models of customer service operations are primarily predicated on a face-to-face or at least voice-to-voice encounter with the customer. Assessing the quality of the service within these encounters is typically problematic as many aspects are highly subjective in nature. Parasuraman, Zeithaml, and Berry (1985) identify 10 dimensions of service quality in face-to-face customer service operations. Of these, only one focuses on the tangible elements of service delivery, whereas the other nine are all intangibles (reliability, responsiveness, competence, courtesy, credibility, security, access, communication, and understanding the customer). Customer service operations must satisfy customers' psychological needs as much as their physical needs. As such, they are reliant as much upon the staff as the technology of the delivery system.

However, the use of the Internet in e-business fundamentally changes the nature of the organization's contact with its customers. Customers now interact with a computer screen rather than a human being. The service deliverer has no control over any other physical elements of the service delivery system. The entire customer encounter takes place within the confines and constraints of the customer's ICT. Most service operations management literature is predicated on service delivery systems with real rather than virtual customer encounters. As yet, there have been few attempts to consider the impact of Internet only encounters on the management of service operations. Furthermore, as Westbrook and Peterson (1998) point out, most of the extant service literature is "grounded and tested on theory rooted at the retail customer level" (p.51). There is a relative paucity of literature that attempts to engage customer service issues from the perspective of organizational customers within the supply chain. Considering customers only as individual consumers in e-business is remiss as the value of business to business (B2B) online transactions far outweighs that of business to consumer (B2C). For example, the most recently available official UK figures estimate that for every £100 of sales over the Internet £25 were to households, while £75 were to businesses (Office for National Statistics, 2005).

It seems clear that the use of the Internet-based technologies that constitute the online environment requires a reconsideration of elements of customer service in e-business. Bitner, Brown, and Meuter (2000) argue that the Internet makes the service encounter more complex and there have been calls for more research into the impact of ICT on customer service (e.g., Parasuraman & Grewal, 2000). One such study assessed the quality of online customer service to be poor and inconsistent in many industries, including those that might be expected to be more customer orientated like travel and retail (Lennon & Harris, 2002).

There is as yet, no agreed method for evaluating the quality of customer interaction with a Web site. One approach is offered by the WEBQUAL instrument developed by Barnes and Vidgen (2002). They have adapted Parasuraman, Zeithaml, and Berry's (1988) well-known SERVQUAL instrument to the online environment by adding questions on usability and information quality. However, like SERVQUAL, WEBQUAL assesses the customer service delivery system interaction from the customer's perspective. From the service provider's perspective it may be more enlightening to follow Walsh and Godfrey (2000) in simply distinguishing between the *functional* and the *emotional* as the dimensions of customer service in e-business. These two terms seem to equate to the hard/soft, structure/infrastructure, tangible/intangible dichotomy of the off-line world. In this vein, Parasuraman et al.'s (1985) 10 elements of service can be recast in accordance with their impact on the customer service encounter (see Table 1).

Arguably, *reliability, responsiveness, competence, access,* and *tangibles* seem to relate to the functional dimension. In the Internet environment, these are tangible rather than intangible elements, which can be assessed elements using objective rather

Table 1. Parasuraman et al.'s (1985) service elements in the online environment

Functional	Emotional
Reliability	Courtesy
Responsiveness	Communication
Competence	Credibility
Access	Security
Tangibles	Understanding the customer

than subjective performance measures. For example, Voss (2003), demonstrates how responsiveness can be determined. In the online service encounter these elements are primarily technology dominated and determined. They facilitate communication and information dissemination and gathering. They particularly rely upon the ICT hardware and software available to the customer and the design and maintenance of the Web site. On the other hand, *courtesy, communication, credibility, security,* and *understanding the customer* seem more related to the emotional, as they are human dominated and determined. These remain intangible elements that can only be assessed subjectively by the customer.

The interplay between the functional and emotional aspects of customer service is likely to have an impact on the success of the customer's online encounter with the organization. If the functional factors operate effectively, then so can the emotional. Similarly, where the emotional factors operate well, customers may be more tolerant of functional (i.e., technical) problems. However, many firms seem to use ICT merely to address and enhance functional elements (Domegan, 1996), mainly in efforts to improve efficiency and reduce costs. Much of the effort to improve customer Web site interactions has primarily concentrated on functionality (Lightner, 2004). Yet, effective engagement with the emotional elements of customer service also seems likely to affect customers' willingness to interact, goodwill, positive feedback, loyalty, and so forth. In their study, Dadzie, Chelariu, and Winston (2005) show that Web site features that address the emotional dimension by supplementing or reducing the imper- sonal nature of online customer service improves customer satisfaction significantly, more than improving functional efficiency. Furthermore, online customer service is a two-way dynamic between customer and service provider. As Laudon and Traver (2002) point out, online customer service is "more than simply following through on order fulfillment; it has to do with users' ability to communicate with a company and obtain desired information in a timely manner" (p.386). Equally, companies are reliant on information provided by customers in order to improve and enhance their service. Such information can be captured through the use of customer relationship management (CRM) systems, chatrooms, intelligent agents, automated response systems, and the like, that companies can use to encourage customer interaction. Such tools can be used not only to enhance functional linkages between producers and customers, but also to strengthen emotional linkages. In the virtual as much as the real world, achieving high levels of satisfaction in customer service operations still holds the key to realizing a sustainable competitive advantage. In e-business, this seems likely to depend on how organizations use technology to enhance their customer service operations as part of their business strategy.

Research Methodology

This research investigated how organizations might create a competitive advantage through the use of Internet-based ICTs to enhance customer service. To do this, the business processes of order fulfillment and delivery were studied in organizations engaged in e-business. The main objective was to identify current emerging practice. It should be noted that the study focused on the service encounter from the organization's perspective and no attempt was made to assess it from the customer perspective. Like much initial e-business research, this study was exploratory and primarily descriptive in nature. This is perhaps unavoidable, for as Christensen and Sundahl (2001) note, at the earliest stages of research "the best that researchers can do is to observe phenomena, and to carefully describe and record what they see" (p.1).

The level of detail required for such a study is almost certainly best achieved through a case study approach. A case study is "an objective in-depth examination of a contemporary phenomenon within some real-life context where the investigator has little control over events" (Yin, 1994). Qualitative case studies also have the advantage of facilitating a contextual understanding of actions and meanings (Bryman, 1988). Research in operations management (OM) has a strong quantitative tradition. However, recent years have witnessed a greater variety in the choice of both research subjects and methods. Many OM researchers have argued for more qualitative case study work (e.g., McCutcheon & Meredith, 1993; Meredith, 1998). However, Voss, Tsikriktsis, and Frohlich (2002) note their greater use in Europe compared to the U.S.

Data gathering in this study was principally affected via semi-structured interviews with relevant company executives. For the smaller companies, the managing director (in the cases of Clothingco and E-Accounting) or other relevant directors (in the cases of Legalco and Shareco) were interviewed. For the larger companies, managers with responsibilities for e-business operations were interviewed (two each in the cases of Rebankco and Metalco and one each in the cases of Equipco and Creditinsure). The interviews, which were conducted in 2001 and 2002, were typically of between 1 and 2 hours duration. This enabled relevant and interesting issues to be explored in some depth, as they emerged. Questions were based on a theoretical framework that focuses attention on the organization's business processes, its supporting information systems, and its business context (Barnes, Hinton, & Mieczkowska, 2002).

Interviews were recorded for subsequent transcription and analysis. Interview data were supplemented by company documentation. All interviews were conducted at company premises, which enabled valuable additional contextual data to be collected through observation. Subsequent phone, e-mail, and letter contacts with interviewees also provided further data. Although limited in scope, this use of multiple sources served to enhance understanding and improve the validity of the interview data. The findings from each case were then compared in cross-case analysis to deepen understanding and explanation (Miles & Huberman, 1994). The analysis particularly focused on identifying and distinguishing between the functional and the emotional dimensions of customer service in e-business.

As access to the organizations was a prerequisite for this study, a major criterion for case selection was willingness on the part of the companies to provide sustained access for interview purposes. The eight case companies constitute, in essence, a convenience sample and one not intended to be representative in any statistical sense. Unlike quantitative research, which uses statistical inference to generalize from a sample to a larger population, qualitative research relies on logical inference. As Yin (1994) points out "case studies are generalizable to theoretical propositions and not populations" (p.10). Where there is more than one case, replication logic can be used to generalize more widely. It is difficult to generalize from a limited number of cases. However, their findings can offer a basis for subsequent testing using quantitative methods, as part of the "normal cycle of research" in which explanation can be built from description, which can in turn be tested as part of an iterative theory building process (Meredith, Raturi, Amoako-Gympah, & Kaplan, 1989).

Results

This section provides a brief description of the empirical findings from each of the eight case companies included in this study. Pseudonyms are used for all case companies, and some case details are disguised to protect company confidentiality. The companies encompassed manufacturers (metal goods and industrial equipment) as well as service providers (clothing retailing, retail banking, financial management, legal services, share-trading, and credit insurance). There were examples of both B2B and B2C markets being served.

Clothingco

Clothingco is a small company that sells specialist clothing, mainly aimed at the older customer as well as those who may have requirements that few other suppliers can meet. It began life as a mail order business in 1999, but very quickly perceived that the Internet could be a major new business channel to help reach customers who find it difficult or undesirable to visit retail stores that supply these types of products. The company still retains its printed catalog alongside its on-line operations, and customers can order online, by phone, or by mail. Because of some initial inappropriate technology choices, there are problems in integrating customer information received from different channels, and data have to be manu-ally reintegrated into the company's information systems. Because its suppliers do not use electronic ordering, Clothingco finds it difficult to monitor supplier stocks (e.g., due to supplier stock shortages or discontinued lines), so it sometimes finds that it cannot supply its customers as quickly as it would like. Use of its online shopping facility enables Clothingco to respond rapidly and individually to every e-mail received and track all communication with individual customers. Although the company itself has some problems with functionality due to inadequacies in some aspects of its technology, this is restricted to its internal business processes. Adoption of e-business has enabled the company to achieve considerable improve-ments in the functional dimension of customer service. In particular it can now offer improved access and responsiveness to those customers that choose to buy over the Internet. Clothingco also seems to be trying to improve the emotional dimension of customer service. At a basic level, its online catalog enables its Web site visitors to look into a virtual shop window, hopefully thereby stirring some positive emotions. The company is trying to deepen its relationship with its customers, by targeted marketing initiatives in the form of personalized e-mails and letters. However, at present the customer base is too small to afford very much in the way of reliable information about customer behavior and purchasing patterns. However, like many online traders, Clothingco is aware that some customers are nervous about ordering and paying online. They hope that such security fears can be allayed as successful transactions build customer confidence.

Rebankco CMO

Rebankco CMO is the central mortgage office of a large retail bank. Previously, customers applying for a loan needed to visit their local branch office to complete an application form manually, which would then be posted to CMO. Alternatively, customers could telephone their details directly to CMO, whose operators would complete an online application form for them. As part of Rebankco's move to In-ternet banking, it is now attempting to move some of its mortgage services online via its Web site. However, this only has a "call me" button to trigger a telephone call to the customer from the central mortgage office. While this is a primitive use of the technology, it is conceivable that customers may like this personal response. Rebankco CMO does accept online applications from one of its subsidiaries (a recently acquired competitor). Because of internal information system integration problems, all applications however received (online, by telephone, or by mail), must be manually rekeyed by the bank's operators into its own system. These technological problems do not currently have high priority in Rebankco because of other business investment requirements. Although, arguably, most of Rebankco's problems with functionality primarily affect its internal operations, it also seems likely that they also impact its customer service operations, because customers accessing the Bank's services via its Web site are likely to expect to submit their application online, rather than have to do so over the phone. The bank does seem to have a clear view of the importance of customer service and is willing to develop its online processes. For example, it is making efforts to make its application process more responsive by using electronic process for property valuation and credit verification. However, because Rebankco retains multi-channel access for its mortgage applicants (they can complete a paper application at a branch, by phone, or on the Web site), there seems to be a greater possibility for error or loss of information in the handling of customer applications. This risks a worse level of functionality in customer service. There is little or no indication that Rebankco has recognized the emotional dimension to customer service, and it is not possible to detect any deliberate actions being taken to address these issues in the online environment.

Metalco

Metalco is a major European metals producer serving a specialist market of relatively few customers. It has developed an industry portal in conjunction with a number of its European competitors. The portal is a one-stop shopping facility offering multiple products to users, specifiers, and buyers by facilitating access to all the participating companies' Web sites. Its intention is to enable all the participating companies to compete more effectively with rival producers in other parts of the world and discourage use of products made from alternative materials. Metalco's own Web site provides customers with a wide range of facilities. They can make enquiries; request and receive quotations; place orders; receive acknowledgements; test certificates; dispatch notes and invoices; register order queries and complaints (whether these concern the quantity or quality of goods dispatched); and track and trace their orders in the manufacturing process. The company hopes its Web site will offer an improved service to its customers, adding value for its customers, thereby encouraging customer loyalty. Although cost reduction remains vital in its highly competitive global markets, Metalco hopes its Web-based services will differentiate itself from its competitors by maximizing customer access to information. The main focus of Metalco's efforts to improve customer service through its Web site is clearly on functionality, seemingly aimed particularly at improving reliability, responsiveness, and access. However, its online actions may also be addressing some aspects of the emotional dimension. Its own Web site certainly improves the level of communication with its customers and the information that can be captured seems likely to improve its understanding of customers. Also, the industry portal may well provide additional credibility and an improved sense of security to customers.

E-Accounting

E-Accounting is a small financial management company established early in 2000 as a dot-com. The company acts as an outsourced finance and accounting function for its clients, who are mostly small and medium-sized enterprises (SMEs), often technology or service based. It also provides some financial consultancy services. Although originally conceived as an entirely online model, e-accounting has had to become a clicks-and-mortar operation because so many of its clients wanted to retain face-to-face dealing. This appears to be partly in response to post-crash skepticism about dot-coms, but more specifically because some prospective clients were very wary of supplying accounting information online. Technology and integration also have been, and remain, key issues. The company's own internal systems are not yet fully integrated because it has been unable to find an appropriate software package. There are also external integration problems because many of its clients' banks have inadequate or incompatible software and technology platforms. E-Accounting appreciates that legacy systems and the costs of changing them are a considerable expense and investment of time and training for its clients. As such it recognizes that it needs to work with the available systems, in tandem with its clients. Being a small business itself, it can empathize with clients about their own particular needs and concerns, particularly having to work with severe financial constraints. The way forward lies both in finding the right technological solution and making the investment commitment to that solution. Despite the problems with technical functionality that e-accounting experienced both internally and externally, it seems that the emotional dimension has presented the biggest problems to using the Internet to enhance customer service. Customers' concerns seem to center on the credibility and security of an online only accounting service provider. As such, in order to address these concerns (and stay in business), e-accounting was forced to move to a clicks-and-mortar model.

Legalco

Legalco is a London based dot-com, providing online legal advice and services, set up by lawyers concerned to make the law more accessible and affordable. Its Web site hosts some free legal information. It also offers a fixed-price e-mail, legal advice service for matters such as employment, family, motoring, housing, and accident law. It sells personalized legal documents (such as wills, tenancy agreements, etc.)

via the Web site. Use of the Internet facilitates 24-hour access to Legalco's services, albeit at a basic level. The Web site also acts as a conduit to other legal services, for both individuals and companies. It can provide a range of prepackaged, fixed-priced legal packages (e.g., conveyancing, divorce proceedings including face-to-face consultations, court representation, etc.). Most clients choose to pay a single annual fee, which allows them to call upon a pool of legal services as required. Most of these services are provided by law firms that are local to the clients. Legalco block purchases legal services from law firms across the UK and works closely with them to ensure the quality of their provision. As a well-funded dot-com start-up, it was able to develop its own bespoke information systems, which, although subsequently modified in the light of greater customer knowledge, have provided a high level of functionality. In fact, for a dot-com start-up, Legalco appears to have remarkably few problems with this dimension of customer service. Its online model also attempts to address the emotional dimension as well, for example, by offering initial anonymity to clients who may be reluctant or nervous in their initial approach for legal assistance. Its increased level of understanding of its customers gained from its Internet operations has enabled it to experiment with its customer service operations in order to improve its offering. It is also experimenting with how best to seek feedback from customers about their experience, using follow-up e-mails and phone calls.

Shareco

Shareco is a London-based share dealer, primarily trading stocks in small and medium-sized companies. Originally the company offered only telephone-based trading, mostly to corporate institutional clients. It introduced its own Web site to facilitate online dealing, aimed primarily at small private investors. Its corporate clients continue to deal mostly by phone. Shareco believes online trading might attract investors from around the world. It sees private investors as a potentially high growth market that can be best served by online trading where it can create "stickiness" through both familiarity with, and ease of use of the technology. To be commercially successful, online trading will need to achieve high volumes, as private investor trades are generally a low margin business. All business, whether obtained through conventional or electronic channels, is handled by its traders operating in its dealing room. The heavy investment in IT made for online trading has facilitated significant efficiency gains, particularly in back office operations, which support its low cost online model. Shareco seems to have had few problems with the functionality dimension of customer service. However, it seems to have done little to address the emotional dimension.

Equipco

Equipco manufactures a range of industrial equipment used mostly in fluid process-ing applications. Its products are technically complex, its customers geographically dispersed, and it sells primarily through local intermediaries who can offer the level of expertise necessary to ensure that customers order the most appropriate equipment for their requirements. Previously, its intermediaries made enquiries and placed orders via letter, fax, or e-mail. Company engineers would advise on product selection us-ing paper-based product performance data. These processes of equipment selection, quotation, and order entry have now been replaced by a Web-based software tool. This is installed on a personal computer, normally that of the intermediary, although some customers have also installed it. Thus, the software tool supports Equipco's intermediaries, ensures the best technical solutions, and reduces lead times and costs. A separate e-business tool supports the sale of spares in a similar fashion, display-ing real-time data on price and availability and speeding up the entire order cycle by invoicing electronically. As a small company in its industry, Equipco believes it cannot compete on price alone. It hopes its use of e-business will differentiate it from its competitors through service enhancement. It aims to be a service leader in an industry that is making increased use of e-business. It sees e-business as a means of locking in customers and distributors to its Web-based processes thereby raising the barriers to exit. The use of online technology to support its distributors has certainly improved the functional dimension of customer service, providing customers with improved reliability; responsiveness and competence; and access, and ultimately perhaps more appropriate products. However, it is perhaps through its decision to enhance rather than replace the role of its distributors that it has suc-cessfully addressed the emotional dimension. The distributors' use of the software seems to enhance its communications and its understanding of its customer, while increasing Equipco's credibility and security with its customers.

Creditinsure

Creditinsure provides business credit insurance, including debt collection and other related services. Creditinsure has incorporated the use of e-business into its existing operations to become a clicks-and-mortar business. It wants to use e-business to enhance its customer service processes. It has developed a Web-based communication tool whereby applications for credit insurance can be transmitted and agreed electronically. The Web site is also used as a marketing device for the company's other services (e.g., debt collection). Creditinsure allows its customers access beyond its Web site, thereby opening up some of its internal information systems so that there is greater visibility of information to customers, for example, through the document and messaging system. This meant that communications, which had previously been for internal consumption only, could now be viewed by external customers. Use of the Web site has undoubtedly improved the functional dimension of customer service, increasing reliability, responsiveness, and access for its customers. However, it may well have helped address some aspects of the emotional dimension. While allowing customers to access its internal communication systems may have resulted in some loss in the frankness of internal communication, Creditinsure believes that the resulting greater transparency will achieve greater customer satisfaction by improving communications and enabling it to capture information that will improve its understanding of its customers. This greater openness may also improve its credibility with customers. However, Creditinsure is aware that it must proceed with caution in its use of the Internet, as many clients are reluctant to move to e-business in what is a very conservative industry. It hopes to draw these reluctant customers into greater use of e-business through "customer-friendly" applications, thereby hoping to address the courtesy, credibility, and security aspects of the emotional dimension. There are, however, other concerns about how e-business will fit with ongoing and developing corporate strategy. The company is particularly concerned about how e-business will affect the role of its intermediaries, primarily insurance brokers, who currently account for 80% of its business. Although its Web site enables Creditinsure to go direct to its clients, bypassing its brokers if required, the company is unsure whether to adopt such a disintermediated business model. If it retains its intermediaries, its online services and communications need to be developed and tailored for these different users. The disintermediation debate acknowledges that customer service is not only about achieving an appropriate level of functionality, but also about addressing the emotional dimension of contact with customers.

Discussion

In all the cases except one, the companies each had a clear strategy for their use of e-business in customer service. Only Rebankco CMO seemed to have no clear objective for its use of e-business, other than as part of a wider adoption of online working throughout the company to improve efficiencies. The other companies were either aiming to penetrate targeted market segments (Clothingco, Shareco, Legalco, and e-accounting) or to defend existing market segments (Metalco, Equipco, and Creditinsure). All these companies would claim to offer a product/service package that was in some way differentiated through its online customer service operations. All saw e-business as a means of adding value for their customers in order to access new online markets or to increase the loyalty of existing customers and raise exit barriers.

The companies varied in their use of e-business within the customer contact process. Clothingco, Rebankco CMO, and Metalco used e-business as an additional channel. Shareco used it as their only channel for the targeted market segment. Legalco and e-accounting used it as a gateway to both their online and their face-to-face offerings. Equipco used e-business to enhance the role of its intermediaries with its end customers. Creditinsure seemed to be using it as part of a gradual process of disintermediation.

The use of e-business in customer service operations seemed to have improved the functional dimension of customer service in most of these cases, with clear apparent improvements in reliability, responsiveness, competence, and access. Rebankco CMO's case is again the exception. Although their Web site offers some potential for improving access to the service by customers, the absence of real interactivity seems more likely to frustrate than satisfy a typical online visitor.

However, the companies' approach to the emotional dimension of customer service offers some marked contrasts. Rebankco CMO and Shareco seem to have done little or nothing to address this dimension. In contrast, the online models adopted by Clothingco, Metalco, Legalco, and Creditinsure seem to address some of the aspects of the emotional dimension of customer service for their respective customers. Clothingco's product displays and personalized support services improve communications and credibility with customers and convey customer understanding. Metalco's extensive range of Web services enhances communications, credibility, customer understanding, and security. The anonymity offered to clients by Legalco addresses potential concerns about credibility and security. Creditinsure has improved credibility and communications by allowing customers access to its internal communication systems.

The cases of Equipco and Creditinsure raise some interesting issues about the role of intermediaries in the customer service process. One of the benefits often claimed for e-business is that it will disintermediate the supply chain thereby getting producers closer to the ultimate consumers of their products. However, by enhancing rather than replacing the role of its distributors, Equipco has arguably strengthened, rather than weakened, the emotional dimension of customer service. Creditinsure's initial and somewhat tentative moves towards disintermediation, on the other hand, threaten to disrupt its existing customer service operations to the detriment of the emotional aspects of customer service.

It is generally recognized that many consumers have security concerns about purchasing online. Clothingco's experiences are typical of Internet traders having to allay purchasers' concerns about releasing credit card details, the credibility of unseen retailers, whether their orders will be fulfilled, product returns, and so on. This issue is generally felt to affect B2C markets. However, the case of e-accounting illustrates that this issue can also apply in B2B markets, albeit in the SME sector. E-Accounting appears to have initially failed to understand the concerns that their potential customers had over online security and credibility. Fortunately, this issue was soon recognized and by offering off-line as well as online services, the future of the company seems to have been secured.

With regard to barriers to the increased use of e-business in customer service operations, Clothingco, Rebankco CMO, and e-accounting offer examples of functionality being impaired by inadequate or inappropriate technology. This might occur internally, or between the company and its suppliers, as well as between company and its customers. This seemed likely to lead to similar emotional barriers being raised, thereby preventing the enhancement of customer service. Clothingco, Metalco, e-accounting, Legalco, Equipco, and Creditinsure offer examples of companies who have gone some way to address the emotional dimension of online customer service to a lesser or greater extent. At a basic level, this relied on good Web site design. However, at a deeper level this also required the Web site to offer a greater degree of interactivity and enable customers to access a wide range of online information retrieval and communication services. This, in turn relies on the Web site having a high degree of technical functionality. The relationship of online with face-to-face and telephone-based services also seems to impact the customer service encounter. All of the case companies enable customers to interact with them through a mix of media if necessary. Assessing this was beyond the scope of this research, but it seems a topic worthy of further investigation.

Conclusion

The advent of e-business seems to offer considerable scope for organizations to gain a competitive advantage by enhancing their customer service operations. The Internet enables service providers to communicate and interact with their customers, both directly and via their supply chain intermediaries, more often, more fully, and more intimately than ever before.

The distinction between the functional and emotional dimensions of customer service has proved a useful basis on which to analyze online customer service operations. The evidence from the case companies in this study demonstrates that it is important to address both dimensions in order to enhance the online customer contact experience.

The technology of e-business provides great opportunities to enhance the functional dimension of customer service particularly with respect to reliability, responsiveness, competence, and access. It seems to be relatively easy to overcome functional barriers to the increased use of e-business to enhance customer service operations. Only one of the companies studied (Rebankco CMO) seems to not have made effective use of the available Internet technologies in this respect.

However, enhancing customer service operations to maximize the value added for customers also seems to require action to address the emotional dimension as well as the functional dimension. It seems as if firms find it more difficult to take action with regard to the emotional dimension. The cases of Clothingco, Rebankco CMO, and e-accounting illustrate that the emotional dimension can be adversely affected if inadequate or inappropriate technology impairs Web site functionality. Examples of companies who have been trying to address one or more aspects of the emotional dimension are offered by the cases of Clothingco (communications, credibility, and customer understanding), Metalco (communications, credibility, customer understanding, and security), and Legalco (credibility and security). Equipco has enhanced the emotional dimension of service with its customers by strengthening its links with its supply chain intermediaries. Interestingly, e-accounting had to address the issues of credibility and security by offering an off-line service alongside its online offering. Thus, the major conclusion from this research is that it does not seem possible to enhance customer service operations in e-business to full effect if the emotional dimension is neglected.

It is important to take note of the limitations of the research reported here. Firstly, its generalizability is restricted due to the limited number of cases that were undertaken. Clearly, it would be dangerous to try to draw general conclusions from such a small number of companies in one national context at one point in time. It is also important to note that customer service operations were only considered from the providers' perspective. As such, it needs to be complemented by an assessment from the customers' perspective, if a richer and more complete understanding is to be achieved.

As it is a relatively new phenomenon, it is perhaps understandable that many aspects of e-business have not received the full attention of academics. This is particularly true of customer service, which remains an under researched area. As such there is considerable scope for further study.

References

Barnes, D. L., Hinton, C. M., & Mieczkowska, S. M. (2002). Developing a framework to investigate the impact of e-commerce on the management of internal business processes. *Knowledge and Process Management, 9*(3), 133-142.

Barnes, S., & Vidgen, R. (2002). An integrative approach to the assessment of e-commerce quality. *Journal of Electronic Commerce Research, 3*(3), 114-127.

Bitner, M. J., Brown, S. W., & Meuter, M. L. (2000). Technology infusion in service encounters. *Journal of the Academy of Marketing Science, 28*(1), 138-149.

Bryman, A. (1988). *Quantity and quality in social research.* London: Unwin Hyman.

Chaffey, D. (2002). *E-business and e-commerce management.* Harlow, UK: FT/ Prentice Hall.

Christensen, C., & Sundahl, D. (2001). *The process of theory building.* (Working Paper). Boston: Harvard Business School.

Dadzie, K. Q., Chelariu, C., & Winston, E. (2005) Customer service in the Internet-enabled logistics supply chain: Website design antecedents and loyalty effects. *Journal of Business Logistics, 26*(1), 53-78.

Domegan, C. (1996). The adoption of information technology in customer service. *European Journal of Marketing, 30*(6), 52-69.

Hayes, R. H., & Wheelwright, S. C. (1984). *Restoring our competitive edge: Competing through manufacturing.* New York: Wiley.

Johnston, R. (1987). A framework for developing a quality strategy in a customer processing operation. *International Journal of Quality and Reliability Management, 4*(4), 37-46.

Kardaras, D., & Papathanassiou, E. (2000). The development of B2C e-commerce in Greece: Current situation and future potential. *Internet Research, 10*(4), 284-294.

Laudon, K. C., & Traver, C. G. (2002). *E-commerce: Business, technology, society.* New York: Addison-Wesley.

Lennon, R., & Harris, J. (2002). Customer service on the Web: A cross-industry investigation. *Journal of Targeting, Measurement and Analysis for Marketing, 14*(4), 325-338.

Lightner, N. J. (2004). Evaluating e-commerce functionality with a focus on customer service. *Communications of the ACM, 47*(10), 88-92.

McCutcheon, D. M., & Meredith, J. R. (1993). Conducting case study research in operations management. *Journal of Operations Management, 11*(3), 239-256.

Meredith, J. (1998). Building operations management theory through case and field research. *Journal of Operations Management, 16*(4), 441-454.

Meredith, J. R., Raturi, A., Amoako-Gympah, K., & Kaplan, B. (1989). Alternative research paradigms in operation. *Journal of Operations Management, 8*(4), 297-326.

Miles, M. B., & Huberman, A. M. (1994). *Qualitative data analysis* (2nd ed.). London: Sage.

Ngash, S., Ryan, T., & Igbari, M. (2003). Quality and effectiveness in Web-based customer support systems. *Information & Management, 40,* 757-768.

Office for National Statistics. (2005). *Information and communication technology (ICT): Activity of UK businesses, 2004.* Retrieved January 19, 2006, from http://www.statistics.gov.uk/downloads/theme_economy/ecommerce_report_2004.pdf

Parasuraman, A., & Grewal, D. (2000). The impact of technology on the quality-value-loyalty chain: A research agenda. *Journal of the Academy of Marketing Science, 28*(1), 168-174.

Parasuraman, A., Zeithaml, V., & Berry, L. L. (1985, Fall). A conceptual model of service quality and its implication for future research. *Journal of Marketing,* 41-50.

Parasuraman, A., Zeithaml, V., & Berry, L. L. (1988). SERVQUAL: A multiple-item scale for measuring consumer perceptions of service quality. *Journal of Retailing, 64*(1), 12-40.

Piccoli, G., Brohman, M. K., Watson, R. T., & Parasuraman, A. (2004). Net-based customer service systems: Evolution and revolution in Web site functionalities. *Decision sciences, 35*(3), 423-448.

Poon, S., & Swatman, P. (1999). An exploratory study of small business Internet commerce issues. *Information and Management, 35,* 9-18.

Porter, M. E. (1980). *Competitive strategy.* New York: Free Press.

Porter, M. E. (1985). *Competitive advantage.* New York: Free Press.

Porter, M. E. (2001, March). Strategy and the Internet. *Harvard Business Review,* 63-69.

Shostack, G. L. (1984, January-February). Designing services that deliver. *Harvard Business Review,* 133-139.

Slack, N., Chambers, S., & Johnston, R. (2001). *Operations management* (3rd ed.). London: FT-Pitman.

Talley, M., & Axelroth, J. (2001). Talking about customer service. *Information Outlook, 5*(12), 6-13.

Voss, C. A. (2003). Rethinking paradigms of service—Service in a virtual environment. *International Journal of Operations and Production Management, 23*(1), 88-104.

Voss, C., Tsikriktsis, N., & Frohlich, M. (2002). Case research in operations management. *International Journal of Operations and Production Management, 22*(2), 195-219.

Walsh, J., & Godfrey, S. (2000). The Internet: A new era in customer service. *European Management Journal, 18*(1), 85-92.

Westbrook, K. W., & Peterson, R. M. (1998). Business-to-business selling determinants of quality. *Industrial Marketing Management, 27*(1), 51-62.

Yin, R. K. (1994). *Case study research* (2nd ed.). London: Sage.

Zeithaml, V. A. (2002). Service excellence in electronic channels. *Managing Service Quality, 12*(3), 135-138.

Chapter II

Firm Value Effects of Web Site Redesign

Raquel Benbunan-Fich, Baruch College, CUNY, USA

Eliezer M. Fich, Drexel University, USA

Abstract

The redesign of a Web site can be classified as both an information technology (IT) investment and an e-commerce initiative. Although the empirical literature provides evidence that financial markets are sensitive to e-commerce announcements, it is still unknown what types of announcements affect the value of firms. We use the event study methodology on a sample of Web site redesigns from 1995 to 1999 to investigate the types of commercial organizations that announce changes to their Web presence and to study whether such redesign initiatives affect the value of publicly traded firms. Our findings indicate that, on average, refining a Web presence does not produce significant firm valuation adjustments. However, cross-sectional analyses reveal that Web site redesign increases firm value in service companies.

Introduction

Web sites are essential business tools to communicate information to the public (Benbunan-Fich & Altschuller, 2005; Lohse & Spiller, 1998) and to provide an "electronic storefront" to support business transactions (Winter, Saunders, & Hart 2003, p. 309). Due to the evolving nature of Internet technologies and changes in the e-commerce strategies of the firms, an organizational Web presence undergoes frequent transformations where the Web site is redesigned to take advantage of new technological possibilities or to reflect new strategic objectives (Palmer & Griffith, 1998).

Articles in the press suggest that Web site redesign can have a significant impact on the firm. For example, in September 2000, shares of NBCi (NBC Internet) increased more than 20% after the company unveiled its redesigned site ("NBC Internet," 2000). However, refining a Web presence is not always successful. For instance, the online magazine Salon.com was forced to pull back a site redesign that generated numerous complaints from its users ("Salon relents," 2000). Despite these and other examples, we are unaware of any systematic study of the valuation impact of Web site changes in commercial organizations. Ideally, an updated Web presence should improve the firm's ability to attract customers and increase its online revenues, and hence augment firm value. However, a redesigned site may also hinder the firm's online performance. This news may be met with unfavorable investor reactions and thus decrease the value of the firm.

As an organizational activity, the redesign of a Web presence can be classified as an IT investment and an e-commerce project. Although recent studies provide empirical evidence indicating that financial markets may be sensitive to the announcement of these initiatives via press releases, it is not known which type of announcements affect the value of firms. This study contributes to this body of literature by examining a particular type of e-commerce announcement: Web presence redesign. Our main research question asks whether refining a Web presence affects the market value of firms. We also investigate whether the market response is different depending upon the type of firm making the announcement and whether the nature (content) of the announcement also affects the direction and magnitude of the reaction.

We begin by reviewing the relevant literature in e-commerce and IT investments and developing our hypotheses. Next, we describe the event study methodology and detail our research design. We follow with the presentation of our results and a discussion of the limitations and implications of this study. Concluding remarks are presented in the last section.

Literature Review and Hypotheses

The emergence of the Internet as a commercial channel has opened new business possibilities for organizations. Traditional brick-and-mortar firms have taken advantage of the new medium and have extended their operations to cyberspace. At the same time, a new breed of pure-play Internet firms or "dot-coms," which conduct most or all of their business activities through the Internet, have joined the economy. For both types of organizations, updating their Web sites can be a crucial activity for the viability of their online operations. However, the improvement of a Web presence is likely to be especially critical for pure Internet firms, because the site is their only interface with customers.

Palmer and Griffith (1998) suggest that the design of a Web presence is the result of the interaction between technical choices and marketing/strategic decisions. Therefore, any change in the technological environment (i.e., evolution of Web technologies) or any shift in the e-commerce strategy of the firm requires a redesign in order to adapt the site to the new conditions. New technological possibilities or changes in the strategic direction of the firm's online operations usually result in the incorporation of new e-commerce features (functionality).

Aside from these strategically or technologically motivated changes, the redesign of a Web presence is also necessary to improve the ease of use (usability) of the site. Usability-based redesigns are due either to the need to expand content to accommodate an increasing user base; to include new features to facilitate navigation and access to information; or to change the appearance of the site in favor of a more pleasant and efficient layout (Guenther, 2000). The goal of a Web presence refinement is to produce a better fit between the firm's objectives and its Web presence, or the site and its visitors, or to make better use of the technology that is available. Since changes in these three fronts are constant, Web site redesign is an ongoing task.

Companies often announce the redesign of a site via a press release to encourage customers' visits and to inform different audiences about changes in their Web presence. According to signaling theory (Eliashberg & Robertson, 1988; Heil & Robertson, 1991; Moore, 1992), firms send messages to their constituents (buyers, competitors, employees, investors, industry analysts, etc.) regarding various projects and initiatives. The objective of such announcements is to influence the attitudes and actions of the different targeted audiences (Calantone & Schatzel, 2000). Using press releases, firms alert market participants about particular investments, projects, managerial changes, and other issues that are likely to affect firm performance. In turn, financial markets adjust the value of the firm in response to the new information.

For publicly traded firms, the value of redesigning a Web presence can be measured by the investors' reaction to such announcements. Web site redesign may increase firm value if investors perceive that the changes made to a Web presence improve the firm's ability to attract customers or generate online sales. Conversely, if investors believe that those changes impair the online performance of the organization, firm value is likely to decrease. It is also possible that a redesign announcement has no material effect on firm value. However, when news about the refinement of a Web presence significantly impacts the value of the firm, the success (or failure) of the redesign can be measured by the increase (or decrease) in firm value.

The emerging empirical literature provides evidence that financial markets are sensitive to the announcement of e-commerce initiatives via press releases. For example, Benbunan-Fich and Fich (2004) find positive stock price reactions on the announcement of Web traffic milestones during the late 1990s. Similarly, Cooper, Dimitrov, and Rau (2000) document a favorable reaction to the announcement of corporate name changes to Internet related ("dot-com" or "dotnet") names. Subramani and Walden (2001) report significant stock price increases for 251 e-commerce announcements about new business-to-consumer initiatives during the last quarter of 1998. However, since a classification of announcements is not offered in their study, the magnitude of the reaction for each type of initiative is not known.

Disclosures of Web site redesign initiatives belong to the general category of e-commerce announcements for which recent empirical literature has found positive market reactions. Moreover, the refinement of a Web presence indicates its evolution with either the incorporation of advanced technological features, new e-commerce strategies, or better understanding of users' needs and preferences. This signal of positive change should trigger a favorable market reaction. Thus, we hypothesize that:

H1: The announcement of a Web site redesign will increase firm value.

In the early days of the Internet as a commercial medium, little was known about how to design Web sites to maximize profits (Hoffman, Novak, & Chatterjee, 1996). Since then, studies find that design features affect consumers' reactions to the site (Jarvenpaa & Todd, 1997), Web site traffic (Goodwin & Marquis, 2000; Lohse & Spiller, 1998), purchase behavior (Liang & Lai, 2002), customer loyalty (Koufaris, Kambil, & LaBarbera, 2001), and sales (Lohse & Spiller, 1998). Consequently, if a Web presence redesign alters key design features, it is also likely to produce significant changes in some of these indicators, which in turn may affect firm value.

From the designers' viewpoint, Web site changes are based on the premise that a refined Web presence improves the firm's online performance. Therefore, Web site redesign decisions are expected to have a favorable effect on traffic, sales, or consumer perceptions. However, the success of a redesign effort may not be immediate because it depends largely upon the users' reactions to the new site and their subsequent behavior. Hence, financial markets may not be able to immediately assess the value of a redesign effort in the absence of other indicators of performance such as increased Web site traffic, better customer satisfaction, or more online sales.

Changes to a Web presence are more critical for pure Internet firms (Net firms), not only because the Web site is their only interface with customers, but also because their performance depends largely on the success of their online activities. Thus, it is reasonable to expect that Web site redesign announcements will produce stronger wealth adjustment effects in Net firms than in traditional firms. Moreover, most of the Net firms generally have a relatively shorter trading life and more uncertain prospects of success and survival than other more established firms do. Hence, any signal that provides investors with additional information about the likelihood of success or failure of publicly traded companies should produce comparatively larger valuation adjustments for Net firms than for more established organizations. This conjecture leads us to:

H2: Pure Internet firms will have larger valuation increases due to Web site redesign announcements than traditional firms will.

Porter and Millar (1985) suggest that the amount of information that goes into the development, delivery, and/or utilization of the product or service affects the overall operations of the firm and the role of information systems (IS). The degree of information intensity in the product and/or service is one of the key drivers of e-commerce strategies in general, and of Web site design, in particular (Palmer & Griffith, 1998). Due to the high degree of information intensity in their products and business processes, financial and service firms may experience comparatively larger advantages in Web-based commerce than manufacturing firms, for whom there is lower information intensity in their core market offer (Palmer & Griffith, 1998; Porter & Millar, 1985). Thus, we expect that refining a Web presence will have a greater impact in service firms that can develop and/or deliver their product or services electronically. Therefore,

H3: Service firms will have larger valuation increases due to the redesign of their Web presences than manufacturing organizations will.

Announcing the refinement of a Web presence is not only an e-commerce signal but also an IT investment communication. The academic literature presents interesting findings regarding the effects of such disclosures on the market valuation of firms. For example, Dos Santos, Peffer, and Mauer (1993) examine the impact of 97 announcements of IT investments between 1981 and 1988. They find no excess returns for firms announcing IT investments; however, their cross-sectional analyses reveal that innovative IT investments increase the value of firms while noninnovative investments do not. Dos Santos et al. (1993) classify an IT investment as an innovation when it represents the first use of a technology in an industry, when it would produce a new IT-based product or service, or when it would result in the development of new IT for an industry. In a follow up study, Im, Dow, and Grover (2001) extend the Dos Santos et al. sample with 141 IT investment announcements from 1989 to 1996. They find that, on average, IT investment announcements do not increase the value of the firms. One plausible explanation for their result is that investors are unable to ascertain the effect of these investments on firm performance.

In the case of Web site redesign, it is likely that the nature of the change—new functionality versus improved usability—influences the direction and magnitude of the reaction. New functionality may be associated with an innovation in the Web site, while usability changes may be perceived by investors as cosmetic changes. Therefore, the claims made in a press release (content of the announcement) regarding the nature of the Web site changes may hold the key to understanding the market's reaction to the announcement. Specifically, the addition of e-commerce functionality, such as ordering capabilities, should produce a stronger positive reaction than layout, navigation, or other usability improvements. Based on these conjectures, we hypothesize that:

H4: The addition of new functionality to a Web presence will produce larger firm valuation increases than usability improvements will.

Methodology: Event Study

An event study measures the economic significance of an announcement or project, by establishing whether the return of a security due to an event is significantly different from the return that would have been forecasted for the same security had the event not occurred. The methodology is based on the efficient market hypothesis (Fama, Fisher, & Jensen, 1969), which predicts that financial markets efficiently process publicly available information to update the expectations of future performance. At any given time, the price of a security is information efficient because it reflects all the available information about the firm's current and future profit potential. Thus, any news resulting from an unexpected event that may materially affect the firm's current and future profitability will produce changes in the firm's stock price to adjust it to the new assessment of the value of the firm. The amount of change in the price of a security due to the event, compared with its forecasted without-the-event price, reflects the market's unbiased estimation of the economic value of the new information (Brown & Warner, 1985). This estimation is used to calculate whether a particular event affects firm value.

Event studies are widely used in many business disciplines to investigate the impact of managerial decision making, shareholder initiatives, and other economic factors on the creation or destruction of firm value. In the IS field, the methodology has been used to study value creation through IT investments (Dos Santos et al., 1993; Im et al., 2001), e-commerce announcements (Subramani & Walden, 2001), and Web site traffic milestones (Benbunan-Fich & Fich, 2004) among others.

We use the event study methodology to examine the excess stock return around the announcement date of a Web site redesign. The impact of the redesign is determined by estimating the price of the stock if the event had not occurred and then calculating the return actually earned by the firm. Abnormal stock returns are then computed by subtracting raw returns around the event date from the market model expected returns. These abnormal or excess returns are then accumulated over a pre-determined period surrounding the announcement (event window), to produce cumulative abnormal returns (CARs). If the difference between the expected stock price and the actual price is statistically significant then it can be concluded that the redesign announcement had a meaningful effect on the market valuation of the firm. Furthermore, the magnitude of this difference provides a quantifiable indicator of the economic value of a Web site redesign project See Brown and Warner (1985) for a more technical explanation of the event study methodology.

A possible shortcoming of the event study method is that stock prices are naturally noisy, and therefore an event of interest must generate a reaction significant enough to be detected above the normal background noise of the stock market. A second limitation deals with the issue of the true event date. For some events, it is very difficult to pinpoint exactly when the actual information becomes publicly available. In some instances, information may leak out of its source before it officially becomes public knowledge, while in other cases the information may be broadcast at the end of the trading day, not giving investors enough time to react and trade.

Another possible limitation arises when different events occur around the same dates. Managers have a tendency to counter bad information with potentially good information, or the firm may experience other newsworthy events simultaneously, such as earnings or dividends announcements. When different news items are communicated at the same time, the reaction captured by the event study methodology may be confounded with events other than the one under study. In these circumstances, it is very difficult to establish which of the events caused the market reaction. Furthermore, some events may offset the impact of others, and the firm may not experience significant changes in value. This offset effect may also occur in a single event situation. Since the market reaction is an aggregation of expectations, when these expectations are not consistent (some investors think it is good news, while others think it is not) the overall effect of the event on the value of the firm may not be significant (Chaney, Devinney, & Winer, 1991). Notwithstanding these limitations, event studies offer an unbiased estimation of the economic value and significance of an announcement.

Research Design

To address the research questions underlying this study, we assemble a sample of firms that announce Web site redesigns. For this purpose, we collect, evaluate, and classify relevant redesign press releases during the 1995 to 1999 period. In order to examine our announcements using stock market data, we select events related to publicly traded companies. Finally, we separate the sample by a criterion that appropriately allows us to test our hypotheses.

Data Collection and Sample Selection

We obtain announcements of Web site redesign through full-text database searches of Lexis/Nexis, from January 1995 to December 1999. Redesign articles are defined as those containing the following keywords: redesign AND (Website OR Web site), and issued as PR Newswires or Business Wires. The initial search yields a total of 630 articles, which includes the redesign of products, magazines, and production facilities. These nonrelevant announcements are eliminated. Duplicate articles (those referring to the same redesign), and press releases announcing intentions or plans of redesign and/or the hiring of consultants for an upcoming redesign project are also excluded. Only articles announcing the completion of a Web site redesign effort, for which there was no preceding announcement of redesign intentions, are selected.

A total of 213 announcements meet these criteria (2 in 1995, 21 in 1996, 39 in 1997, 51 in 1998, and 100 in 1999). Since first generation Web sites were first launched from 1994 to 1995, it is not surprising that the number of redesign announcements in 1995 is extremely small. Beginning in 1996, we find evidence of more Web site redesign efforts. These initiatives steadily increase over the sample period, doubling in magnitude from 1998 to 1999.

Sample Characteristics and Coding of Variables

For each announcement, we code the ownership (public or private) of the companies that redesign their Web sites. Like Subramani and Walden (2001), we differentiate between *Net* and *non-Net* (conventional) firms, where a Net firm is one that derives more than 50% of its revenue from Internet related activities. Table 1 provides information on the total number of announcements for each year, along with ownership (public or private), and type of firm (Net or non-Net) making the announcements.

To investigate which kind of firms make redesign announcements, we count the number of press releases in each cell of a bidimensional contingency table crossing ownership (public vs. private) and firm type (Net vs. non-Net). Table 2 presents the number and frequency of announcements for each category. The highest number of announcements is found in the public/non-Net cell, followed by traditional private firms, and then by private Internet organizations. Notably, the lowest proportion of announcements corresponds to publicly traded Internet firms.

From the 102 publicly traded companies making redesign announcements from 1995 to 1999, we extract the releases referring to firms trading in the major stock exchanges (NYSE, AMEX, or NASDAQ) for which trading data is available from the University of Chicago's Center for Research in Security Prices (CRSP) database. We screen these observations and eliminate those that experience a simultaneous news event (such as earnings, dividends, management, or board changes announcements) on the date of the announcement that could contaminate the reaction to the Web site redesign initiative.

Our screening procedures yield a final sample of 77 usable events. We classify each firm in our sample by whether the company is a manufacturing or a service organization, based on the firms' 2-digit Standard Industrial Classification (SIC). Manufacturing organizations are those located in division D (manufacturing—codes 2000 to 3800), while service firms are those that belong to divisions E (transportation and communications), F (wholesale trade), G (retail trade), H (financial firms)

Table 1. Description of announcements

	1995	1996	1997	1998	1999	Total
Articles retained	2	21	39	51	100	213
Firm ownership						
Public	1	10	17	23	51	102
Private	1	11	22	28	49	111
Type of firm						
Net	0	5	9	20	53	87
Non-Net	2	16	30	31	47	126

Table 2. Number of announcements and firm classification

Firm classification	Number of announcements*	Frequency
Public/Net	35	16%
Public/Non-Net	67	32%
Private/Net	52	24%
Private/Non-Net	59	28%
Sample size	213	100%

* If the same firm made more than one redesign announcement in the period, each announcement was counted separately and classified in the appropriate category.

or I (services). In Appendix 1, we show the distribution of announcements in each industry category. About 35% of the announcements in our sample refer to manufacturing firms, while 65% pertain to service organizations.

In addition, we classify each redesign announcement in the sample into functionality or usability, according to the content of the press release. Functionality announcements refer to the rollout of new functions or features, while usability disclosures describe site redesigns that augment information content, improve navigation, or facilitate access to information. For the purposes of coding, a functionality-based redesign consists of adding a major function that was not present in the earlier version of the site. Examples include new electronic order forms, new online services, new community features (chat rooms, bulletin boards, community of users, etc.), and new interactive options for the users. A usability-based refinement of a Web presence consists of general changes to the information content of the site and/or changes to the access to that information. These enhancements include streamlining of the look and feel, faster and easier navigation, enhanced information content, and improved search capabilities. In Appendix 2, we provide examples of announcements in each of these categories.

Event Study Parameters

The event study methodology requires a set of parameters to calculate the reaction of the market. The first parameter, the estimation period, refers to the length of time prior to the event over which the expected returns are calculated. The duration of the estimation period is often 255 days (about one year of trading data). The second parameter, the event window, refers to the period over which abnormal returns are accumulated. The windows are determined around the date of announcement, which is designated as 0. Although a one-day event window (day = 0) is usually recommended, several empirical studies use larger windows to capture pre-announcement information leakage and post-announcement delays. For example, a (-1, +1) window produces a three-day CARs, from one day before the announcement until one day after the announcement. McWilliams and Siegel (1997) recommend using short event windows around the announcement date because in larger ones other news may affect investors' reactions.

Empirical Tests

To test our first hypothesis, we estimate CARs for our sample of 77 redesign announcements. Although we focus on the (-1, +1) event window, we also compute abnormal returns for longer windows of (-3, +3) and (-5, +5). For each window, we

Table 3. Event study

Event windows*	Average CAR (%)	t-statistic	Positive : Negative	Gen sign Z
(-1, +1)	1.03	1.014	43:34	1.591+
(-3, +3)	1.47	0.946	37:40	0.221
(-5, +5)	1.58	0.812	36:41	-0.008

Significance level: + = 10%
* Estimation periods for each window are 255 days in length. Model used market adjusted returns, equally weighted index.

report the t-statistic, which tests whether these CARs are significantly different from zero, the number of securities with positive and negative returns, and a generalized sign Z statistic. The null hypothesis for the generalized sign test is that the fraction of positive returns is the same as in the estimation period. Table 3 shows the results.

CARs are positive with magnitudes of 1.03%, 1.47%, and 1.58% for the (-1, +1), (-3, +3), and (-5, +5) windows, respectively. However, none is statistically significant. About 55% of the securities experience positive CARs in the (-1, +1) window, but according to the generalized sign test, this is marginally higher than the fraction of announcements experiencing positive returns in the estimation period. Based on the event study results for the full sample over the three windows, firm value does not appear to be affected by Web site redesign announcements. Thus, we do not find support for *H1*.

Univariate Analyses

To test hypotheses *H2, H3,* and *H4*, we use the Net/non-Net firm categorization, the manufacturing/service classification, and the content coding to respectively separate our 77 announcements. Table 4 summarizes the results of the event study for each category in the (-1, +1) window. For each subsample, the table presents CARs, t-statistics, the number of positive and negative returns, and generalized sign tests. In the last column of the table, we report a t-test comparing the CARs in each pair of subsamples.

Our second hypothesis (H2) states that pure Internet firms, but not traditional firms, will experience larger valuation increases due to a Web site redesign. To test this hypothesis, we use the Net versus non-Net classification. As shown in panel A of Table 4, only 21 announcements fall into the Net category, while the remaining 56 fall into the non-Net category. The three-day CARs are 0.83% for the Net group and 1.10% for the non-Net group; however, neither is statistically significant. In the

Table 4. Event study for subsamples

Breakdown category	Sample size	Average CAR (%)	t	Positive: Negative	Gen sign Z	Subsample comparison t
Panel A: Breakdown by firm type						
Net	21	0.83	0.285	12:9	0.915	-0.096
Non-Net	56	1.10	1.130	31:25	1.306 +	
Panel B: Breakdown by industry						
Manufacturing	30	-1.15	-0.934	14:16	0.014	2.228*
Service	47	2.42	1.721*	29:18	2.026*	
Panel C: Breakdown by content						
Functionality	25	0.71	0.465	14:11	0.828	-0.178
Usability	52	1.18	0.892	29:23	1.362+	

*Significance levels: + = 10%, * = 5%.*

Net subsample, the proportion of positive returns is the same as in the estimation period, but in the non-Net group, the frequency of positive returns is marginally higher than in the estimation period. Moreover, our t-test shows that the average CARs in the Net group are not significantly different from the CARs in the non-Net group. Therefore, these results do not support H2.

The third hypothesis (*H3*) predicts that unlike manufacturing firms, service firms will have larger valuation increases due to the redesign of their Web presence. To test *H3*, we use each firm's industrial sector classification. As panel B of Table 4 indicates, about 40% of the announcements are placed in the manufacturing group. Consistent with our expectations, the reactions to Web site redesign announcements from service firms are on the order of 2.4%, which is significantly different from zero at 5% level. In addition, the number of service firm announcements with positive CARs is significantly higher (also at the 5% level) than those in the estimation period. The CARs for low information intensive firms are negative (-1.15%) but not significant. Nevertheless, our t-test of the CARs in the two subsamples shows that average CARs for the service subsample are significantly different (at the 5% level) from average CARs for the manufacturing subsample. Overall, these results support *H3*.

The last hypothesis (H4) indicates that the addition of new functionality to a Web presence will produce larger firm valuation increases than reports of usability improvements. To test this, the authors independently classified the announcements into two categories: functionality and usability. Initial inter-rater reliability was .77 as a total of 12 announcements were placed in different categories. After the disagreements were solved through discussion and consensus, a total of 25 announcements were placed in the functionality category and 52 were classified as usability. Event study results, presented in Panel C of Table 4, show that neither of the content subsamples experience significant market reactions. Average CARs are 0.71% and 1.18% for the functionality and usability subsamples respectively; neither one is statistically significant. However, the frequency of positive returns for usability redesign is marginally higher than the frequency computed in the estimation period. Finally, a t-test shows that the average CARs in the two subsamples are not significantly different from each other. Based on these findings, our results do not support H4.

Multivariate Analyses

To study the joint effects of firm type, industry classification, and information content we examine our three-day CARs in a multivariate context. Specifically, we estimate the following regression models:

$$CAR_i = \beta_0 + \beta_1 net + \beta_2 ind + \varepsilon_1 \tag{1}$$

$$CAR_i = \beta_0 + \beta_1 net + \beta_2 ind + \beta_3 cont + \varepsilon_2 \tag{2}$$

The dependent variable is the CARs over the three day window (-1, +1) for each firm i. In the first model, the independent variables are the Net classification (1 if the firm is a pure-Internet company; 0 otherwise), and firm type (1 if it is service; 0 for manufacturing). The model in equation (2) adds a third categorical variable indicating content (1 if the announcement describes a functionality type of redesign; 0 otherwise). Both regressions are estimated with the full sample of 77 announcements.

Least squares coefficients are reported in Table 5. Model 1 is significant at the 10% level, and coefficient estimates for this model confirm that Web site redesign announcements for service organizations are well received by investors. Indeed, the coefficient estimate indicates that the impact of Web site redesign for service firms is economically meaningful, as CARs are 3.69% higher for service organizations. This result confirms our earlier findings regarding *H3*. Other results are also consistent with our univariate tests, as the firm type indicator (net) does not yield a significant coefficient. In the second model, the inclusion of the content indicator (functionality vs. usability) does not alter our results or improve the estimation.

Table 5. Multivariate analyses

Independent variables[1]	Model 1[2]	Model 2[3]
Intercept	-0.92 (1.20)	-0.74 (1.26)
Net	-1.66 (1.80)	-1.65 (1.81)
Industry	3.69* (1.64)	3.80* (1.67)
Content		-0.74 (1.62)
R^2	0.06	0.07
F-Statistic	2.53+	1.74

*Significance levels: + = 10%; * = 5%. Standard errors are reported in parenthesis below each estimate.*

1. *The dependent variable is the Cumulative Abnormal Return for the ith firm in the sample computed over the (-1, +1) window.*
2. *The explanatory variables in Model 1 are: net (indicator set to 1 if the firm is a pure-Internet firm and 0 otherwise), and industry (indicator set to 1 for service firms and 0 otherwise).*
3. *Model 2 also includes another indicator variable content (set to 1 if the announcement describes a functionality-based Web site redesign, and 0 otherwise).*

Summary

An analysis of 213 public and private firms that make redesign announcements from 1995 to 1999 reveals that non-Net, publicly traded firms tend to make more redesign announcements than Internet and privately owned companies. However, we find no evidence of abnormal market reactions for 77 redesign announcements by publicly traded firms. We control for the effect of other variables, such as firm type (Net vs. non-Net), industry classification (manufacturing vs. service), and nature of the announcement (functionality vs. usability). Using these categorizations, we find that only the industry classification yields statistically significant results. In fact, service organizations experience statistically significant CARs, which are in turn, significantly larger than those experienced by manufacturing organizations. Interestingly, however, CARs related to manufacturing firms are negative but not significantly different from zero.

Discussion, Limitations, and Implications

Overall, the fact that we are unable to reject the null hypothesis (of no changes in firm value due to Web site redesign announcements) at a time when general e-commerce news (Subramani & Walden, 2001) and Web traffic announcements (Benbunan-Fich & Fich, 2004) do prompt significant market reactions, is noteworthy in itself. Several alternative explanations can account for this finding.

First, from the efficient market hypothesis' perspective, investors may not view redesign announcements as new information regarding the firm's ability to conduct business. Instead, it is likely that investors expect Web sites to frequently evolve, taking advantage of new technologies, implementing new strategies, or accommodating a changing user base. Therefore, due to their constantly evolving nature, Web sites may be considered "works in progress," and so the announcement of a redesign may have little wealth adjustment value.

A second explanation is the possibility of time lag factors. On average, investors may have difficulties interpreting the implications of a redesign initiative immediately after it is announced. The success of a redesign depends upon how customers respond to the new version of the Web site, and on how this refined presence affects other indicators of performance such as traffic or sales. It is only when these indicators change that the markets react, as Benbunan-Fich and Fich (2004) document for the achievement of Web site traffic milestones. Although the lack of reaction could be an argument for expanding the event window, a longer window may not unequivocally attribute excess returns to the redesign announcement.

Another explanation is that financial markets may indeed appreciate the value of the redesign, but the reaction is not strong enough to rise above the general noise of the market and to be detected with our sample size. The refinement of a Web presence may be a small event relative to the total value of the firm. In particular, for large publicly traded firms, changing a Web presence in one of the subsidiaries may not be strong enough to generate excess returns for the entire organization. Interestingly, to avoid this problem, Im et al. (2001) select only IT investment announcements that are significant at the corporate level rather than at the division or subunit level. Given the size of our sample, we are unable to follow this approach.

Some limitations of this study warrant mention. The use of press releases as a source to identify the companies that change their sites may introduce some selection bias. First, only companies that announce their redesign activities through PR Newswires or Business Wires are selected. In fact, many more companies may have changed their sites and not issued a press release or used a different medium to communicate the news. Second, although we control for variables such as type of firm, industry, and content of the announcement, the event study technique considers all events alike regardless of particular firm characteristics. Thus, there could be other variables (such as firm size or trading age) that may have a bearing on the results.

A third limitation is the size of the sample. We start with a sample of 213 redesign announcements, but only a fraction are usable for the event study (publicly traded firms that have trading data available and did not experience a simultaneous news announcement).

Notwithstanding these caveats, our results have practical and academic implications. For practitioners, announcing the redesign of a Web presence is part of legitimate promotional efforts aimed at communicating the availability of an enhanced Web presence. Our findings suggest that investors do not assign significant value to such initiatives upon their announcement. However, other constituents may react positively to this kind of communication. For example, customers may want to visit the new version of the site. From the research standpoint, our results calibrate the findings of other empirical studies and contribute to the development of a taxonomy of e-commerce initiatives and IT investments that increase firm value.

There are several possible extensions to this work. One would be to study in more depth the nature of the changes introduced in the redesigned version of the sites. In this regard, Benbunan-Fich and Altschuller (2005) perform a more extensive content analysis of site redesign press releases from public and private firms in the late 1990s. Their findings suggest that the majority of companies redesigned their Web presence to expand information and change navigation protocols, and only a fraction incorporated substantial functionality enhancements.

A second possible extension to the research presented here would be to include more recent observations in the sample. Given the exponential increase in redesign announcements over the years, the addition of the years 2000 to 2002 will increase sample size considerably. In a larger sample, it may be possible to select only re design events that are relevant at the corporate level, or only those who represent radical transformations and investigate whether these produce excess returns. An expanded sample may also enable the separation of service firms into financial and nonfinancial organizations in order to examine whether redesign efforts add more value to financial organizations than to other types of service organizations. Despite these potential advantages, others have augmented their sample to include more recent years without much success. For example, Benbunan-Fich and Fich (2004) do not find significant valuation increases due to Web traffic milestones during 2000 and 2001 even though they find significant firm value increases of the order of 5.5% in a sample of 87 announcements, during the late 1990s.

Finally, another potential extension would be to study the impact of redesign announcements on the Web consulting firms that were hired for the project and are mentioned in the press release. For these consultants, the completion of a redesign initiative may be perceived as an endorsement of their qualifications and expertise.

Conclusion

In this chapter, we investigate whether certain types of e-commerce initiatives, particularly Web site redesign, add value to firms. From an initial sample of 213 press releases announcing the completion of Web site redesign efforts from 1995 to 1999, we observe that traditional (non-Net) publicly traded firms tend to make more announcements than other types of firms. We use the event study methodology to examine market reactions for 77 announcements related to Web site redesigns in publicly traded firms. We cannot reject the null hypothesis that redesign events do not induce significant valuation adjustments when first disclosed. It is possible that over time, successful redesigns affect other variables such as sales or traffic and these, in turn, will increase the value of the announcing firms.

In order to control for the type of industry, we divide the sample into manufacturing and service organizations. Significant CARs are observed for firms in the service sector, indicating that these firms benefit more from Web site redesign initiatives than those that manufacture products. Our multivariate tests reveal that, in fact, three-day CARs are 3.69% larger in magnitude for service companies. Interestingly, however, no significant CARs are observed when the sample is sorted by whether companies are Net or non-Net firms. In terms of content, it appears that the nature of the changes communicated in the announcement, as operationalized here (functionality vs. usability), does not affect the direction and magnitude of the reaction. The value of a redesign initiative appears to be sensitive only to the industry classification of the firm making the announcement.

The empirical literature in IT investments and e-commerce announcements offers a fertile ground to explore the nature of the different signals communicated via press releases by publicly traded companies. Given the results presented here and the mixed evidence recently reported by related studies, there appears to be enough incentive for researchers to investigate which type of IT projects truly affect firm value.

Acknowledgments

We are grateful to Shoshana Altschuller, Mike Gallivan, Marios Koufaris, Detmar Straub, the editor, associate editor, and three anonymous reviewers for very helpful suggestions. We thank May Li and William Hampton-Sosa for capable research assistance. This research was funded in part by a grant from The City University of New York PSC-CUNY Research Program, Grant # 64554-00 33 awarded to R. Benbunan-Fich. The opinions expressed herein are solely those of the authors and not those of the sponsors of this project.

References

Benbunan-Fich, R., & Altschuller, S. W. (2005, June). Web presence transformations in the 1990s: An analysis of press releases. *IEEE Transactions on Professional Communication, 48*(2), 131-146.

Benbunan-Fich, R., & Fich, E. M. (2004, Summer). Effects of Web traffic announcements on firm value. *International Journal of Electronic Commerce, 8*(4), 161-181.

Brown, S. J., & Warner, J. B. (1985, March). Using daily stock returns: The case of event studies. *Journal of Financial Economics, 14*, 3-31.

Calantone, R. J., & Schatzel, K. E. (2000, January). Strategic foretelling: Communication-based antecedents of a firm's propensity to pre-announce. *Journal of Marketing, 64*, 17-30.

Chaney, P., Devinney, T., & Winer, R. (1991). The impact of new product introductions on the market value of firms. *Journal of Business, 64*(4), 573-610.

Cooper, M., Dimitrov, O., & Rau, P. R. (2000, December). A rose.com by any other name. *Journal of Finance, 56*(6), 2371-2388.

Dos Santos, B., Peffer, K., & Mauer, D. (1993). The impact of information technology investment announcements on the market value of the firm. *Information Systems Research, 4*(1), 1-23.

Eliashberg, J., & Robertson, T. (1988). New product pre-announcing behavior: A market signaling study. *Journal of Marketing Research, 25*(3), 282-292.

Fama, E., Fisher, L., & Jensen, M. C. (1969). The adjustment of stock prices to new information. *International Economic Review, 10*(1), 1-21.

Goodwin, U., & Marquis, G. (2000). Effective Web site design: An empirical study. In *Processings of the IEEE International Engineering Management Conference*, 2000. Leading Technology Change: Managment Issues and Challenges, IEEE Press, Piscataway NL, 2000. 313-318.

Guenther, K. (2000, September-October). Evidence based Web redesigns. *Online,* 67-72.

Heil, O., & Robertson, T. (1991). Towards a theory of competitive market signaling: A research agenda. *Strategic Management Journal, 12*(6), 403-418.

Hoffman, D., Novak, T., & Chatterjee, P. (1996). Commercial scenarios for the Web. *Journal of Computer-Mediated Communication, 1*(3). Retrieved March 9, 2006 from http://jcmc.indiana.edu/vol1/issue3/hoffman.html

Im, K., Dow, K., & Grover, V. (2001). A reexamination of IT investment and the market value of the firm—An event study methodology. *Information Systems Research, 12*(1), 103-117.

Jarvenpaa, S. L., & Todd, P. A. (1997). Consumer reactions to electronic shopping on the World Wide Web. *International Journal of Electronic Commerce, 1*(2), 59-88.

Koufaris, M., Kambil, A., & LaBarbera, P. (2001, Winter). Consumer behavior in Web-based commerce: An empirical study. *International Journal of Electronic Commerce, 6*(2), 115-138.

Liang, T. P., & Lai, H. J. (2002). Effect of store design on consumer purchases: An empirical study of on-line bookstores. *Information & Management, 39*(6), 431-444.

Lohse, G., & Spiller, P. (1998). Electronic shopping: The effects of customer interfaces on traffic and sales. *Communications of the ACM, 41*(7), 81-87.

McWilliams, A., & Siegel, D. (1997). Event studies in management research: Theoretical and empirical issues. *Academy of Management Journal, 40*(3), 626-657.

Moore, M. (1992). Signal and choices in a competitive interaction: The role of moves and messages. *Management Science, 38*(4), 483-500.

NBC Internet redesigns its Web site. (2000, September 26). *USA Today,* p. B-1.

Palmer, J. W., & Griffith, D. A. (1998). An emerging model of Web site design for marketing. *Communications of the ACM, 44*(3), 44-51.

Porter, M. E., & Millar, V. (1985, July-August). How information gives you competitive advantage. *Harvard Business Review,* 149-160.

Richtel, M. (2000, June 5)Salon relents and redesigns site to soothe indignant readers. C-3. *New York Times.*

Subramani, M., & Walden, E. (2001). The impact of e-commerce announcements on the market value of firms. *Information Systems Research, 12*(2), 135-154.

Winter, S. J., Saunders, C., & Hart, P. (2003). Electronic window dressing: Impression management with Websites. *European Journal of Information Systems, 12*(4), 309-322.

Appendix I. Industry Classification of Publicly Traded Firms

Category	Division	Industry (two digit SIC)	Count	Percent (%)
Manufacturing				
	D-manufacturing			
		Food (20)	1	1.3
		Textiles (23)	2	2.6
		Paper products (26)	2	2.6
		Printing (27)	9	11.7
		Rubber and plastic products (30)	1	1.3
		Metal (34)	2	2.6
		Computers (35)	6	7.8
		Electronic and electric equipment (36)	3	3.9
		Photo equipment (38)	1	1.3
		Manufacturing total	**27**	**35.2**
Service				
	E-transportation, communication and utilities			
		Water transportation (44)	1	1.3
		Air transportation (45)	2	2.6
		Communications (48)	4	5.2
		Electric, gas, and sanitary services (49)	1	1.3
	F-wholesale trade			
		Durable goods (50)	3	3.9
		Non-durable goods (51)	1	1.3
	E-retail trade			
		General merchandise stores (53)	1	1.3
		Food stores (54)	1	1.3
		Apparel and accessory stores (56)	1	1.3
		Miscellaneous retail (59)	3	3.9
	H-finance, insurance and real estate			
		Depository institutions (60)	1	1.3
		Security and commodity brokers (62)	6	7.8
		Holding companies (67)	3	3.9
	I-services			
		Hotel and lodging (70)	2	2.6
		Personal services (72)	1	1.3
		Business services (73)	16	20.8
		Motion pictures (78)	3	3.9
		Service total	**50**	**65.6**

Appendix II. Content Classification in a Sample of Announcements

Source and date	Content (abbreviated)	Classification
Business Wire, 6/17/96	Psygnosis, Inc., one of the fastest-growing multi-platform gaming developers and publishers worldwide, has reaffirmed its commitment to on-line marketing and customer service with a comprehensive redesign of its Web site. The newly improved website will offer web browsers a first-hand look at Psygnosis' broad product lineup for 1996/1997, complete with comprehensive screen shots, press releases, game demos, preview videos and exciting new sweepstakes and contests. The new site features high speed connections to the Internet and more than 100 pages of unique content encompassing product information, technical support, more than 100 MB of digital video, sound and screen capture files, special interest sections and extensive use of Netscape's features.	Usability
PR Newswire, 6/17/97	JCPenney today launched a newly redesigned Internet Store featuring over 2,000 products, an electronic order form, 19 print catalogs and many special online offers. With Modem Media's assistance, JCPenney developed this new dynamic online shopping destination to make it easier for customers to navigate the site and to provide users with a reason to buy JCPenney merchandise online. One of the most *noteworthy features of the new site is the electronic order form* which provides JCPenney catalog customers with the ability to order any of the more than 90,000 products found in current JCPenney catalogs.	Functionality
PR Newswire, 6/24/97	360 Communications Company, the second largest publicly held cellular company in the United States, today launched a redesign of its World Wide Web site. The new site has an interactive, user friendly format designed to meet the information needs of visitors—from customers and potential customers to shareowners, potential investors and 360 associates.	Usability
PR Newswire, 6/26/97	3Com today launched a new, visually compelling design for its corporate Web site that offers optimal organization of the vast technical and product information provided at the site…Through in-depth research, Studio Archetype helped 3Com determine that the site should be reoriented from a product-focus to a user-focus so that it can better address its audience's diverse needs for information. Studio Archetype's creative team styled a more intuitive graphical user interface with clearly visible and logically defined navigational features. They created news story zones with obvious captions and descriptive images and introduced a concise labeling system that enables users to instantly locate information to meet their specific needs.	Usability
PR Newswire, 11/2/97	Citibank today announced the release of Direct Access 6.1, the next generation of its acclaimed online banking service, and unveiled a new look for its Web site, with features that will dramatically change the way the bank interacts with its customers. The new version of *Direct Access allows, for the first time, Citibank customers to conduct their banking over the Internet* and features a familiar point-and-click interface. Direct Access also establishes Citibank as the only bank to provide a complete Internet banking service that carries no additional charges for customers, including for bill payments.	Functionality

Source and date	Content (abbreviated)	Classification
PR Newswire, 12/22/97	VF Corporation is the largest publicly traded apparel manufacturer in the world. The redesign of VFC's Corporate Web site, active since December 8, 1997, is structured as an aggregate site with sections devoted to VFC's brands, its global reach, its corporate history, and its financial outlook. Each section brings to the forefront information that is critical to the investment community but also provides information for general corporate communications and consumers. In addition, the site design is intuitive for users, enabling them to quickly and efficiently get the VFC information they need.	Usability

Chapter III

Jurisdiction in B2C E-Commerce Dispute within European Union

Ong Chin Eang, Monash University, Malaysia

Abstract

E-commerce jurisdiction has always been an issue because e-commerce exists in a borderless environment, and this e-environment diminishes the importance of physical location and locality. This imposes a great concern over which country's jurisdiction to engage when disputes occur between business and consumer in the e-environment. This is crucial when the consumer is seeking "redress" as there is always the question as to where a court action should be brought in. The current jurisdictions by the European Commission (EC) within the European Union (EU), The E-Commerce Directive—Country of Origin, and Rome II are still in the drafting process. These legislations are not the total solution. This paper reviews the issue of current jurisdiction, whether there is a need to call for a single jurisdiction, and what complications arise when seeking redress in this borderless e-environment. This paper also raises important issues that relate to the gaps and loopholes that exist in Country of Origin and Rome II.

Jurisdiction

Stoney (2001) claims that jurisdiction is a word that has had significant meaning and influence in the off-line world for hundreds of years. The problems posed by jurisdiction are not problems created by the Internet and e-commerce. The global and seamless nature of the Internet has simply added to or compounded the problem as e-commerce (whether it is business-to-business [B2B] or business-to-consumer [B2C]) expands and increasingly gains the confidence of the commercial and consumer sectors.

All the same, it is the fact that the Internet has momentously augmented the potential for jurisdiction around the global e-commerce market, and more importantly it has extended the potential scope of liability through e-commerce to make it practically boundless and immeasurable. There are several phenomena absent from e-commerce relations when compared with face-to-face communication. The presumption of desired relational development is not present, the degree of intimacy possible in an e-commerce relationship is constrained, and the expansion of whatever e-relationship exists in other domains is limited (Johnson, 2001; Podlas, 2000). Consequently, e-commerce radically undermines the relationship between legally significant (on-line) phenomena and physical location. This rise of the cross border e-commerce activity is destroying:

- the link between geographical location;
- the power of local governments to assert control over online behavior;
- the effects of online behavior on individuals or things;
- the legitimacy of a local sovereign's efforts to regulate global phenomena; and
- the ability of physical location to give notice of which sets of rules apply.

Cross border e-commerce thus radically subverts the system of rule making based on borders between physical spaces (Johnson & Post, 1996).

In addition to breaking down barriers between physical jurisdictions, it has no territorially based boundaries. Substantive and procedural laws vary from jurisdiction to jurisdiction. The question of what laws govern transactions over cross-border e-commerce environments and where consumers and businesses are subject to jurisdiction can be important. Notions of jurisdiction are based on a physical reality that does not exist in the e-commerce environment. However, actions in the virtual world of e-commerce have legal ramifications in the tangible world. Disputes occurring from e-commerce transactions introduce the most difficult application of traditional law, when businesses are being contacted via electronic means. Contract formation may require contact of minds, but it does not require an actual meeting of the businesses and consumers involved (Zekos, 2002).

Authorities, businesses, and even consumers know that the liability in global e-commerce is virtually limitless. Hence, there is a need for clear and effective protection (redress) to consumers. This is one of the means for creating consumer confidence in the e-environment. The test to determine and limit liability in the cross border e-commerce environment is jurisdiction. However, the question is:

What test or rules are applied by the courts to determine proper jurisdiction for Internet based transactions in cases where defendants reside or provide goods or services from outside the jurisdiction? (Oosterbaan, Jeekel, & Jonker, 2003)

This e-environment does not simply diminish the importance of physical location; it demolishes locality. In addition to that, e-commerce was contemplated to go beyond the physical boundary; to provide and create the ease of use; and facilitate businesses and consumers to land at unreachable destinations. Thus, it has rendered territorial jurisdiction problematic (Kobrin, 2001).

The principle issues of jurisdiction are which country's laws to engage when disputes occur between businesses and consumers in more than one country, and the questions over which court is able to judge the disputes. At first, this might appear only to be of importance to legal advocates, but there is an actual increase of cross-border e-commerce between consumers in one country buying goods or services from businesses based in other countries. Without certainty over the legal disputes and risks in this business to the consumer e-market, cross-border e-commerce cannot reach its potential (Cable & Wireless, 2003).

Call for a Single Jurisdiction?

The leading complication encountered in the e-environment is that cross-border channels are not always sympathetic to the needs of consumers. There is no certainty for a consumer to know who the business/merchant is. The opportunity to inspect the product before the transaction is nearly zero. In addition, consumers have no control of the technological methods for information sharing of goods in terms of the suitability, quality, and durability. Hence, consumers assert that there is a lack of respect for their rights in this e-environment because high numbers of consumers have no idea by whom or under what jurisdiction they are protected when seeking redress. In this cross-border e-commerce environment, Businesses and consumers are entering into a dangerous minefield, or obliquely, businesses and consumers are engaging at their own risks. From the second a consumer places an online order and businesses accept the payments, businesses and consumers have already moved in and out of numerous regulatory realms. Indeed, businesses and consumers are always in such a rush to go online that they overlook potentially serious legal ramifications. The transaction could be national or international and businesses and consumers do not know when they are leaving a regulated zone and entering unregulated areas (Mitchell & Robertson, 2001).

As a way of illustration, too often businesses and consumers become involved in e-commerce transactions without being aware that they have legally traveled outside their home nation or realizing that what appears to be local actions can result in cross-border consequences. For example, if a business—Amazone, UK Company—maintains a Web site advertising its product, and that site is accessed by a consumer in Singapore who points, clicks, and buys, the Amazone Company may suddenly be selling in Singapore; conversely, the consumer who has never left his/her home, may in fact, be creating a contract in the UK. Because the e-commerce eliminates physical barriers and permits domestic businesses and foreign consumers to consummate commercial transactions, it concomitantly dissolves the traditional methods for determining jurisdiction and which country's law applies. This increases the risk that commercial litigation will take place in countries, and under laws, that are foreign to some businesses and consumers. Thus, e-commerce can increase cross-border dispute, jurisdiction issues (Podlas, 2000).

Added to the aforementioned details, for instance, a former renowned U.S. university professor of computer science decided one day that technology and the Internet is the root of all evil. He began work on "Mickey"—the computer virus of the century. When Mickey was complete, he unleashed it through the Internet where it spread without detection to networks throughout the world. The virus wreaked havoc on numerous businesses, and individuals in the U.S. and a few foreign countries (Australia, Singapore, and Germany) incurred a total loss of $500,000 damage. With plans to file a suit against the professor in the U.S., a media frenzy ensued, and the headlines blaze with the all-important question, "Will Australia, Singapore, and Germany's courts exercise jurisdiction over a U.S. lunatic?" Hence, cross-border dispute jurisdiction is not only limited to B2C e-commerce, in fact it can occur in any online environment (Osen, 2000).

Following the aforementioned discussion, e-commerce transactions can easily cross multiple jurisdiction borders. Businesses and consumers can never be certain which rules of a particular country they could be subjected to. Correspondingly, the authorities are also confronted by a similar situation in regulating their jurisdiction of these e-commerce activities. The Internet and Web sites are not smart enough to distinguish or draw a line to define what rules and regulations are enforceable in the current transaction. Web sites are not static, and e-commerce transactions can be based or formed elsewhere in a matter of seconds (Clark, 2000). In this cross border e-commerce there are no state lines—no signposts on the "cross-border e-commerce highway"—to tell businesses and consumers when they have entered unregulated areas. How then can courts be expected to adjudicate causes of action arising in e-commerce? Hence, e-commerce "increases the porosity of physical boundaries," it is no easy task to determine the "who-what-and-where" in cases involving businesses, consumers, and transactions (Osen, 2000, p. 15).

Thus, consumers claim they are particularly at a greater disadvantage because of distance mobility of the Internet and Web sites and are also weakened by scarcity of knowledge about the local conditions if disputes occur, and consumers enter into an e-commerce marketplace without the sovereign's awareness (De Zylva, 2001).

When a consumer is seeking redress there is always a question as to where a court action should be brought. And the confusion here is how a consumer can enforce ruling when businesses and consumers are allocated in different countries. This is a great concern to businesses and consumers as it affects their decision-making process in the e-environment. The fear among businesses and consumers requires international agreement to clarify this issue. If consumers are seeking redress outside the borders of their country the court must be in the position to enforce a binding decision. This authority must hold jurisdiction over both parties, namely businesses and consumers (Podlas, 2000). There is no single code or internationally recognized jurisdiction. At present, the guidelines such as E-Commerce Directives and Rome II that have been adopted are still very uncertain.

Complication of Jurisdiction

Whose Jurisdiction?

A classical illustration of complicated jurisdiction when seeking redress is the question of:

Has the business created a virtual storefront in the consumer's jurisdiction to make a sale, or has the consumer virtually traveled to the business's jurisdiction to make a purchase? Therefore, it is possible for a consumer to order a book from her home in Malaysia from a seller physically located in Melbourne, it is as if the bookseller boarded a plane and delivered the book to the purchaser (consumer) in Malaysia, or as if the purchaser (consumer) flew to Melbourne to buy the book off the shelf? (International Chamber of Commerce, 2001)

This issue results in businesses confining their markets and reducing their products on offer until redress resolution is more certain and predictable. Eventually, consumers may be embittered with limited choices, face a more competitive price, or be deterred from shopping online due to the basis of their residence.

In reality a complicated jurisdiction could extend to bringing the edge of e-commerce redress into chaos. As an illustration, a merchant/business located in Singapore engaged in a transaction with a business established in Australia through the connection of a server located in New Zealand, which is supported by the Internet service provider headquarters in Hong Kong. He/she executes a transaction with a consumer in Thailand, and the products purchased will be delivered directly to a friend living in Japan. If a dispute arises and there is a need to seek redress, then the question is, in which jurisdiction? This attests that the legal and regulatory complications of the jurisdiction could be far greater than those encountered between just two countries (Ham & Atkinson, 2001).

With all the different jurisdictions implicated, inconclusiveness occurs as to the legislation and mechanisms (redress) that will care for the interests of both businesses and consumers. Once more, in order to avoid these uncertainties, businesses and consumers are presumably going to operate only in the domestic e-commerce market.

There is no surprise that businesses and consumers worry they will be subjected to these uncertainties. For instance, Norway is a member of the European Economic Area Agreement (EEAA) and has established a national E-Commerce Act, which largely supports the EEAA, but realized that full compliance is not easy because there are dissimilarities to that of the EEAA's requirements (American University, 2002). For instance, Norwegian e-commerce laws do provide some fundamental protections in contracts (like terms, conditions, and marketing information); however, there are differences to those of the EEAA's requirements.

In Brazil, specific legislation to e-commerce does not exist. The rules determined for online or e-transactions remain unchanged to those applied to the Code of Customers Defense that was enacted many years before e-commerce existed. Consequently, it is no wonder that jurisdiction remains a restless issue (Tigre, 2003).

The initiatives and demand for legislation on jurisdiction in e-commerce redress is not moving in parallel across the globe. By way of illustration, Vietnam is the case. While other countries such as the EU already enforce the E-Commerce Directive (Country of Origin) among its 15 member states and are fighting to repudiate the ROME II (Country of Destination), Vietnam is to issue its "first" e-commerce regulations. The Vietnamese government will draft e-commerce legislation to endeavor to promote the use of this technology, because e-commerce is growing increasingly familiar, especially in the banking sector. Regulations governing e-commerce do not exist in this country, except a very straightforward stipulation that is only available for e-mail, commercial transactions, and e-payment transactions. Not to mention that such stipulations are still in the middle of the drafting process, thus inadequate to regulate e-commerce transactions. Hence, the judicial bodies are encountered with an invalid legislation when managing any e-commerce disputes. There are 80,000 enterprises in Vietnam, only 3% applied some of the regulation elements, 7% have the plan to use it, and the remainder are unaware of it. Vietnam is one country (The Vietnam Investment Review, 2003; United Nation Development Programme, 2003). Thailand is another example, with 64 million people in the country, only 10% Internet usage, and 22% Teledensity, the concern of privacy rights have not yet been firmly established or accepted with due attention. Hence, the issue of jurisdiction in consumer redress is not yet a matter of contention in the country (Koanantakool, 2003).

How many countries in Asia, Europe, and the U.S. experience a similar issue to that which occurred in Vietnam? On that account, it is undoubted that jurisdiction remains a complicated issue in e-commerce redress.

Where did it Happen?

Before the question of whose jurisdiction to apply is answered, there is another question about "Where online activity takes place?" or "Where did it occur?" It has always been complicated to know in which country the transaction occurred. There is the idea that the e-commerce businesses and consumers now reside in a borderless world. There are doubts about locations or establishment of any redress mechanisms, and yet only a few regions have corresponding laws. Moreover, the questions about authority and effectiveness of enforcement will stop when it reaches the border (Caslon Analytics, 2001). As such, how can one find an answer?

Suppose businesses decide to deal with consumers in any given jurisdiction, they should be prepared to move forward to the courts of that jurisdiction, and this also applies to any consumers who choose to deal with businesses. The sound judgment is that there is nothing about e-commerce that justifies changing this rule. Although the e-commerce environment, the same as with brick and mortar, has different means by which to ascertain where the transaction was located. Can the simplest solution be to ask the businesses or consumers? Nevertheless, it is never easy to define who chose to initiate the transaction when the situation occurs in the borderless e-environment.

In cases when authorities come upon this situation, they usually define the case by the degree to which the business's Web site was "active" or "passive." On account of that, businesses claim that in the e-commerce environment their relationship with the consumers is not considered an active conjunction. Businesses argue they do not appeal to, or try to, captivate the consumers by creating an activity in the consumer's country of residence nor with the intention to push the advertisings or even the transactions directly into the country. E-commerce is accessible globally with no boundaries and does not count on any physical affinity or attachment between businesses and consumers, thus businesses claim that they rely on the consumers to take the "initiative" and decide whether or not to execute the e-transaction with them (businesses) (Barlow, 2003).

As such, it is certain that consumers become eligible for redress only if they are the passive factor in the relationship, that is, consumers should not be the ones to initiate the contact with the businesses. Besides that, businesses assert that any consumers who commit to an e-transaction cannot be regarded as passive because consumers who assert the lead to surf the Internet in search of a specific product or service render themselves active (Rosner, 2002). Other than that, businesses point out that as e-commerce has global characteristics and is accessible to users anywhere and anytime, if the businesses merely post materials on a Web site then this is just a passive activity and this passive factor is insufficient to justify the exercise of personal jurisdiction (Bharuka & Fisher, 2001; European Publishers Council, 2003).

Uncertainty and Trust

Businesses went on to purport the argument that e-commence only started from the beginning of 1993 or 1994, and it was predominantly driven by the private sector. Government involvement stimulated the advancement of the technology, but the real development of e-commerce was due to private sector guidance. Therefore government should leave the issue of jurisdiction to the private sector. Businesses should be aware of the current jurisdiction available to them so that when the relationship between businesses and consumers are contractual the parties can clearly define a governing law. Will the final choice be respected remains an unanswered question. If governments were to leave the issue of jurisdiction to businesses, the controversial argument is, can businesses enforce it (Maxwell, 1999).

Another related point that consumers stressed was that despite the fact a Web site was able to inform the consumers which country's laws and courts determine the redress, it is indefinite whether most consumers could engage in an informed choice concerned with complicated international jurisdiction issues. Thus, it is assumed that the governments will protect their citizens (consumers). However, if there is a jurisdiction available and there is still a need for government involvement, then this indicates that jurisdiction is proving to provide insufficient protection (Pitofsky, 2000) for consumers. Furthermore, it always appears that governments are not in the position to enforce judgment upon foreign cases. Obviously this powerlessness to enforce jurisdiction over foreign redress issues is an additional complication and burden to any government. With the current international jurisdiction—e-commerce directives in the EU and Rome II—it is unlikely to be an effective enforcement alternative for jurisdiction obtained in a consumer's country of residence against businesses located outside the jurisdictions influence (United State Council for International Business, 2000).

In addition to the issue of a lack of enforceability, businesses and consumers further support the argument that jurisdiction failed to buy their confidence and trust because disputes potentially have multiple solutions. With the jurisdiction currently in operation, a single "input" in a particular e-commerce business transaction, can end in multiple different "outputs," or legal jurisdictions. This is due to different private international legislation that engages at an international, regional (i.e., EU), and even a national level. By way of illustration, back in 1997, when the EC and the Japanese Ministry of Industry and Trade delivered policy documents on e-commerce, these parties encountered the same issue—one input, multiple outcomes. In this case, the profoundly broad agreement on e-commerce policy in this document is rather striking given the countries diverse legislation and various cultural traditions (Maxwell, 1999). In addition to that, e-commerce is still developing. Courts do not follow the same thinking when conforming on matters of online dispute and further confuse businesses and consumers with different interpretations by different courts. Consequently, this gives rise to the need to establish certainty on the outcomes of any jurisdiction, and also on the liabilities of businesses and consumers involved (Cable & Wireless, 2003).

Current Issue in Europe

Although there is no easy solution to the problem of jurisdiction and the choice of law to protect consumers in the e-commerce marketplace, the legal approach of Country of Origin and Rome II have been outlined as follows:

EU countries are already using E-Commerce Directive (Country of Origin) such that the provision of services (online transaction) shall be subject to the law of the member states in which the providers (businesses/merchants) of that service (online transaction) is established to govern e-commerce transactions. To illustrate this, if a buyer from Hong Kong purchased a product online from a seller (merchant) based in Denmark and there is a dispute, certainly the dispute shall be subjected or governed by the law of Denmark.

Rome II (Country of Destination), allows transactions to be governed by the laws of the country of the buyer; however, it is still being debated. In this way, if a buyer from Australia purchased a product online from a seller (merchant) based in Germany, and a transaction dispute occurs, the dispute is to be governed by the laws of Australia. Until today, the question of what laws to use to govern this still arise (Goldstein, 2001):

- Should online transactions be governed by the rules in the country where the transaction originated or was completed, or by the laws of the country of the buyer? Who will be fully protected? Businesses or consumers? Or will both parties be shielded from any disputes or claims against business and consumer?

- Allowing the rules of the country of destination to govern is also not without complications. The courts could conceivably make online merchants responsible for complying with hundreds of laws in hundreds of countries. This is because if courts are claiming jurisdiction and applying their countries' laws to Web sites of companies located outside of their geographic boundaries, such reach could subject companies to the courts and laws of virtually any country from which their Web site can be accessed (International Chamber of Commerce, 2001).

Rome II

When the EC put forward the draft of Rome II, businesses claimed that there was no need for the Rome II initiative. Businesses further assert that there is no evidence either from industry or consumers to support that there is a need of a uniform jurisdiction (Rome II) on the judgment of the law applicable to noncontractual redress relations. Businesses strongly opposed Rome II and argue at present that no definite occurrences show that any dispute issues exist that need to be brought to the attention of Rome II regulation (Collins, 2002).

Conversely, the EC claims that the aim of Rome II is to strike a reasonable balance between the benefits of businesses and consumers involved in this e-commerce environment. Businesses agree that with Rome II they will be able to provide consumers with certainty and greater protection, and this could be one of the possible ways to build up their trust and confidence. Theoretically, Rome II is striking a reasonable balance of the interest of both parties. However, in practice this jurisdiction reflects that any business could be subjected to thousands of laws with unforeseeable liability. Understanding and respecting the various laws would place highly restrictive burdens on any business, large or small (Caplan, 2001; Europa, 2003; Out-Law 2003b). This proposal would extend across borders and would considerably augment the sort of contracts to which it is applicable, giving consumers more possibility of taking the other contracting party (businesses) to court. Thus, it also makes it possible for a consumer to go "forum shopping" and choose a place of residence in a country that pays out the best damages.

In general, there is significant criticism of the country-of-destination approach adopted in Brussels I and the draft proposal of Rome II. With this proposal (Rome II), the EC is putting businesses at greater risk than before. With Rome II, the question of passive or active will no longer be an issue and how to define passive or active states is not important to both parties. Businesses are always attached to the risks, and their liability is unavoidable because this EC proposal leaves businesses with no choice. Because this approach subjects businesses to increased litigation costs, businesses may be tempted to pass these costs on to consumers by way of higher prices. Businesses may also choose to decrease the number of choices available to consumers by limiting the use of their Web sites to certain consumers through closed computer systems, or by simply shutting down their Web presence.

In Spain, the government recently decided to require all Spanish-based Web sites engaged in commerce to register with the government in the name of consumer protection. Accordingly, more than 300 Web site owners have taken their pages off-line ("Spanish net law," 2002). Some have just suspended their Web presence temporarily in protest, but others have left for good. Georgeos Diaz-Montexano, the owner of a Web site providing an online course in Egyptian hieroglyphics, says, "With this law, as always, it's the little guy that gets hurt." The International Chamber of Commerce (ICC), in reply to the Spanish law, published a statement remarking that "excessive domestic regulation of internet content creates significant uncertainties for business operating in this global medium, and has a chilling effect on commercial communication" (International Chamber of Commerce, 2002).

The EU approach significantly affects small- and mid-sized companies, which may view the Internet as the perfect medium to grow their businesses. Large conglomerates that operate throughout the EU or on a global basis can more easily afford legal expertise to avoid the various legal pitfalls involved with a worldwide practice. Small- and mid-sized businesses do not have that same luxury and may choose to shut down their Web sites in light of the potential for increased litigation, where the cost of even one lawsuit in a foreign jurisdiction may cause them to go out of business. Ironically, a measure meant to promote consumer confidence in Internet transactions then actually reduces consumer choices (Chen, 2004).

Besides that, the relationship between ROME II and the E-commerce Directive is unclear. Rome II contradicts the single market concept (E-Commerce Directive) proposed by the EC. This regulation would trigger the application of any law other than in the Country of Origin and would seem to create conflict with the whole idea of the E-Commerce Directive (Country of Destination) Internal Market principle. It is believed that businesses will take the opportunity to oppose the argument that there is no need for Rome II at all. Moreover, this draft does not promote the early objective (E-Commerce Directive—Internal Market) of the EC. This draft is full of vague concepts and complicated exceptions, which do not act in accordance with the original objective, thus Rome II will not augment the progress of the single market, nor will it have any other beneficial impact on businesses or consumers. This makes the relationship between these two instruments very unclear (Collins, 2002; E-Radar, 2005; Morrison & Foerster, 2002; Out-Law, 2003a).

Referring to those assertions mentioned previously, businesses are particularly concerned with the internal market and consistently argue that Rome II is not promoting or having any benefits to the single market principle. The point is that businesses are anxious that Rome II might demolish the internal market (EU). If this happens, businesses (merchants) in these 15 states (EU) will encounter disadvantages. Without doubt, businesses are not concerned about consumers' interests in Rome II. Certainly, businesses/merchants in these 15 states (EU) have no intention to strike a balance between the interest of businesses and consumers.

Even the ICC does not understand the EC view of Rome II and ICC believes this will have a harmful impact among the 15 states of the EU (International Chamber of Commerce, 2000). After all, it is possible to argue that the global economy is moving into the digital economies. The volume of e-commerce will continue to grow as the "old economy" increasingly uses the Internet to deliver goods and services to consumers. EC should be aware that the E-Commerce Directive (Country of Origin) is inefficient and is creating barriers to consumers in the cross-border e-commerce environment. People (consumers) are staying away from the EU e-markets. Besides that, the EC possibly realizes that this single-market concept is an advantage to the EU's 15 member states, but in the long term the trade might be unsuccessful to attract or drive the traffic of foreign investors/consumers. Hence, the objective to establish Rome II is to "balance the legal certainty" or what has been mentioned earlier, to "strike a reasonable balance." In point of fact, EC is creating more complications and confusion.

Due to this fact, it is vital to indicate that the issue of applicable jurisdiction has a global dimension. For that reason, when the authority encounters the question whether it should be treated as an international convention with "universal application" instead of "community legislation" (Rome II). In regards to universal application, it seems that a global application receives more attention and respect. As a result, an effective/enforceable should be formed as an international convention, instead of community legislation (Rome II). The international community should be seeking out ways to establish the universal application. With the EC imposing rigid legislation that is contradictory with other countries, it leads to more uncertainty and cost when disputes encounter conflicting rulings (European Union Committee, 2002).

E-Commerce Directive: Country of Origin

In this cross-border environment where nations seem to be tripping over each other with their own jurisdictions, the EC introduced the E-Commerce Directive (Country of Origin) with the principle that any redress or disputes is, in general, subject to the law of the EU member state in which it is established, rather than the law of any other country. The EC believes that this approach builds "legal predictability" among cross-border e-channels.

Businesses believe that any one who wants to promote cross-border e-commerce but does not give any assurances or certainty to consumers will have to understand that consumers may choose not to involve themselves in e-transactions/activities. This is due to the fact that businesses have not set up the global e-market to give consumers "confidence" to trade online. As a matter of fact, the EC asserts that the Country of Origin ensures that the legal framework exists, and this is where consumers can be confident of their basic rights in matters of dispute or redress.

Meanwhile, the objective of the EC with Country of Origin is to make sure the legal framework will help to build Europe's journey towards dot-com riches. With this directive, it is a great opportunity to augment cross-border e-markets as this is vital for EU growth and competitiveness (Interactive Advertising Bureau UK, 2001; Morrison, 2000). Also, the aim was to eliminate existing anomalies and attain a regime in which businesses operate inside the framework of law in their own countries. The directive is, hence, based firmly upon the internal market of mutual recognition. Ultimately, in securing an internal market for this e-commerce environment, it was acclaimed that additional harmonization of specific aspects of existing community law—within the EU member states—would also be necessary (Pearce & Platten, 2000).

However, consumers argue that the achievement of the directive under Country of Origin is not improving or sustaining consumer trust and confidence. In Rome II, businesses claim that under this principle they might be subject to thousands of laws at any one time, from any of the 15 member states, and they are put at greater risk when doing business online. In Country of Origin, a situation is conceivable in which businesses wish to seek redress from consumers. Hence, any consumers that execute e-commerce transactions within the EU might find themselves subjected to the foreign jurisdiction in any one of the 15 member states. Similarly, consumers may find themselves in a risky situation and at anytime could be the defendants under this directive (Lawson, 2001).

What is more, this directive is central to a single or internal market. It is certain that this principle is to ensure that businesses benefit from the free movement of services and freedom of establishment so that their services can be traded everywhere in the EU as long as businesses comply with the law in their home member states. It is more like self-regulation where this jurisdiction is customized for the 15 member states (European Brands Association, 1999). These member states only have to comply with one set of laws, and a set of laws that they are familiar with (Hornle, 2004). Indirectly, this directive is similar to a "club"; as long as you have subscribed and are members then you will have the privilege to enjoy the benefits. Country of Origin is the club and these 15 member states are the members. Thus, these member states have the privilege to govern the e-transactions, disputes, or redress based on the jurisdiction of their home country simply because they are a "member" of the state in conjunction with the principle of this directive. Obviously, the purpose of the E-Commerce Directive—Country of Origin is to secure a favorable legal framework for EU members.

Because of this approach, businesses take for granted that as long as they adhere to their home countries' regulations and are transparent in all transactions by making available all relevant information and stating their policy comprehensively and unambiguously before the consumer executes a transaction, then they will have the privilege to trade throughout all EU countries (Kirk & Hooles, 2002). Government is unable to impose any additional regulation on these e-tailers from other parts of the EU. If an Australian business has complied with Australian regulations, it should be able to sell to consumers in Finland without having to consider the Finnish regulations. This principle is not looking into consumer benefits. It enables activities to be controlled at the business source, and thus it is one of the ways to mitigate their own risks and responsibilities. In actual fact, businesses are magnifying their own protection and passing out the indirect message to consumers that "Under Country of Origin, if any mistakes or errors occur, it will not be my fault and you trade at you own risk" (Theresa Villiers, 2002).

Conclusion

By using the Internet, people can communicate with each other regardless of where they live by utilizing the global language of business, English. Geographic and political borders should largely be irrelevant in the e-environment, if, within a single jurisdiction, everyone is speaking the same language. Ultimately, the linguistic and cultural differences or absence of face-to-face communication is no longer an issue in contributing to misunderstandings or impeding the redress between businesses and consumers.

With the current complexities of the e-environment, single or harmonized jurisdiction, the global redress is believed to achieve an outcome which will enhance consumers and even businesses' confidence in the e-commerce marketplace. Nonetheless, prior to single or harmonized jurisdiction the global redress requires to determines the sovereignty aspect before the decision is reach.

Concurrently, on occasion government has no choice but to exercise control "to reach out" to protect the welfare of the people (business/consumer), the government is doing this not because they believe this is a appropriate action or taking advantages on another side to protect their internal market—but simply because there is no better option available.

Besides that, when enforcing a judgment or any redress decision against someone or something over which the court or authority has no control is a common issue and a limitation that poses to every country, government, authority, and even to any single individual. If a country can extend its perspective jurisdiction or power/redress decision beyond its enforcement jurisdiction, the question is how many countries can do that? The problem or complication is sovereignty. No country wants to be controlled and every country wants to be in control.

Thus, when the world is focusing on formulating laws and regulations on e-commence redress the authority should deal with the differences in legal systems and not conceal technical or legal barriers. The authority should confront the actual issues—uncertainty, enforcement, misunderstanding, and mutual interest, because if the authority entrench a single redress jurisdiction or harmonize the global redress has to be substantiated and collaborated with sovereignty. After all, when the single redress jurisdiction is established and well exercise, sovereignty issues can be slowly offset and resolve.

In the meantime, the matter of contention is still for these days and the time to come. Hence, by drawing up international conventions for settling disputes between business and consumers—with both parties afforded protection (businesses and consumers) and being well defined with no room for a difference in interpretation by various courts—the simultaneous development of cross-border e-commerce transactions will not be discouraged. This is a very long-term solution, but there is no reason why it should not start now.

References

American University. (2002). *E-commerce regulation environment.* Retrieved July 24, 2003, from http://www.american.edu/initeb/bb3747a/Norway%20-%20E-Commerce.htm

Barlow, J. (2003). The continuing evolution of Internet jurisdiction. *Internet Law: Jurisdiction.* Retrieved August 11, 2003, from http://www.internetlawjournal.com/content/litigationarticle01210301.htm

Bharuka, D., & Fisher, W. (2001). *Dispute resolution in cyberspace.* Berkman Center for Internet & Society. Retrieved August 14, 2004, from http://cyber.law.harvard.edu/ilaw/jurisdiction/

Cable & Wireless. (2003). *Jurisdiction.*

Caplan, J. (2001, January 10). *You've got lawsuit.* Retrieved August 11, 2003, from http://www.cfo.com/printarticle/0,5317,1921|A,00.html?f=options

Caslon Analytics. (2001). *Caslon analytic cyberspace governance guide.* Retrieved August 24, 2003, from http://www.caslon.com.au/governanceguide4.htm

Chen, C. (2004). United States and European Union approaches to Internet jurisdiction and their impact on e-commerce comment. *Journal of International Economic Law, 25*(1), 423.

Clark, E. (2000). *Call by expert for global commission to solve e-commerce jurisdiction problems.*

Collins, S. (2002). *Comments of Yahoo! Europe on the draft proposal for a "Rome II Regulation."* Government and Regulatory Affairs Yahoo, Europe. Retrieved July 18, 2003, from http://www.aig.org/r2g/yahoo_position.pdf

De Zylva, M. O. (2001, December 3). Confidence system in e-commerce. *AEDED Seminar,* Madrid. London: Word & Bond. Retrieved August 11, 2003, from http://www.e-global.es/confianza/wordanbod_text.pdf

E-Radar. (2005). *Legal issue Rome II.* Retrieved February 14, 2006, from http://www.e-ra.org.uk/rome_ii_regulation.htm

Europa. (2003). *Non-contractual obligations in cross-border cases.* Retrieved August 28, 2003, from http://www.europa.eu.int/comm/justice_home/news/intro/news_220703_1_en.htm

European Brands Association. (1999). *Effective not theoretical consumer protection in electronic commerce.* Retrieved July 17, 2003, from http://www.aim.be/docs/Marketing/AIM_POSc-o-origin.doc_1.doc

European Publishers Council. (2003). *Position paper of the European publishers council on the draft council regulation on jurisdiction and the enforcement of judgment in civil commercial matters.* Retrieved August 24, 2003, from http://www.epceurope.org/statements/Brussels_Regulation_final_position_paper.shtml

European Union Committee. (2002). *Position paper on the Draft Rome II Regulation.* Retrieved July 25, 2003, from http://www.eucommittee.be/Pops/2002archive/rome102002.pdf

Goldstein, N. (2001). Brussels I: A race to the top. *Chicago Journal of International Law, 2*(2), 521-524.

Ham, S., & Atkinson, R. D. (2001). *A third way framework for global e-commerce.* Progressive Policy Institute Technology & New Economy Project. Retrieved July 15, 2003, from http://www.ndol.org/documents/global_ecommerce.pdf

Hornle, J. (2004). The UK perspective on the country of origin rule in the e-commerce directive—A rule of administrative law applicable to private law disputes? *International Journal of Law and Information Technology, 12*(3), 333.

Interactive Advertising Bureau (IAB) UK. (2001). *An internal market strategy for service: The IAB's contribution.* Retrieved September 5, 2003, from http://www.iabuk.net/index.php?class=news&view=248

International Chamber of Commerce. (2000). *ICC request for re-evaluation of the European Commission's draft proposal for a council regulation on the law applicable to non-contractual obligations ("Rome II").* Retrieved July 13, 2003, from http://www.iccwbo.org/law/jurisdiction/rome2/documents/00004/

International Chamber of Commerce. (2001, June 6). *Jurisdiction and applicable law in electronic commerce.* Retrieved August 24, 2003, from http://www. iccwbo.org/home/statements_rules/statements/2001/jurisdiction_and_applicable_law.asp

International Chamber of Commerce. (2002, November 22). *New Spanish Internet law will stymie e-commerce.* Retrieved December 15, 2006, from http://www. iccwbo.org/icccafb/index.html?cookies=no

Johnson, A. R. (2001). *Will making it easier for consumers to sue help or e-commerce in the European Union?* Retrieved July 27, 2003, from http://www.haledorr. com/publications/pubsdetail.asp?ID=15154610232001

Johnson, D. R., & Post, D. (1996). Law and borders—The rise of law in cyberspace. *Stanford Law Review, 48,* 41.

Kirk, S., & Hooles, A. J. (2002, August), *E-commerce directive.* Retrieved September 5, 2003, from http://aporter.pair.com/articles/ecommerce.pdf

Koanantakool, T. (2003). *Thailand perspective toward self-regulation and government enforcement on privacy issues.* APEC E-commerce Steering Group. Retrieved October 1, 2003, from http://www.export.gov/apececommerce/ privacy/2003workshop/thaweesak_paper.html

Kobrin, S. J. (2001). Territoriality and the governance of cyberspace. *Journal of International Business Studies, 32*(4), 1-25.

Lawson, P. (2001). *Comments on The Draft Hague Convention on jurisdiction and foreign judgment in civil and commercial matter.* The Public Interest Advocacy Center. Retrieved August 24, 2003, from http://www.piac.ca/HagueConvention.htm

Maxwell, E. E. (1999). *19 policies for the emerging e-commerce marketplace.* Retrieved July 26, 2003, from http://www.aaas.org/spp/yearbook/2000/ch19. pdf

Mitchell, J., & Robertson, A. (2001). *The FSA's approach to regulation of e-commerce.* Scottish Advisory Committee on Telecommunications. Retrieved July 25, 2003, from http://www.fsa.gov.uk/pubs/discussion/06/responses/sa_cot.pdf

Morrison, D. S. (2000). *EC's e-commerce directive may be too indirect.* Retrieved September 11, 2003, from Red Herring Web site: http://www.redherring. com/investor/2000/0519/inv-eurocom051900.html

Morrison & Foerster. (2002, May). *Rome II Regulation: Preliminary draft proposal for a council regulation on the law applicable to non-contractual obligations.* Retrieved February 14, 2006, from http://www.mofo.com/news/updates/files/ update710.html

Oosterbaan, D. T. L., Jeekel, C. A., & Jonker, L. (2003). *E-commerce 2003; Netherlands.* Oosterbaan & Van Eeghen.

Osen, J. (2000). The thorny side of jurisdiction and the Internet. *Network Security Journal, 2000*(10), 13-16.

Out-Law. (2003a, June 13). *Commission defends cross-border law.* Retrieved February 14, 2006, from http://www.out-law.com/page-3639

Out-Law. (2003b). *Supreme Court mulls where to sue for Internet defamation.* Retrieved June 18, 2003, from http://www.out-law.com/php/page.php?page_id=supremecourtmulls1051121181&area=news

Pearce, G., & Platten, N. (2000). Promoting the information society: The EU directive on electronic commerce. *European Law Journal, 6*(4), 363-378.

Pitofsky, R. (2001). *Balancing business in cyberspace.* Federal Trade Commission. Retrieved August 24, 2003, from http://ppm.goinfo.com/Action/ppmeditorial.nsf/0/c3fcd50ac137e8098625694d0056031d?OpenDocument

Podlas, K. (2000). Global commerce or global liability? How e-commerce can lead to suit in foreign courts or under foreign law. *The Mid—Atlantic Journal of Business, 36*(2/3), 89-97.

Rosner, N. (2002). *International jurisdiction in European Union e-commerce contracts.* Retrieved August 8, 2003, from Law Library Resources Xchange Web site: http:///www.llrx.com/features/eu_ecom.htm

Spanish net law sparks protest. (2002, October 25). *Wired News.* Retrieved January 5, 2006, from http://www.wired.com/news/culture/0,1284,56021,00.html

Stoney, M. (2001). *Jurisdiction: How does it affect e-commerce—Strategies for virtual organizations.* Paper presented at Second International We-B Conference 2001.

The Vietnam Investment Review. (2003*). New electronic commerce regulations in the pipeline.* Retrieved July 8, 2003, from http://search.epnet.com/direct.asp?an=2W83247546761&db=buh

Theresa Villers MEP. (2002). *E-commerce: A revolution or a legal nightmare?* Retrieved September 16, 2003, from http://www.theresavilliers.com/link_13.htm

Tigre, P. B. (2003). Brazil in the age of electronic commerce. *Taylor & Francis Journal, 19*(1), 33-43.

United Nation Development Programme (UNDP). (2003). *Vietnamese to issue first e-commerce regulation.*

United State Council for International Business. (2000). *Alternative dispute resolution for consumer transaction in the borderless online marketplace.* Retrieved July 29, 2003, from http://www.uscib.org/policy/adrusgfl.htm

Zekos, G. I. (2002). *Legal problem of commercial transactions in cyberspace: An overview.* Retrieved January 5, 2006, from http://www.ciberspazioediritto.org/articoli/zekos.pdf

Chapter IV

Failures of B2C Retailing:
A Services Industry View

Anil M. Pandya, Northeastern Illinois University, USA

Nikhilesh Dholakia, University of Rhode Island, USA

Abstract

Conceptualizing business-to-consumer (B2C) businesses as an innovative class of technology-infused services yields insights into the factors that may lead to success or failure of such businesses. Drawing from services marketing literature and recent thinking on Internet service metrics, this chapter presents a framework for analyzing B2C businesses.

Birth Pangs of B2C: Dot-Com Failures

Looking back from the perspective of 2006, B2C e-commerce appears to be in a wary-yet-thriving mode (Latzer & Preissl, 2005). B2C systems have become parts of consumer lives, despite lingering consumer skepticism and distrust (Numberger & Rennhak, 2005; Robertson, Murphy, & Purchase, 2005). Turning the clock back by less than a decade, however, shows that B2C e-commerce was born via a very traumatic phase—especially in the USA—of the "dot-com crash."

During 1999 to 2001, many B2C e-commerce ventures failed. The B2C market crash was massive and economically destabilizing. It wiped out billions of dollars of market capitalization and led to a huge loss of employment. Between 1995 and 2000 a total of 492 Internet-related companies raised $36.3 billion in capital in the public markets. By 2000, just 11% of these companies traded at prices greater than their offer price. A third of them traded below 80% of the offer price. In 1999, 230 Initial Public Offerings (IPOs) raised $18.2 billion. In 2000, 130 IPOs were offered and raised $12.8 billion; but 133 IPOs representing $10.4 billion were withdrawn from the market. The market capitalization of the Internet sector in 1999 was $881 billion. This fell to $208 billion by December 2000 (Anderson, 2001). Layoffs in the industry in the year 2000 were 4,805 in September; 5,677 in October, and by December, the total layoffs stood at 22,267. Unemployment reached 700,000 for the year 2001 (Corcoran, 2002, Rock, 2000).

Such failures were attributed to causes such as failure to follow time-honored business and marketing principles (Agarwal, Arjona, & Lemmens, 2001; Varianni & Vaturi 2000), wrong or premature timing (Useem, 2000), inadequate financing (Cummings & Carr, 2001), and poor execution of strategies (Kemmler, Kubicova', Musselwhite, & Prezeau 2001).

Another useful way to look at B2C businesses—successes as well as failures—is to conceptualize them as *innovative consumer services*. In essence, B2C e com merce businesses represent new technology-driven ways of providing promotional, retailing, and distribution services to consumers. This paper proposes a services marketing framework to understand why so many Internet-based B2C companies failed to fulfill their initial promise. B2C dot-com crashes represent special types of services failures. Our analysis shows that the B2C e-commerce in its initial in-carnation was flawed. In B2C settings, consumers balance the cost of their time and efforts against services received and make judgments about service quality (Berry, Seiders, & Grewal, 2002). In the B2C environment, service quality depends on: (1) the process by which perceptions about the quality are formed, and (2) the gap between the perception of the service and the experience of the delivered service (Brady & Cronin, 2001; Zeithaml & Bitner 2003). By viewing B2C e-commerce businesses as services, we bring to bear, upon the B2C e-commerce sector, the existing knowledge from services marketing and Internet service metrics research. Recognizing that services require closer functional coordination between market-ing, production, and operations, we adapt the services models of Brady and Cronin (2001) and Gronroos (1984) for the B2C context to glean fresh insights into the success and failure causes of B2C ventures to help future B2C e-businesses to identify problems and manage them better.

The Concept of Services

Despite their ubiquity and diversity, services are hard to produce, market, profit from, or define. Consider a short list of services a person normally may require: doctors, hospitals, schools, colleges, religious services, airlines, taxis, buses, trains, schools, governments, security, haircuts, banks, gas stations, groceries, Laundromats, dry cleaners, car washes, bookstores, movies, video rentals, theaters, lectures, performances, and libraries. Services are deeds, processes, and performances (Zethaml & Bitner, 2003). They are an act or performance offered by one party to another, where the process may be tied to a physical product, but the performance is intangible and does not result in ownership of any factors of production. Most services are economic activities that create value and provide benefits for customers and bring about desired changes in them or on their behalf (Lovelock, 2003). Most services markets are easy to enter, but highly competitive. Creating and sustaining differentiation and maintaining competitive advantage are usually difficult. Low distinctiveness and increasing competition turn most services into commodities, depressing prices. At some point, low margins make it difficult to sustain the business. Unless managers remain customer focused, carefully develop the augmented service product, and differentiate service quality, the pressure to cut prices is difficult to reverse. Marketing and delivery costs rise as service firms try to maintain customers in the light of improving competitor offerings at lower prices. Most individuals and businesses require customized services. Competition, cost, and profit considerations, however, push providers toward reducing costs and standardization of part or all of the services offered. Therefore, it is common for customers to complain about service quality, value received, late deliveries, rude and uncaring providers, long lines, high prices, poor follow-up, bureaucratic procedures, unhelpful and untrained staff, billing inaccuracies, complicated self-service equipment, poor instructions, and inadequate service product. In short, though services are ubiquitous and necessary, they are highly competitive and difficult to sustain as profitable businesses. Using published evidence, we show that failing B2C businesses did not think about their businesses in services terms, whereas successful ones actively managed their firms as services. We conclude that a B2C e-commerce business has a better chance of success if it is managed as an Internet-based service convenience.

Conventional Services vs. B2C Retailing Services

Service Firm Managers: Balancing Three Things

Conventional services are best seen as an inverted triangle (see Figure 1, left side) with the firm's management at the apex of the inverted triangle (at the bottom) and customers and employees at the two vertices at the base of the triangle (on top, because of inversion). To achieve success, service firms are urged to market internally to the employees and externally to the customers (Gronroos, 1982, 1984). When employees interact effectively and amiably with customers, the results are satisfied customers and successful service businesses. This model of services as a triangle, proposed by Gronroos (1984), suggests that the management tasks entail the coordination of three distinct influence processes:

1. "Strategic positioning" of services by the firm's management to its customers

2. "Internal marketing" of the firm's customer service culture by the managers to the frontline employees

3. "Service encounters" wherein the interaction between customers and the frontline employees lead to satisfactory or unsatisfactory outcomes.

In successful service businesses, all three processes work in positive, mutually reinforcing ways.

Figure 1. Service relationships: Conventional and B2C

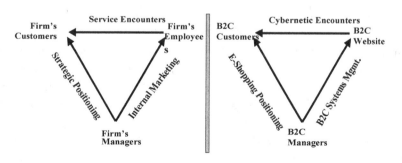

B2C Retailing as New Types of Services

When we conceptualize B2C businesses as e-services (Figure 1, right side), it is evident that most, sometimes all, of the B2C "service encounters" are cybernetic e-encounters rather than direct human interactions. Because of this, these three influence processes, represented on each side of the triangle (Figure 1 left side) of conventional services marketing, must be adjusted as shown (Figure 1 right side):

- Instead of mere "strategic positioning" of services to customers, managers need to position the *e-shopping experience* in the customers' minds as a superior way to obtain promotional, retailing, and distribution services.

- Instead of "internal marketing" to frontline service employees, managers need to sponsor *B2C systems* capable of enabling and assisting employees in providing amiable cybernetic e-encounters and delivering the items ordered.

- Instead of human "service encounters," there is a need to understand and improve *cybernetic service encounters* or *e-encounters*.

How different is such B2C business compared to retail services like ATM banking, telemarketing, and catalog marketing? These older retail modalities do use information technology (IT) to reduce or eliminate human contact. But the similarities with B2C end there. Internet-based B2C business provides customers easy, interactive, global, continuous (24/7), safe, and convenient *access to markets*. ATM is a successful chore-minimizing, self-service innovation—a convenient adjunct to brick-and-mortar banking services. Catalogs address the needs of remote or the time-constrained customers but do not help the price-constrained or the value-oriented customers and do not offer abundant choice and search capabilities. The Internet on the other hand, is an information rich context: providing convenience to the remote or time-constrained buyer, as well as choice and information to the value-oriented, price-constrained, variety-seeking and quality-seeking buyers. Telemarketing is an intrusive selling tool. It takes agency and initiative away from customers. B2C leaves the initiative to the customer as to when to look for a service, without sales pressure. Customers decide whether or not to purchase. Leading B2C firms also provide product reviews, ratings, and discussion forums.

Overall, interactive, information-rich B2C services represent a significant step beyond previous IT-based services such as ATMs, telemarketing, and catalogs. Older direct marketing alternatives grew out of advances in package deliveries, transportation, printing, and information technologies to address niche markets that were poorly addressed by the conventional store. Online B2C firms are an outgrowth of IT that frees all customers from location, time, information, and geographic constraints without the sacrifice of choice or agency. These factors make B2C a different type of service. Later in the paper, we present a technologically elaborated version of B2C service systems and offer suggestions for managing B2C services.

Managing the Quality of Services

Conventional and B2C services face challenges of maintaining high service quality. A study of best practices of successful e-business firms found that successful companies consciously or unconsciously saw themselves as service companies and took pains to find out and deliver what their customers wanted. These B2C companies also believed that they were not selling products but delivering values (Agarwal et al., 2001). Amazon.com and eBay are examples of successful B2C firms that have achieved competitive advantage (Kleindl, 2003; Krishnamurthy, 2003). These firms addressed the conventional *service quality problem* (Parasuraman, Zeithaml, & Barry, 1988).

In an integration of the service quality literature (Parasuraman et al., 1988, Zeithaml & Bitner, 2003), Brady and Cronin (2001) propose a hierarchical schema with three

Table 1. Service quality dimensions: Conventional and B2C (Based on Brady and Cronin, 2001; Parasuraman et al., 1988; Sweiger, 1999; and the authors' research)

Conventional service quality dimension	Conventional subdimension	Corresponding B2C service quality dimension
Interaction quality	Employee attitudes	Ease of use and friendliness of Web pages
	Employee behaviors	Interactivity and responsiveness of Web pages
	Employee expertise	Accuracy of accessible knowledge content of Web pages
Environment quality	Ambient conditions (nonvisual aspects)	Download speeds, otherwise *Not Applicable*
	Facility design (visual aspects)	"Look and feel" of the Web site
	Social conditions (crowds, commotion)	Type, size, quality, reliability, and operating styles of e-communities (users, experts)
Outcome quality	Waiting time	Search times and download times. Also, lead time for item delivery.
	Tangible evidence of service performance	Visible evidence of order completion, order correctness, payment, order tracking through e-mail feedback.
	Valence (positive or negative) of outcome	Positive or negative user experiences regarding item availability, order/payment correctness, match between item's Web description and the item itself, delivery, and returns.

main dimensions: Interaction Quality, Environment Quality, and Outcome Quality; each with three subdimensions. Table 1 compares these conventional dimensions of service quality with their B2C equivalents and highlights the differences between a conventional service and a cybernetic e-service, which a B2C business needs to provide.

There are two views of the concept of service quality and how to manage it. The first is what Brady and Cronin (2001) call the "Nordic" perspective (Gronroos 1982, 1984). Here, service quality is defined in global functional and technical quality terms, where customers judge the service quality based on outcome, and the way the service was delivered. External marketing and positioning the service consists of producing, pricing, promoting, and distributing. Gronroos (1984), chief exponent of the Nordic approach, argued that management of the service firm must also focus on "internal marketing" of a pro-customer service culture to the frontline employees (Figure 1 left side). The Nordic model is parsimonious and emphasizes delivery of service quality to obtain customer satisfaction. The second, the "American" perspective (Parasuraman et al., 1988), argues that customers use service encounter characteristics (reliability, responsiveness, empathy, assurances, and tangibles) to assess satisfaction. Because services are high in experience and credence values, customers typically find it difficult to judge technical quality of service delivery and look for cues elsewhere (Zeithaml & Bitner, 2003). Accordingly, for a consistent high-quality delivery, a firm must manage customer expectations formed by past experience, word-of-mouth, price, and advertising. Perceptions of deviation from expectations lead to dissatisfaction. Five gaps cause dissatisfaction. These are gaps between: (1) consumer expectation and management perception; (2) management perceptions and quality specifications; (3) quality specification and service delivery; (4) service delivery and external communication; and (5) perceived service and expected service. To manage service quality, managers must calibrate, track, and influence such characteristics, thereby reducing the gaps between expected and perceived quality.

Brady and Cronin (2001) integrate elements of the Nordic and American perspectives (see Table 1) and urge managers to pay attention to reliability, responsiveness, and empathy of service providers. In the B2C context, such a multi-dimensional view is useful, but needs to be adapted to the largely cybernetic forms of reliability, responsiveness, and empathy.

Managing B2C Retail Service Quality: A Framework

Since B2C commerce is a self-service technology, dimensions such as ambience, aesthetic, and display are either irrelevant or need to be reinterpreted in terms of Web aesthetics (Table 1). Factors such as Web site look and feel; its attractiveness; display; helpful hints about how to use the site; ease of "surfing" and navigating the site; options available; and ease of ordering the products become important. In the off-line environment, consumers respond to employee attitudes and behaviors. Well-trained employees can sense consumers' response and adjust the service offering. This corrective mechanism is absent in the online environment. Thus, "doing it right the first time" is of paramount importance in the cybernetic context. Attitudes, behaviors, and expertise of providers need to be reinterpreted as dimensions pertaining to friendliness, responsiveness, and knowledge content of Web sites (Table 1). Finally, the outcome-related dimensions also need to be similarly reinterpreted, using both the immediate outcomes of the ordering process (order/payment completion, accuracy) and—in case of nondigital products—delayed outcomes associated with delivery and potential returns (Table 1).

Box 1. Selected B2C service failures in electronic retailing of toys

The following illustrate some B2C failures in toy retailing. The examples are drawn from ZD Net Anchordesk (http://www.zdnet.com):

- David ordered 5 dolls for his daughter on November 29, 1999 with a guarantee from Toys R Us of a 7-10 day delivery. As of December 23, nothing had happened. Repeated phone calls and e-mails produced the response: "We don't know the status of your order."

- Thom's wife ordered toys from Toys R Us for their 8-year-old son on November 30, 1999. By December 15, 1999, the order status was "still in warehouse." The friendly but unhelpful customer service said the order would be shipped by that weekend. The order status was "still in warehouse" as of December 23, 1999.

- Charles, while shopping on eToys' site, found that the much-sought-after doll "Amazing Ally" was in stock, and quickly placed it in his shopping basket. While he was adding other items, the doll apparently went out of stock! His sister, for whom he was shopping, got the bad news only when she received the confirmation by e-mail. Charles felt someone had ripped the item out of his shopping basket without his knowing, on his way to the checkout lane.

- Neil received his order from eToys and a few days later received another huge package containing two Talking "Bubba Bears" he did not order. He contacted eToys to make sure they had not charged him and arrange to have eToys pick up the package of bears. Two months and dozens of phone calls and e-mails later eToys had still not picked up the bears.

B2C Retailing: Back to Services-Related Basics

In the B2C situation, in a sense we are back to the original conception of Gron-roos (1984) about managing service quality (Figure 1) but with strong technology mediation. Just as internal marketing is needed to motivate employees to become excellent service providers, internal managerial processes are needed to create a friendly, high-availability, high-performance Web site, and a smooth delivery and returns process. A big difference between conventional and B2C services is the appearance of complex order taking and fulfillment systems, in place of frontline employees. B2C service problems often arise from the breakdown of such systems (see Box 1).

Figure 2 shows the two sets of processes and personnel that need to be managed effectively in B2C businesses (Sweiger, 1999). Front-end processes are those deal-ing with the design and maintenance of Web sites, luring visitors to Web sites, and converting them into customers and repeat buyers. Back-end processes are those dealing with order fulfillment, delivery, and returns (Figure 2). B2C managers need to integrate and influence both processes to achieve optimum performance. It should be noted that customers only experience those parts of the front-end and back-end processes that impact them directly (see the thick arrows in Figure 2). B2C failures can and do occur in these visible processes (Box 1), but they may also occur in the background—in the inability of managers to direct these processes in proper ways.

Figure 2. Influence processes relating to B2C service quality

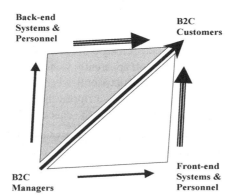

B2C Systemic Connections

B2C e-commerce differs from conventional retail in terms of the customer experiences and the enhanced ability of the B2C service provider to track Web site visitors, whether they are customers or not. According to Sweiger (1999):

While traditional brick-and-mortar commerce enterprises typically have no easy way to record and analyze user behavior until they become customers, if even that, e-commerce enterprises can record and analyze all activities of all types of users, all of the time. (p. 1)

This clickstream tracking ability opens up additional avenues of success and failure for B2C firms. As Figure 3 shows, B2C firms need enterprise-wide information architecture that coordinates front-end processes and personnel; back-end processes and personnel; and the managers and managerial processes responsible for directing both these customer-focused processes. B2C companies can "sink or swim" depending on how well they manage their customer and visitor data warehouses. If there are glitches in the communication of front-end order information to back-end order fulfillment processes, or inadequacies in learning from tracked user behavior, the B2C venture can succumb to competitive pressure or customer apathy.

Figure 3. Critical importance of enterprise information architecture in B2C business

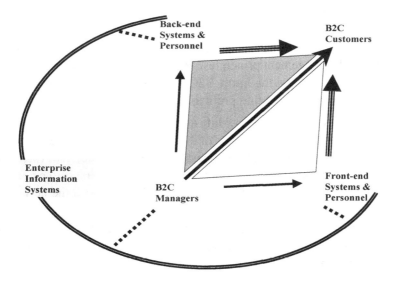

B2C Retailing: Purchase Cycle Calculus

The cost-benefit calculus—and therefore the value of a transaction on the Net—depends on the entire cycle of search, purchase, delivery, assessment, and return. This cycle, although similar to a conventional purchase in the "bricks" environment, is structurally different in the B2C environment. Many of the unsuccessful B2C providers failed to see this difference and assumed that customers will buy because the offering is "inexpensive," or "convenient," or "technically exciting or challenging." Such assumptions usually did not hold. Successful B2C firms escaped these stereotypical follies and saw themselves as providers of a *new technology-infused service*, a service not assessable by traditional retail service metrics.

In most B2C debacles, there was persistent discrepancy between high customer acquisition costs and low revenues. In early 1999, B2C companies spent over $1,100 to acquire a customer, who typically spent only $400. In late 1999, the average cost of customer acquisition was reduced to $800 but customer spending remained at or below $400. The average monthly losses per B2C site were $1 and $1.1 million, respectively, in the first and second half of 1999, despite the increased efficiencies (Agarwal et al., 2001). In the false hope that the Internet was a price elastic market, many B2C businesses maintained low margins. In reality, instead of clicking across multiple sites, 80-90% of buyers of books and CDs visited only one site, even though prices of books and CDs across Web sites varied by as much as 25-30%. In the B2C market structure, instead of deep discounting, astute firms could have charged higher prices without sacrificing revenues and profits (Marn, 2000). Only a small but solid group of companies managed to achieve visitor conversion rates of 12%, customer churn rates below 20%, and repeat purchase rates of around 60% (Agarwal et al., 2001). The majority of the B2C failures were caused by "fatal attraction": luring visitors to the site but failing to convert them into customers. Successful firms generated nearly three times the gross income from repeat customers as from one-time buyers. Why did so many firms, with so much talent and easy access to capital, fail to use time-tested management principles? What was it about this new technology and service delivery method that most B2C managers misread? Why could these companies not convert visitors into profitable and loyal customers?

The Internet implies a revolutionary shift in marketing. From being agents of the seller, B2C firms have to become agents of the buyer (Achrol & Kotler, 1999). B2C firms failed to appreciate that their business was a new service innovation, not a new technology business. This subtle but strategic shift in perspective could have refocused B2C managerial efforts from being preoccupied with the new technology and market share dominance, to providing consistently high-quality customer service and convenience to create buyer loyalty and customer retention. While acknowledging that many B2C firms strayed from services marketing principles, our framework emphasizes the importance of cybernetic e-encounters, captures some of the additional underlying complexity of B2C failures, and identifies ingredients for B2C success.

Amazon.com succeeded in the book business because buyers receive excellent service at low cost. Amazon.com ranked highest of all online and off-line businesses in consumer satisfaction reported by the American Customer Satisfaction Index (ACSI), a difficult feat in any context (Kleindl, 2003). Amazon.com does have problems but these are in the supply chain, where traditional distributors sometimes did not cooperate (Krishnamurthy, 2003).

As a global concept, B2C e-commerce represents a major innovation in the way marketing is done. It offers goods and services to consumers through the Internet. It reduces search costs. It is convenient, quick, easily accessible, and often less expensive. In this sense it is a "new service product" for consumers as well as the world available in a new way. When firms offer traditional products such as books, CDs, groceries, and toys via the Internet, they are not merely marketing known products to known customers. They are offering instead a fast, highly competitive, interactive, and technological means of information access and transaction. By using such means, consumers are able to comparison shop and receive door-to-door service at a reasonably low price. The failure of B2C firms can thus be construed as a failure of a new class of Internet-mediated service where these firms failed to seamlessly integrate the front-end and back-end systems and personnel with the needs of customers.

The Middle Path

Finally, we are ready examine the importance of the middle arrow (Figures 2 and 3) connecting B2C managers to B2C customers. While most of the B2C customer enterprise interactions are cybernetic or quasi-mechanistic (as in package delivery to a mailbox), managers still need to communicate with customers in ways more direct than a Web site. They need to constantly position the B2C shopping experience to the customers using mass media, public relations, and even personal meetings. Only by combining effective traditional media communications, friendly front-end Web interactions, and smooth back-end processes can B2C businesses hope to attract and retain customers. All this, of course, must be done efficiently. Successful companies, as stated earlier, achieved higher visitor conversion rates, reduced significantly the rate of customer defection, and achieved high-repeat purchase rates. These firms generated nearly three times the gross income from repeat buyers as compared to one-time buyers. The superior skills of these firms lay in acquiring visitors, converting them into customers, and retaining them. This requires seamless coordinated execution of the communication, positioning, front-end tasks, and back-end tasks (Figures 2 and 3). Amazon.com succeeds by paying meticulous attention to these strategic details (Kleindl, 2003, p. 134; Krishnamurthy, 2003, p. 123). EBay, the most successful of Internet companies, with profits since 1997, also follows a similar approach (Krishnamurthy, 2003, p. 143). Firms that failed did not follow this approach.

Summary and Conclusion

Boo.com is the prototypical B2C e-commerce startup that failed. It got entangled in creating the best aesthetic site possible but failed to incorporate the basic desire of customers to view and compare fashion products quickly to make a buy decision—a failure to integrate the front-end systems and personnel with customer needs. Launched with a blaze of publicity, it burned through $135 million even before it went public (Isaacs, 2001). Insiders say Boo.com failed because it spent too much money on marketing (Isaacs, 2001). While Boo.com Web designers were fretting about aesthetics, customers were looking for good deals and fast delivery service. Similarly, Petstore.com, Pets.com, Toysmart.com, and other similar ventures failed to take off because they offered nothing new to the customers. These sites had neither inexpensive products, nor inexpensive and reliable delivery. They targeted ultra-thin niches for which demand had never been—and probably, never will be—proven (Isaacs, 2001). Toysmart.com, did not have a chance in a crowded space occupied by Toys R Us and other e-tailers (Isaacs, 2001). These B2C e-commerce companies addressed a known need but their offer did not match either customer expectations of better and cheaper service or match the offers of already existing new and traditional suppliers. E-toys failed first to forecast demand and then overreacted and overstocked products, which quickly became obsolete. They could not fulfill customer expectations, despite the fact that their top management team consisted of experienced Disney executives. In these companies we see a failure of integration at both the front and the back-end systems as shown in Figures 2 and 3.

In summary, to be successful, a B2C e-business must think of themselves as providing service convenience on the Internet, focus on their core customers, find their customers efficiently, offer them what they want, and deliver the products efficiently, reliably, and in a timely manner by integrating systems and people for creating customer friendly and accurate Web access, accurate order processing, and timely order fulfillment. For this, marketing folks must think like information systems people, and vice versa.

References

Agarwal, V., Arjona, L. D., & Lemmens, R. (2001). E-Performance: The path to rational exuberance. *The McKinsey Quarterly, 1,* 31-43.

Bowman, R. J. (2001, February). *Increased European sales for staples? Yeah, we've got that.* Retrieved from http://www.supplychainbrain.com/archives/2.01. staples.htm?adcode=5

Brady, M. K., & Cronin, J. J., Jr. (2001, July). Some new thoughts on conceptualizing perceived service quality: A hierarchical approach. *Journal Of Marketing Research, 65*(3), 34-50.

Cummings, E. M., & Carr, K. S. (2001, August). How does your garden tank? *Darwin.* Retrieved from http://www.darwinmag.com/read/080101/garden.html

Gronroos, C. (1984). A service quality model and its marketing implications. *European Journal of Marketing, 18*(4), 36-44.

Kemmler, K., Kubicova', M., Musselwhite, R., & Prezeau, R. (2001). E-Performance II: The good, the bad and the merely average. *The McKinsey Quarterly*, 3.

Kleindl, B. A. (2003). *Strategic electronic marketing: Managing e-business.* Cincinnati, OH: Thomson South-Western Press.

Krishnamurthy, S. (2003). *E-commerce management: Text and cases.* Cincinnati, OH: Thomson South-Western Press.

Latzer, M., & Preissl, B. (2005). Preface to the focus theme: E-Business impacts revisited. *Electronic Markets, 15*(3), 178-180.

Numberger, S., & Rennhak, C. (2005). The future of B2C e-commerce. *Electronic Markets, 15*(3), 269-282.

Parasuraman, A., Zeithaml, V. A., & Berry, L. (1985, Fall). A conceptual model of service quality and its implications for future research. *Journal of Marketing, 49,* 41-50.

Robertson, G., Murphy, J., & Purchase, S. (2005). Distance to market: Propinquity across in-store and online food retailing. *Electronic Markets, 15*(3), 235-245.

Useem, J. (2000, October 30). Dot-coms: What have we learned? *Fortune,* 82-104.

Varianni, V., & Vaturi, D. (2000). Marketing lessons from e-failures. *The McKinsey Quarterly, 4,* 216-19.

Chapter V

Inducing Online Trust in E-Commerce:
Empirical Investigations on Web Design Factors

Ye Diana Wang, George Mason University, USA

Henry H. Emurian, University of Maryland,
Baltimore County (UMBC), USA

Abstract

Two studies were undertaken to investigate interface design features that might impact customers' trust in an e-commerce vendor's Web site. In a first quantitative survey study, experienced Internet users rated 14 features of a synthetic e-commerce interface for their trust-inducing effectiveness. A factor analysis of the ratings partially confirmed a proposed conceptual model of trust-inducing features and yielded the following three factors: (1) visual design, (2) content design, and (3) social-cue design. The comparatively lower ratings on the social-cue design factor motivated a second qualitative analysis of a different group of users' observations regarding the importance of virtual re-embedding strategies as they may impact trust in an online vendor's Web site. Users' reports from interviews generally supported the importance of socially rich Web sites in promoting online trust, and they deepened our understanding of the functionalities and suitability of various communication media for the adoption of virtual re-embedding strategies. The complementary outcomes from both quantitative and qualitative sources of information are anticipated to contribute to future applications and research in e-commerce interface design considerations affecting online trust.

Introduction and Background

Online trust, defined as an Internet user's psychological state of risk acceptance (Rousseau, Sitkin, Burt, & Camerer, 1998), is essential for the proliferation of e-commerce. If consumers trust online vendors and have confidence in the reliability and integrity of vendors, they will likely feel more at ease in making purchase decisions (e.g., Ang & Lee, 2000; McKnight & Chervany, 2002; Teo, 2002). Consumer trust, which conventional vendors work tirelessly to achieve in off-line situations, is even more difficult to build in online environments. This is due to at least two reasons or disadvantageous characteristics of e-commerce. First, completions of e-commerce transactions are typically separated in space and time, with the exception of the delivery of downloadable digital products, and this situation requires consumers often to disclose personal information and to make a purchase even before seeing a product (Riegelsberger & Sasse, 2000). Second, a Web site, rather than a face-to-face interaction with a sales person, is the primary and direct "contact point" relied upon by online vendors to interact and communicate with their customers (Gefen & Straub, 2003). An important question, then, is how can online vendors attract potential consumers and induce their trust in an online environment?

The answers to this challenge may reside in the online vendors' primary and direct "contact point"—the electronic storefront. According to Ang and Lee (2000), "If the web site does not lead the consumer to believe that the vendor is trustworthy, no purchase decision will result" (p. 3). In other words, one key consideration in fostering online trust is to build a trust-inducing e-commerce interface. In that regard, several studies have reported evaluations of a list of design features that could potentially appear on an interface to impact trust (e.g., Fogg et al., 2001; Lee, Kim, & Moon, 2000; Neilsen, 1999). Related studies have reported evaluations of existing e-commerce Web sites, such as Amazon.com, as a method for determining trust-inducing features (e.g., Cheskin/Sapient, 1999; Gefen & Straub, 2004; Jarvenpaa, Tractinsky, & Saarinen, 1999). However, the trust-inducing features of those sites could not always be accurately measured or generalized to other e-commerce Web sites due to a lack of a standardized interface for evaluation.

This chapter first presents an investigation to identify features, suggested by a conceptual framework as shown in Table 1, of a synthetic e-commerce interface that are evaluated for their trust-inducing influence. A quantitative factor analytic approach was used. Based upon the outcome of that evaluation, a second investigation was undertaken to shed additional light on social cues or interaction opportunities that

Table 1. Conceptual framework of trust-inducing features

Dimension	Explanation	Features	Literature sources
Graphics design	Refers to the graphical design factors on the Web site that normally give consumers a first impression.	• Use of three-dimensional and half-screen size clipart • Symmetric use of moderate pastel color of low brightness and cool tone • Use of well-chosen, good-shot photographs	Karvonen and Parkkinen (2001); Kim and Moon (1998).
Structure design	Defines the overall organization and accessibility of displayed information on the Web site.	• Implementation of easy-to-use navigation (simplicity, consistency) • Use of accessible information (e.g., no broken links and missing pictures) • Use of navigation reinforcement (e.g., guides, tutorials, instructions, etc.) • Application of page design techniques (e.g., white space and margin, strict grouping, visual density, etc.)	Cheskin/Sapient (1999); Karvonen and Parkkinen (2001); Nielsen (1999); Zhang, Von Dran, Small, and Barcellos (1999).
Content design	Refers to the informational components that can be included on the Web site, either textual or graphical.	• Display of brand-promoting information (e.g., prominent company logo or slogan, main selling point) • Up-front disclosure of all aspects of the customer relationship (company competence, security, privacy, financial, and legal concerns) • Display of seals of approval or third-party certificate • Use of comprehensive, correct, and current product information • Use of a relevant domain name	Belanger, Hiller, and Smith, (2002); Cheskin/Sapient (1999); Egger (2001); Hu, Lin, and Zhang (2001); Nielsen (1999); Shneiderman (2000).
Social-cue design	Relates to embedding social cues, such as face-to-face interaction and social presence, into Web interface via different communication media.	• Inclusion of a representative photograph or video clip • Use of synchronous communication media (instant messaging, chat lines, video telephony, etc.)	Basso et al. (2001); Riegelsberger and Sasse (2001); Steinbruck et al. (2002).

may impact trust in e-commerce Web sites. A qualitative approach was used in the second study. Together, the two studies to be presented will indicate features of interface design and functionality that online vendors would be well advised not to overlook when presenting their electronic storefronts to e-commerce shoppers. Although there are almost certainly many potential sources of influence that promote or hinder online trust, our research focuses on evaluations of interface design features and on seeking deeper understandings from Internet users' observations on the potential impact of interface design in inducing online trust. The remainder of this chapter describes the proposed conceptual framework, the research methodology, the results of the two studies, a discussion, and, finally, our conclusions with future directions.[1]

Conceptual Framework of Trust-Inducing Features

The outcome of our previous study (Wang & Emurian, 2005a) was a conceptual framework of trust-inducing features that were identified from the literature on enhancing online trust by Web interface design. The framework classified 14 trust-inducing features into four broad dimensions, namely (1) graphics design, (2) structure design, (3) content design, and (4) social-cue design. Table 1 illustrates the framework in detail, including the explanations, design features, and literature sources for each dimension that was proposed on the basis of a semantic and functional grouping of features obtained from the literature. The first three dimensions are straightforward. The fourth dimension, the social-cue design dimension, relates to embedding social cues into Web site interfaces via different communication media, and it is a relatively recent design strategy being suggested by some human-computer interaction (HCI) researchers (e.g., Basso, Goldberg, Greenspan, & Weimer, 2001; Riegelsberger & Sasse, 2001; Steinbruck, Schaumburg, Duda, & Kruger, 2002). The framework is not exhaustive in the sense that it does not attempt to capture every possible trust-inducing feature the Web designer can apply. It is focused on articulating the most prominent set of trust-inducing features, derived from numerous previous studies, and presenting them as an integrated entity that can be empirically evaluated.

Investigations on Interface Design Dimenstions: A Quantitative Approach

Synthetic E-Commerce Interface

To provide an illustrative example of the framework, a synthetic e-commerce interface (see Figure 1) for a hypothetical online vendor selling plasma TVs was created based on the 14 identified trust-inducing features (Wang & Emurian, 2005b). We chose the selling product to be plasma TVs because of the attractiveness of the image and its unique ability to induce serious reflection and thought on the purpose of the survey, which was to evaluate specific features concerning trust. We gave an imaginary name, "PlasmaTV.com," to the Web site. The interface was tailored such that every feature could be visually illustrated by some element or aspect of the interface. For example, the company logo in the upper left corner and the main selling point in the central image were on the interface to represent "display of brand-promoting information." The VeriSign seal in the lower left corner was used to present "display of seals of approval or third-party certificates." We intention-

Figure 1. Synthetic e-commerce interface

ally created the interface in two languages, namely English and Chinese, so that we could perform cross-cultural analyses of the data. Both versions of the interface were implemented using professional Web page development tools in conjunction with a graphics editing package. The interfaces were accessible to the general public at a subdomain that was provided by the university.

Survey

A Web-based survey was conducted to confirm the proposed framework of trust-inducing features. A text version of the survey is presented in Appendix A. The rationale and advantages of using a Web-based survey in our study were as follows. First, the abilities of a Web-based survey, to make respondents feel anonymous and overcome time and place constraints, helped us to reach respondents more easily than using other data collection methods. Second, the survey was implemented to require mandatory responses for every item, preventing uncompleted answerers from being submitted. Last, the Web-based survey included a hyperlink to the e-commerce interface, providing a convenient way to direct the respondents to the Web interface that needed to be viewed and evaluated in an online setting.

The initial survey instrument was reviewed by four experienced online shoppers and two language experts for consistency, completeness, and readability. The language experts were asked to pay special attention to the accuracy of the translation between the English and Chinese versions. The objectives of this step were to examine the face validity of each item in the survey and to avoid any misleading cultural differences due to inaccurate translation.

The resulting survey instrument is described as follows. As previously mentioned, a link to the synthetic e-commerce interface that opened up in a new window was inserted at the top of the survey so that subjects could examine the interface carefully while completing the survey. Below the link were the three sections of the survey. The first section consisted of seven drop-down menus gathering demographic and experiential information on a respondent's age, gender, current location, highest education attained, weekly hours spent on the Internet, and experience with purchasing online. The second section of the survey consisted of 15 items to rate, of which the first 14 items corresponded to the 14 design features, and the last item assessed the overall level of trustworthiness. The visual element examples representing each design feature on the interface were indicated in parentheses after each item on the survey.

Respondents rated each of the first 14 items using a 10-point Likert-type scale, which allowed them to select a response indicating the trust-inducing importance of each feature. The responses ranged from "1," indicating that the feature was "not important at all," to "10," indicating that the feature was "extremely important." The anchors for item 15, an overall evaluation of the trustworthiness of the interface, were "1 = Not at all trustworthy" to "10 = Totally trustworthy." The last section of the survey was a feedback box provided for comments. Like the interface itself, the survey was also created in both English and Chinese to reach more respondents and to enable cross-cultural comparisons.

In developing the survey, we used the best wording for the features that we could, and our preliminary trials with the survey instrument did not reveal a serious or compromising problem with the survey content. Since the reliability of the item ratings within three identified factors was satisfactorily high, as presented in a subsequent section of this chapter, we conclude that the survey items were understood by the respondents. Aberrant items would have revealed themselves in the factor analysis.

Respondents

To solicit a pool of respondents who would be as close to the general public of Internet users as possible, we distributed the link to the survey through university listservs, online discussion boards, and personal e-mail contacts. No monetary compensation was provided. The participants were volunteers who were also interested in the research topic. We eliminated two respondents who were obviously unconcerned (i.e., giving the same rating for all features), and eventually a total of 181 respondents was included in the final analysis. Table 2 presents the characteristics of the participants based upon the information reported on the survey. Since the survey did not target specific individuals, there is no response-rate calculation. It is also the case that this approach did not yield a truly random sample from a population, but it did produce a representative pool of Internet users. For that reason, the generality of the results best applies to respondents who exhibit the characteristics reported and to those who are disposed to answer a circulated request to participate in a similar survey.

Among the respondents, 108 (60%) were located in the USA. There were 73 (40%) female participants, and 123 (68%) of the participants used the English language interface.[2] Most of them had a bachelor's degree (n = 94, 52%), spent more than 15 hours per week online (n = 105, 58%), and were in their 20s (n = 104, 57%). Most respondents (n = 141, 78%) reported that they had made a purchase online, and 26 (18%) of the purchasers reported that they had been cheated in online shopping.

Table 2. Characteristics of survey respondents

Age		Location of participant	
11-20	17	USA	108
21-30	104	Other	73
31-40	28		
41-50	18	**Gender**	
51-60	13	Female	73
61-70	1	Male	108
Education		**Weekly Internet hours**	
High school	23	1-5	20
Associates degree	10	6-10	35
Bachelors degree	94	11-15	21
Masters degree	40	>15	105
Doctoral degree	14		
Internet purchase		**Purchasers cheated**	
Yes	141	Yes	26
No	40	No	115
Language of interface			
Chinese	58		
English	123		

Results

The data analysis had four major parts: (1) confirming the underlying dimensions in the conceptual framework of trust-inducing features, (2) comparing the magnitudes of the ratings across the dimensions obtained, (3) correlating ratings within the dimensions with overall trust ratings, and (4) comparing overall trust ratings based on demographic and experiential subgroups.

Confirming the Underlying Dimensions

The references from the existing literature used to formulate the 14 features of the conceptual framework, together with the involvement of experienced online shoppers and language experts in constructing the survey, established the content validity of the survey items. However, the classification into the four groupings was based on the authors' informed judgment. Hence, the 14 features were subjected to a confirmatory factor analysis to confirm the underlying dimensions and to assess the construct validity and internal reliability of the framework. The statistical tests presented hereafter are standard in this type of analysis, and information about them is readily available elsewhere (e.g., Lee & Turban, 2001).

Before we conducted a factor analysis, we ran two tests that indicated the suitability of the data for structure detection. The high value (0.81) from the Kaiser-Meyer-Olkin Test, which measures sampling adequacy, indicated that a factor analysis would be useful with the data. The significant Bartlett's Test ($p < .001$), which examines whether the variables are related, indicated that the data were suitable for structure detection. Therefore, a factor analysis was performed.

We used the principal components analysis to analyze the raw matrix of 181 responses with the latent root criterion (Eigen value = 1 criterion). Three components (Eigen values > 1.44) accounted for 56% of the total variance of the data set. The scree test, which showed that there were some bending points at three factors, further verified the number of dimensions. Based on this initial analysis, we tried several rotation methods to determine which features loaded on each of the three dimensions and eventually chose the Varimax rotation method, which revealed the underlying relationship the best. As presented in Table 3, all factor loadings reach the acceptable level of 0.3 (Nunally, 1978), with most of them exceeding 0.6. To examine the internal reliability of each factor (i.e., visual design, content design, and social-cue design dimension), Cronbach's alpha was calculated on each factor, and the alpha coefficients were 0.80, 0.77, and 0.53, respectively. According to Nunally (1978), an alpha of 0.50 or higher indicates a sufficient level of internal reliability.

The factor analysis revealed that none of the 14 features in the proposed framework should be eliminated because each item fell into one of the three factors (all fac-

Table 3. Rotated component matrix (N = 181)

Dimensions	Features	Factor		
		1	2	3
Visual design	V1 - Three-dimensional and half-screen size clipart	.504		
	V2 - Symmetrical, moderate pastel color of low brightness and cool tone	.685		
	V3 - Well-chosen, good-shot photographs	.762		
	V4 - Easy-to-use navigation	.748		
	V5 - Accessible information	.696		
	V6 - Navigation reinforcement	.532		
	V7 - Page design techniques	.636		
Content design	C1 - Brand-promoting information		.447	
	C2 - All aspects of customer relationship information		.795	
	C3 - Seals of approval or third-party certificate		.778	
	C4 - Comprehensive, correct, and current product information		.688	
	C5 - Relevant domain name		.476	
Social-cue design	S1 - Representative photograph or video clip			.744
	S2 - Synchronous communication media			.734

tor loadings ≥ .30). The analysis also showed that the items for each factor loaded unambiguously. The only difference between the confirmatory analysis results and our proposed framework was the number of groupings: The 14 features clustered into three factors (i.e., dimensions) rather than four. The first factor included the first two dimensions of the proposed framework, and the last two factors were consistent with the last two dimensions as proposed. Therefore, we named the first factor "visual design," which reflected both graphics and structure aspects, and we kept the names for the last two factors as "content design" and "social-cue design." Because little covariance existed among these three factors, it may be concluded that these three dimensions reflect different aspects of interface design to promote ratings of trust.

Evaluating Relative Magnitudes

To investigate the relative magnitudes in ratings among the survey items that fell within each of the three identified dimensions, the median rating across those items was determined for each of the 181 respondents. The median is the appropriate index of central tendency for ordinal data. Figure 2 presents boxplots of those ratings for each of the three dimensions. The figure, then, is a boxplot of the medians. Figure 2 shows that all three medians exceed 5, but the median for the social-cue design dimension is graphically lower in comparison to the other two. The result of a Kruskal-Wallis "ANOVA by ranks" Test (Maxwell & Delaney, 2000, p. 703), which is most appropriate for ordinal data and which can be used to assess differ-

Figure 2. Boxplots of medians of the ratings of the features within each factor (The circles are outliers)

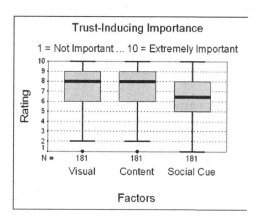

ences across two or more samples, was significant (χ^2 = 42.50, df = 2, p < .001). Pairwise comparisons, Bonferroni corrected, showed significant differences between the social-cue median and the other two medians. These data suggest that all three dimensions were sensitive to the respondents' evaluations, but the social-cue dimension was rated as somewhat less important as the other two dimensions.

Evaluating Correlational Relationships

To evaluate the correlation between each dimension and the respondents' overall trust evaluations toward the synthetic interface, the ratings from item 15 in the survey were collected to represent the overall trust level as a result of the 14 trust-inducing design features. Because only two indicators were available for the social-cue dimension and only one for the overall trust rating, structural equation modeling (SEM) was not appropriate for analyzing these data (Garson, 2004). In its place, a stepwise regression was undertaken using each participant's median rating within each dimension as the predictor variable for the visual, content, and social-cue dimensions, respectively, and using the overall trust rating as the criterion variable. The outcome showed that only the content ratings were significantly related to the overall trust ratings (beta = .198, t = 2.07, p = .008). The visual and social-cue predictors were both excluded by the stepwise regression.

Comparing Demographic and Experiential Subgroups

The overall trustworthiness ratings were compared based on the different characteristics of the respondents. The purpose of this part of the analysis was to investigate whether demographic characteristics and individual experiences are related to users' overall trustworthiness ratings of the e-commerce interface under consideration.

Comparisons based on Demographic Characteristics

The survey asked the subject to indicate his or her age by selecting one of six age categories. The Kruskal-Wallis Test showed no significant differences among the age groups in overall trustworthiness ratings ($\chi^2 = 8.69$, df $= 5$, p $> .10$). A comparison between male (n $= 108$) and female (n $= 73$) subjects was not significant ($\chi^2 = 0.33$, p $> .10$), and a comparison among the five education level categories was not significant ($\chi^2 = 9.40$, df $= 4$, p $> .05$).

Cross-Cultural Comparisons

Because we developed the survey and the e-commerce interface in both English and Chinese, we were able to make cross-cultural comparisons in overall trust ratings. Due to the fact that people's current locations do not necessarily represent their national culture, we divided the respondents into two cultural groups based on the language of the survey that they chose as their mother tongue. A Kruskal-Wallis Test was conducted to compare the difference in overall trustworthiness ratings between English (n $= 123$) and Chinese (n $= 58$) speakers, and the outcome was not significant ($\chi^2 = 0.45$, p $> .10$).

Comparisons based on Online Experience

The respondents selected one of four categories based on their reported weekly hours spent online. The result of the Kruskal-Wallis Test across the four time intervals was not significant ($\chi^2 = 4.02$, df $= 3$, p $> .25$). In this survey, we did not request information about the years of Internet use. We would suggest, however, that it does not take too long to come up to speed on using the Internet, especially for users who were kind enough to answer our survey. Therefore, the "weekly hours" measure is used only to provide a rough sense of the characteristics of the population under consideration.

There was no significant difference in trustworthiness ratings between subjects who did report previous online purchasing experiences (n $= 141$) and those who did not ($\chi^2 = 0.11$, p $> .10$). We also compared the overall trust ratings between the respondents who had been cheated by an online vendor (n $= 26$) and those who had not been cheated. The result showed a significant difference ($\chi^2 = 4.13$, p $< .05$).

Figure 3. Boxplots of overall trust ratings for purchasers who had been and who had not been cheated by an online vendor (The circles are outliers)

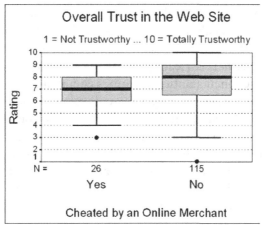

Figure 3 shows that the respondents who had been cheated by an online vendor gave comparatively lower ratings of the overall trustworthiness of the Web site than those who had never been cheated.

Investigations on the Social-Cue Design Dimension: A Qualitative Approach

The results of the statistical tests from the previous study suggest that all three identified dimensions contributed to the respondents' evaluations of the synthetic e-commerce interface, but the social-cue design dimension was rated somewhat less important than the other two dimensions. It is suspected that the lower ratings on the social-cue design dimension items are due to the fact that the two rated features within the social-cue design dimension were the only ones that were not actually implemented as functional examples on the interface, and thus were not understood well by the respondents. Therefore, the results call for a deeper understanding on applying virtual re-embedding strategies to interface design by undertaking further investigations.

As the separation of e-commerce transactions over space and time, commonly known as *dis-embedding* (Riegelsberger & Sasse, 2001), presents a real problem, integrating social presence and interpersonal interactions into e-commerce Web sites by means of virtual re-embedding strategies has been proposed as a possible solution (e.g., Basso et al., 2001; Gefen & Straub, 2004; Hassanein & Head, 2004; Qiu & Benbasat, 2005; Riegelsberger & Sasse, 2001; Steinbruck et al., 2002). While most of the previous research on virtual re-embedding remains preliminary and only focuses on investigating the use of socially rich text and picture design elements in interface design (Riegelsberger & Sasse, 2001; Steinbruck et al., 2002; Riegelsberger, Sasse, & McCarthy, 2003; Hassanein & Head, 2004), the authors conducted an exploratory qualitative study on the functionalities of various communication media in the use of virtual re-embedding strategies. As a huge collection of communication media is presently available to be chosen from and employed in e-commerce, we are particularly interested in how to provide more opportunities for personal contacts and even face-to-face interactions between consumers and the online vendor by using richer communication media. Especially, what are the criteria for an online vendor to select suitable communication media? Which medium is best for supporting what functionality and when? These are some questions of focus.

Methodology

Research Design

Data were collected based on triangulation, which is the use of a variety of methods (Patton, 2002), including (1) online questionnaire, (2) semi-structured interview, and (3) contextual interview. The combination of these methods allowed for obtaining feedback directly from the participants while observing their natural online shopping behaviors and reactions. The three methods are described hereafter.

First, each participant completed an online questionnaire providing demographic information. The questionnaire consisted of three sections as shown in Appendix B. The first section consisted of three drop-down menus gathering demographic information on each participant's age, gender, and education background. The second section included four questions and was used to determine each participant's level of trust propensity, which is a person's degree of trust (Diller, Lin, & Tashjian, 2003). For example, one of the four items was "I almost always believe what people tell me," and the participant would select a rating ranged from "1 = strongly disagree" to "7 = strongly agree." The ratings on all four questions would be used to determine the "overall trust propensity" of the participants. The last section of the questionnaire consisted of three drop-down menus gathering information on each participant's overall online experience, including weekly hours spent on the Internet, numbers of online purchases, and occurrence of being cheated by an online vendor.

Following the questionnaire, a semi-structured interview was conducted to cover the general views and preferences of the participant on virtual re-embedding strategies. During the interview, each participant was asked 5-10 open-ended questions from defining social cues to brainstorming on the various cues, ways, and tools for adding interpersonal interactions and social presence to an e-commerce Web site.

The second contextual interview supplemented the first one by providing concrete, visual examples for earlier discussion of general ideas. The participant was asked to name an existing e-commerce Web site, which he or she considered as most trust-worthy or sociable. While browsing through the Web site, the participant was asked to identify the interface elements and features that provided social cues and induced trust feelings. The participant was also encouraged to think aloud and describe mental reactions upon noticing these elements and cues. In addition, the interviewer asked each participant to perform one or more short tasks, such as finding customer service information on how to contact the online vendor in case of difficulties or problems. Both interviews were audio recorded and transcribed along with the interview notes that the interviewer took for later coding and analysis.

Participants

To sample a diverse and close to the general public of Internet users as a university student population could be, 14 experienced online shoppers of different age groups were recruited on campus. The age distribution was: 11-20 years (n = 5), 21-30 years (n = 4), 31-40 years (n = 2), 41-50 years (n = 2), and 51-60 years (n = 1). In fact, the participants were all 18 years of age or older. Gender representation was equal between female and male. Among the participants, nine of them were undergradu-ate students and the rest were graduate students. Most of them were experienced with using the Internet (eight spent more than 15 hours per week online) and with online shopping (all purchased online more than six times before). Although only one person reported that she had been cheated by an online vendor, the median of the overall trust propensity of all participants was slightly lower than neutral (3.6 in a 7-point scale). Participation was rewarded with monetary compensation.

Analysis

The resulting verbal protocol transcribed from recordings and notes was subject to in-depth qualitative content analysis. The following method was used in analyzing the protocol. First, a file was created for each participant where all the feedback was stored verbatim. Second, the first author summarized all opinions and sugges-tions that were elicited in each participant's file. Third, closely related issues were organized into categories with corresponding descriptive terms. For some significant ideas, the participants' original words were directly quoted for support. In addition, the number of times that each category was mentioned was also noted. Finally, for the sake of brevity and clarity, only the most informative categories and ideas were selected for the presentation.

Results

Deliberations on Communication Media

Based on the discussions with the participants, communication media are found to be needed and used on e-commerce Web sites primarily for three functions:

1. **providing customer services and technical support**, such as answering questions from the customer regarding a transaction problem or order status inquiry;

2. **displaying instructions or demonstrations**, such as showing the customer how to use a product or giving a virtual tour of the store; and

3. **transferring electronic documents and directing online links**, such as sending an online coupon or confirmation to the customer or forwarding the URL of a Web site.

Based on the three dimensions for computer-mediated communication channels that are proposed by Greenspan, Goldberg, Wimer, and Basso (2000), the different types of media in e-commerce are distinguished according to their channel availability, synchrony, and channel symmetry, as shown in Table 4.

Due to the various features of each communication medium, different media are suitable for supporting specific types of usages in e-commerce. Our participants' discussions of their media choices, in conjunction with the examination of media features in Table 4, has led us to a deeper understanding of the best suitability of each communication medium for one of the three e-commerce functions, as depicted in Figure 4. Detailed explanations are as follows, and the participants' original words were directly quoted for support at some places.

Function 1: Voice Chat vs. Videoconferencing

A voice chat medium enables consumers with a microphone and speaker connected to their PC's sound card to talk with a store representative online, while videoconferencing is made possible because of the video telephony technology by which consumers can not only talk to but also see the face of the other party via a Web camera. Because these two media provide more interactive contacts and more channels of communication compared with other media types, they are most suitable for Function 1, where consumers can "have real-time conversation" and "see the representative's face."

The most important features that both the media have are real-time interaction and voice communication. The ability to interact with a real person ensures consumers

Table 4. Features of communication media

Dimensions \ Media	Channel availability			Synchrony		Channel symmetry	
	Contextual	Audio	Visual	Synchronous	Asynchronous	One-way	Two-way
Voice chat		X		X			X
Videoconferencing		X	X	X			X
Video clip		X	X		X	X	
E-mail	X				X		X
Instant messaging	X			X			X

Figure 4. Suitability of communication media

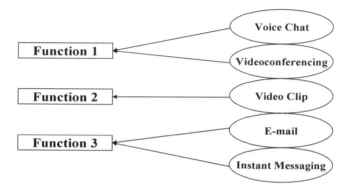

about the existence of the online vendor and thus induces online trust; and the ability to talk by voice increases task efficiency and brings convenience to consumers because most people prefer talking rather than typing. The major difference between voice chat and videoconferencing, of course, is the presence in the latter of the visual communication dimension. Although it is assumed that videoconferencing is inherently superior to voice chat, the participants had mixed opinions on this issue. Some positive feedback on the face-to-face communication in e-commerce included "it is more comforting if I can see the person I can talk to," and "when talking face-to-face, I can find the cues such as facial expressions and body language that I often use in judging whether a person is trustworthy." On the other hand, some participants opposed face-to-face contact because they thought "seeing the store representative could make the customer feel more pressured to buy things," and "people sometimes could be biased based on how a representative looks." Furthermore, 13 out of the 14 participants did not want their own faces to be seen by the other party.

Function 2: Video Clip

A video clip uses streaming video technology to play brief motion pictures online. Because a video clip provides both audio and visual dimensions of communication, it was found to be most suitable for Function 2, such as explaining how a product works, showing how to solve a technical problem, playing a short commercial for a product or service, and giving a virtual tour of a store or Web site.

Because of the asynchronous and asymmetric communicational nature of video clips, they are best for dealing with structured problems and repeating prerecorded messages. According to our participants, using real people to show how to use a product or service helps to build consumer trust online; however, cartoons can also be used in an instructional video clip as long as they provide clear demonstrations. An example of such an animated video clip called "automated demo" was found at Amazon.com, which showed online visitors how to use the Web site.

Function 3: E-mail vs. Instant Messaging

Due to the popularity of e-mail, it has become one of the most frequently used contact methods in e-commerce. Meanwhile, instant messaging (IM) is also attracting an increasing number of users. Both media enable online consumers to type their questions and receive feedback from a store representative online. When dealing with situations such as offering consumers online coupons, sending electronic confirmations, or forwarding Web URLs, e-mail and IM are more capable than any other communication media and, therefore, are most suitable for Function 3.

E-mail and IM share the similarity of a contextual nature, while their major difference lies in synchrony. Instant messaging, which is a synchronous media providing interactive communication, was considered superior to e-mail by our participants. Because the higher synchrony of IM produces more immediate feedback and intuitive actions and leaves less time for manipulating the "smartest" answer, our participants thought the feedback from a representative via IM was more trustworthy than an e-mail.

When asked how important immediate feedback was, most of the participants expressed views such as "it is very important" and "I want feedback right away." In addition, a participant considered immediate feedback as a major indicator for a seller's integrity at eBay.com. However, some participants revealed that they could be much more patient with the online vendors to which they were loyal or if they saw some feedback guarantee on the Web site.

Deliberations on Photographs

A photograph is the simplest form of communication medium, which is repeatedly proposed in the literature to have positive effects on online trust. The discussions with the participants focused on the use of two types of photographs on e-commerce Web sites, as described next.

Employee Photos

Similar to the findings of Riegelsberger and Sasse (2002), participants' responses to displaying employee photos on e-commerce interfaces varied dramatically. Some participants thought that "seeing the people behind the Web site" and "being able to match an employee's name with the face" could add friendliness and trustworthiness to an e-commerce Web site. However, other participants did not find employee photos trust-inducing because it was hard for them to believe that the people in the photos were really the employees working for the company.

Product Photos

Most participants supported the use of product photos. They especially wanted to see photos of real people using the product and photos of the actual product, not a model or image of the product. Multiple pictures that could show a product from multiple angles were also suggested as a way to help consumers to know more about the product and to enhance online trust.

Discussion

In this chapter, we first presented a quantitative study to confirm a conceptual model's validity in characterizing features of a user's perception of a trustworthy e-commerce Web site. A subsequent qualitative study shed additional light on the importance of a social-cue dimension. What follows is a discussion of these outcomes.

The underlying dimensions of the conceptual framework proposed in our previous study (Wang & Emurian, 2005a) were partially confirmed, and the relative magnitudes of respondents' ratings of the three dimensions were further evaluated. The factor analysis revealed the following three underlying dimensions: (1) visual, (2) content, and (3) social-cue design dimensions. The social-cue dimension was rated as somewhat less important than the other two dimensions.

The correlational relationships between each dimension and overall trust ratings were also evaluated. It was found that the content design dimension was the only group of ratings that was significantly related to overall trust ratings, although the small beta weight makes questionable any practical importance of even that relationship. This outcome suggests the insensitivity of a single global rating of trust, and it indicates the importance of collecting information on several features of an interface rather than relying simply on a global rating of trustworthiness.

The results, however, did reveal that having been cheated by an online vendor is influential enough to affect a respondent's overall trust rating of an e-commerce interface. The respondents who had been cheated by online vendors gave significantly lower ratings on the overall trustworthiness of the interface than those who had never been cheated. Other demographic and experiential factors, such as age, gender, language, and time spent online, were not found to have significant relationships with trust ratings in the current study. The lack of significant cultural and other individual difference relationships in the results might be attributable to the sample size and narrow measurement of overall trust, and thus will need more thorough examination and elaboration in the future. However, as suggested by Emurian (2006), there may be more similarities than differences when it comes to shopping online in China and in America. Finally, the fact that the overall trustworthiness ratings of the interface were sensitive to the prior purchasing history of the respondents does suggest that the synthetic interface evoked feelings similar to those that might be expected to occur when using an online vendor's Web site.

Researchers, however, may adopt a theoretical rationale for conjecturing a relationship, based on SEM, between a criterion latent variable and actual future performance, even when the data consist of ratings on multi-item scales (e.g., Bassellier, Benbasat, & Reich, 2003). Although covariance structure models are frequently used to infer the strength of causal relationships from a set of correlations (Meehl & Waller, 2002), proposing an interpretive transition from correlation to causation based upon such models is not free from ongoing controversy (Freedman, 1997). In the present set of correlations, we refrain from inferring that the three uncovered dimensions, or more specifically the content dimension, "cause" trust. Rather, we suggest that similar antecedent variables might be influential in both the rated ingredients constituting the dimensions and the overall rating of trust, with the content dimension ratings showing the most robust correlational relationship with that more general evaluation. The use of self-reported correlational data without predictive validity determinations that are empirically verified leads to sensible restraint in recommending strategic interventions where a purchasing action, not verbal behavior about a potential future action (i.e., "intention"), is the ultimate outcome of interest and importance to an organization.

In addition to the conclusions reached from the quantitative analysis, a further step was taken to seek a fuller understanding from Internet users on applying virtual re-embedding strategies to interface design via various communication media. The qualitative reports generally supported the importance of socially rich Web sites in promoting online trust, and they deepen our understanding on the functionalities and suitability of various communication media in the use of virtual re-embedding strategies.

In summary, the results of the two consecutive studies indicate that e-commerce vendors would be well advised not to neglect the contributions of several aspects of Web site design as those factors act together to promote consumer trust. The design of a trustworthy e-commerce interface, then, requires attention to a wide range of features that synergistically contribute to effective levels of trust in the Web site.

Conclusion and Research Directions

As e-commerce continues to evolve and emerge as a competitive business form, online vendors face the challenge of building and sustaining consumer trust on the Internet. This issue has occasioned numerous inquiries by investigators from diverse disciplines whose research methods and outcomes intend to offer effective solutions. In this vain, the authors adopted an HCI approach in an attempt to address the challenge by applying trust-inducing design features to an e-commerce interface.

The contributions that the present research brings to the field are twofold. First, both the quantitative and qualitative studies provide empirical evidence and indicative support for the importance of interface design in inducing online trust. Second, the unique research approach, which included conducting a Web-based survey and developing a synthetic e-commerce interface for illustration and testing purposes in the first study, as well as the use of triangulation in obtaining qualitative data directly from Internet users and the walkthrough of existing Web sites selected by the users in the second study, supplements the research field that is currently in need of inventive methodological approaches to tackle the relatively new research problem.

The authors hope that the complementary findings from both quantitative and qualitative sources of information will contribute to future applications and research in e-commerce interface design considerations affecting online trust. Future research may continue to elaborate and substantiate the conceptual framework to include more social-cue design features and validate the framework in a more controllable experimental setting. Some of the practical issues for building online trust that evolved from the respondents' feedback are also subject to further investigation for reaching the ultimate goal of helping online vendors to foster optimal levels of trust in their customers.

References

Ang, L., & Lee, B.-C. (2000). Influencing perceptions of trustworthiness in Internet commerce: A rational choice framework. In *Proceedings of Fifth CollECTer Conference on Electronic Commerce,* December 13-14 (pp. 1-12). Brisbane, Australia.

Bassellier, G., Benbasat, I., & Reich, B. H. (2003). The influence of business managers' IT competence on championing IT. *Information Systems Research, 14*(4), 317-336.

Basso, A., Goldberg, D., Greenspan, S., & Weimer, D. (2001). First impressions: Emotional and cognitive factors underlying judgments of trust in e-commerce. In *Proceedings of the 3ʳᵈ ACM Conference on Electronic Commerce* (pp. 137-143). New York: ACM Press.

Belanger, F., Hiller, J. S., & Smith, W. J. (2002). Trustworthiness in electronic commerce: The role of privacy, security, and site attributes. *Journal of Strategic Information Systems, 11*, 245-270.

Cheskin Research and Studio Archetype/Sapient. (1999). *eCommerce trust: A joint research study with Studio Archetype/Sapient and Cheskin.* Retrieved October 19ᵗʰ 2006, from http://www.cheskin.com/cms/tiles/i.articles//17_report-eComm%20Trust1999.pdf

Diller, S., Lin, L., & Tashjian, V. (2003). The evolving role of security, privacy, and trust in a digitized world. In J. A. Jacko & A. Sears (Eds.), *The human-computer interaction handbook: Fundamentals, evolving technologies and emerging applications* (pp. 1213-1225). Mahwah, NJ: Lawrence Erlbaum.

Egger, F. N. (2001). Affective design of e-commerce user interface: How to maximize perceived trustworthiness. In *Proceedings of the International Conference on Affective Human Factors Design.* London: Asean Academic Press.

Emurian, H. H. (2006). E-commerce in China: A personal perspective [Editorial]. *Information Resources Management Journal, 19*(1), i-iii.

Fogg, B. J., Marshall, J., Laraki, O., Osipovich, A., Varma, C., Fang, N., et al. (2001). What makes a Web site credible? A report on a large quantitative study. In Carroll, J.M., & Tanner, P.P (Eds.), *Proceedings of ACM CHI 2001 Conference on Human Factors in Computing Systems* (pp. 61-68). New York: ACM Press.

Freedman, D. A. (1997). From association to causation via regression. In V. R. McKim & S. P. Turner (Eds.), *Causality in crisis? Statistical methods and the search for causal knowledge in the social sciences* (pp. 113-161). IN: University of Notre Dame Press.

Garson, G. D. (2004). *Structural equation modeling.* Retrieved October 19ᵗʰ 2006, from http://www2.chass.ncsu.edu/garson/pa765/structur.htm

Gefen, D., & Straub, D. W. (2003). Managing user trust in B2C e-services. *E-Service Journal, 2*(2), 7-24.

Gefen, D., & Straub, D. W. (2004). Consumer trust in B2C e-commerce and the importance of social presence: Experiments in e-products and e-services. *Omega, 32*, 407-424.

Greenspan, S., Goldberg, D., Wimer, D., & Basso, A. (2000). Interpersonal trust and common ground in electronically mediated communication. In *Proceedings of the ACM2000 Conference on Computer Supported Cooperative Work.* Philadelphia, PA.

Hassanein, K. S., & Head, M. M. (2004). Building online trust through socially rich Web interfaces. In *Proceedings of the Second Annual Conference on Privacy, Security and Trust*, October 13-15 (pp. 15-22). New Brunswick, Canada.

Hu, X., Lin, Z., & Zhang, H. (2001). *Myth or reality: Effect of trust-promoting seals in electronic markets.* Paper presented at Workshop on Information Technologies and System 2001, New Orleans, LA.

Jarvenpaa, S. L., Tractinsky, J., & Saarinen, L. (1999). Consumer trust in an Internet store: A cross-cultural validation. *Journal of Computer Mediated Communication, 5*(2). Retrieved Octoer 19th 2006, from http://www.ascusc. org/jcmc/vol5/issue2

Karvonen, K., & Parkkinen, J. (2001). Signs of trust. In Constantine Stephanidis(Eds.), *Proceedings of the 9th International Conference on HCI.* Mahwah, NJ: Lawrence Erlbaum.

Kim, J., & Moon, J. Y. (1998). Designing towards emotional usability in customer interfaces—Trustworthiness of cyber-banking system interfaces. *Interacting with Computers, 10,* 1-29.

Lee, J., Kim, J., & Moon, J. Y. (2000). What makes Internet users visit cyber stores again? Key design factors for customer loyalty. In *Proceedings of ACM CHI 2000* (pp. 305-312). Amsterdam.

Lee, M. K. O., & Turban, E. (2001). A trust model for consumer Internet shopping. *International Journal of Electronic Commerce, 6*(1), 75-91.

Maxwell, S. E., & Delaney, H. D. (2000). *Designing experiments and analyzing data.* Mahwah, NJ: Lawrence Erlbaum.

McKnight, D., & Chervany, N. (2002). What trust means in e-commerce customer relationships: An interdisciplinary conceptual typology. *International Journal of Electronic Commerce, 6*(2), 35-59.

Meehl, P. E., & Waller, N. G. (2002). The path analysis controversy: A new statistical approach to strong appraisal of verisimilitude. *Psychological Methods, 7*(3), 283-300.

Neilsen, J. (1999). *Trust or bust: Communicating trustworthiness in Web design.* Retrieved from Jacob Nielsen's Alertbox Web site: http://www.useit.com/alertbox/990307.htm/

Nunally, J. C. (1978). *Psychometric theory* (2nd ed.). Englewood Cliffs, NJ: McGraw-Hill.

Patton, M. Q. (2002). *Qualitative research and evaluation methods,* (3rd ed.). Thousand Oaks, CA: Sage.

Qiu, L., & Benbasat, I. (2005). Online consumer trust and live help interfaces: The effects of text-to-speech voice and three-dimensional avatars. *International Journal of Human-Computer Interaction, 19*(1), 75-94.

Riegelsberger, J., & Sasse, M. A. (2000). Trust me, I'm a .com: Reassuring shoppers in electronic retail environments. *Intermedia, 28*(4). Retrieved October 19th 2006, from http://www.iicom.org/intermedia/archive/04_2000/200028.04_ 09trust.html

Riegelsberger, J., & Sasse, M. A. (2001). *Trustbuilders and trustbusters: The role of trust cues in interfaces to e-commerce applications.* Paper presented at the 1st IFIP Conference on E-commerce, E-business, and E-government. Retrieved October 19th 2006, from http://www.cs.ucl.ac.uk/staff/J.Riegelsberger/trust-builders.pdf

Riegelsberger, J., & Sasse, M. A. (2002) Face it: Photographs don't make Websites trustworthy. In *Proceedings of CHI2002.* Minneapolis, MN.

Riegelsberger, J., Sasse, M. A., & McCarthy, J. D. (2003) Shiny happy people building trust? Photos on e-commerce Websites and consumer trust. *Proceedings of CHI2003.* Ft. Lauderdale, FL.

Rousseau, D. M., Sitkin, S. B., Burt, R. S., & Camerer, C. (1998). Not so different after all: A cross-discipline view of trust. *Academy of Management Review, 23*(3), 393-404.

Shneiderman, B. (2000). Designing trust into online experiences. *Communications of the ACM, 43*(12), 57-59.

Steinbruck, U., Schaumburg, H., Duda, S., & Kruger, T. (2002). A picture says more than a thousand words: Photographs as trust builders in e-commerce Websites. In *Conference Extended Abstracts on Human Factors in Computer Systems.* Minneapolis, MN.

Teo, S. H. T. (2002). Attitudes toward online shopping and the Internet. *Behaviour & Information Technology, 21*(4), 259-271.

Wang, Y. D., & Emurian, H. H. (2005a). An overview of online trust: Concepts, elements, and implications. *Computers in Human Behavior, 21*(1), 105-125.

Wang, Y. D., & Emurian, H. H. (2005b). Trust in e-commerce: Consideration of interface design factors. *Journal of Electronic Commerce in Organizations, 3*(4), 42-60.

Zhang, P., Von Dran, G. M., Small, R. V., & Barcellos, S. (1999). Websites that satisfy users: A theoretical framework for Web user interface design and evaluation. *Proceedings of the 32nd Hawaii International Conference on System Sciences* (pp. 1-8). Retrieved from October 19th 2006, http://melody.syr.edu/pzhang/ publications/HICSSpp_Zhang-etal.pdf

Endnotes

[1] The quantitative study reported in this chapter is based upon Wang and Emurian (2005b).

[2] These numbers are accurate, although the identical bifurcation of frequencies within the location and gender categories is obviously notable.

Appendix A: The Abbreviated Survey (English Version)

Instructions

Assume that you are interested in purchasing a product online from PlasmaTV. com, an online vendor. The trustworthiness of an e-commerce Web site refers to your opinion or perception of confidence in a vendor's reliability and integrity. The purpose of this study is to evaluate your perceived trustworthiness of an e-commerce Web site by asking you to rate the importance of several trust-inducing features illustrated by the PlasmaTV.com e-commerce interface, which has been designed for this particular study. Please open the following link in a separate window (best viewed with Internet Explorer): http://userpages.umbc.edu/~ywang8/online_trust/

Demographic Information

(The following choices were implemented by drop-down menus.)

1. Age
2. Gender
3. Current location
4. Highest education attained
5. Average hours per week spent on the Internet
6. Have you ever purchased anything online?
7. Have you ever been cheated by an online vendor?

Features to Rate

Please indicate how unimportant or important each feature, is to affect or influence your perceived trustworthiness of an e-commerce Web site. An example of the feature to evaluate is given in parentheses. The range of your rating is from 1 = "Not important at all" to 10 = "Extremely important." You may choose any number from 1 to 10 to rate the importance of the feature to you. Please refer to the example feature on the PlasmaTV.com interface before you make your evaluation and be sure to choose only one number for each feature.

(The following choices were implemented by checkboxes.)

1. Use of three-dimensional and half-screen size clipart (see the main picture of a plasma TV)

2. Symmetric use of moderate pastel color of low brightness and cool tone (see the overall color of the Web page)

3. Use of well-chosen, good-shot photographs

4. Easy-to-use navigation (see the drop-down menus and pay attention to the simplicity and consistency in fonts, symbols, and text)

5. Accessible information (assume there are no broken links and missing pictures on the main interface and all subpages)

6. Use of navigation reinforcement (see the navigation anchor "You are here >> HOME" on the upper left corner and the drop-down menu of "How To Documents")

7. Application of page design techniques (see the use of ample white space and adequate margins; also strict grouping of related information; low visual density)

8. Display of brand-promoting information (see the company logo on the upper left corner and main selling point in the main picture.)

9. Up-front disclosure of all aspects of the customer relationship (see the drop-down menu for "Store Policy")

10. Display of seals of approval or third-party certificates (see the VeriSign seal on the lower left corner)

11. Comprehensive, correct, and current product information (see "Most Popular Models")

12. Use of a relevant domain name (assume the domain name is www.PlasmaTV.com)

13. Inclusion of representative photograph or video clip (see the picture in the lower right corner)

14. Use of synchronous communication media (see "Sales Chat" where users can exchange instant messages with a sales representative)

15. Rate your opinion or perception of the overall level of trustworthiness of the PlasmaTV.com Web site.

Appendix B:
Demographic Information Questionnaire

Introduction

The purpose of this research is to investigate the social cues that are perceived as effective in inducing people's trust toward e-commerce. The demographic information requested from you is strictly anonymous. Since the reliability of this research depends upon your help, your sincere and honest answers will be greatly appreciated.

General Information

(The following choices were implemented by drop-down menus.)

1. Age
2. Gender
3. Highest education attained

Propensity to Trust

This section will determine your propensity to trust others. Please indicate the level of your agreement/disagreement with the statement. The range of your rating is from 1 = "strongly disagree" to 7 = "strongly agree."

(The following choices were implemented by checkboxes.)

1. Most people are trustworthy.
2. It is better to trust people than to be suspicious of others until they prove themselves trustworthy.

3.   I almost always believe what people tell me.

4.   I have few difficulties trusting people.

Online Experiences

This section reviews your online experiences.

(The following choices were implemented by drop-down menus.)

1.   How many hours on average per week do you spend on the Internet?

2.   How many times have you made purchases over the Internet?

3.   Have you ever been cheated by an online vendor or had a credit card number stolen?

Chapter VI

Public Perception— A Newspaper Medium Perspective: E-Commerce in Australian Manufacturing (Revisited)

Jing Gao, University of South Australia, Australia

Abstract

This chapter will present evidence to show that there is an absence of informed, broad, media discussion on e-commerce initiatives in Australia. As pointed out by several authors (e.g., Gittins, 1995), the newspaper medium is one of the main vehicles through which advisers and policy makers seek to influence society. Thus this medium takes on the role of a public forum on national issues. However, it was found that newspapers in Australia have failed in their role of preparing manufacturing industries for the impact of new technologies. In this interpretive study, major Australian newspapers were examined for public discussions about e-commerce in manufacturing industries. The political-legal, economic, social, and technological (PEST) framework was used as a lens to subdivide issues, problems, and opportunities identified in the academic e-commerce literature. This lens was then used to examine 103 newspaper articles identified using the keywords Australian manufacturing and e-commerce in what was believed to be all the major Australian newspapers. It was found that some articles merely report vendors' promises of potential cost savings while overlooking the need for investment in technology, training, and maintenance costs, while other discussions focused on "users as victims" issues such as security and privacy. In-depth issues such as reliability, communication protocols, bandwidth availability, and integration problems were overlooked. In particular, the problem of business strategies was ignored.

Introduction

Background: E-Commerce is Growing

The emergence of e-commerce and Internet technologies means that organisations have changed the way in which they conduct their business. Gunasekaran and Ngai (2005) suggest that the e-commerce concept and related technologies, essentially offer an open communication platform and a globally interactive marketplace.

The rapid growth in e-commerce has been attributed to the presence of the Internet as an integrated distribution, financial, and communications infrastructure (Haley, 2002; Kalakota & Whinston, 1996). E-commerce may transform business in ways similar to industrialisation, electricity, the telephone, the internal combustion engine, and numerous other infrastructure inventions and has a great impact on our daily lives (Roehl & Standifird, 2001). This transformation process takes time, but it seems safe to agree with Prasad (2000, p. 26) that e-commerce is "here to stay" as one thread in the overall fabric of commerce as both businesses and individuals are showing signs of appreciating the advantages of using the Web to buy and sell in a global marketplace.

Many Problems to Overcome

Adopting e-commerce is a complicated issue and is not a risk-free investment. For example, while acknowledging the benefits of e-commerce, Chen, Lee, and Mayer (2001, p. 139) suggest that there also exists a "dark underbelly" to e-commerce that is becoming more of a concern as the Internet becomes increasingly competitive and congested. However, Qimei (2000) asserts that the question challenging today's entrepreneur is not whether to have a Web site but how to win in the Internet competition.

Gunasekaran and Ngai (2005) identified several perceived barriers of the Internet for e-commerce (summarised from a survey study). For example, they point to the lack of a legal framework for conducting e-commerce on the Internet; the lack of trained and qualified people; and the lack of security. In particular, the authors note that many companies hesitate to implement the Internet for e-commerce due to a lack of a legal framework for conducting e-commerce on the Internet, which results in a consequent lack of confidence. Lawson, Alcock, Cooper, and Burgess (2003) present a similar view; barriers in doing business online can be categorised as having a technical (including inadequacy of telecommunications infrastructure and security of transactions) or a social perspective (including not trusting information technology [IT], a lack of knowledge about conducting business online, the lack of IT skills in staff, and a lack of awareness about possible uses of the Internet).

Additionally, there are many problems associated with revising existing business models for the new online environment. For example, Truman (2000) states that managers have not actively incorporated or planned for applications such as Electronic Data Interchange (EDI). Secondly, management has not considered internal integration as a risk factor during e-commerce implementation. Further, Wright (2001) indicates that information security is significant, as traditional approaches are no longer working, or workable, in e-commerce business models. To maximise the use of e-commerce, a more thorough understanding of e-commerce problems and opportunities is required. Therefore there is a need for a leading discussion of e-commerce issues by experts or in the news media.

Aim of This Study

This research starts with an exploration of the leading role of the newspaper medium. With respect to this role, the researcher argues that good media leadership may facilitate e-commerce in industries, especially traditional industries such as manufacturing. The Australian manufacturing industry is selected as the research subject and the PEST framework is used to analyse the newspaper medium coverage of e-commerce issues in this industry. In total, 103 newspaper articles (from 1999 to 2002) are identified from all Australian newspapers. Based on the findings, this research explores the proposition that newspapers in Australia have failed to take a leading role to provide an in-depth discussion in preparing manufacturing industries for the impact of new technologies. It is thought that the lack of awareness of various e-commerce problems as a result of the poor coverage in the mass media can slow down the e-commerce movement.

The Newspaper Medium

Potential for Leading Discussion

The newspaper medium has a leading role in informing society. Thompson (2000) suggests that the information individuals use to construct a sense of reality comes from four sources: (1) personal experience, (2) other individuals, (3) social groups and institutions, and (4) the mass media. Individuals in complex post-industrial societies have become especially dependent on the mass media as a resource in the formation of a sense of social reality. According to Stein (1972), "the media furnishes our consciousness with the people, places and events that we call reality." Hannigan (1995), therefore, asserts that most individuals depend on the media to help make sense of the deluge of information presented to them, especially information about environmental risks, technologies, and initiatives (Dispensa & Brulle, 2003). Thompson (2000) suggests that newspapers (one type of mass media) contribute greatly to the social construction of reality by participating in the rhetoric of social problems discourse. That is, the repetitive rhetorical tools used by reporters and the claims makers to whom they give voice, help define and shape individual perceptions of the problems they discuss. An analogy can be drawn from the newspaper coverage during the election time. Often individual perceptions of particular nominees are influenced by the stories presented in the newspaper articles. For example, if President George W. Bush's Army service history is discussed in the U.S. news media, this may have a great impact on the number of votes that he can receive.

Newspapers also serve the function of opening up discussion and persuading society. Gittins (1995) suggests that the newspaper medium is one of the main vehicles through which advisers and policy makers seek to influence their society. Aiex (2000) and Walker (1990) indicate that, whatever its positive or negative effects, exposure to the news media does influence public awareness of government policies. For example, Gilens and Hertzman (2000) have provided an example of how media power has been critical in influencing public opinions of the U.S. Telecommunications Act (1996).

The news media play a very important role in creating and leading discussion in society. Throughout the literature, this view is supported by a number of authors. For example, Luttberg's (1988) study concludes that newspaper articles can persuade individual and public opinions. Gade, Abel, Antecol, and Hsueh (1998) strongly argue that the newspapers' primary role should be as "windows to the world," (p. 4) pointing out issues and holding problems up for scrutiny. According to Hoge and James (1994), the news media can be regarded as a discussion-forum provider in society.

Perspectives on Reality

Industrial perspectives of e-commerce can be obtained from the newspaper medium, because Gittins (1995) argues the medium is concerned primarily with the reporting of news: the recording of facts about events and the recording of opinions expressed by people with some form of authority. Erikson, Baranek, and Chan (1987) further claim that news consumers also participate in the news-making process by formulating actions on the basis of the news they consume, thus playing a part in the creation of subsequent events, some of which will be deemed newsworthy. The researcher also feels that people working in industry will read newspaper articles relating to e-commerce more carefully, in order to develop their own e-commerce perspectives, which may guide business practice. Subsequently these perspectives or business practices will be reported as industry perspectives in newspaper articles again. Therefore the researcher believes that in this news-making process, industry perspectives on e-commerce will be reflected in the newspaper medium.

Reporters' perspectives are also included in newspapers. Harris (2001) suggests that the use of newspaper stories might be challenged on the basis that the analysis will reveal the journalists' perceptions and not those of the prime agents. It is a difficult problem to avoid in newspaper studies. Hence, extra care in this research was taken to ensure that newspaper analyses incorporated both the perspectives of the journalists and perspectives of people in the business world. For example, "who says so" is considered when collecting empirics.

The Australian Manufacturing Industry

Clark, Geer, and Underhill (1996) suggest that the Australian manufacturing industry started in the early 19th century. According to the Australian Bureau of Statistics (2001), this sector includes machinery and equipment manufacturing (which has the largest employment number); food, beverage, and tobacco manufacturing; and metal product manufacturing. Non-metallic mineral product manufacturing is the smallest employer in the manufacturing sector, accounting for only 3.8% of manufacturing employment. Food, beverage, and tobacco manufacturing is the largest contributor to total manufacturing turnover and to total industry value added (IVA). Bloch's (1996) research shows that the manufacturing industry in Australia is generally growing more slowly than the overall economy; thus the initiatives of e-commerce may present new opportunities for the growth of this industry.

E-Commerce in Manufacturing

E-Commerce in Australian Manufacturing

"The impact of E-commerce on the economic activity and even the development of wealthy fully industrialised nations is impossible to deny," Murillo (2001 p. 370). Soliman and Youssef (2001) also indicate that the development of Internet-based e-business has already emerged as a fast growing trend in business. Based on their research, these authors believe that manufacturers' key strategies need to (and will) include broader implementation of business-to-business (B2B) e-commerce in their operations, in particular supply chain management operations. Bakos and Treacy (1986) and Pouder, John, and Cannon (2001) further suggest that manufacturing firms have to use the Internet to gain access to extra competitive advantage.

Table 1. Applications of e-commerce in functional areas

Organisational functional areas	E-Commerce applications and/or contributions	E-Commerce tools and systems
Marketing	Product promotion, new sales channels, direct savings, reduced cycle time, customer services	B2B e-commerce, Internet ordering, Web site for the company
Purchasing	Ordering, fund transfer, supplier selection	EDI, Internet purchasing
Design	Customer feedback, research on customer requirements, product design, quality function deployment, data mining and warehousing	Web-integrated computer aided development (CAD), Hyperlinks, 3-D navigation, Internet for data and information exchange
Production	Production planning and control, Scheduling, inventory management, quality control	B2B e-commerce, ERP (Web integrated)
Sales and distribution	Distribution of Internet sales, selection of distribution channels, transportation, scheduling, third party logistics	Electronic funds transfer (EFT), online TPS, bar-coding system, ERP, Web-integrated inventory management, Internet delivery of products and services
Human resource management	E-recruiting, benefit selection and management, training and education using the Web	E-mails, interactive Web sites, Web-based multimedia applications
Warehousing	Warehousing inventory management, forecasting, scheduling of work force	EDI, EFT, Web-integrated inventory management
Supplier development	Partnership, supplier development	Web-assisted supplier selection, communication using Internet (e-mails), research on suppliers and products with Web and intelligent agents

Gunasekaran, Marri, McGaughey, and Nebhwani (2002) have provided a table (Table 1) to summarise the applications of e-commerce to operations. It is particularly relevant to manufacturing firms as it contains all the key functional areas.

Benefits of Applying E-Commerce in Manufacturing

Mathew and De (1999) have put the e-commerce benefits for manufacturing into three categories: (1) tangible, (2) intangible, and (3) strategic benefits. Examples of tangible benefits, which can be quantified and measured, include various kinds of cost savings resulting from automated order processing, Web-based publications for marketing purposes and electronic processes of billing and payments. Intangible benefits are obtained from the reductions in time or effort achieved in the primary functions of the Web site, in the area of customer service, order management, inventory control, and resource sharing for projects. Moreover, the Internet and e-commerce can help organisations collaborate with customers or vendors over the Web to extend their value-added chain, which may refine organisational strategic alliances. Furthermore, Nath (1998) suggests that the manufacturing sector, dominated by the automotive industry, has embraced the Internet as a new medium for growth and customer expansion. By providing consumers with the ability to shop and even finance a new purchase online (excluding actual signing of the final papers), the companies have managed to turn purchasing a car into a fun and interesting experience.

Moreover, Soliman and Youssef (2003) suggest that the introduction of Internet-based e-commerce and its superiority over traditional EDI is adding a new dimension to reducing the cost of manufacturing. The authors find that improvements in the movement of raw material, work-in-process, and finished goods are likely to occur as a result of using the Internet-based e-commerce. The reduction in time and costs in the whole manufacturing chain make it possible to gain competitive advantages in price, product innovation, and service.

However, Mackay, Altmann, and McMichael (2003) find that the level of e-commerce support provided by Australian firms is considerably less (less than half) than that of their U.S. counterparts. This suggests that Australian firms have a long way to go in providing electronic support to their key B2B customers. This chapter will try to examine the related issues through a newspaper perspective.

PEST Framework of E-Commerce Problems and Challenges

The author's approach involves canvassing e-commerce issues using the traditional PEST framework. According to Prasad's (2000) study of e-commerce challenge factors, the author thinks that using the PEST framework is an appropriate way to summarise e-commerce issues found in various sections of the literature, applied to both B2B and business-to-consumer (B2C) e-commerce. This framework will then be used to review Australian newspaper media's perspectives on e-commerce and manufacturing.

The origin of the PEST analysis (framework) is unknown. However, Johnson and Scholes (2003) point out that PEST analysis is a popular strategic analysis method used since the 1990s, which aims to identify and evaluate environmental influences on strategy, significant trends, developments, opportunities, and threats for any organisation and industry. A number of reasons for choosing this framework are listed as follows:

1. The purpose of this study is to explore newspaper influences on various e-commerce issues in the Australian manufacturing industry. These influences are regarded as external factors (outside of the industry). The PEST analysis is designed to provide an overall environmental scan, and the results of the analysis will possibly lead to discussions of the question of how the industry is likely to change under these influences. Therefore, the choice of the PEST analysis is in line with the purpose of this study.

2. The PEST framework contains four dimensions: (1) political-legal, (2) economic, (3) social and (4) technological issues. These four dimensions cover a comprehensive range of factors. For example, political factors can have a direct impact on the way business operates. Government decisions will certainly affect the industry's operations. National and global economic factors will also affect the business strategies. Social factors (such as how individuals think and live) are critical for any business. Additionally, adopting new approaches (technologies) for tackling problems is vital for competitive advantage. After reviewing a number of studies, which use the PEST analysis, this range of factors (issues) is considered to be adequate and sufficient to address various external influences on e-commerce in manufacturing.

3. Prasad's (2000) study of e-commerce challenge factors provides a successful example of PEST analysis. A broad discussion of various e-commerce problems and challenges is found in his study. Similar approaches are found in many studies including Nabil, Dogramaci, and Gangopadhyay (1999), Wright

(2001), Clarke (1996), and Hughes and Glaister (2001). According to these studies, it is believed that PEST analysis is a useful tool for studying e-commerce issues.

The PEST framework has four dimensions. The analysis requires the user to identify issues/factors under these dimensions. In this study, these issues are extracted from two sources within the literature. Firstly, many of them are extracted from Prasad's (2000) study. Secondly, as a result of a literature review, extra issues are added to the table. For example, Hughes and Glaister (2001) outline the taxation concerns within e-commerce. Jarvenpaa and Tiller (1999) highlight the lack of Internet regulations. These issues are summarised in Table 2. However, the boundaries between these dimensions are not hard and fast, nor are the categories exhaustive.

The researcher is aware of the limitations of the PEST analysis, with its aim being to identify and evaluate environmental influences. In most cases, internal influences (e.g., within the organisation or within the industry) are often neglected. Additionally, in an unstructured discussion, it may be difficult to identify the exact issue (as listed in Table 2). For example, users' concerns about security in e-commerce can be a technical issue and a social issue of trust. Alternative approaches can be found, such as Thompson and Strickland (1990), who suggest that strengths, weaknesses, opportunities and threats (SWOT) analysis (for internal factors) is an appropriate management approach for analysing an organisation's internal factors. Linstone's (1999) technical, organisational and personal (TOP) model is another useful method that can be used to address various levels of concern regarding a particular problem. The TOP model also requires users to look at the same problem from multiple viewpoints (perspectives) in order to obtain rich insights.

The current focus in this research is the coverage of e-commerce issues in newspaper articles (as an external influence). Moreover, the PEST framework essentially covers all necessary elements in the TOP model. Therefore, the PEST framework is regarded as the most appropriate for this research.

Table 2. Modified PEST framework for e-commerce, based on Prasad's (2000) PEST research issues

Economical	Technical	Social	Political
Cost justification, Internet access, Telecommunication infrastructure, Skill shortage, Performance measurement	Security, Reliability, Bandwidth, Integration	Privacy/security—Trust, cultural diversity, Absence of "touch/feel"	Intellectual property, Legal validity of transactions, Taxation issues Policing/regulation, Business strategy (with an e-commerce focus)

Economic Dimension

Cost Justification

Prasad (2000) finds that the initial investment in developing an e-commerce Web site is relatively high. For example, the initial investment for creating an e-commerce Web site usually includes the cost of hardware and software, future maintenance, and training for staff. Whether or not the initial investment can be returned remains uncertain for a long period. Quite often, manufacturing firms do not want to participate in e-commerce because of the fear of losing their investment. Thus, Poon and Swatman (1999 p. 10) point out that "cost effectiveness" is a key issue that organisations concentrate upon.

Internet Access

Internet access is the first step in e-commerce practice. Typical Internet access includes the use of e-mails, browsing Web sites, and so on. It is possible that organisations may not use the Internet for any commercial purposes, but Internet access still can benefit the organisation through effective information exchange. However, it is believed that a manufacturing industry that is familiar with the Internet may be more aware of the potential benefits to be derived from e-commerce activities.

Telecommunication Infrastructure

Telecommunication infrastructure is the backbone of e-commerce. Prasad (2000) argues that a major area of concern for e-commerce is the construction of a telecommunications infrastructure that can support its explosive growth. For example, the establishment of a national broadband network may pass on the message to organisations: the network is ready, are you ready for e-commerce?

Lack of Knowledge and Skilled Personnel

Kathuria, Anandarajan, and Igbaria (1999) indicate that many organisations lack information technology literacy, especially in the area of e-commerce. In their study (Kathuria et al., 1999), the authors found that managers generally lack understanding of the most appropriate technology or applications. In addition, from a questionnaire survey, Martin (2002) highlights that Australian manufacturing firms, especially small and medium-sized enterprise (SMEs), have urgent educational needs and preferences when it comes to assimilating and diffusing information on new technologies. Kakabadse (2000), and Soliman and Youssef (2001) indicate that many manufacturing firms are experiencing some difficulty in finding skilled Web developers, content providers, and knowledgeable professionals to manage and maintain a customer hotline. As suggested by these authors, the lack of skilled personnel accounts for the slow progress of e-commerce uptake.

Performance Measurement

E-commerce performance measurement is a difficult task. Based on a comparative study of e-commerce across the UK, USA, Japan, and Germany, undertaken on behalf of the UK government by the consultancy firm, Chaston, Badger, Mangles, and Sadler-Smith (2001) suggest that studying the Internet and e-commerce is hampered by a lack of validated tools for measuring the degree to which firms are able to benefit from exploiting the technology. Further, Nath (1998) points out that companies adopt Internet and e-commerce technologies at different levels. Many companies are merely using e-mails. Hence, measures of how efficient and effective the companies could be are often uncertain.

Technical Dimension

Security Issues

Security problems and challenges (as a technical issue) that are associated with e-commerce applications and the Internet can never be ignored. Nath (1998) suggests that, when an organisation uses the Internet to engage in e-commerce, it exposes itself to security risks. Although many security protection technologies such as data encryption, firewalls, and virus checking can be found in the commercial market, no one can claim that security is no longer a problem.

Reliability

Successful e-commerce services depend on access to a reliable platform including the use of a reliable system (hardware and software) and a reliable network. However, Prasad (2000) indicates that current online systems may not be totally reliable, especially when the transaction volume goes northbound.

Bandwidth

Bandwidth has become a major issue in the development of e-commerce solutions, because it determines the speed and capacity for communication. Due to the current limitations on Internet bandwidth, organisations may not be able to deliver rich media information such as video and audio information. Bandwidth not only restricts communications between end customers and manufacturers, but also restricts the information exchange between manufacturers and their suppliers. For example, if there is a large volume of inventory information to be exchanged, low bandwidth may result in a traffic jam, which disables the manufacturers' just-in-time (JIT) inventory management initiatives.

Integration Difficulties

Technological integration is not an easy task. Fujii, Kaihara, Morita, and Tanaka (2000 p. 4113) highlight that, as manufacturing systems become automated, so-called "automation islands" have appeared in factories. This concept refers to various individual units and their respective headquarters, each having a different platform for their information systems (IS). If various units use different types of computer hardware and software systems, managers will have only a partial view of the data and overall information gain will be reduced. With such a lack of accurate information, the decision-making process will not gain significantly from the tremendous investments made in building the e-commerce technology and other IT.

Social Dimension

Security (as a Social Issue), Privacy/Trust

Security and privacy issues are major hurdles for the growth of e-commerce. According to the survey conducted by Ng, Pan, and Wilson (1998) on the problems that e-commerce was facing during the period 1995-1997, 60% of participants were not convinced by assurances of e-commerce security. As a result, consumers are hesitant to transact with companies and to disclose confidential data such as their home address, social security number, and credit card number over the Internet.

According to Kao and Decou (2003), lack of trust in the security of electronic communication is identified as an e-commerce obstacle. Security threats could arise from either attacks against information in transit or attacks against the site storing information. Although it is impossible to have 100% security control, efforts should still be made to minimise the negative implications.

Cultural Diversity

E-commerce practitioners in the manufacturing industry are concerned with the cultural diversity of consumers. Prasad (2000) indicates that the ability to customise the interface for individual and group needs is one of the greatest assets of e-commerce, especially for the global market.

Absence of "Touch and Feel"

Furthermore, due to the current technology, the absence of touch and feel on Web sites is always a big issue for online service providers. For example, automotive manufacturers cannot provide their customers with test drives on their Web sites. Compared to buying a computer online, purchasing a car is an expensive transaction. Thus, further assurance (such as a trial drive) is required; however, this kind of service cannot be provided by online services.

Political Dimension

Intellectual Property

During the implementation of e-commerce projects, a manufacturer may recognise the intellectual property as an important asset in their organisation. This intellectual property may include the organisation's new vision (i.e., new target market), details of the current market, and information regarding new products (new designs). Thus, whether or not the organisation is aware of this sensitive information, and whether or not adequate protection is in place, can be critical.

Taxation

The taxation system for the e-commerce market is still under development. In Australia, most online retailers are selling goods and services with Goods and Services Tax (GST) inclusive, but many transactions are still processed without any contribution to the taxation system. For example, eBay treats individual transactions as private auctions, which do not include any taxes.

Policing and Regulation

The Australian manufacturing industry has legal protections in the traditional market. For example, various laws (Retail Sales Tax Act) and regulations (related to quality assurance, public liability and warranty issues) have been passed. However, when conducting business in the e-commerce market, particularly in the areas of security and privacy, relevant legal protection is also essential.

Kao and Decou (2003) point out that e-commerce has potentially opened the marketplace globally. Organisations, therefore, need to examine the legality of their products, services, and practices in all areas because what is legally acceptable in one place may not be acceptable in other places.

Lack of IT Focus in Business Strategies

Manufacturing organisations have strong focuses on production processes instead of customer focuses. As a result, Gilbert, Arthur, Pick, Roger, Ward, & Sidne (2000) assert that the manufacturing sector has failed to realise the same level of benefits from IT that the non-manufacturing sector has enjoyed. Gordon and Gordon (2000), and Closs and Xu (2000) suggest that IS applications in manufacturing firms lack a strategic orientation because the customers are often separated from the organisation. Mohanti and Deshmukh (1999) assert that technological importance is overlooked. The authors indicate that IT is not always viewed as an important input to the organisational strategy in many medium and small manufacturing firms.

Internet and E-Commerce Strategies

Traditional industries, such as manufacturing or mining industries, view the Internet merely as an information tool for their customers. Dutta and Biren (1999) studied business transformations on the Internet over different industries in 1999. They argue that firms in old industries, such as manufacturing, recognise the use of the Internet by new economy firms, but fail to see the potential for their own business. For example, Sarkis and Sundarraj (2002) point out that most large manufacturing companies have done little to leverage these technologies other than as a publishing medium.

Research Design

Applying the PEST Framework

I have put various e-commerce issues, noted previously, into the traditional PEST framework, using the framework as a lens to review the Australian newspaper medium's coverage of e-commerce and manufacturing. Thus this research used major daily newspapers as the text to be examined. The use of this medium as a source of the reality, against which the conceptual description is to be checked, is believed consistent with its use by historical researchers as a "faithful mirror of reality" (Franzosi, 1995). Harris (2001 p. 191) and Franzosi (1995 p. 158) also suggest that "newspaper articles ... can form a major research resource," and it is anticipated that the major dailies will contain articles on a wide variety of topics, including management, politics, and community organisations, while containing items of sufficient length for useful analysis. Therefore, the choice of the Australian newspaper medium is adequate for the study of the Australian manufacturing industry.

Data Collection

In total, 103 newspapers articles were collected from Factiva.com by searching the keywords (as shown in Table 3) in both title and content and specifying the date range (from 1999 to 2002). Factiva.com is a Web-based newspaper archival search engine that contains over 8,000 publications from the period between 1990-2002. The data obtained covers a complete collection of Australian newspapers including: *The Australian, Australian Financial Review, Canberra Times, Courier-Mail, Sunday Telegraph,* and local newspapers such as *The Adelaide Advertiser, Perth Sunday Times, The Age—Melbourne, The Sydney Morning Herald,* and *The West Australian.*

The articles were gathered from different sources as shown in Table 4.

Table 3. Key words for searching newspaper articles (including combinations of 1&3, 1&4, 2&3, 2&4, etc.)

Key words:	1.	E-business (Electronic business)
	2.	E-commerce (Electronic commerce)
	3.	Manufacturing
	4.	Australian manufacturing

Table 4. Sources of data

Newspaper Name	Number of Articles
The Australian	34
Australian Financial Review	26
Canberra Times	4
Courier-Mail	5
Adelaide Advertiser	3
The Age	12
Sydney Morning Herald	19
Total	103

Findings

The Economic Dimension

Cost Justification

Cost justification is an important issue in the manufacturing industry. However, according to the analysis, no newspaper articles addressed the issue of the initial cost of setting up e-commerce. Instead, the concern of "Cost-Saving" has been discussed many times as shown next:

Companies in the manufacturing and transport sectors were the least involved. The manufacturing industry was said to be missing **an opportunity to reduce costs.** (Needham, 2001)

Many of the newspaper articles highlight the vast array of costs associated with manufacturing organisations and that these costs can be minimised through the use of e-commerce, for example, transaction cost saving, resulting from automated business processes:

Oracle marketing director Paul Rushton says that companies, especially manufacturing concerns, are already making big gains from automated supply chains. "Transaction costs drop dramatically," Rushton says. "There is a simplification, even elimination, of paperwork". (Bennett, 2001)

Other benefits include transportation cost savings, resulting from the ability of searching an optimised route:

BHP announced its "new economy" spin-off, OneSteel. Its very name suggested a readily accessible online brand and service. Freight costs are a huge issue for the steel manufacturer, with the system it **now uses a mapping tool that highlights the most cost-effective routes across the country.** (Cant, 2002)

An integrated supply chain produces cost savings in raw materials:

Companies looking to make savings in procurement processes should examine internal systems and relationships with suppliers before looking to join an online marketplace, said John Brand, e-business strategies program director at research company Meta Group. **Using the Internet for purchasing goods used directly in the manufacturing process would offer the largest savings**, *he said.* (Cresswell, 2001)

Though many articles address cost-saving issues, the lack of discussion of the setup and ongoing costs of e-commerce projects creates concern as to whether or not Australian manufacturing organisations have conduct a cost-benefit analysis before taking a step into e-commerce.

Skill Shortage

The problem of skill shortage is rarely mentioned in the newspaper articles. Only one article overtly discusses this problem. It suggests that the owners of small manufacturing organisations do not have basic computer literacy. Many owners view computers merely as office automation tools.

If someone could come and just set my computer up so it works and show me how to do it in 10 easy steps, we'd be doing it. (Sinclair, 2001)

Internet Access

Internet access is the first step of e-commerce practice, and research has shown that most manufacturers currently have Internet access, but most firms are using the Internet primarily for information exchange:

The survey conducted by Australian Chamber of Manufacturers – a forerunner of the Australian Industry Group—showed only 20 per cent of Australian firms were using the Net. However the survey released in 18 July 2000 by the Australian In-

dustry Group and PricewwaterhouseCoopers shows that **more than 80 per cent of firms were now using the Internet, mainly for gathering and disseminating information.** (Gettler, 2000)

Telecommunication Infrastructure

Telecommunication infrastructure is the backbone of e-commerce. Many countries need to completely revamp their telecommunication networks and equipment to take advantage of this new medium. However, in this study, the issue of government-wide telecommunication infrastructure has not been addressed in any of the articles. The question of how the Australian telecommunication infrastructure supports e-commerce activities in the manufacturing industry is not discussed.

E-commerce issues in this dimension have not been addressed properly as shown in Table 5.

Table 5. Summary of findings—Economical dimension

Economical	*No. of articles addressing the issue*
Cost justification	0 (5 for cost-saving)
Internet access	1
Telecom infrastructure	0
Skill shortage	1
Performance measurement	0

Technical Dimension

Security

The issue of security is a dominant topic in newspaper discussions. The manufacturing industry not only views this issue as a technological issue, but also as an important social consideration. Within the discussion, possible solutions such as using encryption methods are recommended. The newspaper articles further indicate that manufacturing organisations are still waiting for a proper solution—security has not yet been convincingly demonstrated:

Australia's first industry-wide automotive extranet has been launched. Called the AANX (Australian Automotive Network Exchange), the extranet has just entered its testing stage and will allow large manufacturers and supplies to trade components as well as exchange plans and critical business information. It is designed to conduct business-to-business E-commerce, but includes more than just buying and selling. There is collaboration in the development stage, support of just-in-time manufacturing. **However the problem the AANX has was its inability to deliver PKI digital certificates, which will be provided with the AANX exchange. The large manufacturers don't want to transmit confidential data over the unsecured Internet.** (Kaufman, 2000)

According to Cap Gemini Ernst & Young's surveyed (2001) 166 CEOs and senior executives of the top 1000 Australian and New Zealand corporations. "Manufacturing companies were least active. **Organizations were cautious about E-commerce because of security issues and privacy concerns**". (Brown, 2001)

Reliability

Within this study, of 103 articles, only two addressed the issue of technological reliability. However these two articles did not discuss the reliability issue in great detail. For example, the inefficiency of IS handling due to the large volume of online transactions is not discussed.

A study of Australian manufacturers last year found that 25 per cent were using the Internet to buy and sell but another quarter had no interest at all in electronic business. Heather Ridout, Australian Industry Group Director for public policy, said that there is an element of "wait and see" **as manufacturers wait for technology to stabilise.** *She goes on to say that as the industry becomes more familiar with the Internet, she expects technology spending to rank alongside spending on new manufacturing processes.* (Sinclair, 2001)

A constant issue for large corporates entering the E-commerce world is deciding which technology to invest in as it is changing so rapidly ... .(Hunt, 2001)

Integration

There are often significant problems in integrating Internet and e-commerce software with the existing applications and databases, as discussed by Prasad (2000). Newspaper articles address this issue many times:

In the future, the competition may be between supply chains. In other situations the owners of brands may concentrate activities on designing products and marketing, leaving the manufacturing to specialised manufacturing operations that also supply their marketing and design competitors. **Enterprises that jump into e-business before getting their systems right are likely to suffer badly.** (Gottliebsen, 2001)

KPMG believes firms in the industries such as automotive/manufacturing, financial services, communication and others **are struggling with system integration, maintaining a high level of security and bundling products and services** *online.* (Marriner, 2000)

ERP basically means the integration of high-end applications, usually based around manufacturing or accounting systems. One of the reasons that can explain the decline in ERP was the greater publicity given to applications such as electronic commerce and customer relationship management (CRM). These were often spoken of as if they were separate applications but they were not. They were simply different aspects of ERP. (Philipson, 2002)

Bandwidth

In this study (1999~2002), no newspaper articles presented any information related to problems with low bandwidth, with current Internet access options. In particular, no discussion is found in relation to the limitations of low bandwidth on the design of multimedia-based Web sites. However, due to the fast growth of communication technology, bandwidth issues may be addressed adequately in the near future.

According to the researcher's analysis, security issues dominate thinking in this dimension.

Table 6. Summary of findings—Technical dimension

Technical	No. of articles addressing the issue
Security	18
Reliability	2
Bandwidth	0
Integration	6

Social Dimension

Security, Privacy—Trust

Security and privacy issues are major hurdles for the growth of e-commerce. As found in the newspaper articles, reporters, and manufacturing firms expressed their concern and hesitancy on the issue of security; however, few attempted to present solutions. Nevertheless one article (as shown hereafter) suggested that a well-designed privacy policy would help to minimise security and privacy problems:

The manufacturing, retail, travel and entertainment sectors had the poorest knowledge of the privacy laws, while financial services, health and education industries took the laws most seriously. ... Bennett from KPMG says **there are some basic steps companies can take: Appoint a privacy officer, then adopt a general privacy policy, establish a privacy access procedure to provide customers' details and then establish a privacy complaints handling procedure.** (Mclachlan & Connors, 2001)

Cultural Diversity

E-commerce practitioners in the manufacturing industry are concerned with the cultural diversity of consumers. There was one article found in this study, which addressed the issue of customisation of e-commerce Web site interfaces to adjust to cultural diversity. This article also shows that Australian manufacturers are now targeting a global market when implementing e-commerce projects.

According to Alby McCraken, chief executive of Para-Anchors, which manufactures parachute sea anchors and sells to boat owners in the UK, Europe, New Zealand and South Africa over the Internet ... **"if your prices are in Australian dollars, then consider a currency converter, and transactions into their languages if you are trying to attract non-English-speaking customers.** (Lavelle, 2002)

Touch and Feel

Manufacturing firms are not concerned with the absence of touch and feel on their Web sites. However it is always a big issue for online service providers. From this study, it seems that Australian manufacturers give very little recognition or attention to touch and feel. However, there was one indirect discussion on this issue. According to this article, BHP has researched the buying habits of its customers,

Table 7. Summary of findings—Social dimension

Social	No. of articles addressing the issue
Privacy/Security (as a social issue)—trust	12
Cultural diversity	1
Absence of touch/feel	1

but has not gone far enough to discuss the reality of the current online services; that is, the absence of touch and feel.

BHP announced its "new economy" spin-off, OneSteel. Its very name suggested a readily accessible online brand and service. While the company geared up for the online world, **the reality, the company's reporter person Dines says, was that steel customers remain traditional store buyers.** (Cant, 2002)

Table 7 shows the key findings in this dimension.

Political Dimension

The legal dimension of e-commerce is concerned with intellectual property rights and the legal validity of electronic transactions as well as strategic considerations.

Policy and Regulation, Legal Validity of Transactions

It was found that many articles address the legal issues of e-commerce, but most of them only attempt to discuss the legal issues in general terms, without discussion of the possible solutions and potential implications for the manufacturing industry.

A fundamental problem of E-commerce is the laws. For example, those of Austra-lia, and the reach of courts, have been defined traditionally in terms of geography; yet, a web site can cross multiple jurisdictional borders easily. This in turn poses a problem for Internet sites because they can never be sure when their site might subject them to the laws of a specific country or state. Similarly, law-enforcement bodies have great difficulty in policing their jurisdictions when E-commerce activi-ties, including some fraudulent or other illegal activities, can invade the jurisdiction so readily and evade law-enforcement efforts. Another issue is how to determine what law applies. (Clark, 2000)

Electronic exchanges, all the rage in the manufacturing industry, are set to invade Australia's legal practices following an arrangement between Clayton Utz and a big American law firm. Privacy is the area of emerging E-commerce law. (Cochrane, 2000)

Jurisdictional issues must be resolved soon or they will threaten the viability of online commerce. This is especially so as international transactions increase and the present case-by-case approach will prove to be dysfunctional. There are two fundamental issues of E-commerce activities: whose law is to apply and how much sovereignty or control should governments exercise over Internet commerce. (Clark, 2001)

Intellectual Property

During the implementation of e-commence projects, manufacturers recognise intellectual property as important assets in organisations. Now they are seeking to protect their assets. The following article introduces a recent case relating to intellectual property. The manufacturer, Maggbury, is concerned about its company's confidentiality with external service providers.

Australian technology entrepreneurs are being advised to review their confidentiality agreements with venture capitalists, investment banks and manufacturers following a recent High Court case which has thrown into doubt the effectiveness of such contracts. In July 1995, Maggbury approached Hafele wanting the manufacturing group to help produce its invention, a type of mechanical hinge used primarily in wall-mounted ironing boards. To protect its intellectual property, Maggbury entered into a confidentiality agreement with Hafele which stated that Hafele must not disclose information about Maggbury's invention to any person and that Hafele would forever observe this obligation unless released from the agreement by Maggbury. (Nicholas, 2002)

Taxation Issues

The taxation system for the e-commerce market is still under developed. In Australia, most online retailers are selling goods and services with GST inclusive, but many transactions are still processed without any contribution to the taxation system. With respect to researching e-commerce taxation issues in the Australian manufacturing industry, it was found that this issue was not being addressed in any newspaper articles.

Strategic Considerations

Many articles promote e-commerce technology as a new business strategy for the Australian manufacturing industry. Furthermore, many reporters suggest that the industry has already engaged in e-commerce activities.

Australia's manufacturing industry is pushing ahead with leading edge business-to-business strategies and already is churning $12 billion of transactions through the Internet. The latest study conducted by the Australian Industry Group and PricewaterhouseCooper shows that almost one in two Australian manufacturers are using or preparing to use Internet e-business. It was found that 44 per cent of manufacturers have Internet strategies in place, 10.3 per cent already use e-business exchanges and a third are preparing E-commerce initiatives. (Zampetakis, 2000)

The growth of e-business and the Internet will change and expand the structure of core business across key industry sectors, according to a third of global executives surveyed by KPMG consulting. (Caruana, 2000)

While promoting e-commerce as a new business strategic orientation, few articles suggest that there is an industry-wide inefficiency in participating in e-commerce. For example, the following article suggests that, compared with other industries, e-commerce in Australian manufacturing industry is only taking off slowly.

Most companies were found to have e-business strategies and active involvement by senior management in formulating e-business strategies but some of the traditional manufacturing sectors were lagging behind, KPMG consulting partner Nigel Montgomery said. The survey found the financial services and communica-

Table 8. Summary of findings—Political dimension

Political	No. of articles addressing the issue
Intellectual property	3
Legal validity of transactions	10
Taxation issues	0
Policing/regulation	3
Business strategy (with an e-commerce focus)	8

tion industries were undergoing significant e-business change, **with the chemical and automotive industries lagging in terms of readiness for e-business growth.** (Caruana, 2000)

Key findings in this dimension are listed in Table 8.

Summary of Findings

Most issues identified by the PEST four dimensions framework were found in the newspaper articles, but the majority of articles have not provided detailed discussions or depth on these issues. Within the four dimensions identified, the technical dimension is the one that has been most thoroughly discussed, while security and privacy issues (as a technical issue and a social issue) have gained the most attention (about 20 distinct articles addressed these concerns). However, compared with security issues, it was found that there is a lack of discussion of the topics related to B2B e-commerce movements and supply chain management techniques. The keywords appeared in the article, but the details were overlooked.

Discussion

Dominant Thinking: Security

The newspaper discussions on security and privacy issues were found to be very comprehensive. In total, 18 articles (17% of 103 articles) addressed the security issue as a technical problem. The newspaper articles not only addressed this issue, but also provided further details on possible solutions such as the use of an encryption method know as public key infrastructure (PKI) for transaction transmissions. Manufacturers appear to be aware of these issues and are actively seeking legal protection for newer technologies. It was also suggested that the relevant legal framework is not yet mature enough to satisfy manufacturers, customers, and their suppliers' requirements regarding security. Security concerns therefore become a barrier in organisations undertaking e-commerce projects. On the other hand, the security concern is also an important social issue. Twelve articles (11%) presented this issue as a social concern (whether or not the users or organisations trust the current e-commerce services). Consumers' confidence with e-commerce is extremely critical and a lack of adequate security may impede the motivation that the manufacturing industry has towards e-commerce. It is suggested that security and privacy concerns are the first problems that the manufacturing industry must overcome, and they are still awaiting an appropriate solution.

Lack of Discussion on Other Issues

Unlike the coverage for security, many other issues have been overlooked in the newspaper articles, as is evident from the quantity of discussion. For example, in many e-commerce research papers, technical issues such as reliability, communication protocols, bandwidth availability, and integration problems are mentioned as significant in e-commerce. However, only a few newspaper articles addressed these issues. For example, of the 103 articles, only two articles included a simple discussion of the reliability issue; just six articles mentioned the integration problems; but none discussed the issue of bandwidth.

Moreover, the quality of discussion is also poor. For example, the newspaper medium has overlooked the problem of skills shortage. Only one article briefly addressed this issue but, even in that article, the issue of skill shortage was viewed as a lack of understanding and skills in basic computer literacy. It is obvious that e-commerce involves more than mastering basic computer skills. In addition, the priority given to these issues is unclear, as is the level of effort the industry is making to resolve these issues. Thus, the risk of overlooking fundamental issues, such as a skills shortage, telecommunication infrastructure, and others, may block industry attempts and waste previous investments in e-commerce.

The Absence of Leading Discussions

More importantly, while the key words such as *B2B e-commerce* and *supply chain* appeared in many articles, the newspaper medium does not present or lead further discussion on these topics. For example, although it is found that the Australian manufacturing industry has built its e-commerce supply chain management network—AANX—the role, function, advantages, and disadvantages of the AANX network have not been discussed in depth. The problem of the lack of scrutinised discussion also applies to other issues such as taxation, performance measurement, and so on.

Although eight articles address business's strategic considerations of e-commerce, the discussion is very simple: essentially, all eight articles simply propose that adopting e-commerce is a good business strategy. In-depth discussion (e.g., how to implement e-commerce, adopting e-commerce changes, current strategies) is not presented in the newspaper articles. In fact, these strategic considerations and the impact due to the Internet-based, supply-chain management are areas where the manufacturing industry requires expert advice or at least must be able to increase general awareness.

Unfortunately, I feel that if the newspaper medium is trying to lead the public forum for issues associated with e-commerce in manufacturing, they have had very limited success, because the detail covered in the newspaper articles is not sufficient to create an awareness of e-commerce problems and challenges.

Recommendations

The majority of organisations in the manufacturing industry have expressed enthusiasm for adopting e-commerce as a new business opportunity. The newspaper medium in Australia has certainly picked up on this interest. However, this medium has failed to use its power to raise or lead further discussion in the public and private domains. Instead of over selling e-commerce, or telling only success stories, more effort could be invested in creating general awareness about a comprehensive range of e-commerce problems and challenges.

This comprehensive, in-depth coverage would consistently remind the industry, and the public, that e-commerce is a problematic issue which requires continuous investment of effort and resources. An analogy can be drawn from the immigration issue in Australia. The newspaper medium has presented in-depth coverage of all aspects of immigration (e.g., the positive and negative consequences of accepting refugees). The newspaper articles often lead to public debates on the national policy development of immigration. Over time, immigration becomes a key issue in Australia, and the government is forced to deal with it carefully. Therefore, when considering the case of e-commerce, a similar effort should be expected from the newspaper medium. If the discussion of e-commerce only remains at the surface level, e-commerce will not be regarded as a serious topic that strikes individuals, governments, and industries as a matter of concern. ("It is not important, so why bother?")

Additionally, newspaper reporters may not have professional knowledge and skills to deal with various e-commerce aspects. Since they are playing an important role in leading the public forum on e-commerce, training is absolutely essential. Expert advice (e.g., from industry consultants, IT professionals) must be brought into the articles for further scrutiny and discussion. With all these efforts, the newspaper articles should no longer be only a reproduction of what is happening "out there," but also an informed and comprehensible interpretation about why it occurs in such ways.

The passion for e-commerce may fade, but the e-commerce movement will continue. The exploration of the media's role in this movement will contribute to the development of future policy and strategies on how to facilitate e-commerce activities. Therefore, further studies are required. For example, the primary source of data in this research is the Australian newspaper medium. Similar studies using international newspaper articles can enrich the findings. Moreover, when exploring the role of the mass media in preparing the industry for the e-commerce movement, the studies of another medium (e.g., TV news) can be very useful.

Year 2003-2005 Revisited

The original research was completed in 2003, but the article is being republished in 2006, requiring updates to that year. I applied the same methodology (using the same PEST framework with the same keywords) to complete the second-round study in 2006, for the period between 2003 and 2005. An additional 87 Australian nation-wide newspaper articles were collected from the factiva online newspaper database (http://infoweb.newsbank.com).

Although, during the past 3 years, Internet and Web technologies have advanced tremendously, and the concepts of e-commerce and e-business have obtained much awareness, the research findings still showed a lack of scrutiny in the newspaper medium. There is limited discussion of the issues that prohibit the Australian manufacturing industry from taking advantage of e-commerce. Instead of modifying the original study, the highlights are provided hereafter with a specific focus on the most and the least popular issues published in the previous study.

Overall, the newspaper medium projected a strong and positive message that encourages the industry's moves towards e-commerce and the e-business domain. The majority of articles include the same positive comments as shown in the following examples:

Automation and the move to e-commerce is key to the company's forward plans. (Mills, 2003)

The technology now used in e-commerce has made it possible for a supplier to be integrated with its clients. (Chong, 2003)

Among the economical political dimension, the skill shortage problems have gained a little more attention. Several articles discussed the problem (however, with a negative view, which shows the issue has yet to be resolved), as exemplified hereafter:

Smaller businesses are having trouble getting good IT advice ... *many of the people who run small and medium-sized businesses do not know enough about IT and end up resorting to a combination of do-it-yourself, vendor support and independent advice ... Often people who have another profession have other expertise. I haven't seen any cases where that's worked very well.* (Timson, 2003)

Within the technical dimension, security and broadband issues still attracted the most attention. In particular, a number of articles identified that security is the biggest barrier to adopting e-commerce.

The major reason given for not engaging in e-commerce was the security issue ... *businesses said they had a major concern with computer hacking ... Like any other resource available to business, the internet must prove that it can operate securely and efficiently—something it currently cannot guarantee. Until the problem can be overcome, the internet will continue to be a great source of information and a marketing medium, but not a major new way of conducting business.* (Newnham, 2003)

The greatest barrier to adopting e-commerce centred around concerns over online security. (Ellis, 2004)

Unlike the previous findings, bandwidth issues have been addressed many times during the last 3 years, perhaps due to the development of the broadband technology. Some strong arguments were found, as shown hereafter:

Wakim [managing director for an organisation] said he and staff **were frustrated with slow and unreliable dial-up internet**. *It's [broadband] desperately needed for the local businesses. ... It will improve our efficiency for exports, which is limited at the moment. ... Small Business Minister [of Australia] Marsha Thomson said the council had recognised* **broadband was a necessary business tool.** (Vainoras, 2004)

Smaller companies and many regional manufacturers **weren't taking up broadband and indicated they were at risk of being left behind**. *... An Australian Industry Group study identified a strong business uptake of broadband technology by medium to large-sized manufacturing organisations. The companies said they had been rewarded with competitive benefits relating to performance and productivity.* (Ellis, 2004)

Only one article tackled the reliability issue during this period. In particular, this newspaper article suggested that many manufacturing organisations were lacking awareness in adopting appropriate technologies and developing strategies in coping with data backup and disaster recovery.

One in three companies are operating without a disaster recovery plan… Companies surveyed also admitted their data backup and disaster recovery plans have "significant vulnerabilities." … Executives now realise the dangers because downtime on their computers costs corporations some $1 million an hour in lost revenue. (Suzukamo, 2003)

Radio rrequency identifier (RFID) became a new integration issue for e-commerce/e-business adoption that concerned manufacturers in Australia. Companies were considering how to fit the technology into their existing business processes. For example:

The use of RFID on toll tags is well established in Australia. … In Australia, most RFID projects are popping up in manufacturing and agriculture. (Mills, 2004)

A lot of manufacturing chief financial officers will grit their teeth when they crunch the numbers on supply-chain RFID projects, but will at some point be forced to sign off on them anyway. … Forward-thinking IT executives, therefore, will already be working hard to identify every opportunity to squeeze organisational value out of the technology to make the business case respectable, or at least to ensure the pain is tolerable, when the time comes". (McCable, 2005)

Similarly to the previous findings, this study still showed that the social and political dimensions were not well discussed. In fact, during the past 3 years, the Australian newspaper medium still has not taken the leading role to inform the public and the private sector with various e-commerce issues. Even one of the newspaper articles suggested that:

Email is handy and access to online information is great, but e-commerce is still struggling for acceptance. … There are more than 1.6 million small businesses in Australia employing about 4 million people. It is therefore surprising how little attention is paid, and help given [support of E-commerce adoption], to small businesses. (Newnham, 2003)

Perhaps the newspaper medium has never intended to undertake the leading role such as they often exercise in elections. Nevertheless, this research raised an open question: Who will take the role in informing and supporting the general public regarding e-commerce adoption?

References

Aiex, N. K. (2000). Political communication via the Media. *ERIC Digest, 1*(3), D151.

Australian Bureau of Statistics. (2001). *Manufacturing special article—Manufacturing in the twentieth century*. Canberra: Year Book Australia.

Bakos, J., & Treacy, M. (1986). Information technology and corporate strategy: A research perspective. *MIS Quarterly, 10*(2), 107.

Bennett, B. (2001). Behind closed doors. *Sydney Morning Herald*.

Bloch, H. (1996). Changes in the international competitiveness of Australian manufacturing: 1968 to 1989. *Australian Economic Review, 3*(115), 308.

Brown, P. (2001). A Website, an intranet and that's e-business. *The Australian*.

Cant, S. (2002). Steeling themselves to work outside the square. *Sydney Morning Herald*.

Caruana, L. (2000). Gearing up for revolution. *The Australian*.

Chaston, I., Badger, B., Mangles, T., & Sadler-Smith, E. (2001). The Internet and e-commerce: An opportunity to examine organisational learning in progress in small manufacturing firms. *International Small Business Journal, 19*(2), 13-30.

Chen, K. L., Lee, H. M., & Mayer, M. W. (2001). The impact of security control on business-to-consumer electronic commerce. *Human Systems Management, 20*(2), 139.

Chong, F. (2003). Chain gangs get back-end into gear. *The Australian*.

Clark, C., Geer, Y., & Underhill, B. (1996). *The changing of Australian manufacturing*. Industry Commission.

Clark, E. (2000). What law governs whom in the net's fuzzy world? *Canberra Times*.

Clark, E. (2001). Jurisdiction looming threat to e-commerce. *Canberra Times*.

Clarke, R. (1996). Internet privacy concerns confirm the case for intervention. *Communications of the ACM, 42*(2), 60-67.

Closs, D. J., & Xu, K. (2000). Logistics information technology practice in manufacturing and merchandising firms: An international benchmarking study versus world class logistics firms. *International Journal of Physical Distribution & Logistics Management, 30*(10), 869.

Cochrane, N. (2000). Australia joins e-consortium of worlds' legal firms. *The Age*.

Cresswell, E. (2001). Exchanges "number juggling. " *The Australian*.

Dispensa, J. M., & Brulle, R. J. (2003). Media's social construction of environmental issues: Focus on global warming—A comparative study. *International Journal of Sociology and Social Policy, 23*(1), 74-105.

Dutta, S., & Biren, B. (1999). Business transformation on the Internet: Results from the 2000 study. *European Management Journal, 19*(5), 449-462.

Ellis, G. (2004). City of innovation falls behind—News extra. *Illawarra Mercury*.

Erikson, R. V., Baranek, P. M., & Chan, J. B. L. (1987). *Visualizing deviance: A study of news organizations.* Toronto: University of Toronto Press.

Franzosi, R. (1995). Computer-assisted content analysis of newspapers. *Quality & Quantity, 29,* 157-172.

Fujii, S., Kaihara, T., Morita, H., & Tanaka, M. (2000). A distributed virtual factory in agile manufacturing environment. *International Journal of Production Research, 38*(17) 4113-4128.

Gade, P., Abel, S., Antecol, M., & Hsueh, H. (1998). Journalists' attitudes toward civic journalism media roles. *Newspaper Research Journal, 19*(4), 10-26.

Gettler, L. (2000). Industry lags in e-biz. *The Age.*

Gilbert, A. H., Jr., Arthur H., Pick, R. A., Roger A., Ward., & Sidne G. (2000). Continuing information systems issues: A comparison of the manufacturing and non-manufacturing sect. *Journal of Applied Business Research, 16*(4), 21.

Gilens, M., & Hertzman, C. (2000). Corporate ownership and news bias: Newspaper coverage of the 1996 Telecommunications Act. *The Journal of Politics, 62*(2), 369-386.

Gittins, R. (1995). The role of the media in the formulation of economic policy. *The Australian Economic Review, 5*(4) 5-15.

Gordon, J. R., & Gordon, S. R. (2000). Structuring the interaction between IT and business units. *Information Systems Management, 17*(1) 7-16.

Gottliebsen, R. (2001). Huge rewards for those who get IT right. *The Australian.*

Gunasekaran, A., Marri, H. B., McGaughey, R. E., & Nebhwani, M. D. (2002). E-commerce and its impact on operations management. *International Journal of Production Economics, 191*(8) 185-197.

Gunasekaran, A., & Ngai, E. W. T. (2005). E-commerce in Hong Kong: An empirical perspective and analysis. *Internet Research, 15*(2), 141-159.

Haley, G. T. (2002). E-commerce in China: Changing business as we know it. *Industrial Marketing Management, 31*(2), 119-124.

Hannigan, J. A. (1995). *Environmental sociology.* Routledge.

Harris, H. (2001). Content analysis of secondary data: A study of courage in managerial decision making. *Journal of Business Ethics, 34*(3/4), 191-208.

Hoge, J., & James, F. (1994). Media pervasiveness. *Foreign Affairs, 73*(1), 136-144.

Hughes, J. F., & Glaister, K. (2001). Electronic commerce and international taxation: A square peg in a round hole? *European Management Journal, 19*(6), 651.

Hunt, J. (2001). Big names move in to e-markets. *The Age.*

Jarvenpass, S.L., & Tiller, E.H. (1999). Integrating market, technology and policy opportunities in e-business strategy. *Journal of Strategic Information Systems 8*(3), 235-249.

Johnson, G., & Scholes, K. (2003). *Exploring corporate strategy.* Prentice Hall.

Kakabadse, A. (2000). Future role of IS/IT professionals. *Journal of Management Development, 19*(2), 97-154.

Kalakota, R., & Whinston, A. B. (1996). *Frontiers of the electronic commerce.* Addison-Wesley.

Kao, D., & Decou, J. (2003). A strategy-based model for e-commerce planning. *Industrial Management & Data Systems, 103*(4), 238-252.

Kathuria, R., Anandarajan, M., & Igbaria, M. (1999). Selecting IT applications in manufacturing. A KBS approach. *International Journal of Management Science, 27*(6), 605-616.

Kaufman, D. (2000). Car parts market picks up steam on the net. *Sydney Morning Herald.*

Lavelle, P. (2002). Online sales a matter of untangling the Web. *Australian Financial Review.*

Lawson, R., Alcock, C., Cooper, J., & Burgess, L. (2003). Factors affecting adoption of electronic commerce technologies by SMEs: An Australian study. *Journal of Small Business and Enterprise Development, 10*(3), 265-276.

Linstone, H. A. (1999). *Decision making for technology executives: Using multiple perspectives to improve performance.* Artech House Publisher.

Luttberg, N. R. (1988). Role of newspaper coverage and political ads in local elections. *Journalism Quarterly, 65*(4), 881-888.

Mackay, D. R., Altmann, G. L., & McMichael, H. (2003). How intimate are Australian e-business retail supply chains? *Logistics Information Management, 16*(1), 48-55.

Marriner, C. (2000). Electronics firms in the box seat for e-business: Survey. *Sydney Morning Herald.*

Martin, C. (2002). *Technological diffusion in Australian industry.* Adelaide, University of South Australia.

Mathew, B., & De, R. (1999). Issues in the management of Web technologies: A conceptual framework. *International Journal of Information Management, 41*(9), 427-447.

McCable, B. (2005). Transponderosa's rough riders. *The Australian.*

Mclachlan, M., & Connors, E. (2001). Evasion of privacy. *Australian Financial Review.*

Mills, K. (2003). Caravaner switches gear. *The Australian.*

Mills, K. (2004). BYE BYE BARCODE—Time for RFID to prove itself. *The Australian.*

Mohanti, R. P., & Deshmukh, S. G. (1999). Evaluating manufacturing strategy for a learning organisation. *International Journal of Operations & Production Management, 19*(3), 308-327.

Murillo, L. (2001). Supply chain management and the international dissemination of e-commerce. *Industrial Management & Data Systems, 101*(7), 370-377.

Nabil, R. A., Dogramaci, O., & Gangopadhyay, A. (1999). *Electronic commerce: Technical, business, and legal issues.* Upper Saddle River, NJ: Prentice Hall.

Nath, R. (1998). Electronic commerce and the Internet: Issues, problems and perspectives. *International Journal of Information Management, 18*(2), 91-101.

Needham, K. (2001). No such thing as e-business at the big end of town. *Sydney Morning Herald.*

Newnham, M. (2003). Security still holds back SMEs from embracing the Internet—Small business. *The Age.*

Nicholas, K. (2002). Ruling puts confidentiality deals at risk. *Australian Financial Review.*

Ng, H.-I., Pan, Y. J., & Wilson, T. D. (1998). Business use of the World Wide Web: A report on further investigation. *International Journal of Information Management, 18*(5), 291-314.

Philipson, G. (2002). Reports of ERP's death exaggerated. *The Age.*

Poon, S., & Swatman, P. M. C. (1999). An exploratory study of small business Internet commerce issues. *Information & Management, 35*(1), 9-18.

Pouder, R., John, C. H., & Cannon, A. R. (2001). Change drivers in the new millennium implications for manufacturing strategy research. *Journal of Operations Management, 19,* 143-160.

Prasad, B. (2000). The challenges facing global e-commerce. *Information Systems Management, 17*(4), 26-34.

Qimei, C. (2000). Attitude toward the site. *Journal of Advertising Research, 39*(5), 27.

Retail Sales Tax Act, R.S.O 1990, C. R.31, ss. 7(4), (5), 9, 48(4).

Roehl, T. W., & Standifird, S. (2001). Globalization and electronic commerce: Inferences from retail brokering. *Journal of International Business Studies, 32*(4), 749.

Sarkis, J., & Sundarraj, R. P. (2002). Evolution of brokering; paradigms in e-commerce enabled manufacturing. *International Journal of Production Economics, 75*(1/2), 21-31.

Sinclair, J. (2001). Web leaves small business in e-commerce spin. *The Age.*

Soliman, F., & Youssef, M. (2001). The impact of some recent developments in e-business on the management of next generation manufacturing. *International Journal of Operations & Production Management, 21*(5/6), 538-564.

Soliman, F., & Youssef, A. M. (2003). Internet-based e-commerce and its impact on manufacturing and business operations. *Industrial Management & Data Systems, 103*(8), 546-552.

Stein, R. (1972). *Media power.* Boston: Houghton Mifflin.

Suzukamo, L. B. (2003). Most firms not disaster ready—Storage: IT business special peport. *The Australian.*

Tellecommunications Act of 1996 (1996). Pub. PA. No. 104-104, 110 Stat. 56.

Timson, L. (2003). Next plus—Technology for small and medium enterprises. *The Age.*

Thompson, A. A. J., & Strickland, A. J. (1990). *Strategic management: Concept and cases.* Homewood, IL: BPI/Irwin.

Thompson, C. Y. (2000). Representing gangs in the news: Media constructions of criminal gangs. *Sociological Spectrum, 20*(4), 409-432.

Truman, G. E. (2000). Integration in electronic exchange environments. *Journal of Management Information System, 17*(1), 10.

Vainoras, T. (2004). Businesses gain a load of Internet. Leader. *Whittlesea Post.*

Walker, J. R. (1990). Developing a new political reality: Political information and the 1988 Southern Regional Primary. *Southern Communication Journal, 55*(4), 421-435.

Wright, A. (2001). Controlling risks of e-commerce content. *Computer & Security, 20*(2), 147-154.

Zampetakis, H. (2000). Australian manufacturers go for the net—Hook, online and sinker. *Australian Finanical Review.*

Chapter VII

Netrepreneur Simulation:
The Development of Realism in Virtual E-Entrepreneurship Learning

Salim Jiwa, The Manchester Metropolitan University, UK

Dawn Lavelle, University of the Arts London, UK

Arjun Rose, University of the Arts London, UK

Abstract

Entrepreneurship, or the move towards self-reliance, is increasingly seen as an important driver of economic growth and development in the UK. Enterprise education is seen as an expedient means of increasing both the number and quality of entrepreneurs. However, the nature, content, and relevance of entrepreneurship education have been subject to increasing scrutiny. There has been a growing interest in the process by which practitioners learn and the creation of entrepreneurial learning environments that emulate practitioner learning. The need to incorporate realism in educational requirements through a sense of presence experienced by learners has seen an increase in the use of virtual learning contexts. This chapter reviews the pedagogic requirements of entrepreneurial education within one specific context of e-commerce. Netrepreneur simulates the initial start-up phases of e-business creation and, through the modelling and electronic simulation of the e-commerce environment, it aims to create a holistic understanding of the entrepreneurial process as well as encouraging participants to learn by doing. This chapter documents the underpinning objectives of design conceptualisation and the integration of the real and virtual worlds within system development. The later section of the chapter reports on the user survey responses to Netrepreneur, which demonstrates a strong sense of presence experienced by participants. The sense of presence experienced by learners in a virtual environment can be considered to be a key feature in ensuring the efficacy of learning and the following transfer of knowledge and skills from the learning context to the "real world."

Introduction

Entrepreneurship or the move towards self-reliance is increasingly seen as an important driver of economic growth and development. In common with other industrially developed nations, policy makers in the UK have developed an awareness of "entrepreneurship" and "enterprise education" as pragmatic and expedient solutions for a growing range of contemporary socioeconomic and political challenges. Numerous government publications (e.g., Small Business Service, 2005) on competitiveness have confirmed the importance of innovative entrepreneurship and the development of micro and small businesses as a necessary component of driving forward a knowledge-based economy and an enterprising society.

Small businesses in the UK make a major contribution to the health of the economy and to the diversity of opportunity in society. The UK has almost 3.8 million small businesses, accounting for 99% of the total number of UK firms and generating 52% of total turnover. They employ 12.6 million people, representing 56% of the private sector (Small Business Service, 2005). It is now widely acknowledged that the success of the small business helps to enhance competition by challenging incumbent businesses and provides an important source of innovation and new techniques. Despite a generally supportive environment and positive attitudes towards enterprise, the UK continues to lag behind the U.S. and many countries in Europe in terms of entrepreneurial activity (Minniti, Bygrave, & Autio, 2005).

The government's main objective in building an enterprise culture is to provide people with sufficient understanding to enable them to make informed choices regarding employment and enterprise. However, there is increasing recognition that career choices for graduates and others with higher skills and knowledge have not traditionally included business creation (Careers Service Unit, 1999). Without the motivation of highly skilled people and their movement into business, it is recognised that societal and economic aspirations will only be partially achieved. Enterprise education is increasingly seen as an expedient means of increasing both the number and quality of entrepreneurs in a given economy, and as such is seen as a key element of the success of the national policy agenda.

The high value-added and high-tech end of the small and medium-sized enterprise (SME) sector is now seen as providing an important impetus for the UK's policy drive towards breaking a low skills equilibrium that has dominated the national economy. The development of the SME sector is seen as representative of, and synonymous with, economic shifts that have been described as being from industrial to post-industrial, from Fordism to post-Fordism, from low skill economy to a high skill economy. Government policy is committed to supporting sectors that represent and champion these shifts, and e-business is increasingly being seen as the "new economy." The proportion of SMEs in the UK retail sector that own a Web site has risen sharply from 7% in 2004, and according to Actinic (2006) may be as high as 25%. Gartner predicts the UK is on a second wave of internet adoption, with predictions of a growing number of companies planning to adopt e-commerce in the future (Actinic, 2006).

However, the nature, relevance, content, and appropriateness of entrepreneurship education has been subject to increasing scrutiny (Henry, Hill, & Leitch, 2005). There has, in parallel, been a growing interest in the process by which practitioners learn, the creation of entrepreneurial learning environments that emulate practitioner learning, and the requirement to tailor realism to educational requirements through a sense of presence experienced by learners in virtual learning contexts.

The process of entrepreneurship has been defined as managerial behaviour which consistently exploits opportunities to deliver results beyond one's capabilities (Parston, 1998). Enterprise capability is the "capacity to handle uncertainty and respond positively to change, to create and implement new ideas and ways of doing things, to make reasonable risk/reward assessments and act upon them in one's personal and working life" (Davies, 2002, p. 8). An entrepreneur is therefore someone with vision who spots a new opportunity and is minded to act on it. Successful entrepreneurial ventures will inevitably require innovation through the exploitation of new ideas, be they cultural, organisational, or technological. The e-commerce paradigm is in a constant state of invention and renewal in the creation of innovation and brand involvement. The challenge in structuring such a learning environment for the education sector concerns the ability of conventional teaching techniques to meet the needs of e-entrepreneurial start-up; the exploitation of new ideas in virtual settings, in conditions of increasing uncertainty. McHardy and Allan (2000), contend that the pressures faced by practitioners as they innovate are not easily replicated by conventional teaching means. Further, Fiet (2000) has noted that "there is an ongoing debate in the entrepreneurship academy about whether we can actually teach students to be entrepreneurs" (p. 1).

This chapter reviews the design development of Netrepreneur, an interactive simulation-based instructional technique designed to encourage entrepreneurs to innovate experientially by facing the uncertainty and ambiguity of e-business creation. It is designed to emulate the way practitioners learn to innovate, allowing participants the opportunity to experiment via action learning, replicating the real world experience but in a relatively risk free environment. The latter section of the chapter reports user survey responses collected from questionnaires. The questionnaires collected information concerning the degree to which learners experienced a sense of presence, that is, realism, through first person experience within the virtual learning context

Entrepreneurship

Successful entrepreneurial ventures require creativity and innovation, which call for enterprising people to interpret "what is possible" into reality (Kao, 1989). In order to meet the demands of chaotic modern environments and harness the potential of new technologies these ventures necessitate learning and change. Prospective entrepreneurs develop their own ways of dealing with opportunities, hindrances, and reservations to "creatively create" new services, products, organisations, and ways of satisfying customers or doing business.

Paradoxically, the learning process for entrepreneurs is notably different to conventional approaches adopted within education. Visionaries are those people who are able to synthesise the available information and clarify patterns that escape others. Motivated by the desire to be successful, entrepreneurs prefer perceptual movement and improvement, continually hoping to find and exploit manageable risks and opportunities (Churchill, 1997). They are comfortable with ambiguity, and they can bring transparency by piecing together unrelated messages and signals. Their approach to strategy is a quick but careful initial screening of data, using only limited analysis, to evaluate the quality of the idea. Their success lies in vigilance, learning, flexibility, and change during implementation (Bhide, 1994). Inadequate thought and appreciation will increase their sensitivity to the unexpected or unanticipated event (Thompson, 1999).

As such, to make people more enterprising, it will be necessary to foster creativity, innovation, and learning through the implementation process. This implies that the learning environment will be required to emulate a coaching instead of telling style, in order to allow entrepreneurs to take initiatives and accept responsibility for the decisions they take. Bruyat and Julien (2000) observed that while entrepreneurship has to do with a process of change, emergence, and the creation of new value, it is also a process of change and creation for the entrepreneur.

Action Learning

The implications behind the creation of this entrepreneurial learning environment are far reaching for educators with respect to emulating practitioner learning. Practitioners are inclined to rely on hunch, intuition, and implied knowledge when relevant facts are limited. Revans (1982), argues that action learning is primarily a way of managing this change through the learning process. Action learning involves participants in a situation in which they attempt to solve realistic problems in a purposeful and logical way. It allows participants to become empowered, to act rationally, and to develop critical thinking skills. This enhances their capacity to investigate, understand, and if necessary, change the ongoing situation, all with minimum external assistance (McHardy & Allan, 2000). Action learning works in the context of real issues and develops the whole person to apply broad skills for use in a wide range of situations. In doing so, this learning process helps make long-standing, inferred issues far clearer. Critten (1993) cites Revans equation for action learning L (action learning) = P (programmed learning) + Q (questioning insight) to describe the ways practitioners learn, "they act, then reflect, by questioning insight, the latter relying on qualities beyond the purely factual level." Q therefore reflects the need for decision making that relies on intuition and "feel." Confirmation of the value of questioning requires action to be taken in order to solve the problem.

McHardy and Allan (2000) proposed that "under real world conditions of stability and slow change, P is necessary and maybe sufficient, however under conditions of rapid change, uncertainty renders the tradition of proven techniques necessary but insufficient"(p. 497). McHardy and Allan (2000), describe P as "facts gleaned from yesterdays problems, such as case studies"(p. 498). Roberts (1996) cites that programmed instruction leaves practical understanding untouched because of "a gap between explicit knowledge and tacit knowledge that informs practice" (p. 72). To Pedler (1983), Q is the real world chaos and uncertainty with no definitive answers.

In contrast to the learning environments of practitioners, Pedler (1983), contends that educational establishments have over emphasised thinking (P) at the expense of "feeling" the need. In exploring the relationship between education and entrepreneurship, Gibb (1987) contrasted the classroom learning situation with the real world learning environment of the entrepreneur. The classroom situation involves a high level of dependence on authority and on what Gibb termed "expert validation"(p. 5), whereas in the real world entrepreneurs must rely on the validity of their own knowledge and personal values. The main differences between the classroom and the real world entrepreneurial learning situation are outlined in Table 1. Further Kirby (2002), proposes that reliance on traditional approaches to education may in fact inhibit the development of requisite entrepreneurial attributes and skills. Coaching learners beyond the realms of the thinking mode, into a mindset where activity and risk taking occurs, requires different teaching methods.

Table 1. Learning processes (Adapted with permission from Henry, Hill, & Leitch, 2005)

University/Business school—Classroom	Entrepreneurial—real world
Critical judgement after analysis of large amount of information	"Gut feel" decision making with limited information
Understanding and recalling the information itself	Understanding the values of those who transmit and filter information
Assuming goals away	Recognising the widely varied goals of others
Seeking verification of the truth by study of information	Making decisions on the basis of judgement of trust and competence of people
Understanding basis principles of society in the metaphysical way	Seeking to apply and adjust in practise to basis principles of society
Seeking the correct answer with time to do it	Developing the most appropriate solution under pressure
Learning in the classroom	Learning while and through doing
Gleaning information from experts and authoritative sources	Gleaning information personally from any and everywhere and weighing it up
Evaluation through written assessments	Evaluation by judgement of people and events through direct feedback
Success in learning measured by knowledge-based examination passed	Success in learning by solving problems and learning from failure

Figure 1. A knowledge/skills matrix

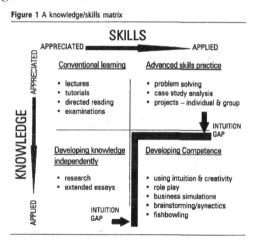

Source: McHardy, P, Allan, T., (2000), Closing the gap between what industry needs and what HE provides, Education and Training, Vol. 42 No. 9 pp.496-508

McHardy and Allan (2000) developed a knowledge skills matrix (Figure 1) for facilitating creativity, a pedagogic framework of two axes: (1) one a continuum for knowledge and (2) the other for skills (in each case from appreciated to applied). Of the four quadrants, the first three represent a focus on either knowledge or skills, but with neither integrated. When moving into the final quadrant the crossing of an "intuition gap" is required, where "feeling" cues associated with Pedler's (1983) and Revan's (1980) action learning can be activated using techniques such as simulation.

Simulation and Virtual World Contexts

In the real world, one of the most effective ways of acquiring knowledge and skills is to be immersed within a situational context. While this concept of "learning by doing" is widely acknowledged as an effective mode of acquisition; it is often difficult to replicate within classroom and training instructional contexts. Greeno, Smith, and Moore (1993) contend this problem occurs due to the fact that the knowledge of how to perform a task is embedded in the contextual environment within which the task is to be performed.

However, for time-restricted learning contexts, the real world dynamic offers too many unanticipated factors (Engel, Blackwell, & Miniard, 1993), introducing too many complexities for any specific lessons to be learned effectively. The use of virtual environments which compress time and space as microcosms of real settings, can be tailored to develop knowledge and skills to give participants an experiential taste of reality.

Simulations are constructed situations that simulate the problems, constraints, and resources of the everyday environment and insert the learner into the midst of the maze, challenging them to find a way to the designated final objective. The generally accepted definition of simulation given by Guetzkow (1963) is; "an operating representation of central features of reality" (p. 10). Thus, to qualify as a simulation an exercise must have two essential features, namely, it must represent a real situation of some sort (or an imaginary situation that might be real) and must be ongoing, that is, dynamic.

Simulation can be used as a response to situations in which participants have to display skills, take risks, and provide a structured environment for learning complex problems. Virtual environments are constructed as recognisably like the reality, while contrasting from it in its outcome. Participants are therefore encouraged to "feel" risk taking, but as Keys, Fulmer, and Stumpf (1996), propose they "learn through experimentation ... without the do or die consequences encountered in real life" (p. 44). Therefore, virtual worlds have the potential to provide a powerful learning environment in between reality and fiction: real enough to be relevant and involving for the user/trainee, so to be sure he/she will be able to fix the experience and to recall it in a professional context; and at the same time "not real" enough to allow users to make severe mistakes in the virtual environment without feeling too depressed or lowered in self-esteem afterwards (so that they are able to reflect on the experience, or be ready to look for and receive help). In synthesis, trainees can have a protected environment in which they experience success and failures and are much more likely to put themselves at risk. In order to gain a recallable learning experience, it is important to act behaviours, and consequently to succeed or make mistakes as a consequence to these actions, feeling emotions connected to success or failure and developing and elaborating appropriate thoughts over this experience.

According to Schon (1987) constraints that would prevent or inhibit experiment in the built world are greatly reduced in the virtual world, "permitting different paces in doing different things, different ways of doing the same thing, and above all permits reflection in action" (p. 102). Pfeiffer (1995) proposes that participants may learn more from simulation, "we remember more from what we know from being told about, or from reading about." (p. 209). Furthermore, active involvement through simulation is intrinsically motivating and engenders critical enquiry (Gallo, 1987).

Presence in Virtual Environments: Tailoring Realism to Educational Requirements

Presence has been defined as a psychological state of "being there" mediated by an environment that engages our senses, captures our attention, and fosters our active involvement. The environment that mediates presence can be real, virtual, symbolic, or some combination thereof (Witmer, Christian, & Singer, 2005).

The learning potential of virtual environments depends on the possibility for learners to actively and personally experience the situation. As underlined by educational constructivist models; first-person experience; activity and interactivity; together with narrative dimension represent important dimensions to learning. Schank (1997) has clearly pointed out how feeling present or a sense of presence, that is feeling that the consequences of actions played in virtual environments and simulations are real (emulate practitioner learning) can dramatically improve learning outcome.

The more an individual feels present in a virtual environment, the more real the experience will seem to them; they will experience thoughts, emotions, and behaviour similar to those they could experience in a real-life situation, thus allowing the creation of recallable experience (Mantovani & Castelnuovo, 2003). In order to gain a recallable experience, it is important to act behaviours, succeed and make mistakes as a consequence of these actions, feeling emotions connected to success or failure, and developing appropriate thoughts over this experience.

Virtual environment applications in learning are many and varied, differing according to area, technology used, type of skill, and the specific training goal for the virtual experience. As recognised by many authors (Banos et al., 2000; Jacobson, 2001; Riva, 2000; Romano & Brna, 2001), in learning environments presence is a result of a complex web of interrelationship of various factors and does not depend only on graphic or perceptual cues. This technological and perceptual realism has dominated the concept of presence research, but now the physiological state described as a subjective feeling depending on many environmental, contextual, and personal characteristics/factors is growing in importance. Mania and Chalmers (2001) refer to this presence as a "state of consciousness"(p. 249). It is these cognitive abilities such as problem solving, coping skills, and so forth that are more relevant in the psychological state of presence than technological aspects connected with graphic realism. Case realism is more connected with the possibility of creating interactions between persons, complex problems till reaching an "ecologically valid" (Riva, 2000, p. 353) reconstruction of the social and cultural context where people live and act.

As noted by Nowak (2001) "presence is not a unidimensional construct, but instead is a collection of several correlated constructs, each taping in to a small part of the sense of presence." The complex web of interrelationships that leads to a sense of presence therefore depends on several factors: the fidelity of its sensory components; the nature of the required interactions and tasks; the focus of the user's attention/concentration; and the ease with which the user adapts to the demands of the environment. It also depends on the user's previous experiences and current state. According to Witmer and Singer (2005) both involvement and immersion are needed to experience presence. *Involvement* is a psychological state experienced as a consequence of focusing one's mental energy and attention on a coherent set of stimuli or meaningfully related activities or events. Involvement is increased by performing tasks and participating in activities that stimulate, challenge, and engage the user either cognitively, physically, or emotionally. *Immersion* is a psychological state characterised by perceiving oneself to be enveloped by, included in, and interacting with an environment that provides a continuous stream of stimuli and experiences. Immersion in a virtual environment (VE) is reduced by extraneous distractions and is increased by factors that facilitate direct interaction with the VE and the performance of VE task activities.

The sense of presence experienced by learners in virtual environments can thus be considered as a key feature in ensuring the efficacy of learning and the following transfer of knowledge and skills from the learning context to the real world.

E-Commerce Environment

Many tried and untried business models have been hypothesised for implementation in the quest for e-market success. However, there are no guarantees that what is created, as an online enterprise with expectations of being a successful, viable long-term businesses, will be anything but an empty digital environment tomorrow. Many analysts have predicted hardship for e-businesses because of poor planning and understanding of the market and technological challenges.

Despite the fatalistic trial-and-error approach being employed by many e-businesses, the Internet is still recognised as a revolutionary technology with the potential to change the traditional business environment and steer the future of e-commerce. This future will accelerate the shift of power towards the consumer, which will lead to fundamental changes in the way companies relate to their customers and compete with each other (The Boston Consulting Group, 2000). The immense popularity of the Internet in recent years has been fuelled largely by the prospect of performing business online. Actinic (2005), propose that in 2005 e-commerce in the UK "finally came of age, riding a second wave of business internet adoption. The percentage of companies allowing customers to purchase online more than doubled, to 8%, with most sites becoming profitable within twelve months." The virtual world has the ability to bring down physical barriers to commerce, almost immediately giving the smallest business and entrepreneurs access to untapped markets, where the size differential of bricks and mortar no longer matters in brand development and involvement. These reduced barriers to entry are of obvious benefit to potential entrepreneurs.

Against the background of the potential for commercial transformation and the realisation of the reality, the need for online businesses to learn the lessons needed to survive and prosper becomes an imperative. It is recognised that enduring e-enterprises require a sound business proposal underpinned by an understanding of e-commerce buying behaviour, and a Web presence that translates into brand involvement.

The Netrepreneur Simulation

The relevant research reviewed provides strong support for learning strategies which actively involve participants in the process, and for those activities that accurately simulate real world practices, that is, provide a sense of presence for the participant. The review further highlights the necessity of incorporating these pedagogical considerations in the creation of a virtual world, whereby entrepreneurs can learn about e-start-up venture creation and the complex causes of casualties in the online economy, and in doing so fulfil governmental aspirations of building an enterprise culture.

The simulation, therefore, aims to foster creativity innovation and learning through the implementation process. With this in mind the project development sought to incorporate the following objectives:

1. Design a simulation that blends the real and virtual worlds allowing participants to develop the ability to learn the way practitioners do.

2. Encourage participants to cross the "intuition gap" by replicating Q-type factors of chaos and uncertainty, thereby encouraging risk taking.

3. Facilitate the incremental discovery of e-commerce dynamics leading to viable predictive business proposals in the creation of brand value and active involvement.

Pedagogic Considerations

The simulation has two target groups: firstly, the creation of a learning environment for would-be entrepreneurs wishing to establish a presence in the online economy, and secondly, the simulation should be utilised as an experiential learning programme for university students, recognising that increasingly many students need to create their own jobs and can not expect secure employment from large, established organisations. This will allow them to understand the basic e-enterprise dynamics behind the theory. Beyond this, participating graduates will develop a mindset that appreciates the need for the incorporation of creativity and innovation in developing business solutions, in increasingly undefined and changeable operating environments.

The requirements of new approaches to learning (L) highlight a different role for the educator in structuring the learning environment. Learning must now be enabled, with participants left to derive their own conclusions. In such less conventional environments, students still need guidance in knowledge assimilation (P-type approaches) but also in the context of making sense of learning by doing (Q-type approaches).

Thompson (1999), commenting on entrepreneurship, highlights that while creativity and strategic awareness are important, they are only partial. Instead, he proposes that people need to be encouraged to look at things around them in a more critical way, observing events and incidents more closely and questioning how things might be done differently and thereby improved for greater commercial benefit (Q-type approaches).

With this in mind, the learning process was designed to encourage participants to innovate experientially by facing the ambiguity and uncertainty of open-ended change.

An important aspect of process development therefore was the synchronisation of both P- and Q-type learning environments.

The programme of instruction is designed in three successive parts (see Figure 2). In the first part participants are on conventional learning paths. In the second, participants experience action-learning principles through simulation as proposed by Revans (1982), triggering feeling cues allowing participants to cross the intuition gap. The third part returned to more standard pedagogic techniques, in particular those of reflecting to gain understanding. Participants therefore move from comfortable P-type learning environments to the Q-type zone of risk taking and back to a semi comfortable zone (P/Q), where they can conceptualise their experience.

The simulation requires participants to operate the business for several iterations. These e-cycles allow entrepreneurs to learn from initial mistakes, improve an existing business design for the next cycle, or start a new business. This process of incremental improvement coincides with Churchill's (1997) view that entrepreneurs prefer perceptual movement and improvement in the quest of exploiting manageable risks and opportunities. To this effect, the simulation allows participants to operate their online presence in much the same way as an e-commerce business. This strong sense of presence is essential to ensure the quality of learning since the experience in the virtual environment leads to recallable knowledge in the real world as a consequence of an engrossing experience acquired in the virtual world. It is this sense of presence that gives the virtual experience the same value as a corresponding real experience.

Figure 2. Netrepreneur programme of instruction

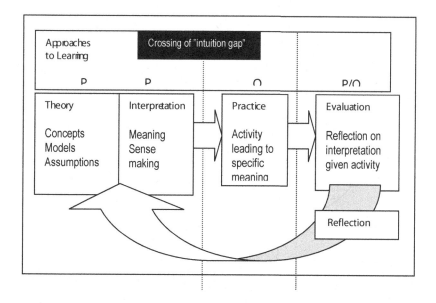

As such, the learning process consists of a phase more focused on *action* (behavioral) eliciting *emotions* (emotional), followed by a process of reflection and reframing (*cognitive*). Netrepreneur ensures this type of process through moments of high sense of presence in the more behavioral-emotional phase and moments of "absence" or shift of focus during cognitive reflection.

Uniquely, Netrepreneur dispenses with the time-restricted periods found in many existing business simulations, allowing both consumers and entrepreneurs to carry out their activities on a 24-hour a day, seven days a week basis. By adding this real-time aspect, the simulation is able to enhance learning and adapt emphasis that facilitates the incremental discovery of e-commerce dynamics at a pace that is suitable to the entrepreneurs learning style.

Simulating E-Start-Up

Netrepreneur is designed to simulate the initial start-up phases of entrepreneurial activity in the online e-commerce economy. Participants devise a viable business within the context of an e-commerce "virtual world," and review business performance in light of market data.

To this extent each e-cycle consists of the following stages of business planning and Web site development (theory informs interpretation), implementation (practice),

Figure 3. E-cycle

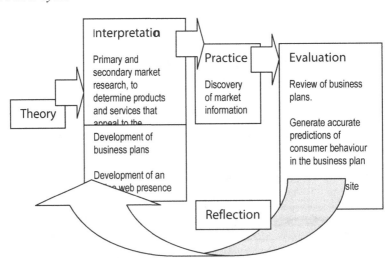

evaluation, and review (reflection on theory and interpretation). This is illustrated in Figure 3.

The Simulation

The "micro world" is represented by a virtual shopping mall (Figure 4) within which entrepreneurs can design and implement Web-based companies to market (virtual) goods and services online to a large group of consumers.

For the entrepreneur, the goal of each e-cycle is to design and implement (online Web site development) companies with a product/service offer that consumers will visit and purchase from and, in doing so, accurately predict their purchasing behaviour in the business plan. For the consumer, the objective is to examine the company Web pages and purchase goods and services that would appeal to them in the real world. Consumers are not required to spend all of their money or to buy anything at all if they do not find anything of interest. Alternatively, the facilitator of

Figure 4. Virtual shopping mall

the learning programme can provide role-play scenarios to consumers and instruct them to maximise their welfare.

At the end of each e-cycle a reflection period allows entrepreneurs the opportunity to analyse the information collected from the activities within the e-cycle. Based upon this information entrepreneurs can improve their approach to the next business cycle. This reflection period is based on a review of the business plan with respect to:

- financial status of the online business;
- consumer Web site statistics (hits versus purchase);
- consumer segmentation characteristics; and
- forecast versus actual market share/sales.

The Netrepreneur business plan allows prospective entrepreneurs the opportunity to run through the main elements considered within a real business plan. The structure of this business plan assists them not only in designing a Netrepreneur business but also in evaluating its success after each e-cycle. This evaluation process is based on comparing the predictions made in the business plan on market share, cash flow, sales, and profits with those actually attained during the consumer purchase phase of the simulation.

Netrepreneur provides entrepreneurs with the following information as part of each e-cycle to facilitate the incremental improvement process:

Consumer Web site statistics: Statistics and data on sales and hits include information about: actual transactions, hits per page, and the time spent by a consumer visiting each site. As part of the business plan entrepreneurs would be expected to forecast anticipated market share, cash flow, sales activity, and profits. These forecasts can be tested during each e-cycle with respect to forecast versus actual market share and sales activity.

Consumer segmentation characteristics: Information is collected through a questionnaire completed by consumers upon entry to the simulation, which includes information such as gender, age status, earnings, and so forth. This facilitates the development of the marketing component in the business plan.

Financial status of the online business at the end of each e-cycle: Companies are created with an initial fund to facilitate the start up cost of the business. Entrepreneurs are given a personal bank account and, over the course of the simulation, payments are made each day for the company's Web presence

Figure 5. The simulation in context

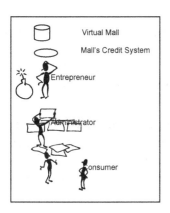
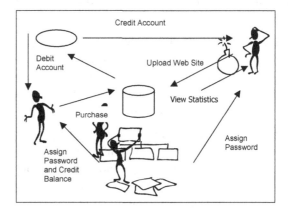

and the cost of products and services sold. Also from each e-cycle, income is derived from each day's purchases. Netrepreneur then provides a cash flow statement for each company. The administrator may alter Netrepreneur fixed expenses; these include, for example, costs incurred in Web site development and hosting fees. The variable cost component of the cash flow requires the entrepreneur to generate a percentage profit on sales estimates within their business plan. This is then used to determine the gross profit margin given the net sales revenue attained in the simulation.

The simulation is divided into three areas, allowing access to facilitators, entrepreneurs, and consumers (Figure 5).

The Administration Panel

Through the administration panel, facilitators are able to perform four functions:

1. Assign company names, passwords, and restricted upload areas to entrepreneurs.
2. Provide user logins and passwords to consumers.
3. Enable virtual credit balances for consumers.
4. Input venture start-up cost component (fixed and variable)

For facilitators the set up and maintenance of the administration system has been made as simple as possible, with no technical expertise required and all hosting being done remotely.

The login facility used in Netrepreneur utilises a combination of usernames, passwords, and secret access levels, which are assigned prior to the simulation by the facilitator. By designing the login function in this way, facilitators are able to restrict certain areas of the upload facility and therefore prevent entrepreneurs from altering any stores which are not their own.

The company names, which have been selected by entrepreneurs in their business plans, are then inputted by facilitators and will appear in the retailer selection menu on the main entry screen to provide a direct link for consumers to access the Netrepreneur stores. The cash balance option in the simulation has been provided to introduce a start-up cost component to the game.

Facilitators will also provide up to 150 shopper accounts with usernames, passwords, and cash balances. Cash balances have been made user specific, as facilitators may choose to vary the funds available to different consumers, therefore adding additional realism to the simulation; alternatively the cash balances could remain constant to truly gauge concept success.

Entrepreneurs

Once logged in to the simulation, entrepreneurs are able to perform four functions:

*   upload their e-commerce sites,
*   gain access to the mall's virtual credit system to sell their goods and services,
*   view mall sales and hits statistics, and
*   gain access to the cash flow statement at the end of the e-cycle.

The virtual shopping mall is essentially a landlord for up to 10 entrepreneur Web businesses. The aim for the entrepreneurs is to select their product concept, determine a pricing structure, and design their store presence.

The system is designed to facilitate all levels of technical expertise, from those with no Web design experience to those who are fully experienced in complex Web design methods, thereby removing any constraints for curriculum design and/or prior knowledge. Designs created in Microsoft Word and can be uploaded directly to the Netrepreneur site, with no need for Web design or file transfer protocol (FTP) software. Netrepreneur also supports complex Web design methods and the use of any programming language with an FTP facility, to the Netrepreneur mall. It is envisaged that this will facilitate greater access to Netrepreneur within the university and from other interested institutions.

Competing entrepreneurs, as commercial tenants, are also provided with access to the mall's virtual credit system, thus allowing consumers to purchase their goods. This credit system is developed using SQL stored procedures and integrates this with credit values assigned by the simulation facilitator.

Following consumer evaluation and purchase, entrepreneurs will be able to assess both their concept marketability and the design of their Web sites through various hits and sales figures provided by the simulation. This will enable entrepreneurs to reflect on the objectives of the business proposition and then provides the opportunity for them to review and change accordingly. This process of improvement will facilitate an understanding of the consumer's propensity to seek into an "optimal experience" and its dependency on the business concept and interpretation of Web presence.

Consumers

The selection criteria for consumers are dependent on the set objectives of the instructional context. For example, in the use of Netrepreneur as part of enterprise and Web design undergraduate curriculum, entrepreneurs are briefed to design business propositions targeted at the student population of the university, and as such, students will form the consumer population.

For consumers, the simulation provides the ability to login and access all stores in the mall. Consumers may purchase products from these stores with a virtual credit balance assigned by facilitators. To prevent misuse, the simulation recognises returning customers and provides only remaining credit balances after what has been spent on the previous visit.

On entry into Netrepreneur consumers complete a registration questionnaire. This registration questionnaire provides entrepreneurs with information on customer characteristics, such as demographics and lifestyle. Netrepreneur provides the entrepreneurs with this information, not only on the consumer population accessing the virtual mall, but also on consumers actually purchasing goods or services.

Application of Netrepreneur

Successful pilots of the simulation have seen both the University of the Arts, London and Manchester Metropolitan University adopting Netrepreneur within e-enterprise curriculum. Further, Retail Enterprise Network, an organisation created to develop ways of protecting and promoting diversity within the SME retail sector, is utilising the simulation within training in e-entrepreneurship, with both British and Spanish users.

Transfer of Learning to the Built Environment

In the real world, one of the very natural ways of acquiring knowledge in a practitioner domain is to be immersed in a situation related to this domain and to practice. Value in the entrepreneurial venture is added through the transformation process (Thopmson, 1999). Effective control of the value adding process will require sound performance measurement, which is outcome driven. To this end the simulation encourages participants to understand which factors are critical for success and ensure that performance in respect of these is measured and any failings remedied prior to "live" trading. The simulation makes this possible by allowing:

- the recognition of customer behaviour profiles,
- the identification of valuable segments,
- the discovery of patterns of consumer "stickiness" when engaged in Web site usage,
- the forecasting of customers' reactions, and
- the decision support in business planning.

This allows entrepreneurs the opportunity to entice prospects into active involvement with brands by allowing them to successfully:

- design Web sites better tailored to customer needs,
- alter or reposition the proposition, and
- embark on the first stages of e-trading.

The main learning outcomes are shown in Appendix I.

Post Experience Feedback: Survey Methodology

Presence plays a very important role in the process of learning and the transfer of skills by emulating the behaviour of the practitioner. The main rationale for the use of virtual environments such as simulation in enterprise learning contexts relies on the possibility of making significant first person experiences of the knowledge and skills. In order to achieve this goal, the learning experience should seem real and engaging to the participant, as if they should feel emotionally and cognitively present in the situation. The sense of presence experienced by learners in virtual environments can thus be considered as a key feature in ensuring the efficacy of learning and the following transfer of knowledge and skills from the learning context to the real world.

A field evaluation of the Netrepreneur simulation was undertaken with an undergraduate e-enterprise management module of 100 students. Lectures were first introduced to participants centring on the standard textbook range of business-to-consumer (B2C) e-commerce topics. During the lecture programme *e-commerce trading success factors* were introduced and reinforced by visual on-screen excerpts from successfully established e-enterprises. These excerpts also served as a brief operational demonstration of the simulation exercise.

In the week following the presentation of the lecture material, students in tutorial groups of around four persons, each with their respective tutors, were set the challenge of designing and launching an e-enterprise targeting a specific segmentation niche market. Participants were then shown how to engage with the simulation to review the success of the proposition created and, more importantly, how to reposition the proposition in the light of an evaluation. Success was measured according to the teams that had achieved the highest sales given their target audience market. At the end of the instruction programme participants completed two presence post-experience evaluation survey questionnaires.

Presence was measured by the Presence Questionnaire (PQ) (Witmer & Singer, 2005). It consists of 29 items and includes the following four factors or subscales: (1) Involvement, (2) Sensory Fidelity, (3) Adaptation/Immersion, and (4) Interface Quality. In Witmer and Singer (2005), involvement is defined as a psychological state experienced as a consequence of focusing one's mental energy and attention on a coherent set of stimuli or meaningfully related activities or events. Immersion is defined as a psychological state characterized by perceiving oneself to be enveloped by, included in, and interacting with an environment that provides a continuous stream of stimuli and experiences. The sensory fidelity scale includes auditory and haptic items. Interface quality refers to the degree that participants

Figure 6. Factor relationships

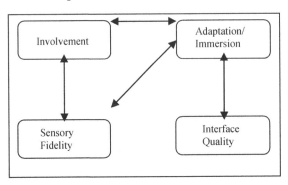

readily adapt to the virtual environment. The relationships among the factors are illustrated in Figure 6.

All the variables from PQ, excluding items referring to sensory fidelity were included in the analysis. Sensory fidelity measures sound and the ability to touch and move objects in a virtual environment. The experimental scenario did not include auditory or haptic cues, therefore the results obtained from the sensory subscale are not included in the total score.

Previous studies have demonstrated that presence scores are affected when participants fail to understand the relationship between a question and experience, and hence generate a score based on personal interpretation of the question (Freeman, Avons, Pearson, & Ijsselsteijn, 1999). To this extent the language used for the PQ questions was altered to better match the experimental scenario. The PQ has been shown to measure a subjective construct (Witmer & Singer, 1998), not simply a score for specific questions. Thus, by preserving the focus of the questions themselves, it is assumed that the conceptual construct is unaffected by minor language changes.

Secondly, Witmer and Singer's (1998) Immersive Tendencies Questionnaire (ITQ) was administered. ITQ is aimed to examine individual differences in the ability to experience presence and is a companion questionnaire to the PQ. For example, it aims to measure the capability or tendency to be involved or immersed, and the ability to focus on a particular activity. It consists of three subscales, Focus, Involvement, and Games. According to Witmer and Singer (1998), the Focus items are related to mental alertness, participants' ability to concentrate on enjoyable activities, and their ability to block out distractions. Involvement items, in turn, are related to the participants' propensity to get involved passively in some activity. The Games items ask how frequently participants play video games and whether they get involved to the extent that they feel they are inside the game.

Results

Assessing the PQ's scale for reliability, with Cronbach's alpha test for internal consistency, gave a result of 0.82 ($N=100$).

A Pearson correlation was calculated between the total score for the PQ without the questions that related to sensory fidelity (mean = 77, s.d. = 18.5) and the score for each of the subscale clusters identified during the previous study undertaken by Witmer and Singer (2005).

A significant correlation was found for the Involvement subscale (r (100) = 0.82, p = 0.01), the Adaption/Immersion subscale (r (100) = 0.68, p = 0.01) and the Interface Quality subscale (r (100) = 0.63, p = 0.01). Significant correlations were also found between the Involvement and Adaptation/Immersion subscales (r (100) = 0.64, p = 0.01).

A reliability analysis and subscale analysis was conducted on the ITQ. The Cronbach's alpha test generated a score of 0.84 (N = 100).

A Pearson correlation was calculated between the total score for the ITQ (mean = 138.69, s.d. = 21.48) and the score for each of its subscale clusters as identified by Witmer and Singer (1998).

A significant correlation was found for the Focus subscale (r (100) = 0.83, p = 0.01), the Involvement subscale (r (100) = 0.57, p = 0.01), and the Game subscale (r (100) = 0.62, p = 0.01).

There was a nonsignificant, almost zero, Pearson correlation between the ITQ score and the PQ score (r (100) = 0.10, p = 0.13). When divided by gender, scores for men exhibited a nonsignificant positive trend (r (70) = 0.18, p = 0.12), whereas women exhibited a nonsignificant negative trend (r (30) = -0.28, p = 0.16).

Pearson correlations conducted between the questionnaires' subscales showed no significant results. However, when divided by gender, the situation changed. For men, the ITQ's Focus subscale significantly correlated with the PQ's total (r (70) = 0.54, p = 0.01), Involvement subscale (r (70) = 0.29, p = 0.02), and Adaptation/Immersion subscale (r (70) = 0.26, p = 0.05). The PQ's Involvement subscale also significantly correlated with the ITQ's Involvement subscale (r (70) = 0.24, p = 0.05) and total (r (70) = 0.23, p = 0.05). However, for women, a significant negative correlation was found between the PQ's Involvement subscale and the ITQ's Involvement subscale (r (30) = -0.46, p = 0.01). In addition, the PQ's Adaption/Immersion subscale negatively correlated with the ITQ total (r (30) = -0.55, p = 0.01) and Game subscales (r (30) = -0.33, p = 0.05).

Discussion

One of the measures of the effectiveness of learning in a virtual environment is the extent to which a user feels presence. By supporting the user in a "realistically natural way," presence enhances the user's ability to utilise real-world skills for a virtual task and helps to transfer learning from the virtual task back into the real world. This post-experience feedback from Netrepreneur is used to evaluate presence as a reliable and valid construct in the process of learning and the transfer of skills by emulating the first person behaviour of the practitioner. The results highlight that a strong sense of presence is experienced by learners in the Netrepreneur learning environment, and this measure can thus be considered as a key feature in ensuring the efficacy of learning and the following transfer of knowledge and skills from the learning context to the real world.

The modified version of the Singer and Witmer (2005) PQ used to assess presence had a Cronbach's alpha of 0.84 ($N = 100$), which indicates that it does indeed form a reliable scale, and the correlations between the PQ score and its subscales indicate that the questionnaire is measuring a unified construct. The PQ measure suggests that users feel immersed and involved in the Netrepreneur virtual environment.

The reliability analysis on a participant's inherent propensity to become immersed in conventional media or situations, as measured by the ITQ score, confirms that it is a valid tool for the experimental population used. The correlation between the ITQ and PQ total was nonsignificant. This result is disappointing, though unsurprising. Previous studies undertaken with an earlier version of the PQ also demonstrate variable correlation (Witmer & Singer, 1998). However, results grouped by gender seem to indicate an interesting trend: Results for men exhibit a positive trend, whereas results for women exhibit a negative trend. This type of correlation however could be down to sample bias for women (n = 30).

Although inconclusive, the possibility of gender bias raises two important issues for further investigation. The first concerns whether the ITQ measure is biased towards one gender. For example, the ITQ includes a question that assesses whether a participant has "ever gotten excited during a chase or fight scene on TV or in the movies?" Part of this question requires empathy with an aggressive emotional response, which may be considered a more masculine trait. Therefore, to reduce bias, a subjective measure should assess a more representative set of emotions. Secondly, the object under investigation or the task to be completed, that is, e-entrepreneurship, could also be a factor for consideration. It is possible that men found this subject, or even the simulation display itself, as more relevant and therefore more involving. While this finding remains inconclusive, it could provide support for the growing interest in research into female entrepreneurs entering into the SME sector and their business knowledge and skills deficit. The Manchester Business School, for example, concludes that standard business support delivery does not always meet the needs of women. They have embarked on a project funded by the European Social Fund to provide support for female entrepreneurs to overcome the issues of discrimination relating to self-employment by increasing the employability of women through entrepreneurial activity (Manchester Business School, 2006).

Conclusion

Entrepreneurship is increasingly seen as an important element of economic growth and development for the UK, and innovative entrepreneurship and the development of the micro and small business is viewed as a necessary component of driving forward a knowledge-based economy and an enterprising society.

But, more new enterprises require more entrepreneurs, but just how are entrepreneurs created? A traditional response to such a labour-market need is to use the educational system to address skill and occupational deficiencies in the workforce. However, the nature, relevance, content, and appropriateness of entrepreneurship education have been subject to increasing scrutiny (Henry et al., 2005).

There has been a growing interest in the process by which practitioners learn and in the creation of entrepreneurial learning environments that emulate practitioner learning. The requirement to tailor realism to educational requirements through a sense of presence experienced by learners has seen an increase in the use of virtual learning contexts. The main rationale for the use of virtual environments such as simulation, in enterprise learning contexts, relies on the possibility of making significant first person experiences of the use of knowledge and skills. In order to achieve this goal, the learning experience should seem real and engaging to the participant, as if they feel emotionally and cognitively present in the situation. The sense of presence experienced by learners in virtual environments can thus be considered to be a key feature in ensuring the efficacy of learning and the following transfer of knowledge and skills from the learning context to the real world.

The purpose of this chapter was to review the pedagogic requirements of entrepreneurial education within one specific context of e-commerce. It documents the development of the Netrepreneur simulation, which creates an experiential virtual world that user groups can run to learn the general dynamics of B2C e-commerce venture creation and the complex causes of casualties in the online economy. The post-evaluation feedback from Netrepreneur demonstrates that a strong sense of presence was experienced by participants, and that this plays an important role in the process of learning and transfer of skills by emulating the behaviour of the practitioner.

It is our hope that by describing the background to the development of this product and its evaluation by the user group we facilitate more of this type of innovation in e-entrepreneurship education and learning.

References

Actinic. (2005). *SME E-commerce report.* Retrieved March 2006, from www.actinic.co.uk/2005

Banos, R. M., Botella, C., GarciaPalacios, A., Villa, H., Perpina, C., & Alcaniz, M. (2000). Presence and reality judgement in virtual environments: A unitary construct? *Cyberpsychology and Behaviour, 3,* 327-335.

Bhide, A. (1994, March-April). How entrepreneurs craft strategies that work. *Harvard Business Review, 72*(2), 150-161.

Bruyat, C., & Julien, P. A. (2000). Defining the field of research in entrepreneurship. *Journal of Business Venturing, 16*(2), 165-80.

Careers Service Unit. (1999). *Moving on: Graduate careers three years after graduation.* Report to the Department for Education and Employment, Career Service Unit, Manchester.

Churchill, N. C. (1997). Breaking down the wall; scaling the ladder. In S. Birley & D. Muzyka (Eds.), *Mastering enterprise* (pp. 143-148). London: Financial Times/Pitman.

Critten, P. (1993). *Investing in people: Towards coprorate capability.* Oxford, Butterworth-Heineman.

Davies, H. (2002). *The Howard Davies review of enterprise and the economy in education.* Norwich: HMSO.

Engel, J., Blackwell, R., & Miniard, P. (1993). *Consumer behaviour.* New York: Dryden Press.

Fiet, J. O. (2000). The theoretical side of teaching entrepreneurship theory. *Journal of Business Venturing, 16*(1), 1-24.

Freeman, J., Avons, S. E., Pearson, D., & Ijsselsteijn, W. (1999). Effects of sensory information and prior experience on direct subjective ratings of presence. *Presence: Teleoperators and Virtual Environments, 8,* 1-13.

Gallo, D. (1987). Empathy, reason and the imagination: The impact of their relationship on education. In D. N. Perkins, J. Lockhead, & J. Bishop (Eds), *Thinking: The 2nd International Conference.* Mahwah, NJ: Lawrence Erlbaum.

Gallo, D. (1989). Educating for empathy, reason and the imagination. *Journal of Creative Behaviour, 23*(2), 98-115

Gartner Group, (2006). *PC forecast analysis, worldwide.* Retrieved June 2006, from www.gartner.com

Gibb, A. A. (1987). Enterprise culture—Its meaning and implications for education and training. *Journal of European Industrial Training, 11*(2), 1-38.

Greeno, J., Smith, D., & Moore, J. (1993). Transfer of situated learning. In D. K. Detterman & R. J. Sterberg (Eds), *Transfer on trial: Intelligence, cognition and instruction* (pp. 99-167). Norwood, NJ: Ablex.

Guetzkow, H. (1963). *Simulation in international relations.* Englewood Cliffs, NJ: Prentice Hall.

Higher Education Careers Service Unit (HECSU). (1999). *Moving on: Graduate careers three years after graduation.* Higher Education Career Service Unite, Manchester, report to the Departed for Education and Employment. http://www.prospects.ac.uk/downloads/csdesk/members/reports/strategyfinal.pdf

Henry, C., Hill, F., & Leitch, C. (2005). Entrepreneurship education and training: Can entrepreneurship be taught? *Part 1, Education and Training* (Vol. 47, No. 2, pp, 98-111). Emerald Group.

Jacobson, D. (2001). Presence revisited: Imagination, competence and activity in text-based virtual worlds. *Cyberpsychology and Behaviour, 4*(6), 653-674.

Kao, J. J. (1989). *Entrepreneurship, creativity and organisation.* Englewood Cliffs, NJ: Prentice Hall.

Keys, B. J., Fulmer, R. M., & Stumpf, S. A. (1996, Spring). Microworlds and simuworlds: Practice fields for the learning organisation. *Organizational Dynamics, 24*(4), 36-49.

Kirby, D. (2002, November 21-22). *Entrepreneurship education: Can business schools meet the challenge?* Paper presented at the Research in ENTrepreneurship (RENT) XV1 Conference, Barcelona, Spain.

Manchester Business School, CDWP. (2006). *E-coaching for women business-owners.* Retrieved March 2006, from www. Mbs.ac.uk/research/diversity-work-psychology/ecoaching.htm

Mania, K., & Chalmers, A. (2001). The effects of levels of immersion on memory and presence in virtual environments: A reality centred approach. *Cyberpsychology and Behaviour, 4,* 247-64.

Mantovani, F., & Castelnuovo, G. (2003). Sense of presence in virtual training: Enhancing skills acquisition and transfer of knowledge through learning experience in virtual environments. In G. Riva, F. Davide, & W. A. Ijsselsteijn (Eds.), *Being there: Concepts, effects and measurement of user presence in synthetic environments* (Chapter 11). Amsterdam: Ios Press. http://www.vepsy.com/communication/book4/4_11MANTOV.pdf

McHardy, P., & Allan, T. (2000). Closing the gap between what industry needs and what HE provides. *Education and Training, 42*(9), 496-508.

Minniti, M., Bygrave, W. D., & Autio, E. (2005). *Global entrepreneurship monitor (GEM)*. Babson College and London Business School.

Nowak, K. (2001). Conceptualising, differentiating and measuring copresence and social presence. *Fourth Annual International Workshop Presence 2001,* Temple University, Philadelphia.

Parston, G. (1998). Quoted in Leadbeater, C. & Gross, S. (Eds.), Civic Entrepreneurship, London: Demos/Public Management Foundation.

Pedler, M. (1983, June). *Action learning in practice.* Gower Company, Aldershot.

Pfeiffer, J. W. , (1995), *Perspectives on human development, Simulation and Gaming,* 207-218.

Revans, R. (1980). *Action learning—New techniques for management.* New York: Anchor Press.

Revans, R. (1982). *The origins and growth of action learning.* London: Chartwell-Bratt.

Pfeiffer, J.W. (1995). *Action learning in practice.* Aldershot: Grower Company

Riva, G. (2000). Design of clinically oriented virtual environments: A communicational approach. *Cyberpsychology and Behaviour, 3,* 351-357.

Romano, D. M., & Brna, P. (2001). Presence and reflection in training: Support for learning to improve quality decision-making skills under time limitations. *Cyberpsychology and Behaviour, 4,* 265-77.

Schank, R. (1997). Virtual learning: A revolutionary approach to building a highly skilled workforce. New York: McGraw-Hill.

Schon, D. D. (1987). *The reflective practitioner.* San Francisco: Jossey-Bass.

Small Business Service. (2005). *A government action plan for small business.* DTI Publications, http://www.sbs.gov.uk/SBS_Gov_files/researchandstats/evbas-eenterprise.pdf

The Boston Consulting Group. (2000). *Winning the online consumer: Insights into online consumer behaviour.* Retrieved March 2005, from www.bcg.com

Thompson, J. (1999). The world of the entrepreneur—A new perspective. *Journal of Workplace Learning: Employee Counselling Today, 11*(6), 209-224.

Witmer, B.G., & Jerome, C.J., & Singer, M.J. (2005). The factor structure of the presence questinnarie. *Presence, 14*(3), 298-312

Witmer, B. G., & Singer, M. J. (1998). Measuring presence in virtual environments: A presence questionnaire. *Presence: Teleoperators and Virtual Environments, 7,* 225-240.

Appendix I: Netrepreneur Learning Outcomes

Learning context	Learning outcomes
Market opportunity analysis	• Analyse marketing strategy and plan with reference to electronic markets • Research customer behaviour profiles and forecast sales demand • Critically assess marketing opportunities and threats • Identify market segments and specify e-market and non e-market elements
Development and integration of e-marketing plan	• Develop strategy for positioning and e-branding of products and services
Development of e-presence Implementation of e-marketing plan	• Implement key activities of e-marketing plan • Identify range of electronic marketing options • Critically assess electronic marketing options against marketing needs • Selection of most appropriate option
Monitoring e-presence Alter or reposition the proposition	• Monitor e-presence, sales activity and competitive environment • Re-assess e-market segmentation and prioritization in line with competitive environment

Appendix II: The Adapted Presence Questionnaire (PQ)

Netrepreneur Learning Environment = From business start-up principles to evaluation of the e-business enterprise

Virtual world = the simulator

Involvement

1. How much were you able to control events in the Netrepreneur Learning Environment?
2. How responsive was the virtual world to actions that you initiated (or performed)?
3. How natural did your interactions with the net learning environment seem?
4. How much did the visual aspects of the virtual world involve you?
6. How natural was the mechanism that controlled movement through the virtual world?
7. How compelling was your sense of objects moving through the virtual world?
8. How much did your experiences in the net learning environment seem consistent with your real world experiences?
10. How completely were you able to actively survey or search the virtual world using vision?
14. How compelling was your sense of moving around inside the virtual world?
17. How well could you move or manipulate objects in the virtual world?
18. How involved were you in the net learning environment experience?
19. How easy was it to identify objects through physical interaction, like touching an object, walking over a surface, or bumping into a wall or object?

Adaptation/Immersion

20. Were you able to anticipate what would happen next in response to the actions that you performed?
21. How quickly did you adjust to the net learning environment experience?

22. How proficient in moving and interacting within the net learning environment did you feel at the end of the experience?

23. How well could you concentrate on the assigned tasks or required activities rather than on the mechanisms used to perform those tasks or activities?

24. How completely were your senses engaged in this experience?

25. Were there moments during the net learning experience when you felt completely focused on the task or environment?

26. How easily did you adjust to the control mechanisms used to interact with the virtual world?

27. Was the information provided through different senses in the net learning environment (e.g., vision, hearing, touch)

Interface Quality

28. How much delay did you experience between your actions and expected outcomes?

29. How much did the visual display quality interfere or distract you from performing assigned tasks or required activities?

30. How much did the control mechanisms interfere with the performance of assigned tasks or with other activities?

Source: Witmer, B. G., Christian, J. J., & Singer, M. J. (2005). The factor structure of the presence questionnaire. Presence, 14(3), 298-312.

Appendix III: Immersive Tendency Questionnaire (ITQ)

1. Do you ever get extremely involved in projects that are assigned to you by your boss or your instructor, to the exclusion of other tasks?

2. How easily can you switch your attention from the task in which you are currently involved to a new task?

3. How frequently do you get emotionally involved (angry, sad, or happy) in the news stories that you read or hear?

4. How well do you feel today?

5. Do you easily become deeply involved in movies or TV dramas? FOCUS

6. Do you ever become so involved in a television program or book that people have problems getting your attention? INVOL

7. How mentally alert do you feel at the present time? FOCUS

8. Do you ever become so involved in a movie that you are not aware of things happening around you? INVOL

9. How frequently do you find yourself closely identifying with the characters in a story line? INVOL

10. Do you ever become so involved in a video game that it is as if you are inside the game rather than moving a joystick and watching the screen? GAMES

11. On average, how many books do you read for enjoyment in a month?

12. What kind of books do you read most frequently? —

    (CIRCLE ONE ITEM ONLY!)

    Spy novels Fantasies Science fiction

    Adventure Romance novels Historical novels

    Westerns Mysteries Other fiction

    Biographies Autobiographies Other non-fiction

13. How physically fit do you feel today? FOCUS

14. How good are you at blocking out external distractions when you are involved in something? FOCUS

15. When watching sports, do you ever become so involved in the game that you react as if you were one of the players?

16. Do you ever become so involved in a daydream that you are not aware of things happening around you? INVOL

17. Do you ever have dreams that are so real that you feel disoriented when you awake? INVOL

18. When playing sports, do you become so involved in the game that you lose track of time? FOCUS

19. Are you easily disturbed when working on a task?

20. How well do you concentrate on enjoyable activities?

21. How often do you play arcade or video games? (OFTEN should be taken to mean every day or every two days, on average.) GAMES

22. How well do you concentrate on disagreeable tasks?

23. Have you ever gotten excited during a chase or fight scene on TV or in the movies? FOCUS

24. To what extent have you dwelled on personal problems in the last 48 hours?

25. Have you ever been scared by something happening on a TV show or in a movie? INVOL

26. Have you ever remained apprehensive or fearful long after watching a scary movie? INVOL

27. Do you ever avoid carnival or fairground rides because they are too scary?

28. How frequently do you watch TV soap operas or docu-dramas?

29. Do you ever become so involved in doing something that you lose all track of time? FOCUS

Note. Subscales: INVOL—Tendency to become involved in activities, FOCUS—Tendency to maintain focus on current activities, GAMES—Tendency to play video games

Source: Wintmer, B. G., & Singer, M. J. (1998). Measuring presence in virtual environments: A presence questionnaire. Presence: Teleoperators and Virtual Environments, 7, 225-240.

Chapter VIII

Conceptualizing Failed B2C Dotcoms as Innovation Failures

Anil M. Pandya, Northeastern Illinois University, USA

Nikhilesh Dholakia, University of Rhode Island, USA

Abstract

During the 1998-2003 dot-com bust, many Internet-based business-to-consumer (B2C) companies failed to fulfill their initial and alluring promises. Concepts derived from the investigation of product and services innovation failures can provide a valuable strategic market framework to understand why so many dot-com B2C ventures crashed so fast. Early B2C ventures represented an entirely new class of technology-driven services. These B2C dot-coms sought to inform, promote, sell, and deliver consumer items in radically unfamiliar ways. In doing so, many B2C firms did not follow time-tested business precepts. In particular, the failed B2C firms did not realize they were marketing innovative services. Our framework uses the continuum of need-solution context in conjunction with the notion that seller/buyer perceptions about the scope of innovations are not necessarily concordant. Matched or "concordant" perceptions lead to success, and mismatched or "discordant" perceptions often breed failures. Using short cases and historical data, this chapter illustrates the explanatory power of the framework.

Introduction

In the advanced economies, B2C e-commerce has become entrenched in many ways and yet consumer skepticism and distrust are expected to persist in some aspects of B2C transactions (Numberger & Rennhak, 2005; Robertson, Murphy, & Purchase 2005). Of course, as is well known, this contemporary state of wary-but-nonetheless-thriving B2C e-commerce was born via a traumatic labor process of the dot-com crash.

This chapter proposes an innovation theory-based conceptual framework to help explain why so many Internet-based B2C companies failed to fulfill their initial promise. B2C dot-com crashes represent special types of innovation failures. Our analysis shows that the product innovation called *B2C e-commerce,* in its initial incarnation, was flawed.

In innovative B2C settings, consumers balance the cost of time and efforts against services received and make judgments about service quality (Berry, Seiders, & Grewal, 2002). In the B2C environment, service quality depends on:

1. The process by which perceptions about the quality are formed, and
2. The gap between the perception of the service and the experience of the de-livered service (Brady & Cronin, 2001; Zeithaml, Bitner, & Gremler, 2006).

Furthermore, in high-tech marketing contexts, two factors shape perceived vs. ex-pected performance. These are the need-solution context (Leonard-Barton, Wilson, & Doyle, 1995), and the congruence of perceptions between technology innovators and technology consumers (Rangan & Bartus, 1995). In this paper it is proposed that in the initial wave of B2C service innovations, buyers and sellers marched down very divergent paths. Technology innovators and sellers saw B2C technologies as being capable of radically exceeding buyers' expectations, while buyers saw B2C innovations as relatively inconvenient ways of performing familiar shopping tasks. Many B2C firms in the first wave focused more attention on marketing and front-end technology and less on timely delivery and customer satisfaction. The results were persistently high customer acquisition costs without sufficient revenues (Agarwal, Arjona, & Lemmens, 2001). Research shows that most B2C firms failed to adhere to conventional management principles (Varianini & Vaturi, 2000). It also suggests that many dot-coms failed because of lack of basic customer knowledge and failure of implementation, logistics, and service follow-up (Howell, 2000). The question is: why so many firms with resources and talents failed to use time-honored princi-ples? What was it about this new technology and service delivery method that these managers misread? We argue that the firms failed to realize they were dealing with a new innovative situation, which needed a new managerial orientation (Achrol

& Kotler, 1999). The Internet did not alter the customer's expectations for service quality, for dependable outcomes, easy access, responsiveness, flexibility, apologies, and compensation when things went wrong (Bitner, 2001; Pandya & Dholakia 2005). As we argue later in the paper, the innovative technology required B2C firms to alter their view of business-customer relations. We develop a framework to show how innovation context can lead to problems of concordance of perceptions between buyers and sellers. Managers have to figure out how to navigate this maze of perceptions to be successful.

The paper is organized as follows. The next section examines the scope of the B2C failure problem and reflects on some early diagnoses of it. The section that follows presents the proposed innovation theory-based framework and provides illustrative evidence. The concluding section draws together the main arguments and makes recommendations for managers and researchers.

Scope of the B2C Problem

B2C e-commerce failure was a system-wide failure. It was not the case where a few managers in a few start-up firms made poor judgment calls. The finding that managers of these firms failed to follow well-known management truths—that costs cannot consistently exceed revenues, pricing correctly is critical, or customer services are important for long-term success (Agarwal et al., 2001; Marn, 2000; Varianini & Vaturi, 2000)—is important and necessary but not in itself, sufficient. Incompetence is not a satisfactory answer when a large number of firms fail. This section first describes the enormity of the B2C failure, followed by a brief review of the empirical findings that have carefully looked at the B2C failures. This discussion sets the stage for our contribution and develops our framework to addresses the question: why these managers in all these firms, failed.

The Size of the Crash

The B2C market crash was massive and economically destabilizing. It wiped out billions of dollars of market capitalization and led to a huge loss of employment. Between 1995 and 2000 a total of 492 Internet-related companies raised $36.3 billion in capital in the public markets. By 2000, just 11% of these companies were trading at prices greater than their offer price. A third of them were trading below 80% of the offer price. In 1999, 230 Initial Public Offerings (IPOs) raised $18.2 billion. In 2000, 130 IPOs were offered and raised $12.8 billion; but 133 IPOs representing $10.4 billion were withdrawn from the market. The market capitalization of the Internet sector in 1999 was $881 billion. This plunged to $208 billion by December 2000 (Anderson, 2001). Layoffs in the industry in the year 2000 were 4,805 in September; 5,677 in October, and by December, the total layoffs stood at 22,267. Unemployment reached 700,000 for the year 2001 (Corcoran, 2002; Rock, 2000). Table 1 shows profiles of some of the B2C firms that failed during the 1999-2000 period.

Table 1. Examples of B2C failures in 1999-2000

B2C Firm	Internet business	Lifespan	Status	Failure date
Redrocket.com	Nickelodeon's toy sales site	January 1995-May 5, 2000	Acquired by Viacom in 1999	May 2000
BBQ.Com	Grilled meats and sauces	June 15, 1999-May 15, 2000.	Standing as Barbequemall.com	May 2000
DEN	Digital Entertainment Network	1996-May 17, 2000	Investment $50 million. $75 million IPO shelved.	May 2000
Toysmart.com	Smart "good" (not destructive or faddish) toys. Encouraged parents to "click on your child's potential."	January 22, 1999-May 19, 2000.	Controlling interest by Disney in August 2000 with $50 million investment.	Disney stopped support
Pixelon	An investment scam	1996-August 2000.	Bilked $30 million from investors. Promoter lived in his car. Spent half the capital on launch.	Turned himself over to the police.
Pop.com	Received $50 million from Paul Allen of Microsoft.	The 80-employee content site never launched.	The site—backed by Steven Spielberg, Jefferey Katzenberg, David Giffen, Ron Howard and Brian Grazer—burned $18 million.	Closed 14 days prior to the launch

Source: Authors' research based on multiple sources in the reference list.

Table 1. continued

B2C Firm	Internet business	Lifespan	Status	Failure date
Pseudo.com	Streaming Media	1994-September 18, 20000	Received $18 million in 1999 and $14 million in Spring 2000.	With 10 channels chasing 10 different genres with streaming rich-media content across broadband, Pseudo could not establish its core audience.
Ingredients.com	The company developed and manufactured personal care products for Web distribution.	1998-October 2000	Received $4.5 million in funding.	Many beauty sites. Competition from major brands and lack of originality or funding saw to its demise.

Source: Authors' research based on multiple sources in the reference list.

Preliminary Diagnosis

In most B2C debacles, there was persistent discrepancy between high customer acquisition costs and low revenues. In early 1999, B2C companies spent over $1,100 to acquire a typical customer, someone who spent only $400 on the B2C company Web site. In late 1999, the average cost of customer acquisition reduced to $800 but customer spending remained at or below $400. The average monthly losses per B2C site were $1 million and $1.1 million, respectively, in the first and second half of 1999, despite the reduction in customer acquisition costs (Agarwal et al., 2001).

As supplemental revenue sources, B2C Web sites relied on subscription fees and advertising. But by the end of 1999, advertising revenue per visitor had declined from about $1 to $.50 and the rates charged to advertisers had declined between 3 and 12%. Among the content providers, fewer than 10% were garnering subscription revenues in late 1999 (Agarwal et al, 2001).

In the false hope that the Internet was a price elastic market, many B2C businesses maintained low margins. However, in reality, instead of clicking across multiple sites, 80 to 90% of buyers of books and CDs visited only one site, even though prices of books and CDs across Web sites varied by as much as 25 to 30%. Hence it appears that in this segment of the B2C market, instead of deep discounting, astute firms could have charged higher prices without sacrificing revenues and profits (Marn, 2000).

Only a small but solid group of companies managed to achieve visitor conversion rates of 12%, customer churn rates below 20%, and repeat purchase rates of around 60% (Agarwal et al., 2001). The majority of the B2C failures were caused by "fatal attraction": luring visitors to the site but failing to convert them into customers. Successful firms generated nearly three times the gross income from repeat customers as from one-time buyers. This difference in performance was the result of superior skills in acquiring (keeping the customer acquisition cost low), converting (keeping the purchase process simple), and retaining customers (making operational execution satisfactorily reliable, that is, sites download quickly, on-time delivery, and ease of return or exchange of purchases). Additionally, the successful companies followed the tried-and-true principles from the brick-and-mortar world:

1. focus on core product or service propositions that fit the needs of well-defined customer segments;

2. control extensions of product lines and business models and focus on the core products; and

3. avoid "bleeding edge technologies" (i.e., leading but unproven technologies) and focus on basic product presentation features, customer service tools, and logistics.

In short, to be successful, a firm must find its natural customers efficiently, offer them what they want, and deliver it reliably (Agarwal et al., 2001).

B2C Internet businesses were hemorrhaging money because they failed to follow basic marketing principles. When e-commerce was young, it seemed that marketing expertise could be cast aside. A speedy grab for a large share of the market with the aim of getting as many visitors as possible to the site became the immediate objective. It was assumed, falsely by most B2C firms, that at some stage these visitors would translate into profitable repeat customers (Varianini & Vaturi, 2000).

Collectively, these findings confirm that most B2C firms failed to adhere to conventional management principles of efficiency and consumer focus. This raises important questions. Why did so many firms with so much talent and easy access to capital (some profiled in Table 1), fail to use time-tested management principles? Why did they fail to realize that managing a B2C e-commerce required acumen similar to that required in the conventional brick-and-mortar world? What was it about this new technology and service delivery method that most B2C managers misread? Why could these companies not convert visitors into profitable and loyal customers? The following section addresses these questions.

Toward Innovation Theory-Based Diagnosis

The Internet implies a revolutionary shift in marketing approach. From being agents of the seller, B2C firms have to become agents of the buyer (Achrol & Kotler, 1999). The Internet allows B2C firms to get close to their customers in ways not possible before. For the first time these firms can represent buyers to the producers of goods rather than the other way around. They can figure out what their customers want and communicate that demand to the producers. B2C firms failed to appreciate this change and did not quite grasp that their business represented a radical service innovation, not new technology business. Additionally, they were offering known products to customers in a new, more convenient, and faster way than what was possible before. This new service concept emerged of the new technology but that is not the whole story. Old retail knowledge about assessing demand, buying, managing inventory, developing displays, and improving delivery technology all have to be seamlessly integrated to create a satisfied customer. This subtle but strategic shift in perspective could have refocused B2C managerial efforts from being preoccupied with the new technology and market share dominance, to providing consistently high quality customer service and convenience geared towards fostering buyer loyalty and customer retention. While acknowledging that many B2C firms strayed from simple and conventional—but nonetheless vital and relevant—management principles, we present a theory-based framework to capture some of the additional underlying complexity of B2C failures and to identify ingredients for B2C success.

Innovation Theory-Based Framework and Evidence

The classical theory of innovation diffusion (Rogers, 1995) identifies four criteria: (1) relative advantage, (2) comparability, (3) complexity, (4) communicability and divisibility for successful new products. This suggests that, to be widely adopted, innovations must be compatible with existing habits; provide incentives to change; and pose low physical, technical, social, economic, and psychological risks to adopters. Overlaying these barriers is the inherent difficulty of maintaining consistent service quality. Recent research shows that technical functionality and reliability contribute to perceptions of product superiority, and product quality has a strong effect on customer satisfaction (Tatikonda & Montoya-Weiss, 2001). Service quality by definition is more difficult to sustain and the difficulty is exacerbated in the context of innovation represented by the high technology-based B2C firms. At the front-end of a B2C operation, not all customers are equally savvy about technology and hence their involvement can lead to frustration when it comes to navigating Web sites. Thus B2C managers face serious problems involving customer perceptions and behavior change when purchasing goods on the Internet. The service quality model, well known in the services marketing literature, identifies four gaps: (1) not knowing what customers expect; (2) not knowing the right service design and standards; (3) not delivering to standards; and (4) not matching performance to standards (Zeithaml & Bitner, 2003). While these approaches are insightful, they do not fully address the problems that B2C technology innovations pose to sellers as well as buyers. We argue that in part, B2C firms failed because they failed to perceive correctly the nature and scope of their innovation and this eventually led to the problems of matching consumer expectations as the context of innovation changed. This is particularly important in the context of high technology innovations where the question of the precedence of technology voice or customer voice remains a contested issue. We extend the current discussion on innovations and combine high technology product development literature and present a new framework to show an additional dimension of difficulty regarding perceptual problems created by the nature and scope of the innovation itself. Our model explores the problem of concordance and discordance between buyers and sellers about the innovation in different innovative contexts. Our model adds texture and substance to the theory of diffusion and service quality model in the context of technology innovation.

Viewing the Initial B2C Wave as Innovation

As a global concept, B2C represents a major innovation in the way marketing is done. It offers goods and services to consumers through the Internet. It reduces search costs. It is convenient, quick, easily accessible, and less expensive. In this sense it is a "new service innovation" for consumers as well as the world. When firms offer traditional products such as books, CDs, groceries, and toys via the Internet, they are not merely marketing known products to known customers. They are offering instead fast, highly competitive, interactive, and technologically facilitated *means* of information access and transaction. Using such means, consumers are able to shop, make comparisons, and receive door-to-door service at a suitable price. The failure of B2C firms can thus be construed as a failure of an entirely new class of Internet-mediated service, not just a failure of the particular firms involved. Conceptually, therefore, we propose that the B2C debacle needs to be seen as a failure of a new service product as a consequence of failure to recognize that B2C Internet-based firms (1) were essentially new services marketing firms; (2) failed to integrate the back and the front-end operations to produce a consistently reliable product quality; and (3) the failure resulted from the lack of perceptual concordance between the service offer and the needs of the buyers.

Putting this observation into the overall context of innovation research, however, it is evident that this experience is not unique. Failure rates of new products generally continue to be as high as 95% (Brown & Eisenhardt, 1995; Goldberg, Lehmann, & Mazursky, 2001; Krishnan & Ulrich, 2001; Tatikonda & Montoya-Weiss, 2001). When viewed as a major innovation in marketing methods, B2C systems are equally, if not more, susceptible to such punishing rates of failure.

Newness of Innovative Solutions and Needs Addressed by Innovations

In the 1980s, Hewlett-Packard (HP) found that successful innovators had a deep understanding of user needs. HP also found that the primary cause of difficulties was a failure to understand user needs, and the clarity reached in understanding user needs was the key determinant of new product success (Leonard-Barton et al., 1995). But the process of figuring out needs in varied market contexts is difficult. The difficulty is compounded when product-markets are new.

New products entering existing markets address known needs. In such cases, satisfaction gaps with existing products can be identified with relative ease and incorporated in the new product. But in new markets, customer needs are uncertain, and the needs and products co-evolve giving rise to four need-solution contexts (as elaborated in Table 2). These are respectively an *improved solution* for a *known need*; a *new solution* for a *known need*; a *new solution* for an *anticipated need*; and an *evolving solution* for an *uncertain need* (Leonard-Barton et al., 1995).

Concordant and Discordant Perceptions of Innovations

What should drive new product development: technology or customers? Views of innovators and customers regarding the nature of product "breakthroughs" may not be concordant. Such mismatch in innovator-customer perceptions could lead to failure of innovations (Rangan & Bartus, 1995).

Breakthroughs usually employ new technology, create new markets, and represent conceptual change. Conversely *increments* represent a continuation of existing products or practices. Furthermore suppliers and customers find it easy to understand increments (Rangan & Bartus, 1995) while breakthroughs, requiring technology and applications development, are driven by technologists (and may be less readily understood by customers). Hence, increments tend to evolve from the demands of customers and the customer's voice (rather than the technologist's voice) guides incremental innovations.

Additionally, performance at a price rather than performance per se, usually becomes a design criterion for incremental innovations. Hence, when one side thinks a particular innovation is a breakthrough while the other thinks it is an increment, we have the potential for discordance. Clearly failures are more likely in such discordant settings.

In the initial B2C wave, there were many possibilities for discordance:

- Large firms treated B2C extensions lightly, as mere increments, but their customers did not.

- B2C start-ups were enamored of the technology and thought they had break-throughs on hand. Conversely customers felt they were buying regular products (clothes, detergents, books, CDs, toys). The difference was that these familiar goods were being presented through a different channel, and the process of buying was new and had to be learned.

Understanding of the B2C e-commerce success versus failure phenomenon increases substantially when we integrate concordance in buyer/seller perceptions with the need-solution context (see Table 2). If innovations are to succeed, not only must the perceptions of sellers and buyers of innovations match, but innovators must also recognize the inherent uncertainty in finding solutions for customer needs in situations where contexts change.

Table 2. Concordant and discordant states of innovations/markets

Technology Continuum	Buyer/Seller concur that the innovation category is:		Buyer/Seller Disagree about newness
NEED-SOLUTION CONTEXT	BREAKTHROUGH	INCREMENTAL	MISMATCH
Incremental Solution/ Known Need	FALSE DAWN	CONCORDANT INNOVATION	DISCORDANT INNOVATION
Innovative Solution/ Known Need	MINOR BREAKTHROUGH	UNDERESTIMATED INNOVATION	DISCORDANT INNOVATION
Innovative Solution/ Anticipated Need	CONCORDANT INNOVATION	UNRECOGNIZED PROMISE	DISCORDANT INNOVATION
Incremental (Evolving) Solution/Uncertain Need	PERILOUS OPTIMISM	CAUTIOUS OPTIMISM	DISCORDANT INNOVATION

Source: Authors' integration of ideas from Leonard-Barton, Wilson, and Doyle (1995) and Rangan and Bartus (1995).

The Integrative Innovation Theory Framework

Table 2 is thus constructed using four dimensions: (1) customer need (known to uncertain); (2) nature of solution (improved to evolving); (3) the scope of innovation (incremental to breakthrough); and (4) buyer-seller agreement (concordance to discordance). These four dimensions on which the framework is constructed give rise to 16 cells. Table 2 shows only 12 cells because the right hand column (where buyer/sellers disagree about newness) shows only four cells instead of eight cells. To save space, unlike the left column, we have not bifurcated the right most column into breakthrough and increment columns. Also, each of the eight cells in this right column has a "Discordant" entry. Thus looking at Table 2 as a whole we see that in the Buyer/Seller agreement column there are only two concordant situations: one under breakthrough and the other under increment. The remaining six cells are false perceptions, overly optimistic assessments, or overly pessimistic assessments. These cases are unlikely to lead to success. In the Buyer/Seller disagreement column on the right all eight cells (only four of which are shown), show discordance with high chance of failure.

The three right-hand columns of Table 2 characterize the level of concordance or discordance of the buyer and the seller about the perceived newness of the innovation. The left-hand column reflects a kind of technology continuum, ranging from the relative comfort of low-tech/known-need to the opposite extreme of high-tech/high-uncertainty.

Concordant innovations occur when needs are known, and both sellers and buyers agree the solution is incremental (and therefore understandable and quickly adopted) and chances of success are high. But when one party thinks it is a breakthrough while the other thinks it is an incremental solution, we have discordant expectations, with greater chances of failure. In rare cases, there may be the possibility of a "false dawn," when an incremental innovation is misperceived as a breakthrough by both sides and there is concordance; where failure occurs after a bubble of enthusiasm.

When needs are unknown, both parties must think it is a breakthrough otherwise perceptions will be discordant and success will be unlikely. There is also the rare possibility of "unrecognized promise," when sellers and buyers both see only incremental benefits in a truly innovative solution which may remain under promoted and under appreciated. As Table 2 shows, for each solution/need pair, there are concordant and discordant conditions. However, it is proposed here that the concordant condition is more likely to lead to success, while the discordant condition will most likely lead to failure.

It should be noted that the framework presented here will behave differently in different market conditions faced by buyers and sellers. Competitive conditions will make the problem of new services and goods marketing certainly more complicated. We are, however, addressing a central issue in high technology products and services development literature, which argues that—for success of innovations—concordance between buyers and sellers is essential. How that concordance is to be created depends on the need/solution context of the innovation. It should be further noted that the framework in Table 2 also suggests that if all cells were equally likely, concordance is possible in only 2 out of 16 possibilities, or about 12% of the time. Discordance is likely 88% of the time, a number that is close to the empirically observed new product failure rate. It is not surprising therefore to find that most innovations fail. When we see the first wave of B2C e-commerce in this light as a service innovation, we can explain the high failure incidence of this wave. Understanding such failure then will help managers to conceive and plan the development of their innovations better. In the next section we examine published evidence to validate the various dimensions of this model.

Evidence of B2C Innovation Discordance

There is evidence of considerable discordance in B2C settings. In early 2000, Josh Harris, founder of the streaming-media company Pseudo.com declared with certitude on the CBS television show *60-Minutes* that he was there to take companies like CBS out of business (Useem, 2000). At the time the Internet was seen as a "disruptive" or "breakthrough" technology that would favor new entrants and send old-line brick-and-mortar companies scurrying for cover. Pseudo.com of course no longer exists but streaming media are being used extensively on the Internet along with other media. In hindsight, the discordance inherent in such views is obvious.

Many established merchants perceived B2C as breakthrough innovation and deliberately created "pure play" (i.e., purely Internet-based commerce) divisions, insulated from the parent. Examples include Borders.com and Grainger.com. Subsequent learning has apparently changed these perceptions. For example, after the first flush of enthusiasm, WW Grainger, a Chicago-based warehousing company, later reabsorbed Grainger.com. According to Grainger's president, it became obvious that the Internet unit needed *greater interdependence* with the originating company (Useem, 2000).

Michael Dell was far more insightful. He created an independent online division within the firm. Scott Eckert, the CEO of the Internet company, used highly creative strategy to get the organization as a whole to adopt the fledgling unit once it became a success and integrated the division in their existing business groups and made it a part of the larger firm (Dell on Line, 1998). Dell clearly saw B2C as a new growth opportunity for their firm but only as an extension of their existing Dell-Direct business and not a breakthrough. He saw it as an extension of their direct distribution model where customers used an 800 number to order computers and accessories of their choice. Now they could do the same thing on their Web site.

Dell began attracting customers who were knowledgeable about computers and knew what they wanted and did appreciate the time and hassle saved by not having to talk to a customer representative on the phone. This is an excellent example of "concordance" between the seller and the buyer. In 3 months Dell reached a sales level of $3 million per day on their new Internet channel.

In direct contrast to Dell, many B2C start-ups mostly assumed they were break-throughs and spent enormous capital on acquiring new customers and upgrading technologies. Some estimate that customer acquisition costs of online firms were four times as high as those of off-line companies (Useem, 2000). Agarwal et al. (2001) also found that companies spent three to four times the amount a customer spent at the Web site to acquire a new customer. The presumption here was that cus-tomers, once acquired, will soon learn the wonders of the breakthrough technology and eventually will spend enough money at the Web site to justify the acquisition costs. Customers were probably looking for price and good delivery experience. Discordance in perception set the stage for gaps in expectations to arise, leading to dissatisfaction with the firms. It is not surprising that Amazon expanded its product offer from books to CDs to almost anything you may want! About 28% of Amazon's unit sales volume is not from its own shelves, but from its third-party sellers, a part of the business that is highly profitable. A fact that is especially relevant in the present context, when Amazon's 2005 fourth quarter profit declined by 43% and the stock fell by 22% (Stross, 2006).

Boo.com is the prototypical breakthrough-enamored B2C start-up. It got entangled in creating the best aesthetic Web site possible but failed to incorporate the basic desire of customers to view and compare fashion products quickly in order to make the buying decision. Launched with a blaze of publicity, it burned through $135 million even before it went public (Isaacs, 2001). Insiders say Boo.com failed be-cause it spent too much money on marketing (Isaacs, 2001). While Boo.com Web designers fretted about aesthetics, customers were actually looking for good deals and fast delivery service. Discordance carried the day.

Petstore.com, Pets.com, Toysmart.com, and other similar ventures also failed to take off. They offered nothing new by way of services to the customers. These Web sites had neither inexpensive products, nor inexpensive and reliable delivery systems. They targeted ultra-thin product niches for which demand had never been proven (Isaacs, 2001), and they also did not augment their offers with high quality and timely service. Toysmart.com did not have a chance in a crowded space oc-cupied by Toys-R-Us and other e-tailers (Isaacs, 2001). These B2C e-commerce companies addressed a known need but their offer did not match either customer expectations of better, cheaper, and timely service or match the offers of already existing new and traditional suppliers. E-Toys failed first to forecast demand and then overreacted and overstocked products, which quickly became obsolete. It could not fulfill customer expectations, despite the fact that their top management team consisted of experienced Disney executives. Here again we see examples of innovative companies and their customers, where perceptual discordance eventually led to service quality failure.

Misperceptions about Breakthroughs and Network Externalities

The breakthrough notion, prompted by the idea that the Internet was a disruptive technology, also spawned the "Instant-Company" approach (Useem, 2000), resting on illusory first-mover advantages and nonexistent "network-externality" effects (i.e., the positive impact on all members of an ever-expanding network). These ideas led companies to build major brands supported by marketing and advertising expenditures. Only some networks, however, are capable of positive network externalities (Arthur, 1996). Networks where members are not interdependent do not exhibit positive externalities. B2C seller-buyer networks are usually star shaped, where each buyer is connected to a single seller. An increasing membership base does not therefore necessarily confer network externality benefits.

In the first wave, B2C players did not have specialized partners—transporters, parcel couriers, third-party logistics providers, fulfillment houses, payment systems, and producers of main and peripheral products. Lacking such services, "the eyeballs the websites managed to attract did not turnout to be loyal" (Useem, 2000, p. 84). For example, CDNow, a music e-tailer, had 83% name recognition but only 17% loyalty. Under such conditions, brand promotion did not turn into first mover or network advantage.

A notable trend is that these hard learned lessons have made subsequent and surviving B2C players attentive to how networks function. The survivors created partnerships to provide interdependent services and have learned to differentiate their products on the Internet.

Misperceptions about First-Mover Advantages

Because the Internet offers instant market access, it can also instantly wipe out the first-mover advantage of B2C pioneers. In general, "me-too" competitors can enter just as rapidly as the first movers did. Only firms capable of creating sustainable competitive advantages can hope to build customer loyalty. Perceptions that B2C offerings in a sector are interchangeable commodities, quite logically, generate commodity-like response from the customers. In such contexts, savvy second movers sometimes can win the competitive game.

Breakthrough is on the Customer Relationship Side

While B2C methods may not be the disruptive breakthroughs that the initial wave of B2C players believed them to be, they are certainly different because they bring the sellers and the buyers together in new ways. B2C methods disrupt old ways of doing business and change the customer-company relationships. Given this, in B2C settings the customer's voice must take precedence over technology's voice. B2C settings create new demands on managers regarding listening and responding to the "voice of the customer." This is not easy. A Deloitte Consulting study of 850 top firms (Reed, 2000) found that only 13% of the companies paid attention to creating customer loyalty networks (integration of marketing and servicing activities through technology) and supply chain collaborations (streamlining of finance and human resources, and the creation of e-chain connectivity involving collaboration and customization of manufacturing and supply processes among supply chain partners). Travelocity, Expedia, and other similar firms responded to the customer need to easy access to inexpensive air travel. These firms have substantially changed the way customers search for and buy tickets, forever changing the nature of competition, pricing, and marketing in the airline industry.

In practice the first-wave, failed B2C firms appear to have seen themselves merely as providers of goods by alternative means. Late entrants and survivors were substantially more customer centric. They focused on basic product presentation, customer service, on-time and efficient delivery, no hassle returns, and so on. In other words, they designed their services and aligned them with the needs of the customers, thus creating concordance.

Implications for Managers and Further Research

B2C retail methods offer low start-up costs, ease of entry, and greater geographic exposure, but these advantages do not make B2C business models simple. For example, Amazon.com, the leading B2C survivor, has increased the assortment of goods offered. Amazon is continually augmenting the B2C innovation by adding features such as full-text search of books; recommendation engines; reviews and ratings; time-based Gold Box specials; referral bonuses; payment system discounts; political campaign coverage and contribution channels; and so forth. Amazon has realized that:

1.   the first wave B2C innovation was an increment, and

2.   it is essential to keep pushing this innovation so that the "Amazon.com shopping experience" moves towards the two highlighted concordant cells of Table 2.

By 2004, Amazon had still not met conventional rubrics of retail profitability but it was inching towards that goal. By the end of the fourth quarter 2005, the Amazon story has not changed and many investors have begun to walk—its share price dropped by 22% when Amazon showed fourth consecutive decline in profit for 2005.

The foregoing discussion has several implications for B2C managers. In relation to its bricks-and-mortar counterpart, the B2C operation must be viewed and studied as an innovation. In most cases, such an innovation would turn out to be more incremental than breakthrough in nature, at least from the customer perspective. It therefore becomes necessary to figure out the segments of customers to whom the B2C option will deliver clear (and more than incremental) advantages. Amazon found this segment among book buyers. The B2C advantages, however, cannot be static. Such advantages need to be constantly augmented and communicated to the customers. Rather than lapsing into techno euphoria, the baseline position of B2C managers should be this: it is going to be exceedingly difficult to create and meet high customer expectations.

E-Toys thought they would present serious competition to brick-and-mortar toy sellers like Toys-R-Us by removing the hassle of shopping, especially during frenzied holiday periods. This created expectations of a fail-proof service. In practice, however, E-Toys ran out of key inventories, stocked the wrong inventories, and failed to process orders correctly. The result was that customers were subjected to serious delays, particularly during the busy holiday gift-giving season. If E-Toys had positioned its innovation incrementally, say as an online birthday toy gift registry, perhaps it could have engendered and successfully met the lower expectation levels, and thus remained in business.

In summary, we have used historical examples in an eclectic cross-sectional fashion across the B2C retail sector to illustrate our proposed innovation theory-based framework for B2C success and failure. We started by questioning the findings of recent empirical studies as to why so many firms, with so much talent and easy access to capital, failed to use time-tested management principles? Why did they fail to realize that managing a B2C e-commerce required acumen similar to that required in the conventional brick-and-mortar world? What was it about this new technology and service delivery method that most B2C managers misread? Why could these companies not convert visitors into profitable and loyal customers? We have argued that it is not incompetence that led to the collapse of many of these ventures but a misperception of their basic business on the one hand and a mistaken positioning of their innovative services for their customers. These errors, we believe, led to discordance in perceptions between buyers and sellers, misallocation of resources within the firm, more so at the front end for customer acquisition and technology than on customer retention and delivery. These problems eventually resulted in serious lapses in service quality, and customer desertion and the customers' abandonment of the B2C method. Our framework captures the problem of creating concordance between buyers and sellers in the context of high-tech innovations and shows by implication that managers have to be aware of the nature and scope of the innovations and then ensure that they are in concordance with their customer base. The framework underlines the necessity of correctly choosing between the voice of the customer and the voice of technology. For known needs and improved solutions, attention to customer voice tends to lead to concordance. But as needs become uncertain and solutions are evolving, customers know less about the needs and will depend on the technology to address their problems. But if managers assume they have breakthrough innovations, and chances of this are high in high-tech settings, they will alienate their clients and will not succeed. The framework thus can be of great use to managers involved in developing and marketing innovative products and services, especially in the e-commerce context. They can carefully assess the need-solution context in which they are operating and then strive for concordance and avoid false optimism or pessimism.

While such an approach has value, it also has obvious limitations. First, there are reasons other than innovation failure that potentially help to explain the dot-com B2C crash phenomenon. These alternative approaches warrant further continuing and in-depth study to understand the colossal economic collapse of the dot-com era. Second, even within the innovation theory framework that we offer, there is need for further systematic in-depth studies that go deep into specific B2C cases. More systematic comparisons of B2C failures are also needed.

References

Achrol, R. S., & Kotler, P. (1999). Marketing in the network economy [Special Issue]. *Journal of Marketing, 63,* 146-163.

Agarwal, V., Arjona, L. D., & Lemmens, R. (2001). E-performance: The path to rational exuberance. *The McKinsey Quarterly, 1,* 31-43.

Anderson, J. (2001, January). Carnage.com. *Institutional Investor, 35*(1), 90.

Arthur, W. B. (1996, July-August). Increasing returns and the new world of business. *Harvard Business Review.*

Berry, L. L., Seiders, K., & Grewal, D. (2002, July). Understanding service convenience. *Journal of Marketing, 66,* 1-17.

Bitner, M. J. (2001, Spring). Self-service technologies: What do customers expect?" *Marketing Management,* 10-11.

Brady, M. K., & Cronin, J. J., Jr. (2001, July). Some new thoughts on conceptualizing perceived service quality: A hierarchical approach. *Journal of Marketing Research, 65*(3), 34-50.

Brown, S. L., & Eisenhardt, K. M. (1995). Product development: Past research, present findings, and future directions. *Academy of Management Review, 20*(3), 343-383.

Corcoran, E. (2002, February 15). Digital diaspora. *Forbes, 169,* 74-80.

Dell on Line. (1998). Boston: Harvard Business School.

Goldberg, J., Lehmann, D. R., & Mazursky, D. (2001). The idea itself and the circumstances of its emergence as the predictors of new product success. *Management Science, 47*(1), 69-84.

Hallowell, R. (2000, May 31). Service in e-commerce: Findings from exploratory research (Module Note, N9-800-418). Boston: Harvard Business School.

Isaacs, N. (2001, March). Crash & burn. *Upside, 13*(3), 186-192.

Krishnan, V., & Ulrich, K. T. (2001). Product development decisions: A review of the literature. *Management Science, 47*(1), 1-21.

Leonard-Barton, D., Wilson, E., & Doyle, J. (1995). Commercializing technology: Understanding user needs. In K. Rangan, B. P. Shapiro, & R. T. Moriarty, Jr. (Eds.), *Business marketing strategy: Cases, concepts, and applications* (pp. 281-305). Chicago: Irwin.

Marn, M. (2000). Virtual pricing. *The McKinsey Quarterly, 4,* 128-130.

Numberger, S., & Rennhak, C. (2005). The future of B2C e-commerce. *Electronic Markets, 15*(3), 269-282.

Rangan, K. V., & Bartus, K. (1995). New product commercialization: Common mistakes. In K. Rangan, B. P. Shapiro, & R. T. Moriarty, Jr. (Eds.), *Business marketing strategy: Cases, concepts, and applications* (pp. 63-75). Chicago: Irwin.

Reed, J. (2000, October). For success, building a customer-centric strategy is key. *Electronic News, 46*(42), 54-59.

Robertson, G., Murphy, J., & Purchase, S. (2005). Distance to market: Propinquity across in-store and online food retailing. *Electronic Markets, 15*(3), 235-245.

Rock, J. (2000, November 20). The hostile market hurts more than just dot-coms. *Weekly Corporate Growth Report, 11068*(1118), 11057.

Stross, R. (2006, February 12). Trying to get a read on Amazon's books. *New York Times,* p. 3.

Tatikonda, M., & Montoya-Weiss, M. M. (2001). Integrated operations and market-ing perspective of product innovation: The influence of organization process factors and capabilities development performance. *Management Science, 47*(1), 151-172.

Useem, J. (2000, October 30). Dot-coms: What have we learned?" *Fortune*, 82-104.

Varianini, V., & Vaturi, D. (2000). Marketing lessons from e-failures. *The McKinsey Quarterly, 4,* 85-97.

Zeithaml, V. A., & Bitner, M. J. (2003). *Services marketing: Integrating customer focus across the firm.* Boston: McGraw Hill-Irwin.

Zeithaml, V. A., Bitner, M. J., & Gremler, D. D. (2006). *Services marketing: Inte-grating customer focus across the firm.* Boston: McGraw Hill-Irwin.

Chapter IX

Implementation of Privacy Protection Policies:
An Empirical Perspective

Noushin Ashrafi, University of Massachusetts, USA

Jean-Pierre Kuilboer, University of Massachusetts, USA

Abstract

Based on U.S. census data, more than three quarter of Internet users are concerned about having control over the release of their private information when using online services. To ease consumers' concerns, the Internet industry has come up with self-regulatory practices. The effectiveness of self-regulatory practices and the commitment of the Internet industry to online privacy are yet to be evaluated. The questions regarding self-regulation, what it means from the industry point of view, and to what extent it is implanted remains unclear. This study is exploratory in nature and attempts to examine privacy issues in the context of fair information practices and how they are perceived and practiced by the top 500 interactive companies in the United States. Our results confirm that most companies ask for consumer trust by claiming benevolence. However, they fall short when it comes to costly implementations of comprehensive privacy protection policies.

Introduction

The e-commerce phenomenon, in conjunction with other advancements in technology, has promoted the development of entire information systems dedicated to analyzing and finding patterns among personal data (Cranor, 1999). Customer relationship management; business intelligence and knowledge management; and mass customization are some of the areas that rely on personal data and used by corporations to serve customers better while helping companies reach their profit targets. The bottom line is that the advanced technology allows consumers to search for information and make transactions online with unprecedented ease while the aggregation of data that makes this service possible also allows significant profiling of Internet users.

Businesses argue that mining personal information is used to advance customer convenience via personalization and mass customization, while furthering their own business objectives (Flammia, 2000). Balancing consumers' rights to privacy and the move to a dossier society—in which the corporate world wants to know everything about the individual and base many of its business decisions upon these presumed facts—is not easy. Privacy advocacy groups have a spectrum of concerns ranging from the collection of information in the first place to how it is aggregated and used, and its disclosure and security. They fear the risks of secondary use by entities outside of the corporation and profiling. National and international apprehensions have been expressed in widely disparate edicts about personal privacy data and the means of its safe handling (Bennett, 1992; Bygrave, 2002; Reidenberg, 2000).

Despite this tension between the interests of the consumer and those of the e-commerce operation, the overall Internet-based economy is on the rise. By the end of 2005, the number of Internet users worldwide reached 1.08 billion and is expected to attain 1.8 billion by 2010 (Clickz, 2006).

Additionally, the value of goods and services bought and sold over the Internet is increasing exponentially; in 2002 it exceeded $2 billion, a 50% rise from 2001 (Rohde, 2002) and in the October-December 2005 period, purchases over the Internet, by e-mail, or through other electronic networks rose to a seasonally adjusted $22.94 billion (Reuters, 2006).

According to the Forrester Research Group (2005), the U.S. will continue to lead the global e-commerce market. They also predict that traditional "brick-and-mortars" will become the dominating players. Powerhouses such as Federated Department Stores, General Electric, American Airlines, Southwest Airlines, and Staples have entered the online trade and are changing the dynamics of e-commerce (McCormick, 2000). The presence of traditional companies with their established brand names creates a tough and competitive environment. Industry leaders such as Orbitz and American Airlines, originally distanced themselves from e-commerce, but are trying to regain their leadership position with their strong online presence in the airline reservation market. In such an environment, luring customers from competitors will not be easy and requires giving consumers something that they have been asking for: the protection of their privacy.

Online privacy laws and regulations are debated and discussed extensively in the literature, but the questions regarding self-regulation, what it means from the industry point of view, and to what extent it is implemented remains unclear. This study is exploratory in nature and attempts to examine privacy issues in the context of fair information practices and how they are perceived and practiced by the top 500 interactive companies in the United States. In the next section we provide a brief discussion on how privacy issues became a source of concern and what actions the international community has taken to deal with them. We then provide a summary of prior research in this area followed by a brief description of self-regulatory practices. We look into privacy issues covered by the top 500 interactive companies to determine the depth and breadth of the self-regulatory practices in these companies. Our empirical study reveals very interesting results that could be of interest to the readers as consumers and to online businesses who are interested to learn about the status of such important issues and practices. Finally, we offer conclusions and report some limitations with this study. The limitations stem from the fact that there is no standard categorization of privacy policies and clear understanding of fair information practices. We strongly believe that studies such as ours should draw attention to this deficiency and prompt the research community to come up with such standards.

Background

Individual privacy has been the subject of debate for years, and concerns have been raised about the sources and destinations of personal data. The potential for mischief has been augmented since the information revolution brought by the Internet, a medium that allows the consolidation of many sources of data and the assembly of a full profile on an individual (Berghel, 2001). Identity management is developing as a management issue worth attention as identity theft has increased rapidly during the past 5 years. This crime became so prevalent that it prompted congress in 1998 to create a new federal offense for identity theft. Despite this law being passed, in 2003 the Federal Trade Commission estimated that 3.2 million consumers had become victims of identity theft during the previous year (Katel, 2005). It is clear that identity management will continue to be an ongoing concern for consumers.

How such a situation has evolved is not a mystery. Security and privacy were afterthoughts grafted onto the Internet architecture, and years of neglect have allowed the accumulation of public and private data that can be mined at will. Following the initial research-oriented use of the Internet (i.e., before 1994), the commercialized World Wide Web (WWW) has occurred through a succession of rapid growth phases. In the first generation of this computing evolution, data collection occurred largely through government agencies, and the centralized but not integrated system was less likely to lead to the violation of individual privacy. In contrast, today the private sector is the prevalent collector of personal information—directly or through derivation and "knowledge data discovery." For example, a large corporation such as WalMart has a data warehouse that tracks consumer buying habits, which exceeds 500 terabytes of data—in contrast to the mere 40 terabytes accumulated by the Internal Revenue Service (IRS) (Owen, 2002). Others, like The Reader's Digest, have made it their trademark to know about the public. Of course, with the establishment of a new government agency such as Homeland Security, the government could still be the ultimate owner of personal data; yet, the collectors of the data are still predominantly from the private sector.

During the period of 1994-1998, a number of issues were uncovered with the operation of the modern Web. Among these, security and the ensuing privacy problems have increased in notoriety. Today, according to a number of polls by different institutions such as the Georgia Institute of Technology, the Wall Street Journal, and a Harris poll (Garfinkel, Gopal, & Goes, 2002; Lawton, 2001), privacy is one of consumers' most important concerns about using the Internet for e-commerce and other purposes. While consumers are increasingly aware of the privacy risks associated with publicized crime such as identity theft, they are still quite ignorant of other largely unethical but legal risks. A survey conducted by Forrester Research (2005) reveals that—despite federal protections under HIPAA—two out of three Americans are concerned about the confidentiality of their personal health information and are largely unaware of their privacy rights. A report from the Annenberg Public Policy Center shows that consumers are largely unaware of how their personal information is used by businesses and falsely believe that the presence of a privacy policy on a Web site means the site cannot share their personal information with others (Electronic Privacy Information Center, 2005). Many Web sites dedicated to health information do not even disclose privacy notices to the public (Sheehan, 2005). Another survey reveals that 64% of American adults do not know that it is legal for online stores to charge different people different prices at the same time of day for the same product based on information mining patterns (Turow, Feldman, & Meltzer, 2005).

Governments around the world have been working on legislation to deal with privacy issues (Erbschloe & Vacca, 2001). Over the past quarter century, government agencies in the United States, Canada, and Europe have studied the way personal information is collected and used and have come to the realization that there is a need for safeguards to assure that these "information practices" are fair and provide adequate privacy protection. The result has been a set of standards governing the collection and use of personal data and addressing issues of privacy and accuracy. The Organization for Economic Cooperation and Development (OECD) has been the leading international body to address privacy issues. In late 1980, the OECD issued a set of guidelines concerning the privacy of personal records. Although broad, these guidelines underpin most current international agreements, national laws, and self-regulatory policies. "These guidelines represent a consensus on basic principles which can be built into existing national legislation, or serve as a basis for legislation in those countries which do not yet have it (OECD, 1981, p. 5). Since then, different organizations and countries have come up with series of reports, guidelines, and model codes that represent widely accepted principles concerning fair information practices.

In contrast to other industrialized countries, the United States has not codified the fair information principles (FIP) into an omnibus privacy law at the federal level. Instead, the principles have formed the basis of many individual laws at both federal and state levels. The current U.S. definition of FIP consists of five principles: (1) notice, (2) choice, (3) access, (4) security, and (5) enforcement (Milne & Culnan, 2002). In 2005 the U.S. Internet Industry Association (USILA) proposed the adoption of 10 principles. The additional principles focus on network providers and complement the FIP's objective (Telecommunications Reports, 2005). The major objective of FIP is to fairly balance business' needs for data collection and consumers' need for data privacy, and it entails the full disclosure of privacy policies to help the user match his or her privacy concerns with those addressed by the firm. The FIP principles address a wide range of issues, from the protection of personal medical or financial information, to protecting children under the age of 13, to informing users about how their information is shared and with whom. The companies that are engaged in self-regulation practices may adopt policies that they deem important to their customers. Therefore, it is quite important that the user checks this information to find out whether his or her privacy concerns are addressed by a particular corporation. While one consumer may worry about cookies—electronic files that permanently contain information about users and their activities—another consumer may be concerned about children accessing inappropriate content.

To categorize these privacy issues into FIP principles, we looked into various federal and state privacy laws and were able to compile different perspectives by various agencies and groups such as the Federal Trade Commission (Federal Trade Report, 1999), the Center for Democracy and Technology (WWW. CDT.org/privacy/guide/basic/fips.html), the Electronic Privacy Information Center (EPIC), the Privacy Act of 1974, Department of Health, Education, and Welfare (HEW). We compiled an exhaustive list of privacy issues addressed by these agencies and categorized them under four FIP principles. We, however, did not address the fifth principle, enforcement, because it is not part of self-regulation; rather, it is the responsibility of a regulatory body to ensure that organizations comply with their own policies and address consumer complaints. Table 1 shows four principles of FIP and 14 issues.

Table 1. Contents of fair information practices

Notice	Choice	Access	Security
Personal information: The organization posting the privacy policy should clearly state why information is collected, what information is collected, how it will be used, and the information retention policy. **Cookies:** The user should be notified that when visiting a site, information might be fed to a "cookie" file, either as a session cookie to track visits, or as a permanent cookie on the user's computer that is stored for future reference. **Privacy policy amendment:** The user should be notified of any changes to existing policies. An amendment should clarify the changes and specify the date they are to be implemented. **Public forum:** Marketers or others can get e-mail addresses or identify visitors from bulletin boards and newsgroups. Visitors should be warned to this effect, so they can use available anonymizing technology in order to keep their privacy.	**Opt-Out/Opt-In:** Users should be able to opt-out not only from the collection of personal, nonnecessary data, but also from direct communications about additional products and services. In "opt-in" the client chooses what to share and with whom. **Third-Party privacy policy:** When a company contains links to other sites, it should not share users' personal information with those Web sites. **Third-Party advertising practices:** Companies allowing advertising on their Web sites should not allow any identifiable information to pass to advertisers. **IP address:** When the Web site records the referrer and destination of a visitor, the data should not be personalized in order to complete the profile of clients. **Children:** An organization should not contact children under age 13 about special offers or for marketing purposes without a parent's permission. **Survey and questionnaire:** The information collected via surveys and questionnaires online should be aggregated. Nonpersonally identifiable information may then be shared with third parties without hampering personal privacy.	**Contact information:** The organization should offer means to remediate potential errors in the data collection, retention, or use. Convenient points of contact should be available so that the user can review, change, and/or correct his/her information. **Registration:** When a user is registered and has an account with a firm, he/she should be able to review their personal information and request the deletion of their account, or any of their personal information held by the company in an easy and convenient way. **Correction to personal information:** The user should be given the opportunity to examine his or her personal information and be able to correct it in a convenient and inexpensive manner.	**Security:** Organizations should take steps to secure clients' personal information from hackers while no security system is absolutely impenetrable, software, systems, and security procedures should be constantly reviewed, refined, and upgraded to reflect new tools, laws, and information as they become available. To this effect, encryption and authentication should be used when appropriate.

Prior Research

The question of privacy online has been addressed in a wide range of publications. This range includes the academic point of view on the protection of individuals' right to their personal data, and practitioners' concerns about privacy practices and their impact on e-commerce (Friedman, Kahn, & Howe, 2000; Gabber, Gibbons,

Kristol, Matias, & Mayer, 1999; Garfinkel et al., 2002; Goldschlag, Reed, & Syverson, 1999; Lawton, 2001; Meeks, 1999; Reiter & Rubin, 1999). Additionally, privacy policies have been the subject of research and discussion. An ongoing argument is that although most organizations have drafted privacy policies, the effective deployment of these policies is not evident (Benassi, 1999; Buchholz & Rosenthal, 2002; Clarke, 1999; Greisiger, 2001; Reagle & Cranor, 1999).

One of the most comprehensive works on Internet privacy policy is by Culnan (1999), who conducted the Georgetown Internet Privacy Policy Survey on 300 Web sites and prepared a progress report, which was presented to the Federal Trade Commission in June 1999. The study addressed three questions: (1) What personal information do Web sites collect from consumers? (2) How many Web sites posted privacy disclosures? (3) Do these disclosures reflect fair information practices? The report did not draw any conclusion, nor it made any recommendation regarding the protection of online privacy; instead, it provided information on the status of online privacy for the commercial Web sites that were visited for the survey. This study was the basis of an article in 2002 where Milne and Culnan (2002) visited 300 commercial Web sites in three consecutive years 1999, 2000, and 2001 and compared their voluntary deployment of fair information practices.

While very useful for providing a progress report on the use of FIPs over three consecutive years, this study did not address all aspects of self-regulatory practices and fell short of covering the full content of its main concern: fair information practices. As the authors suggest, "further research is needed to segment websites by company size, industry, or membership in a trade association or privacy seal program to see if any pattern emerges" (p. 357). Our research attempts a comprehensive investigation of self-regulatory practices that to the best of our knowledge have not been addressed by any researcher yet.

Self-Regulatory Practices

Basically, self-regulatory practices refer to the voluntary deployment of fair information practices. Specifically, it points to what topics belong in a corporate privacy policy, what fine points need to be clearly stated, and choosing avenues to protect personal data. Joining a self-regulatory program, in which *privacy seal programs* certify that companies are indeed complying with privacy requirements, reinforces that companies are serious about establishing and enforcing online privacy. And, of course, consumers need to be informed up front that the company has such privacy protection policies in place. These efforts, when fully deployed, should help enhance the restoration of consumer trust. However, to date there is little concrete evidence to show that companies are truly committed to the deployment of all of these measures.

Our work attempts to address these areas. We start by looking at our set of data on the top 500 interactive companies—companies with Internet transactions—collected in 2002 and examining to what extent self-regulatory practices were deployed. Since our data included information on the company size, industry, and the association with privacy seal programs, we were able to categorize the Web sites based on these criteria. We also scrutinized the content of the four principles of FIPs and analyzed their implementation in detail.

Method of Data Collection and Analysis

In its November 2000 issue, *Interactive Week* magazine published a list of 500 interactive companies. (McCormick, November 13th 2000) "keeping score." From Interactive week. The listing was based on online sales over four quarters ending June 30, 2000. The listing included public and private companies in business at the end of June 2000. The list was compiled in July with a survey conducted by Advantage Business Research. The pollster sent out questionnaires to more than 40,000 e-commerce executives, interactive managers, chief executive officers, and chief information officers. A team at PricewaterhouseCoopers (PWC) helped to retrieve online sales figures. The companies were asked questions about their total revenue, online revenue, and their type of business. Information on nearly 1,500 companies was compiled and ranked based upon their online revenue, and the top 500 companies were published in the November issue. We were fortunate that this listing also included the Web sites for the top 500 companies, which we used as the starting point for our study. In the spring of 2002, we first visited these 500 Web sites and conducted our research to find out what percentage of the top 500 companies had privacy policies published on their Web sites. In the fall of 2002, we visited the Web sites again to check how many of the top 500 companies still had an online presence. At that point, the authors, separately, investigated the contents of the privacy policies of those companies that had published privacy policies and recorded which issues were covered by each company. Although this was a time consuming and tedious task, it was not very difficult because each policy is well defined, and it was easy to see whether the company had addressed the issue or not. However, to increase the reliability of coding, each author checked the Web sites separately and the results were compared. There were few discrepancies, which were checked again and a consensus was reached.

We then checked to see whether nonprofit privacy seal programs such as TRUSTe and BBBOnline validated their privacy policies. We were also interested to find out if company size (based on total revenue), type of business, and the percentage of online business versus off-line business were factors in determining the depth and breadth of adopting self-regulatory practices. The results of these investigations were quite intriguing and are described next.

Published Privacy Policy

The first step in gaining the trust of a consumer is to inform him or her that the company has a published privacy policy (PPP). Recent studies (Liu, Marchewka, Lu, & Yu, 2005) reveal that the presence of a privacy policy is an important factor of trust and possible behavior; comparing two sites that differed only by their privacy notice, the researchers found that posted privacy policies has a strong influence on whether an individual trusts an e-commerce business.

An examination of the top 500 interactive companies as of 2002 indicated that the majority of them have some sort of published privacy policy on their home pages. Table 2 summarizes this information.

Two thirds (67%) of the companies examined had privacy policies published on their Web sites; 37% had PPP and were engaged only in online trade; while 30% had PPP and were conducting business both online and off-line (brick-and-mortar).

Table 2 also shows that less than one third (25%) did not have privacy policies published, with 10% consisting of companies who were only online, and with 15% consisting of companies who had online and off-line business. Between the year 2000, when the data were collected, and the year 2002, when we checked to see whether they had privacy policies published, 8% of the companies had gone out of online business. Further analysis revealed that 5% of the top 500 interactive companies had only online business and were among the dot-com debacle, having perhaps failed to sustain a profit and gone bankrupt; 3% of the top 500 were still in

Table 2. Percentage of companies with a published privacy policy on their Web sites

Have published privacy policy on their Web site		Do not have published privacy policy on their Web site		Out of online business	
67%		25%		8%	
Internet only	37%	Internet only	10%	Internet only/ assume out of business	5%
Both	30%	Both	15%	Both	3%

business, but no longer had an online presence. It is interesting to see that roughly 70% (5 out of 7) of those companies that failed were only online businesses.

Privacy Policy Seal Programs

The next step to gain a user's trust is to seek certification by a credible independent third party. Posting a logo on the screen shows that a third party such as a privacy seal program has certified the privacy protection practices of the company. Privacy seal programs are independent, nonprofit organizations that try to boost users' trust in the Internet by promoting the principles of disclosure and information consent. We found that TRUSTe and BBBOnline were the leading seal programs in terms of adoption. Table 3 summarizes the percentage of the top 500 companies that participate in privacy seal programs.

Table 3 indicates that most companies do not have any logos, indicating that they do not participate in a privacy seal program. Although two thirds of the companies examined had published privacy policies on their Web sites, only 22% felt that they needed a third party to validate their claim, while 14% were certified by TRUSTe and 10% by BBBOnline. Multiple logos included mostly TRUSTe and BBBOn-line, and just a few included TRUSTe and PWC. Others included Direct Marketing Association (DMA)- http://www.dmconsumers.org/privacy.html, WebTrust, and Alliance for Privacy. The results are disappointing, but indicative of the failure of the adoption of privacy seals. As per February 2006, Better Business Bureau Online (BBBOline)- http://bbbonline.org/, is vouching for only 641 sites, and TRUSTe-http://www.truste.org/, reported 1,975 participating Web sites by the end of 2005, with less than 30 Fortune 500 as members.

The next step of this study was to find out the depth of privacy protection offered by the top 500 interactive companies. To analyze this aspect of privacy protection,

Table 3. The percentage of companies that have privacy seal programs

Logo				No logo
22%				
Truste	BBBOnline	Multiple seals	Other	78%
14%	10%	4%	2%	

Note: The percentages do not add up to 100% because of the overlap that multiple logos creates.

we examined the Web sites of these companies and tabulated the privacy issues they had addressed. We were interested in finding out what percentage of companies claiming to have privacy policies had indeed addressed each of these policies. Note that since the categorization of the privacy issues into FIP principles was subjective, we did not look for the percentage of companies that had published policies on the five principles; rather, we looked for the coverage of each of the 14 issues. Table 4 summarizes our findings in this area. This table is significant in revealing which privacy policy issue is perceived as the most important issue and hence is implemented by a large percentage of the firms and which policy is perceived as least important.

Table 4 conveys that almost all of the companies (98%) that claimed they had a privacy policy in place had clearly stated why personal information was collected, what information was collected, and how it would be used; however, only 65% of all 500 companies had such statements. Table 4 is organized by FIP codes and provides in-depth data on the content of FIPs. It appears that companies considered the protection of personal information the most crucial issue, while they regarded issues regarding public forums as the least important to cover.

At this point, we found it interesting to see what percentage of companies with posted privacy policies covered all 14 topics, what percentage covered 13 topics, 12, 11, and so forth. We recognize that it is unlikely that many companies would comply with all of these policies. They would only choose to enforce policies that they consider applicable to their business and important to their customers. Taking these into consideration, one would still be curious to find out what percentage of

Table 4. Percentage of companies that covered 14 privacy issues of FIP

Contents		Companies with PPP		All companies	
Notice		Yes	No	Yes	No
1	Personal information	98%	02%	65%	35%
2	Cookies	80%	20%	53%	47%
3	Privacy policy amendments	57%	43%	37%	63%
4	Public forums	19%	81%	13%	87%
Choice					
1	Opt-Out/Opt-In	73%	17%	48%	52%
2	Third-Party privacy policies	62%	38%	41%	59%
3	Third-Party advertising practices	53%	47%	35%	65%
4	IP address	53%	47%	35%	65%
6	Children	37%	53%	24%	76%
5	Surveys and questionnaire	31%	69%	20%	80%
Access					
1	Contact information	89%	11%	59%	41%
2	Registration	63%	37%	41%	59%
3	Corrections to personal information	57%	43%	37%	63%
Security					
1	Security	78%	22%	51%	49%

Figure 1. Cumulative distribution number of issues covered

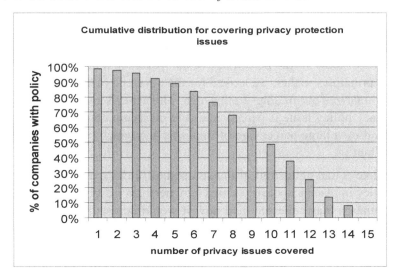

top 500 interactive companies would find all or part of these topics important or relevant to their business and customers. Figure 1 depicts a histogram that conveys this information. Less than 8% of the top 500 interactive companies claiming to have a privacy policy covered all 14 topics, but 98% covered at least one topic. This is consistent with our earlier findings that 98% of companies with PPP cover personal information policy. Figure 1 gives a distribution of coverage.

Company size (total revenue). Data provided by *Interactive Week* magazine included some giant companies such as Intel, IBM, Cisco, GE, Lucent, Dell, United Airlines, and many more, and some smaller companies such as NetZero, The Global Group, and Pets.com. We were interested to see if larger companies would be more inclined to have privacy policies than medium or small companies. We used total revenue as the clustering for size and divided companies into three categories: (1) large companies (total annual revenue exceeding $1 billion), (2) medium (between $100 million to $1 billion), and (3) small (less than $100 million). Companies that

Table 5. Percentage of companies with PPP and privacy seal program logos by size

	Large companies		Medium companies		Small companies		Unknown
% by size	14%		14%		61%		
Privacy policy	89%		84%		60%		11%
Privacy seal	BBBOnline=11%	TRUSTe= 9%	BBBOnline=6%	TRUSTe=11%	BBBOnline= 7%	TRUSTe= 10%	

did not report their total annual revenue are labeled as unknown. The results are depicted in Table 5.

Table 5 shows that a higher percentage of large- and medium-sized companies posted that they had privacy policies, as compared to smaller companies. However, the percentage of large, medium, and small companies that were certified by privacy seal programs do not show a significant difference.

Industry type. The next step in our analysis was to investigate the correlation between the type of business and concerns for online privacy. We separated organizations based on the type of their business into eight categories. Table 6 shows the eight categories and the percentage of the top 500 interactive companies that fall into each category.

Note that 81% and 23% of the retail stores, which constitutes 23% of the total of the interactive companies, had published privacy policies and privacy seal program logos, respectively. According to Table 6, travel and retail companies on the top 500 interactive list are the most sensitive to privacy protection, since 83% and 81% respectively have PPP, and 26% and 23% have privacy seal program logos. Health care organizations seem the least sensitive; however, one needs to realize that financial and health care industries are regulated—hence, self-regulatory practices seem to be redundant for them.

Content. The final step in our analysis was to explore the percentage of different types of companies that cover each of the privacy topics. Table 7 shows these percentages.

Again, note that these are the percentages of each category—not of the total 500. For example, 79% of the retail stores had policies on personal information. It should be noted that not all topics are relevant to every industry or site. For example, a low percentage for public forums or surveys and questionnaires could be indicative of the fact that many sites do not have a public forum, or they do not offer surveys and questionnaires.

Table 7 indicates that, on average, retailers and travel agencies are on the top of the list in terms of covering any of the privacy topics. This makes sense, because these companies are mainly involved in business-to-consumer (B2C) interactions, and are most concerned with gaining the trust of millions of users. Advertising

Table 6. Percentage of different types of companies with PPP and seal program logo

	Retail	Financial	Health	Travel	Communication	Advertising	IT	Other
% by type	23%	7%	3%	5%	20%	7%	15%	20%
PPP	81%	70%	50%	83%	68%	57%	69%	50%
SP logo	23%	14%	6%	26%	18%	26%	14%	3%

Table 7. Percentage of different types of companies that cover each of the 14 privacy issues

Content	Retail	Financial	Health	Travel	Communication	Advertising	IT industry	Other
Notice								
Personal information	79%	70%	50%	78%	66%	57%	64%	48%
Cookies	61%	46%	44%	61%	59%	51%	53%	39%
Privacy policy amendments	46%	38%	44%	39%	49%	34%	35%	19%
Public forums	12%	3%	25%	9%	24%	6%	9%	10%
Choice								
Opt-Out/Opt-In	64%	54%	25%	78%	51%	49%	39%	29%
Third-Party privacy policies	45%	24%	44%	57%	48%	31%	44%	34%
Third-Party advertising practices	36%	24%	44%	48%	48%	26%	35%	24%
IP address	42%	22%	19%	57%	43%	26%	35%	24%
Children	38%	8%	25%	30%	40%	14%	19%	7%
Surveys and questionnaire	26%	5%	13%	44%	31%	26%	12%	12%
Access								
Contact information	70%	54%	50%	74%	64%	57%	56%	43%
Corrections to personal information	53%	38%	31%	57%	43%	40%	26%	20%
Registration	45%	24%	38%	65%	50%	32%	35%	39%
Security								
Security	69%	57%	38%	78%	50%	49%	46%	31%

companies appear to be least concerned with privacy protection issues. This also seems logical, because the nature of their business requires the distribution of user information and thus entailing the risk of jeopardizing consumer trust. Companies in the IT industry were in the middle of the road—somewhere between retailers or travel agencies and advertising. The reason could be that IT companies are involved both in business-to-business (B2B) and B2C interactions. Therefore, some of their interactions are with suppliers, with whom they probably have ongoing business relations and a mutual trust. Health care and financial companies were at the same level as the IT industry, and they, too, are usually involved in a mixture of B2C and B2B interactions. They are also regulated on some aspects of privacy protection. Our results also indicate that companies who are in a competitive business, such as retailers and travel agencies and are in need of customers' trust, were more inclined to implement privacy protection practices. Conversely, those that are most likely to be perceived as using personal data for profiling purposes such as advertising were less inclined to commit themselves. These findings provide some predictable and some surprising insights into the question of self-regulation on privacy protection practices.

Conclusion and Limitations

The emergence of e-commerce and the ensuing burst of the dot-com bubble have strengthened the necessity to cover both computer security and privacy. A common belief is that companies have to address privacy issues more seriously or jeopardize the success of their businesses by losing customer trust. Although we had assumed that having privacy policies should be commonplace, partly because of the fear of regulation, and partly to enhance business through image improvement, our empirical investigation shows otherwise. Only two thirds of companies, regardless of their size or type of business, had informed customers that they have privacy policies in place; less than one fourth had their practices certified by a third party; and less than 10% had covered all 14 aspects of privacy protection.

Noting that these are the top 500 interactive companies, we may conclude that with all the hype about privacy issues, not many companies demonstrate a full commitment to spending resources on privacy protection. There is a good chance that if this trend continues, government regulation will become an inevitable alternative.

There are some limitations with self-regulatory practices. We used the general framework provided by Culnan's (1999) progress report to the Federal Trade Commission, but over the course of our research, we realized that the categorization of privacy issues is not that clear cut. The second problem is the existence of privacy seal programs as independent third parties to certify the sincerity of interactive companies. These programs have received sharp criticism about their own practices, which limits their abilities to supervise the deployment of FIPs by interactive companies.

The third and the most important limitation is the difficulty with enforcing self-regulatory practices. Although we considered this topic out of our research scope, it is important to point out that the key to successful self-regulation is the standardization of policies and procedures to monitor the deployment of policies according to the standards.

Having mentioned these limitations, it is important to note that online privacy protection, although immensely important, is in its infancy and additional research is needed to draw attention to its strengths and limitations.

References

Benassi, P. (1999). TRUSTe: An online privacy seal program. *Communications of the ACM, 42*(2), 56-59.

Bennett, C. J. (1992). *Regulating privacy. Data protection and public policy in Europe and the United States*. Ithaca, NY: Cornell University Press.

Berghel, H. (2001). Cyberprivacy in the new millenium. *IEEE Computer, 34*(1), 132-134.

Better Business Bureau Online. (2003). Retrieved October 2003, from BBBOnline Web site: http://www.bbbonline.org/

Buchholz, R. A., & Rosenthal, S. B. (2002). Internet privacy: Individual rights and the common good. S.A.M *Advanced Management Journal, 67*(1), 34-40.

Bygrave, L. (2002). *Data protection law: Approaching its rationale, logic and limits*. New York: Kluwer Law International.

Clarke, R. (1999). Internet privacy concerns confirm the case for intervention. *Communications of the ACM, 42*(2), 60-67.

Clickz. (2006). *Trends & statistics: The Web's richest source*. Retrieved February 2006, from http://www.clickz.com/stats/web_worldwide/

Cranor, L. F. (1999). Internet privacy. *Communications of the ACM, 42*(2), 29-31.

Culnan, M. J. (1999, May). *Draft. Georgetown Interent Privacy Policy Survey: Privacy Online in 1999: A report to the Federal Trade Commision*. Washington D.C.

Culnan, M. J. (1999, June). The Georgetown Internet privacy policy survey: Report to the Federal Trade Commission. Washington, DC: Georgetown University.

Electronic Privacy Information Center (EPIC). (2005). *EPIC public opinion and privacy page*. Retrieved February 2006, from http://www.epic.org/privacy/survey/

Erbschloe, M., & Vacca, J. (2001). *Net privacy*. New York: McGraw-Hill.

Flammia, G. (2000). Privacy versus convenience. *IEEE Intelligent Systems, 15*(3), 12-13.

Forrester Research. (2005). *National consumer health privacy survey 2005*. Retrieved February 2006, from http://www.chcf.org/topics/view.cfm?itemID=115694

Friedman, B., Kahn, P. H., Jr., & Howe, D. C. (2000). Trust online. *Communications of the ACM, 43*(12), 34-40.

Gabber, E., Gibbons, P. B., Kristol, P. B., Matias, Y., & Mayer, A. (1999). Consistent, yet anonymous, Web access with LPWA. *Communications of the ACM, 42*(2), 42-47.

Garfinkel, R., Gopal, R., & Goes, P. (2002). Privacy protection of binary confidential data against deterministic, stochastic, and insider threat. *Management Science, 48*(6), 749-764.

Garfinkel, S. (2002). *Web security, privacy & commerce* (2nd ed). Sebastopol, CA: O'Reilly.

Goldschlag, D., Reed, M., & Syverson, P. (1999). Onion routing for anonymous and private Internet connections. *Communications of the ACM*, 42(2), 39-41.

Katel, P. (2005, June) Can congress give Americans better protection? *CQ Researcher, 15*(4) 22.

Lawton, G. (2001). Is technology meeting the privacy challenge. *IEEE Computer, 34*(9), 16-18.

Liu, C., Marchewka, J. T., Lu, J., & Yu, C.-S. (2005). Beyond concern: A privacy-trust-behavioral intention model of electronic commerce. *Information & Management, 42*(2), 289-304.

McCormick, J. (2000). Keeping score. *Interactive Week, 7*(48), 56-78.

Meeks, B. N. (1999). The privacy hoax. *Communications of the ACM, 42*(2), 17-19.

Milne, G. R., & Culnan, M. J. (2002). Using the content of online privacy notices to inform public policy: A longitudinal analysis of the 1998-2001 U.S. Web surveys. *The Information Society, 18*(5), 345-359.

Organisation for Economic Copperation and Development. (OECD) (1981). *Guidelines on the Protection of Privacy and Transborder Flows of Personal Data.* Paris.

Owen, T. (2002). Lord of the things. In E. Brynjolfsson, M. D. Smith, & J. H. Yu (Eds.), Consumer surplus in the digital economy: Estimating the value of increased product variety at online booksellers. *Management Science, 49*(11), 20-23.

PriceWaterhouseCoopers. (2003). *Privacy practice.* Retrieved from http://www.pwcglobal.com

Reagle, J., & Cranor, L. F. (1999). The platform for privacy preferences. *Communications of the ACM, 42*(2), 48-55.

Reidenberg, J. (2000). Resolving conflicting international data privacy rules in cyberspace. *Stanford Law Review, 52,* 1315-1371.

Reiter, M., & Rubin, A. D. (1999). Anonymous Web transactions with crowds. *Communications of the ACM, 42*(2), 32-38.

Reuters. (2006). E-commerce sales rise in fourth quarter. *Information Week.* Retrieved from http://www.informationweek.com/industries/showArticle.jhtml?articleID=180204097

Rohde, L. (2002, November 21). UN: Worldwide use of Internet, e-commerce still growing. *IDG News Service.* http//www.networkworld.com/news/2002/1121unreport.html

Sheehan, K. (2005, Fall). Privacy policies at direct-to-consumer Websites. *American Marketing Association, 24*(2), 273-283.

Telecommunications Reports. (2005, September). USIIA proposes 10 principles for IP industry self-regulation. *71*(18), 7-8.

TRUSTe. (2003). Retrieved from Truste Web site: http://www.truste.org/

Turow, J., Feldman, L., & Meltzer, K. (2005). *Open to exploitation: American shoppers online and offline*. Annenberg Public Policy Center, University of Pennsylvania.

Chapter X

Design Considerations in the Development of an Online Course in E-Business

Wing Lam, U21 Global, Singapore

Abstract

This chapter describes how U21 Global (U21G), an e-university formed by a consortium of traditional brick-and-mortar universities, approached the design of MBA650, its online course in e-business. MBA650 is a core course in U21G's MBA program. Gagne's theory (Little, 2001), a pedagogical framework taken from the literature, is used to frame and explain the rationale for the design of MBA650. Gagne's theory identifies a number of instructional events including the identification of learning objectives, presentation of content, provision of learner guidance, feedback, and performance assessment. An evaluation of MBA650 based on student feedback is presented. Finally, several key design considerations in the development of e-business courses are discussed such as including attention to learning outcomes, the student audience, syllabus, key messages, theory vs. practice, team working, and the use of case studies.

Introduction

Over the last few years, electronic business (e-business) has fundamentally changed the way in which many organisations conduct business. Universities realise this, and courses in e-business are now commonly found in the curriculum of both business and technology programs (Etheridge, Hsu, & Wilson, 2001; Ngai, Gunaskaran, & Harris, 2005). Despite the interest paid to e-business by academics, however, the design of courses in e-business remains challenging for a number of reasons:

- The relatively recent emergence of e-business and the lack of an established e-business curriculum or agreed "body of knowledge" (Dunning, Vijayaraman, Krovi, & Kahai, 2001; King, Frank, & Platt, 2001).

- Rapid change within the field of e-business and the rate at which concepts become quickly outdated (Davis, Siau, & Dhenuvakonda, 2003; Petrova & Claxton, 2005).

- The close attention to e-business paid by media and marketing interests, accompanied by inevitable distortions of data (Drew, 2002)

- The multi-disciplinary nature of e-business, which requires academics to understand both business and technology concepts.

At the same time, online academic programs are becoming increasingly commonplace (Castro et al., 2001; Evans & Haase, 2001). Not only are campus-based universities offering online programs, e-universities which deliver programs wholly online have emerged onto the education scene (Schooley, 2001). U21G is one such e-university. Established in 2001, U21G is owned by the 19 research-intensive universities in the Universitas 21 network which includes the National University of Singapore, Edinburgh University, University of Hong Kong, Melbourne University, and the University of Virginia. U21G launched its first program, the MBA, in August 2003, which currently has approximately 650 registered students. A second major program, the Master of Science in Information Systems Management, was launched in late 2005. Degrees offered by U21G are accredited by U21 Pedagogica, a quality assurance body established by U21 that independently reviews all of U21G's programs.

This chapter describes how U21G faced the dual challenge of not only designing a course in e-business as part of its MBA program, but designing one that could be successfully delivered online. The structure of the chapter is as follows. Section 2 of the chapter gives a brief introduction to U21G's pedagogy and presents the pedagogical framework for examining MBA650, U21G's online course in e-Business. Section 3 describes, in detail, the design rationale of MBA650. Section 4 reflects upon some of the design considerations involved in the development of a course in e-Business. Finally, Section 5 concludes with a summary of key points.

Pedagogy and Framework

Online education has several benefits over more traditional face-to-face education, particularly in terms of providing greater flexibility and convenience. Such benefits that make online education particularly well suited as a delivery model for working adults who wish to study on a part-time basis (Petrides, 2002; Schrum, 2002). U21G's programs are aimed exclusively at such an audience. Significantly, U21G's pedagogy is intended to be learner centric, that is, one in which the student is responsible for their own learning and is required to play an active role in the learning process (Berlanger & Jordon, 2000; Dringus, 2000). This type of pedagogy is viewed as highly appropriate to U21G's MBA students, who are adult learners (with an average of 35), disciplined, and highly motivated.

The online classes at U21G typically have between 25-35 students, are 12 weeks in duration, and are facilitated by a professor. There is no physical face-to-face interaction as U21G students can be based anywhere in the world (indeed, the global nature of U21G's online classes is one of its distinguishing features). However, a high degree of interaction is expected between students, and between the students and the professor, using the Web-based communication tools provided within the learning environment such as online discussion boards, chat, audio-conferencing, and e-mail. Research has indicated that, in some cases, the level of interaction in classes conducted online can be significantly higher than in classes conducted face-to-face (Dringus & Scigliano, 2001; Smith, Smith, & Boone, 2000).

Students are provided with comprehensive online courseware that presents them with online access to all the materials required for completion of each course. The design of the online courseware at U21G has been influenced by the significant body of instructional design theory in the literature (Andrews & Goodson, 1995). Gagne's theory (Little, 2001) neatly summarises much of this theory and proposes nine instructional events necessary for effective adult learning:

1. gaining attention in order to engage the learner;
2. identifying the learning objectives to set the learner's expectations;
3. stimulating recall of prior learning to build upon what should already have been learned;
4. presenting the content using an appropriate range of delivery and interaction;
5. providing learning guidance;
6. eliciting performance to facilitate rehearsal, practice, and application of new knowledge;

7.   providing feedback to reinforce learning progress and promote learner attention;

8.   assessing performance to monitor mastery; and

9.   enhancing retention and transfer to enable new knowledge to be contextualised.

In the following section, Gagne's theory (Little, 2001) is used as a framework for explaining the design of MBA650.

Design of MBA650 E-Business

Gaining Attention, in Order to Engage the Learner

A necessary condition for gaining, and importantly maintaining leaner attention, is when the subject matter is relevant to the personal interests of the learner, that is, it has immediate application to the individual's job or personal life. An analysis by the author of the Web sites of 12 institutions revealed significant differences in the content of graduate-level e-business courses as illustrated by the range of topics listed as follows:

- E-business strategy and e-business models
- Value chain analysis
- Strengths, weaknesses, opportunities, and threats (SWOT) analysis of e-business opportunities
- Supply chain management and e-procurement
- Business-to-consumer (B2C) commerce
- Business-to-business (B2B) commerce and marketplaces
- Alliances and partnerships
- Security and cyber-trust
- Transformation from bricks-and-mortar to e-business
- Personalization and customer relationship management (CRM)
- E-marketing
- Online stores and merchants

- E-payment
- Architecture of the Internet (TCP/IP, Web services)
- Web site design and development (e.g., html, php, ASP, CGI, etc.)
- Web technologies (e.g., Java, Coldfusion, .NET)
- Web site usability
- E-business outsourcing
- Wireless technologies and m-business
- E-business in industry verticals: logistics, financial services, manufacturing, healthcare
- E-government

This diversity encompasses topics which are essentially business oriented in nature, such as e-business strategy and SWOT analysis, to technical topics such as Internet architecture and Web technologies. U21G's MBA students are more business rather technology inclined, so it was decided that a business orientation should be adopted for MBA650. The content of a U21G subject is divided into segments, essentially modules or chapters, as illustrated by the screen shot (Figure 1).

Figure 1

The navigation bar on the left depicts the individual segments and clicking on the segments reveals the course content in the main window. MBA650 contains five segments:

1. **E-strategy.** Students study the elements of traditional business strategy, learn how these are applied in an online business setting, and discuss how they would develop an e-strategy for their organisation.
2. **E-commerce.** Students study the basic concepts surrounding the Internet and learn how to make informed decisions about how the functionality of the Internet can be exploited to benefit their organisation.
3. **B2B-commerce.** Students are introduced to Internet exchanges and marketplace and examine how such structures are employed to increase profits, streamline supply chain activities, and create new efficiencies.
4. **B2C-commerce.** Students study the challenges faced by businesses trying to succeed in the online business-to-consumer marketplace, from transforming a traditional business into an online business to creating and maintaining channel alliances.
5. **E-business leadership.** Students gain insights into sound leadership and cultural requirements particular to the new economy and learn to translate them into human resource policies and practices.

Identifying the Learning Objectives, to Set the Learner's Expectations

Students on the MBA program are expected to transfer and apply what they have learned in during their studies into real-world practice. As such, the learning objectives for U21G subjects tend to be procedural rather than declarative in nature. The overall learning objectives for MBA650 e-business are as follows:

Upon completion of the subject you should be able to

- identify and apply various strategic e-business elements in order to strengthen business;
- assess the strategic fit of e-business models to organisational operations;
- match e-business initiatives to organisational strategy;

> - apply e-business impacts and practices gleaned from approximately 10 industries and 20 organisations to other organisational contexts; and
> - recognise from a leadership as well as a managerial perspective the practical implementation challenges associated with e-business strategies.

There is a strong emphasis on relating e-business to a wide variety of organisational situations. The importance of strong leadership in e-business is also recognised, as characterised by the teaching cases of Amazon.com and Dell.

As mentioned earlier, the online courseware is structured into segments. Within each segment, more granular learning objectives are defined. This is consistent with the view that high-level learning objectives should be broken down into more detailed ones (Savenye, Olina, & Niemczyk, 2001). Here, for example, are the learning objectives defined for the segment on B2C commerce.

> Upon completing the segment, students should be able to
>
> - apply the concepts of e-business to formulate and implement B2C e-business initiatives;
> - move customers to online channels and services;
> - construct and implement business models that drive B2C value in their organisation;
> - use appropriate applications of automated customer interaction and integrate automated interaction with human customer interaction;
> - mitigate online channel conflict when possible; and
> - integrate Web site strategies with online alliance channel strategies.

As before, learning outcomes are predominantly procedural in nature, placing emphasis on students being able to apply what they have learned to real-world problem solving.

Stimulating Recall of Prior Knowledge, to Build Upon What Should Already Have Been Learned

At the end of each segment, students are generally required to perform a case study analysis to reinforce the concepts presented within the segment. Case studies are a well-established approach to learning (Parikh, 2002), and their use is considered important at U21G for several reasons:

- Case studies ground concepts of an abstract or theoretical nature to real-world situations and settings.
- Case studies enable students to reinforce their understanding of a particular set of topics within a segment, a whole segment, or a set of segments.
- Case studies draw out the lessons to be learned from both successful and unsuccessful e-business initiatives (positive and negative case studies).
- Case studies illustrate how similar concepts applied in different contexts can lead to different results.
- Case studies serve as meaningful assignment items that can be done either individually or as part of a team.

Case studies are carefully selected to provide the greatest pedagogical value at specific points in a subject. For illustration, at the end of the segment on B2B commerce, students are asked to analyse Citibank's B2B strategy.

The questions here are designed to challenge the student's ability to reason about a company's B2B strategy in a given situation. Typically, questions do not have a right or wrong answer; rather the open-ended nature of the questions allows a student to formulate an answer based on a well-constructed argument.

Title: Citibank's E-Business Strategy for Global Corporate Banking.

Case No.: #HKU197

Date: 7 June 2002

Authors: Yu, J., Farhoomand, A. F., McCauley, M., and S. Khan.

Publisher: Harvard Business School case (field) study.

Questions

1. Could Citibank have used the same strategy in all parts of the world?
2. How should it customise its strategy for different market segments be they regional or based on other socioeconomic factors. How would you formulate such a strategy and implement it in detail?
3. Comment on the effectiveness to date of the e-business strategy at Citibank. Do you think it was ahead of or behind the rest of the leaders in its industry?
4. What should be the reasonable expectations of the return on investment for the money that is put into e-business strategies such as Citibank's?
5. Did Citibank have reasonable expectations, and were they met?

Submit one response document by email to your instructor. Your submission should be no more than 1000 words. Your instructor will announce when to submit.

Presenting the Content Using an Appropriate Range of Delivery and Interaction

One of the tenets often associated with online courseware is that it should be interactive and engaging. While this may hold true under many circumstances, early feedback from pilot U21G students suggested that too much interactivity and engagement was undesirable for the following reasons:

- Requiring a student to continually engage and interact with the courseware over the entire duration of a subject can become extremely exhausting.

- When interactive exercises were over used, students began to "skip" them rather than engage in them.

- Sometimes the value from doing an interactive exercise was minimal; there was a dangerous tendency to have interactivity for interactivity sake rather than for any real pedagogical purpose.

- Students need to reflect on and assimilate what they have learned, suggesting that breaks away from interactive content should be explicitly built into the courseware at specific points.

Figure 2

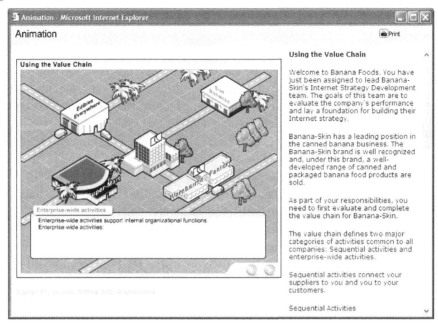

As a consequence, we have been very careful and deliberate about the extent to which interactivity is used in MBA650. One way in which students interact is through structured animations, as shown in Figure 2.

Here, the objective of the animation is to help students understand the concept of value chains. The animation describes a fictitious company, and as the student steps through the animation, the flow of materials between the company and its suppliers is visually constructed. The interactivity serves the specific purpose of incrementally introducing a concept to the student. Figure 3 shows another example of an interactive exercise that is used in MBA650.

In this animation, the student solidifies their understanding of value chains by working through three steps each supported by a sequence of interactive activities. The first of these activities, creating a value chain from a SWOT analysis, is shown where the student drags items from the SWOT analysis onto the appropriate parts of the value chain. The student is therefore tested on how well they understand the relationship between the two that would have otherwise been hard to establish without an interactive exercise.

Unlike the trivial interactivity often seen in courseware designed for the corporate market, the interactive exercises used within MBA650 are carefully crafted to convey a significant pedagogical purpose. This also suggests that courseware originally designed for an academic programme may not be entirely appropriate in the context of a corporate training programme and vice versa.

Figure 3

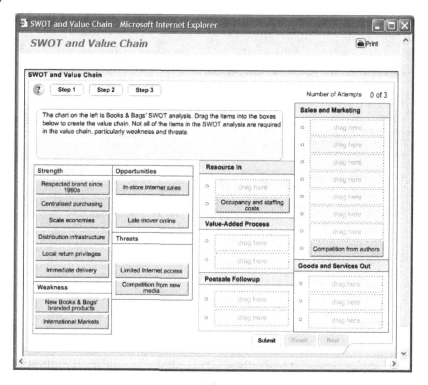

Providing Learner Guidance

Self-assessment is particularly important in an online setting, where a student is not typically in a position where they can immediately clarify their understanding with an instructor. In MBA650, self-assessment is used at many points in the courseware, but particularly so at the end of topics. Self-assessment serves a number of related purposes:

- As a type of test, self-assessment enables a student to quickly determine how well they have understood a particular concept.

- In some cases, it enables the instructor to keep tabs on the progress of individual students and highlight areas where they need further assistance.

- Self-assessment provides a student with reassurance that they have understood a concept in the way that an instructor may provide reassurance in a face-to-face setting.

- Used intelligently, self-assessment can provide a mechanism for allowing students to apply critical thinking skills in a problem-solving situation.

Figure 4

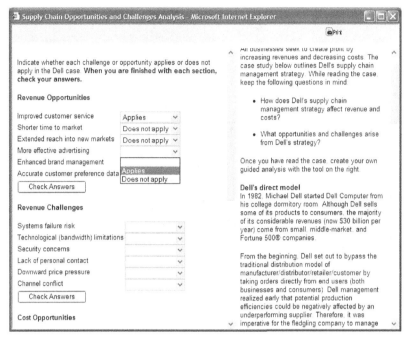

The type of self-assessment typically seen in online courseware is multiple choice questions (MCQ). While in MBA650 MCQ has a place, we have also included more sophisticated types of self-assessment activities. Animations, such as that described previously, are one example of this type of self-assessment. Another example of a self-assessment activity is shown in Figure 4.

In this example, the student reads a case-study on Dell's direct selling model and is then asked to indicate whether or not specific revenue opportunities, revenue challenges, and cost opportunities apply in the case of Dell direct. Notably, the self-assessment exercise is moulded around a case study, and so requires the student to become more involved in the exercise than would be the case for regular MCQ.

Eliciting Performance to Facilitate Rehearsal, Practice, and Application of New Knowledge

One way in which student performance is elicited is through problem solving as part of a virtual team, as is often the way teams operate in today's workplace. Virtual teams are also seen as a way to support community building (Johnson, Suriya, Yoon, Berrett, & La Fleur, 2002) and addressing the lack of community sometimes associated with online education (Song, Singleton, Hill, & Myung, 2004). An example of a team assignment in MBA650 is as follows:

Instructions

Read the following case and work with your team to answer the questions that follow. For the segment assignment, analyse the Eastman Chemical company case study and answer the following questions.

Title: Constructing an E-Supply Chain at Eastman Chemical Co.

Case No.: #HKU222

Date: 25 September 2002

Authors: Yen, B., Farhoomand, A. F., and P. Ng.

Publisher: Harvard Business School case (field) study

To view this case, go to the private Harvard Web site. If you are a new user, click here for instructions on how to enter the site.

Questions

1.   What were the key success factors facing Craig Knight in his quest to sell Eastman's approach to e-business?
2.   What were the major choices of alternatives that Mr. Knight had?
3.   List and describe the risks facing Knight and Eastman in their e-business initiative and suggest for each risk what you would have done to reduce or mitigate that risk.

Submit one response document by e-mail to your instructor. Your submission should be no more than 1000 words. Your instructor will announce when to submit.
Click on the link below to read some helpful tips for working with your team.

Collaboration Tips

Here, the nature of the assignment is not an unfamiliar one: to analyse a case study and respond to specific questions. Team workspaces that include tools such as discussion boards, file repositories, and online chat are provided within the learning platform to support team-based collaboration. Teams are also given general advice on how they should organise themselves and the need to apportion work in an appropriate manner. Where needed, teams can also seek advice from the instructor.

Collaborating as a team in an online setting does of course pose significant challenges, not least due to the lack of face-to-face engagement. However, an online setting does immerse students in a different group dynamic where dominant personalities are neutralised and greater equity can be achieved in proposing ideas.

Providing Feedback to Reinforce Learning Progress and Promote Learner Attention

Over the 12-week duration of a class, students can expect to receive a variety of feedback. Much of this feedback will be from the professor in terms of feedback on submitted assignments. Professors will also provide feedback, both to individuals and to the class as a whole, in the facilitation of the online discussion forums. The extent of professor involvement in online discussions has a major impact on learning and learner satisfaction (Blignaut & Trollip, 2003; Mazzolini & Maddison, 2003). Professors at U21G therefore receive comprehensive guidelines on the facilitation of online discussion forums (Lam, 2005). A professor, for example, may prompt students to think about an alternative dimension of a problem or steer the direction of a discussion towards a new focus. A professor may also highlight and summarise the key points raised during a discussion to help reinforce important ideas. In addition, much peer learning takes place in the online discussion forums, so students also receive feedback from other students in the class.

Assessing Performance to Monitor Mastery

As well as continuous assessment, students are required to take an Open-Book Open-Web (OBOW) examination at the end of the 12 weeks (Williams, 2004; Williams, 2005). The OBOW exams used at U21G represent a significant departure from the conventional, closed book, invigilated model for examinations in that they are situated in an authentic context. In keeping with the constructivist tradition, the OBOW exam comprises a case story that invites students to draw upon all they have learned throughout the subject, and in assembling this knowledge, they demonstrate what they know rather than what they do not know. There is no call for individuals to memorise and regurgitate facts and concepts in a controlled setting. Such case stories are recognised as powerful learning instruments as well as assessment instruments (Hung, Tan, Cheung, & Hu, 2004; McBride, 2005).

An example of an OBOW exam used in MBA650 is given in the Appendix. It is quite unique and will not be used again for examination purposes. The length of an OBOW exam paper is deliberately kept relatively short and succinct, and typically, the exam comprises three components; namely, "The Context," "The Task," and the "Guide to the Task." The Context introduces the case and provides some background information. The Task specifies what students are required to do while the Guide to the Task outlines the approaches students may take in response to The Task.

Students can complete the OBOW exam at any physical location of their choosing within a 75-hour window over a designated weekend (usually the end of week 14). Once the OBOW exam paper has been downloaded from the U21G LMS, the students have 24 hours to submit their response (via the LMS). A wide range of resources such as the text books, electronic library, and the World Wide Web are at the students' disposal throughout the duration of the examination.

Enhancing Retention and Transfer to Enable New Knowledge to be Contextualised

Mazoue (1999) argues that designing effective online courses involves implementing learning strategies that provide students with ample opportunities to discuss, interpret, and integrate their exposure to new concepts. As such, participation in online discussion forums is an important component of the learning process for U21G students. The peer learning that takes place within the discussion forums enhances knowledge retention and transfer, particularly when a student brings to

Figure 5

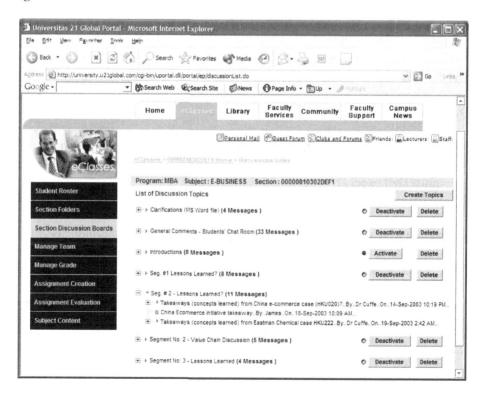

the discussion problems they are facing in their own workplace. A snapshot of the interface to a U21G discussion forum is shown in Figure 5.

Generating discussion in an online setting can be a challenge (Clark, 2001). To stimulate discussion, U21G uses discussion-based assignments.

Here, students are presented with a case study of Dell Direct at the end of a topic on e-marketing. Students are requested to read the case study and post their response to a number of questions on the online discussion forum. By defining a specific set of questions, the discussion starts off in a precise and directed manner with the student being clear about what they are meant to discuss. This is important as our experience has shown that precision early on is conducive to achieving the momentum

---

Read the following case and respond to the question below.

Title: Dell: Selling Directly, Globally.

Case No.: #HKU069

Date: 29 March 2002

Authors: Ng, P., Farhoomand, A. F., and P. Lovelock

Publisher: Harvard Business School case (field) study.

To view this case, go to the private Harvard Web site. If you are a new user, click here for instructions on how to enter the site.

Questions

1. Provide a summary of how the Dell Direct to Consumer model works.
2. Looking inside the Dell organisation, what key organisational capabilities must Dell excel at?
3. What are the disadvantages of the Dell business model relative to traditional business models?
4. If you were starting a brand new competitive company in this industry, what features, structure, and strategy would you employ in order to out compete Dell computer?

To respond to the questions, post your comments on the class discussion board (100-150 words per question).

---

required for discussions to become self-sustaining, that is, when instructor support is no longer required. During the course of discussion, however, new threads may naturally emerge. Online discussion can be conducted in several different modes:

- The instructor facilitates the discussion among a group of students by providing feedback on specific postings, prompting responses from other students, summarising key points, and steering the discussion as necessary.

- The instructor assigns a particular student to facilitate the discussion, with the professor assuming a more passive role where they contribute postings on an occasional basis. Such an approach has been shown to have a strong positive effect on student participation (Corner & Corner, 2003; Poole, 2000).

- The instructor assigns a team to both facilitate and lead the discussion where the team is expected to contribute the majority of the postings. Other students are free to contribute postings but are not required to do so.

- Students within a team engage in private discussions which the instructor has no control or visibility of. This typically occurs in team assignments.

The professor will often employ a variety of different modes during a class. Participation in online discussions typically contributes between 15-25% of a student's summative assessment. The motivation for students to participate therefore clearly exists. It should be noted that the quantity of postings to an online discussion does not necessarily correlate with student learning or effort (Salter, 2000). Therefore, in assessing online discussions, the professor attaches greater weight to the quality rather than quantity of a student's postings. In particular, "deep" discussion that includes "challenge, reflection and debate" will tend to attract a high score (Desanctis, Fayard, Roach, & Jiang, 2003).

Another example follows of how online discussion is encouraged in MBA650 e-business.

Read this article by Sawhney and Parikh and respond to the question below.

How is value created and who gets it in the new economy?

To respond to the question, form a team of two to three students with your fellow classmates and post your answer to the Discussion Board. Your instructor will announce when to post.

Follow up this activity by reviewing the postings by your fellow students. This should be done individually. Select at least two postings that are different from your team and respond to them through the Discussion Board. Your comments and feedback should be thoughtful and helpful in expanding the response to the question.

A similar pattern is repeated here, where the student is asked to read a case study and post their response to specific questions. In many instances, further discussion is encouraged by asking the student to comment on the postings of other students, especially when there are differences in opinion. However, care must be taken to draw out the diversity of viewpoints on a particular issue and to avoid narrowing in on an absolute answer which can create a confrontational atmosphere. Students are encouraged to use discussion forums to ask questions rather than e-mail. This tends to encourage a sense of openness and transparency among members in the class.

Evaluation

Two instruments have been developed to enable U21G to collect feedback from students on the learning experience after every MBA subject. These two survey-based instruments are the student evaluation of subject (SES) and student evaluation of teaching (SET). The SES is designed to capture student feedback on the quality of the courseware, and the SET is designed to capture student feedback on the quality of the instruction given by the instructor. The questions in the SES, which are more relevant to the discussion here than the SET, are shown in Table 1 together with the average score based on seven class sections of MBA 650 (with approximately 25 students per class section).

Note that the SES (and SET) is the same for all MBA subjects. The first category of questions—subject organisation—deals with how well the subject was organised including the use of tools for peer learning. The second category, subject content and workload, focuses on the quality of the content itself. The third category, subject assessment, asks students about the assessment items and methods used on the subject. Finally, students are asked about their overall opinion on the quality of the subject as a whole. After the SES and SET, students are asked about their overall level of satisfaction with the learning experience. Responses to each question are collected on a 5-point Likert scale, where 1=strongly disagree and 5=strongly agree. In addition, spaces on the survey form are provided for students to provide additional written comments.

The data collected so far indicates a high level of overall satisfaction. The aims, structure, and relevance of MBA650 were perceived very positively by students. However, two specific areas of concern relate to questions A4 and A5. The researcher suspects that the relatively low average scores for A4 and A5 might be attributed to the poor usability of the current discussion board and chat tools having a detrimental effect on the student learning experience; a number of students from other subjects

Table 1

	Average Score
A. Subject organisation	
A1 The aims of the subject were clearly articulated.	**4.6**
A2 There was a clear overview of the segments, readings, and assignments.	**4.5**
A3 The subject was structured in a way that helped me to understand.	**4.3**
A4 The various learning tools were used effectively (e.g., chat, threaded discussion, assignments).	**3.3**
A5 The peer interaction in this subject contributed to my learning.	**2.8**
B. Subject content and workload	
B1 The content of the subject was relevant to my learning needs.	**4.5**
B2 The content of the subject was engaging.	**4.3**
B3 The writing style of the subject material was clear and easy to read.	**4.4**
B4 The subject content was appropriately linked to the textbook and/or the readings.	**3.7**
B5 The textbook used in this subject was useful for my learning needs.	**4.5**
B6 The subject workload was appropriate for a reputable MBA programme.	**3.8**
C. Subject assessment	
C1 The assessment items were thought provoking and challenging.	**4.4**
C2 The relative weightings of assessment items (e.g., assignment, final project, examination, etc.) were appropriate.	**4.1**
C3 The ratio of individual to team assignments was appropriate.	**3.9**
C4 The formats for assignments and the examination in this subject were clearly explained.	**3.9**
C5 The assessment methods and feedback in this subject helped my learning.	**3.8**
C6 The assessment criteria for the assessment items in this subject were clearly delineated.	**3.9**
C7 Assessment methods were compatible with the stated learning outcomes.	**3.9**
C8 The assessment was sufficiently flexible to accommodate my learning style and nonstudy-related activities (e.g., career, family).	**3.9**
D. Overall rating	
D1 Overall, how would you rate the quality of your learning in this subject? (1= poor, 5 = excellent)	**4.3**
Overall satisfaction	
Overall, how would you rate your satisfaction level in this subject? (1 = poor, 5 = excellent)	**4.0**

had also commented on this in addition to separate e-mail communications that were received from students. The finding emphasizes the importance of usability of learning tools in an online environment and how this can act as an impediment to peer learning and learning in general.

Discussion of Experiences

E-Business Course Design

There is considerable debate about whether e-business is a new discipline warranting its own programmes or whether it should be weaved into the curriculum of existing programmes (Bartholome & Olsen, 2002). Proponents of the first approach argue that e-business represents a new approach to business that is impossible to confine within a single course. Proponents of the latter approach argue that e-business is inseparable from a broader business curriculum and relies on a sound apprecia- tion of general business methods. Interestingly, one institution decided to drop its e-business programmes after the dot-com bust but retained individual courses in e-business (Rob, 2003).

Another design issue is whether a course in e-business should have a technology or business focus (Durlabhji & Fusilier, 2002). A course that is overly technology centric may result in students who are uncomfortable with creating a business case for e-business or defining an organisation's e-business strategy. Conversely, a course that is overly business centric may result in students who know little about the design and implementation of e-business solutions.

Design Issues

The experience that U21G has gained in the development of MBA650 e-business has raised many interesting questions, reflecting a broad range of design issues. Many of these design issues are pertinent to the teaching of e-business, whether such teaching is conducted online or via a traditional classroom setting, and are discussed in Table 2.

U21G has also come to realise that the skills required of a "virtual" professor are not necessarily the same as those required of a professor conducting face-to-face teaching (Coppola, Hiltz, & Rotter, 2002). Virtual professors not only have an instructional role, but also an affective role in developing student relationships and atmosphere in the virtual classroom, and a managerial role in class and course management (Coppola et al., 2002). Development programmes designed to assist faculty in becoming a competent virtual professor therefore are important (Save- nye et al., 2001). At U21G, professors undergo a 3-week faculty training program, conducted online, that introduces them to U21G's pedagogy and good practices in online education.

Table 2

Learning outcomes	What are the overall learning outcomes, or instructional aims, for the particular e-business subject? A subject may have a number of different purposes, such as demonstrating mastery of a knowledge domain, acquiring a skill set, promoting creativity, or developing analytical and critical thinking (Mazoue, 1999). Should the learning outcomes be more oriented towards business or technology, or should they encompass both aspects and the relationship between the two? Should the outcomes be declarative in nature, providing a theoretical account of e-business concepts or should they be procedural reflecting a more applied approach? In MBA650, there is a mixture of declarative and procedural outcomes, but with a strong bias towards procedural ones. Procedural learning outcomes appear appropriate where a student is required to achieve well-defined performance outcomes.
Student audience	What is the expected profile of a student taking the e-business subject? Are the students undergraduate or graduate students? Are they required to already have a degree in business, IT, or another discipline? What type of academic programs will the e-business course be situated in? In U21G's case, the student audience is MBA students with significant work experience so the courseware and assignments have been written to challenge students' thinking at an advanced level. Also, what kind of work experience, if any, will the students be expected to have? U21G MBA students are required to have at least 2 years work experience at a managerial or supervisory level, and the course has been designed in way that allows students to bring in and share any relevant work experience. However, students may not necessarily be familiar with e-business and may be studying the subject for the first time. As such, MBA650 serves as an introductory rather than advanced presentation of e-business.
Syllabus	What should be the scope and coverage of the e-business syllabus, bearing in mind the terminal qualification, learning outcomes, and anticipated student audience? MBA students for example, will differ from IT students, and the syllabus may need to be oriented differently for students with and without work experience. In addition, how should an e-business subject be structured and organised? MBA650 e-business identifies segments on e-strategy, e-commerce, B2B commerce, B2C commerce, and e-business leadership but this is only one of many possible ways of organising the syllabus.
Key messages	What key messages should an e-business subject resonate? Potential messages include the dissection of existing value chains, the threat that e-business poses to existing brick-and-mortar businesses, and the critical importance of technology innovation in successful e-business. In addition, how differently should e-business be taught given the bursting of the dot-com bubble? In MBA650, the bursting of the dot-com bubble has been used to illustrate specific points, such as the need for sound business models and the ease at which pure-play e-business start-ups are susceptible to collapse.

Table 2 continued

Theory vs. practice	Will students be given a purely theoretical treatment of e-business concepts, or are students expected to apply theory in some practical way? If there is a practice component to the subject, how is this realised in terms of specific assignments or exercises? In the case of MBA650, we rely heavily on a case-study-based approach to ground e-business concepts in a real-world setting. However, this does not necessarily provide students with practical experience, for example, creating an e-business strategy for an organisation or managing the operations of an e-business start-up. The use of simulations appears as an ideal tool for delivering this type of experience and has been successfully used in the context of engineering education (Chung, Harmon, & Baker, 2001) and project management (Collofello, 2000).
Team working in an online setting	How can team and collaborative activities be utilised to teach e-business in an online setting? What types of activities are appropriate and will most likely lead to useful learning outcomes? In MBA650 e-business, group-case analyses are frequently used as a form of collaborative activity. Also, should teams be assigned by the professor or be self-established? In an online setting, where students may not know each other, it may be more appropriate for the professor to make the initial assignment of students into teams.
Case-study usage	Case studies appear as an effective way of teaching e-business concepts. However, to what extent should case studies be used and under what situations are they best utilised? MBA650 uses case studies extensively, typically at the end of a segment or after a set of important topics within a segment. In addition, in MBA650 e-business students typically read a case study and are then prompted to answer specific questions. An alternative mode of use would be to use the case studies as a role-playing exercise whereby team members assume roles relevant to the case study and are asked to respond to questions pertaining to that specific role.

Conclusion

This chapter has described how U21G has designed MBA650, its online course in e-business. The approach contrasts sharply with the rather primitive practice of making electronic copies of presentation slides and documents viewable online or available for downloading. Rather, an instructional design approach has been used consistent with what is understood to be best practice which encourages a high level of collaborative learning and interaction. As more universities begin to offer online academic programmes, it will be important for them to develop and implement instructional approaches that are pedagogically sound. Universities who fail to do this run the risk of student dissatisfaction and attrition, with potentially harmful effects on the reputation of the university in the long run.

References

Andrews, D. H., & Goodson, L. A. (1995). A comparative analysis of models of instructional design. In G. J. Anglin (Ed.), *Instructional technology: Past, present and future* (pp. 161-182). Englewood, CO: Libraries Unlimited.

Bartholome, L. W., & Olsen, D. (2002). A practical approach for implementing e-commerce programmes in business schools. *Communications of the ACM, 45*(1), 19-21.

Berlanger, F., & Jordon, D. H. (2000). *Evaluation and implementation of distance learning: Technologies, tools and techniques.* Hershey, PA: Idea Group Publishing.

Blignaut, S., & Trollip, S. R. (2003). Developing a taxonomy of faculty participation in asynchronous learning environments—An exploratory investigation. *Computers and Education, 41,* 149-172.

Castro, M., Lopez-Rey, A., Perez-Molina, C. M., Colmenar, A., Mora, C. D., Yeves, F., et al. (2001). Examples of distance learning projects in the European community. *IEEE Transactions on Education, 44*(4).

Chung, G. K. W. K., Harmon, T. C., & Baker, E. L. (2001). The impact of a simulation-based learning design project on student learning. *IEEE Transactions on Education, 44*(4).

Clark, J. (2001). Stimulating collaboration and discussion in online learning environments. *Internet and higher Education, 4,* 119-124.

Collofello, J. S. (2000). University/industry collaboration in developing a simulation-based software project management training course. *IEEE Transactions on Education, 43*(3).

Coppola, N. W., Hiltz, S. R., & Rotter, N. G. (2002). Becoming a virtual professor: Pedagogical roles and asynchronous learning networks. *Journal of Management Information Systems, 18*(4), 169-189.

Corner, J., & Corner, P. D. (2003). Teaching OR/MS using discussion leadership. *Interfaces, 33*(3), 60-69.

Crawford, C. (2003, January-March). Web-enhancing university coursework: An innovative professional development model to support a step-by-step approach towards Web-enhancing courses and empowering instructors. *International Journal of E-Learning.*

Davis, S., Siau, K., & Dhenuvakonda, K. (2003). A fit-gap analysis of e-business curricula vs. industry needs. *Communications of the ACM, 46*(12), 167-177.

Desanctis, G., Fayard, A., Roach, M., & Jiang, L. (2003). Learning in online forums. *European Management Journal, 21*(5), 565-577.

Drew, S. (2002). E-business research practice: Towards an agenda. *Electronic Journal of Business Research Methods, 1.*

Dringus, L. P. (2000). Towards active online learning: A dramatic shift in perspective for learning. *The Internet and Higher Education, 2*(4), 189-195.

Dringus, L. P., & Scigliano, J. A. (2001). From early to current developments in online learning at Nova South Eastern University: Reflections on historical milestones. *The Internet and Higher Education, 3*(1-2), 23-40.

Dunning, K. A., Vijayaraman, B. S., Krovi, R., & Kahai, P. S. (2001). Graduate e-business programme design and evaluation. *Journal of Computer Information Systems, 42*(1), 58-64.

Durlabhji, S., & Fusilier, M. R. (2002, January/February). Ferment in business education: E-commerce master's programmes. *Journal of Education for Business.*

Etheridge, H., Hsu, K. H. Y., & Wilson, T. E. (2001). E-business education at AACSB-affiliated business schools: A survey of programmes and curricula. *Journal of Education for Business, 76*(6), 328-331.

Evans, J. R., & Haase, I. M. (2001). Online business education in the 21st century: An analysis of potential target markets. *Internet Research: Electronic Networking Applications and Policy, 11*(3).

Hung, D., Tan, S. C., Cheung, W. S., & Hu, C. (2004). Supporting problem solving with case-stories learning scenario and video-based collaborative learning technology. *Educational Technology & Society, 7*(2), 120-128.

Johnson, S. D., Suriya, C., Yoon, S. W., Berrett, J. V., & La Fleur, J. (2002). Team development and group processes of virtual learning teams. *Computers and Education, 39,* 379-393.

King, C. G., Frank, S. L., & Platt, R. G. (2002). E-commerce courses: Overview of nature and content. *Journal of Education for Business, 76*(6).

Lam, W. (2005). Teaching tip: Encouraging online participation. *Journal of Information Systems Education, 15*(4).

Little, B. (2001). Achieving high performance through e-learning. *Industrial and Commercial Training, 33*(6), 203-207.

Masters, K., & Oberprieler, G. (2004). Encouraging equitable online participation through curriculum articulation. *Computers and Education, 42,* 319-332.

Mazoue, J. (1999). The essentials of online instruction. *Campus-Wide Information Systems, 16*(3).

Mazzolini, M., & Maddison, S. (2003). Sage, guide or ghost? The effect of instructor intervention on student participation in online discussion forums. *Computers and Education, 40,* 237-253.

McBride, N. K. (2005). A student-driven approach to teaching e-commerce. *Journal of Information Systems Education, 16*(1), 75-83.

Ngai, E. W. T., Gunaskaran, A., & Harris, A. L. (2005). The maturing of e-commerce education in our curricula. *Journal of Information Systems Education, 16*(1), 5-8.

Parikh, M. A. (2002). Knowledge acquisition through case-study development. *Communications of the Association of Information Systems, 8.*

Petrides, L. A. (2002). Web-based technologies for distributed (or distance) learning: Creating learning-centred educational experiences in the higher education classroom. *International Journal of Instructional Media, 29*(1), 69-77.

Petrova, K., & Claxton, G. (2005). Building student skills and capabilities in information technology and eBusiness: A moving target. *Journal of Information Systems Education, 16*(1), 5-8.

Pool, D. M. (2000). Student participation in a discussion-oriented online course: A case-study. *Journal of Research on Computing in Education, 33*(2), 162-177.

Rob, M. (2003). The rise and fall of an e-commerce programme. *Communications of the ACM, 46*(3), 25-26.

Salter, G. (2000). Making use of online discussion groups. *Journal of Australian Council for Computers in Education, 15*(2), 5-10.

Savenye, W. C., Olina, Z., & Niemczyk, M. (2001). So you are going to be an online writing instructor: Issues in designing, developing and delivering an online course. *Computers and Composition, 18,* 371-385.

Schooley, C. (2001). *Online universities introduce alternatives for online education.* Giga Information Group.

Schrum, L. M. (2000). Guarding the promise of online learning. *Education Digest, 66*(4), 43-47.

Smith, S. B, Smith, S. J., & Boone, R. (2000). Increasing access to teacher preparation: The effectiveness of traditional instructional methods in an online environment. *Journal of Special Education Technology, 15*(2).

Song, L., Singleton, E. S., Hill, J. R., & Myung, H. K. (2004). Improving online learning: Student perceptions of useful and challenging characteristics. *Internet and Higher Education, 7,* 59-70.

Williams, J. B. (2004). Creating authentic assessments: A method for the authoring of open book open Web examinations. *Proceedings of the 21st ASCILITE Conference, 2,* 934-937. Retrieved November 3, 2005, from http://www.ascilite.org.au/conferences/perth04/procs/williams.html

Williams, J. B. (2005). The place of the closed book, invigilated final examination in a knowledge economy. *Educational Media International, 42*(4), 375-387.

Appendix

The Context

ABC Engineering Limited is a precision engineering company that provides precision machining, fabrication, tool-making, and assembly services to a wide range of industries. The company began as a two-person business in 1971 and since then expanded to become one of Australia's largest precision engineering companies. ABC Engineering employs over 270 personnel with a turnover of A\$200 million in 2004. Over half of the company's employees are skilled tradesmen, or trades apprentices, fully capable of manufacturing parts from drawings with a minimum of supervision.

There are two core streams of business for ABC Engineering. One stream is the manufacturing and delivery of precision parts based on customer specifications. The second stream is machine maintenance, upgrade, and repair where complex machines are stripped and rebuilt. Ninety percent of ABC Engineering's customers are in the aeronautical, automotive, and naval industries.

Source: http://airy.pec.ncsu.edu/PEC/images/cryomat.jpg

New Strategic Directions for ABC Engineering

Ed Paters, the managing director for ABC Engineering, was aware that many companies had gone into e-business, some with dramatic success. However, he had noted that most of these companies were retailing companies selling standardized products like books, music CDs, and computers. Until now, Ed had resisted from going into e-business because the majority of ABC's Engineering business involved the manufacture of custom precision parts.

However, Ed's attendance at a recent trade conference made him began to think differently about e-business. At the conference, he noted that some progressive engineering companies had already moved into the e-business space, with some success. Ed managed to speak to one of the keynote speakers during the break session, who highlighted several different ways in which e-business could help a manufacturing company:

E-tailing is just one aspect of e-business. Many companies are also using the Internet to improve customer service, such as online order tracking. This is really about value-add but customer service differentiates companies from one another. B2B commerce is also another strategic avenue for manufacturing companies, where the procurement of raw materials for manufacturing can be made more streamlined and cost-effective. Some companies I know have reduced their procurement costs by 20-40%.

If ABC Engineering was to maintain its position as one of the leading and most advanced precision engineering companies, it would have to ensure that it took full advantage of the new possibilities that e-business offered. Ed asked his secretary to arrange a meeting with his senior managers to discuss his conference findings when he was back in the office.

Meeting with Senior Managers

Ed decided to use the meeting with his senior managers as a brainstorming session to generate ideas about how the company should approach the e-business market. They were aware that they needed to formulate an e-business strategy, and had read a report about some of the challenges organisations face when they embark on an e-business strategy.

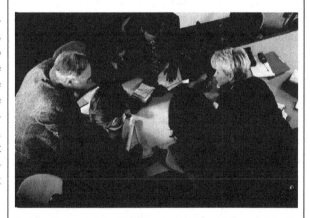

Image Source: http://office.microsoft.com/clipart/default. aspx?lc=en-us

At the meeting, several ideas were discussed. Sue Ping, director of sales and support, said e-business might be used to automate order generation and processing for regular customers whose precision parts the company already had specifications for. Sue also indicated that e-business might be used to expand the company's customer base, although was not sure how this could be best implemented. Customer service was another area of improvement, where Jon Ash, the director of customer services, indicated customers often inundated his department with telephone calls and faxes about the status of orders.

Concerns Over the Strategy

Several brainstorming sessions followed involving Ed and the senior managers. Although many ideas had emerged, there was as yet no clear cut strategy. Kathy Romm, the chief IS manager at ABC Engineering was concerned about the lack of direction:

I know that the Internet provides great potential for our business, but I just don't know what would be the best approach for us. Everyone I talk to has a different answer and no one I think quite understands how ABC can capitalise.... Sometimes I feel overwhelmed by all this talk of e-business....Everyone I speak to says the new economy is the e-economy, but I want to see a clear e-business strategy before we invest in technology solutions.

Kathy had done quite a lot of research in e-business. Although e-business provided lots of opportunities, she had come across articles that cautioned about rushing into e-business without a sound business model. ABC Engineering could not afford to make the same mistake.

Your Task

You are a consultant for a major consulting firm which has a reputation for helping organisations transform their business. You have also recently completed the MBA 650 e-business subject at Universitas 21 Global as part of your firm's continuing education program. Ed of ABC Engineering has approached your firm for advice and has asked you to help develop the company's e-business strategy.

You have agreed to analyse the company's situation and submit a discussion paper with recommendations for ABC Engineering's strategic direction. In your paper, you will evaluate the present situation and suggest ways the company can move forward. Your report will identify the potential opportunities and threats faced by the company and the industry as a whole. The focus should be on the e-business strategy.

Guide to the Task

You have discussed the matter with other senior colleagues within the firm, and, among other things, they recommend that you:

- Analyse the features and functions of relevant existing Web sites and identify the e-business models used. For example, what transactional capabilities do they provide, and do they compete or complement brick-and-mortar business models?

- Identify key areas of improvement and growth for the company. How would undertaking an e-business initiative support the company's mission?

- Describe the building blocks of your recommended e-business model and justify your recommendations.

- Highlight the core competencies and critical success factors of your new strategic e-business initiative.

Chapter XI

E-Recruiting System Development and Architecture

In Lee, Western Illinois University, USA

Abstract

At this time of hyper-competition and rapid environmental changes, one of the most critical sources of competitive advantage is to attract and retain talented workers. E-recruiting is one of the most rapidly growing e-commerce areas. Since the mid-1990s, a number of e-recruiting methods such as job boards, corporate career Web sites, and e-recruiting consortia have been introduced into the labor market. Recruiting through corporate career Web sites has been touted as the most efficient and cost-effective recruiting method. While most of large- and medium-sized organizations have deployed corporate career Web sites, many of them have failed to achieve the maximum benefits because they do not have the appropriate architecture and business practice in place. While e-recruiting methods have been widely used since the mid-1990s, no formal classification system has been developed for a wide variety of e-recruiting sources. This study proposes six categories of e-recruiting sources and presents the architecture of the next-generation, holistic e-recruiting system. This architecture consists of eight distinct yet interrelated subsystems: (1) applicant tracking management subsystem; (2) job requisition management subsystem; (3)

job agent management subsystem; (4) prescreening/self-assessment management subsystem; (5) e-recruiting performance analysis subsystem; (6) candidate relationship management subsystem; (7) workflow management subsystem; and (8) database management subsystem.

Introduction

One of the most profound changes of the past decade in the business environment was the emergence of e-commerce that revolutionized the way companies conduct business. As a part of the e-commerce revolution, Web-based online recruiting has also changed the way companies hire employees. Currently, Web-based online recruiting (e-recruiting) is one of the most successful e-commerce applications as a method for quickly reaching a large pool of potential job seekers. E-recruiting has enjoyed explosive growth since the late 1990s when the strong economy produced a high demand for qualified employees that the labor market could not satisfy (Thomas & Ray, 2000). E-recruiting has driven companies to redesign the recruiting process and to move quickly to Web-based integrated human resource systems that provide standardized frameworks for key personnel processes (Cullen, 2001). The capability of advanced e-recruiting tools enables recruiters to quickly identify and hire qualified candidates and to build ongoing relationships with prospective employees.

Major advantages cited for the rapid and successful adoption of e-recruiting methods include cost savings, efficiency, and convenience for both recruiters and job seekers (Gale, 2001; Miller, 2001; Tomlinson, 2002). In a poll in 2001 of 400 recruiters by Recruiters Network (www.recruitersnetwork.com), 46% indicated that online recruiting was the most effective way to get the most hires and best resumes, followed by referrals (35%), and newspaper classifieds (11%).

According to Forrester Research, the average cost to hire an employee via the Internet is $183, whereas the average cost to hire an employee via traditional methods (i.e., newspapers or magazines) is $1,383. Forrester Research predicts that corporate recruiters will increase their e-recruiting budget by 52% by 2004, while cutting their budget on traditional recruitment by 31%. Forrester Research estimates the e-recruiting market size to be between $2 billion and $4 billion by 2005.

There has been a fundamental shift in the way companies use e-recruiting methods since its inception in the mid-1990s. While most companies utilize at least one third-party job board, more and more companies are creating their own corporate career Web sites. According to iLogos' research, 29% of Global 500 companies had corporate career Web sites and 57% subscribed to third-party job boards in 1998. In 2002, that figure had changed to 91% and 9%, respectively.

E-recruiting has fundamentally changed corporate recruiting processes from batch mode into continuous mode. Traditional recruiting processes are typically paper-based and characterized by numerous hard-copy forms, hand-written signatures, and internal and external communications performed in a batch mode throughout the hiring process. The traditional recruiting process, while still working in most industries, suffers from a long hiring cycle time, high cost per hire, low advertisement coverage, and ineffective candidate management. E-recruiting improves the recruiters' ability to handle job applications and job postings by minimizing paperwork and automating key recruiting activities. Due to the round-the-clock collection of job applications and a continuous recruiting process, microrecruiting and on-demand recruiting became practical and reduced the hiring cycle time significantly. As an example of anecdotal evidence, e-recruiting enabled Dow Chemical to reduce their hiring cycle from 90 days to 34 (Gill, 2001). Dow Chemical was also able to drop costs per hire by 26%. Dow Chemical no longer accepts paper job applications from professional workers residing in the United States. They hire all new salaried workers, who are typically knowledge workers, from a pool of candidates who submitted applications online via either its career Web site or third-party job boards.

While early adopters achieved a short-term competitive advantage by reaching a broader pool of qualified candidates in times of labor shortage, they could hardly create a sustainable competitive advantage. Why are e-recruiting technologies alone not the source of sustainable competitive advantage? Barney (1991) suggested that advantage-creating resources must have four conditions: (1) value, (2) rareness, (3) inimitability, and (4) nonsubstitutability. E-recruiting technologies are now widely available in the form of in-house systems or integrated off-the-shelf software packages. As e-recruiting technologies become commoditized and easily substitutable, early adopters' advantage will be rapidly eroded. Companies that constantly create unique value through superior management skills, innovation, and business process re-engineering are likely to enjoy sustainable competitive advantage.

In summary, we believe that standardized technology infrastructure and system integration are two prerequisites for a seamless exchange of data between the recruiting and other human resource processes. New technological developments in Web standards such as HR-XML and Web Services are quickly integrated into the e-recruiting tools. These new technologies improve the interoperability and communication between legacy human resources applications and new e-HR systems. If clear technological architecture has not been established, it is difficult to fully realize the e-recruiting potential. Having established a comprehensive architecture, companies can then undertake development and integration of various e-recruiting technologies that are likely to lead to their desired results.

The main purposes of this study are to investigate the evolution of e-recruiting systems and to develop a comprehensive e-recruiting architecture for a corporate career Web site. This study proceeds as follows: Section 2 of this study discusses six major categories of e-recruiting source. Section 3 classifies the evolution of e-recruiting systems into five stages and discusses what Fortune 100 companies belong to each stage. Section 4 presents the architecture of the corporate career Web site that takes into consideration both recruiting processes and technologies. Section 5 illustrates the relevance of the architecture to the e-recruiting project with a case study of DaimlerChrysler. Finally, the last section concludes with managerial implications, limitations, and future research directions of this study.

Categories of E-Recruiting Source

While e-recruiting methods have been widely used since the mid-1990s, no formal classification system has been developed for different e-recruiting sources. In order to give recruiters and job seekers a better understanding of the e-recruiting industry, we propose six categories of e-recruiting sources: (1) general purpose job board, (2) niche job board, (3) e-recruiting application service provider, (4) hybrid (online and off-line) recruiting service provider, (5) e-recruiting consortium, and (6) corporate career Web site. Table 1 summarizes six categories of the e-recruiting sources from recruiters' perspectives.

Disintermediation refers to eliminating middlemen/distributors in the supply chain to sell products/services directly to consumers. Examples include Maytag selling home appliances directly to individual customers and Delta Airline selling airline tickets directly to travelers. E-recruiting also enabled companies to disintermediate conventional recruiting firms and newspapers' classified ads by posting job openings directly on their career Web sites. While disintermediation threatened conventional recruiting media, a third-party job board emerged as a new e-recruiting intermediary between recruiters and job seekers.

General-purpose job boards provide a comprehensive online recruiting solution to both employers and job seekers across different industries. Monster, HotJobs, and Careerbuilder are leaders in this category. Job seekers can search for jobs by category, experience, education, location, or any combination of these job attributes. Most of the leading job boards employ agent technology to increase utility to job seekers and recruiters. Personalized job agents match job seekers' profiles with the latest job postings and e-mail the list of jobs to the job seekers. Recruiters can search the job boards' database by skills, experience level, job preference, salary, education, and any combination of keywords to find qualified candidates. When qualified job applicants are available, the recruiter's job agent notifies the recruiter of a list of available applicants. To address job seekers and recruiters' rising dissatisfaction with services and costs, general-purpose job boards have evolved into comprehensive career services where customized placement services, assessment, and candidate relationship management are provided.

Table 1. Summary of six categories of the e-recruiting sources: Recruiters' perspectives

E-Recruiting source	Advantages	Disadvantages	Sample participants
General-Purpose job board	Brand recognition; E-Recruiting Experience; High traffic; Industry best tools; Large candidate base; Large recruiter base	Relatively high job posting cost; Potentially low-quality applications; Limited content control; Stickiness of the job board; Limited candidate relationship	Monster.com; HotJobs.com; CareerBuilder.com
Niche job board	Gathering of passive job seekers; Focused search; Community of professionals	Low brand recognition; Possibility of identity theft	Dice.com; Erexchange.com; Taonline.com; JournalismJobs.com; MarketingJobs.com; TexasJobs.com
E-Recruiting application service provider	Low application development cost for recruiters; Quick application development	Integration issues with existing systems; Possibility of closeout due to competition; Possibility of lock-in; Low traffic	Recruitsoft; Brassring; RecruitUSA; PeopleClick; TalentFusion; Lawson
Hybrid recruiting service providers	Expertise in advertising industry; Portfolio of recruiting media; Price bundling with conventional media	Strong image as a conventional media; Low traffic; Low technology	*New York Times, Wall Street; Chronicle of Higher Education*
E-Recruiting consortium	Low service cost; Direct and immediate link to corporate career site	Potential conflicts among members; Low exposure; Low technology	DirectEmployers.com; NACElink
Corporate career Web site	Candidate relationship management; High interests in jobs by job applicants; Integration with exiting systems	Needs for IT specialists; High upfront development cost	94 percent of Fortune 100 companies; 81 percent of Fortune 500 companies

Niche job boards serve highly specialized job markets such as particular profession, industry, education, location, or any combination of these specialties. Sample profession-oriented job boards include JournalismJobs.com, MarketingJobs.com, AllRetailJobs.com, and JobsInLogistics.com. Location-oriented job boards include NJ.com, TexasJobs.com, and ArizonaJobs.com. The advantage of the niche job boards is a focused search with which recruiters can reach a large pool of qualified candidates most effectively. Most niche job boards operate specialized online communities or newsgroups that draw professionals such as engineers, programmers, and journalists who share specific interests, skills, experience, and knowledge.

Job boards generate revenue by providing recruiters with an applicant tracking service, hiring tools, job posting, career Web site hosting, prescreening tools, and advertisements. As the success of job boards depends on the critical mass of job applicants, job boards typically provide job seekers with free access to the services. Advanced services such as resume writing and interview guides may be accessible to job seekers at a charge. Advantages of using job boards include an access to a large pool of recruiters and job seekers and the availability of state-of-the-art e-recruiting tools. Medium- and small-sized recruiters with low name recognition can access a pool of qualified job applicants at a reasonable cost.

Because of the ease of entry into the e-recruiting market and tight labor market, general purpose and niche job boards overcrowded the e-recruiting industry in the late 1990s and went through a series of mergers and acquisitions in the early 2000s. TMP, a parent company of Monster, acquired FlipDog, the high-profile company in search technology, in 2001. CareerBuilder acquired CareerPath in 2000 and Head-hunter.net in 2001 to gain competitive advantage in the general-purpose job board market. Yahoo! acquired HotJobs, resulting in HotJobs becoming a wholly-owned subsidiary of Yahoo!

E-recruiting application service providers (ASPs) develop and market to recruiters and job boards a combination of specialized services in recruitment software, recruitment process management, education and training, and management expertise. The tight labor market for IT professionals has led many small- and medium-sized recruiters to ASPs. Specialized recruitment software for the in-house development of larger-scale e-recruiting Web sites is available for recruiters who want to quickly develop career Web sites on their own server. Some service providers also support the hosting of corporate career Web sites. Some widely known e-recruiting ASPs include Recruitsoft, BrassRing, RecruitUSA, PeopleClick, TalentFusion, Lawson, and Development Dimensions International Inc. These e-recruiting ASPs are competing with larger enterprise system developers such as Oracle, PeopleSoft, and SAP which also have developed recruiting software as part of enterprise-wide human resource systems.

Hybrid recruiting service providers are traditional media or recruiting firms which provide e-recruiting services to both recruiters and job seekers. Employment advertising in newspapers has suffered historic percentage declines as recruiters switch to more efficient and cost-effective recruiting methods. The Help Wanted Index, a measurement of how many help wanted ads run in newspapers, has registered a continuous decline in the past few years. In the face of losing significant revenue sources, media organizations such as *New York Times, Chronicle of Higher Education,* and the *Wall Street Journal* now provide e-recruiting services as well as paper-based job advertisement services in order to compensate for the job ad revenue lost due to the rapid expansion of alternative e-recruiting services.

Traditional media companies have reduced job ad prices and introduced new services to differentiate themselves from job boards and corporate career Web sites. The *New York Times* now offers a variety of e-recruiting services including resume builders, search engines, and job market research reports to both employers and job seekers. CareerJournal.com developed by the *Wall Street Journal,* focuses exclusively on the career needs of executives, managers, and professionals, leveraging the *Wall Street Journal* brand. CareerJournal.com provides recruiters and job seekers with a database of job openings and resumes as well as salary information, career news, and industry trends. Advantage of the hybrid (online and off-line) recruiting service provider comes from the sharing of existing resources and expertise developed in the traditional job ad industry. The premier content of CareerJournal.com comes from the editorial resources of the *Wall Street Journal* as well as from the Career-Journal.com editorial team.

E-recruiting consortium is a cost-effective alternative to the services provided by job boards. DirectEmployers.com is the first cooperative, employer-owned e-recruiting consortium formed by DirectEmployers Association—a nonprofit organization formed by executives from leading U.S. corporations. According to a recent press release by Recruiters Network (February 20, 2003), DirectEmployers Association achieved a 500% increase in membership in just one year since its launch in February 2002. At the time of this study, DirectEmployers Association has 98 member companies approximately 45% of which are Fortune 500 companies. While job boards place much importance on the stickiness of their Web sites because job seekers who stay longer will have a greater chance of reading employment opportunities, DirectEmployers' search engine merely drives traffic directly to a member's career Web site. A vast majority of members reported that DirectEmployers.com is driving more traffic to their Web sites than any job boards.

NACElink is another e-recruiting consortium that was created as a result of an alliance between DirectEmployers Association and the National Association of Colleges and Employers (NACE) (http://www.naceweb.org). NACElink—a national, integrated, Web-based college recruiting system—was designed to better meet the placement and recruiting needs of colleges, students, and employers. At the time of this study, 137 colleges use the NACElink system, and more colleges are joining daily. Cost saving was the greatest incentive for forming NACElink. For example, depending on the company size, members of DirectEmployers Association pay annual dues of $6,000 to $60,000, which is only a fraction of job ad costs paid to job boards.

Corporate career Web site is the most widely used hiring source used by Fortune 500 companies (iLogos Research, 2000). While the majority of companies (64%) used a combination of job boards and their career Web sites to advertise openings, they posted more jobs on their Web sites than on job boards. On average, corporate career Web sites listed 184 jobs compared to 118 on CareerBuilder, 99 on Monster, and 37 on HotJobs. Deployment of the corporate career Web site is a natural extension of the portfolio of e-commerce applications when the company has already established an e-commerce Web site and enjoyed high Internet traffic. The exposure of the career Web site to visitors is almost as great as the exposure of the home page as long as the home page has the career information with a hyperlink to the Web site. The cost of posting additional job openings is marginally increased, whereas, fees for posting additional job openings are considerably higher at job boards. Career Web sites also have cost advantages and flexibility when compared to job boards in publishing corporate information such as university recruiting, workplace, diversity, benefit, career, and culture with which applicants can make informed decisions about job applications. Considering the significant impact of the corporate career Web site on the corporate recruiting strategy, the following section focuses on the evolution of the corporate career Web site.

Five-Stage Evolution of E-Recruiting Systems

In this section, we classify the evolution of corporate career Web systems into five stages. E-recruiting systems have evolved through numerous technological developments since their introduction in the mid-1990s. Our recent survey shows that Fortune 100 companies are in various stages of development. At the early stage of corporate e-recruiting systems, the purpose of the career Web site was to simply post job openings on the static Web page for job seekers' information. As the e-commerce technologies advance and recruiters gain more e-recruiting experience, the front-end e-recruiting systems add new features and functions, target job seekers better, and integrate with a back-end human resource management system. An advanced e-recruiting system of large companies has been powered by an enterprise-wide system and incorporated best practice recruiting methodologies to achieve strategic advantage. In the following, we discuss what technological and managerial changes characterize each stage of the e-recruiting system. Table 2 summarizes five stages of the e-recruiting systems.

Stage 1 Information Delivery E-Recruiting System

Stage 1 Information Delivery E-Recruiting System simply posts job opening or contact information on the corporate Web site. It is an inexpensive solution to recruiting because of its simple technical features, low implementation cost, and limited functions. Job seekers can simply click on the button/hyperlinks to a Web page containing a list of jobs or contact information. Information delivered is static in nature, and updates can be time-consuming and error-prone.

Table 2. Summary of five stages of the e-recruiting systems

Stage	Technology features	Management practices	The number of fortune 100 companies*
Stage 1 Information delivery e-recruiting system	Static HTML code; E-mail; Fax	Priority on conventional media; Use of third-party job boards	10
Stage 2 Search engine e-recruiting system	Query languages; Centralized job database	Focus on process automation	43
Stage 3 Job agent e-recruiting system	Applicant tracking; Job requisition system; Agent technology; Job basket	Focus on technology applications; Focus on streamlining processes	36
Stage 4 Decision support e-recruiting system	Prescreening/self-assessment tool; Recruiting performance analysis tool	Focus on decision making of recruiters and job applicants; Focus on financial/operational efficiency	5
Stage 5 Holistic e-recruiting system	Candidate relationship management system; workflow management systems;	Strategic use of e-recruiting; Emphasis on system integration/standardization; Employees as human asset; Long-term candidate relationship	0

Note. Six companies did not have corporate career Web sites, but subscribed to third-party job boards for recruiting

Submitting job applications via regular mail and hard copy is encouraged and online job application is limited to an e-mail application. Client side scripting languages and HTML are the dominant languages used to develop the stage 1 e-recruiting system. Currently, AmerisourceBergen, Alberston's, Kmart, and Costco are among 10 Fortune 100 companies in stage 1. Given the widespread adoption of e-recruiting, it is surprising that six Fortune 100 companies have not yet deployed stage 1 e-recruiting systems yet.

Stage 2 Search Engine E-Recruiting System

Stage 2 Search Engine E-Recruiting System includes the stage 1 features and functions. Stage 2 e-recruiting system provides a site search engine for both recruiters and job seekers to expedite the complex job search and candidate search. Interactive search engine helps job seekers compare multiple jobs available based on category, location, experience, types, or any combination of keywords. Data about job seekers are collected through the use of online application forms or resume builders and analyzed for candidate profiling. A personalized search engine is easily configured based on the individual preference and accessed with a user ID and password. As companies collect data about job applicants and link internal databases to the career Web site, concerns over security and privacy emerge as important issues to be addressed. For example, unless the recruiter is a reputable company, job seekers are likely to be wary of fraudulent job postings aimed at stealing personal identities.

Technology behind the search engine is a server-side database management system and database query languages. The recruiters' search engine performs a keyword search on resumes collected online, matches qualifications with the hiring criteria, and yields a list of the best candidates for the job. While the search engine makes the job search and candidate search more efficient, and the update of candidate profiles and job openings is more dynamic, the search engine e-recruiting system is quantity oriented in that a lot of disqualified job applicants can easily flood the corporate career database with resumes. Forty-three Fortune 100 companies including Pfizer and Wal-Mart Stores are in stage 2.

Stage 3 Search Agent E-Recruiting System

In addition to the support of stage 2 functions, Stage 3 Search Agent E-Recruiting System provides advanced job agents for both job seekers and recruiters. While a stage 2 search engine pulls information on job openings and candidates, search agent pushes information to job seekers and recruiters based on predefined criteria. For example, personalized job agent periodically or continuously searches job openings with predefined criteria and notifies candidates of job availability when jobs are identified that match their qualifications.

Job seekers and recruiters can stay informed of all opportunities without searching the job database themselves. Search agent is a critical tool for recruiters who want to build an active ongoing relationship with qualified job seekers whose jobs are not currently available, but are likely to be available in the future. Stage 3 search agent e-recruiting system also supports a job basket tool for simultaneous applications for multiple jobs available in the company. Thirty-six Fortune 100 companies have implemented job agent technology including AT&T, Bank of America, and Target Corporation.

Stage 4 Decision Support E-Recruiting System

In addition to the support of stage 3 functions, Stage 4 Decision Support E-Recruiting System facilitates decision making for job seekers and recruiters by providing an array of decision support tools that perform customized analyses and create reports. The technologies used to support decision making include Web-based prescreening, self-assessment tools, applicant tracking tools, and data warehousing. Decision support e-recruiting system enables job seekers to find a match with target jobs with the help of an online self-assessment tool before submitting applications. Online self-assessment tools help job seekers determine what areas they should target and what they should improve.

Recruiters also utilize decision support tools to narrow down a pool of candidates and to perform an analysis of the candidate's match with jobs based on the applicants' response to prescreening questionnaires. When job seekers apply for a job, the online application procedure leads applicants to fill out a prescreening questionnaire that helps the recruiters and hiring managers determine early in the candidate selection process whether job applicants are qualified or not. While the previous three stages focus on the efficiency of the e-recruiting system, stage 4 e-recruiting system emphasizes the effectiveness of the recruiting system and requires intense involvement of hiring managers in the decision support tool development. Despite the potential benefits of the decision support e-recruiting system, only five Fortune 100 companies have adopted this technology, including Ford, HP, and Bank One.

Stage 5 Holistic E-Recruiting System

The purpose of Stage 5 Holistic E-Recruiting System is to leverage an e-recruiting system to increase the value of corporate human asset to the maximum extent possible. To this end, stage 5 holistic e-recruiting system supports candidate relationship management, streamlines complex interrelated recruiting activities, and integrates the recruiting process with other human resource processes in the enterprise-wide systems environment. Candidate relationship management program promotes a two-way, long-term relationship between employers and prospective employees. Prospective employees include passive applicants who are currently employed but may have interests in the new job opportunities in the future. In the holistic e-recruiting system approach, the corporate career Web site is the center of online and off-line recruiting activities and a single data entry point to all recruiting sources.

Holistic e-recruiting system is in its infancy in 2003. While leading companies understand the strategic value of this holistic e-recruiting system in achieving competitive advantage, none of them have fully adopted it yet. The development of the holistic system would be very complicated and confusing without a comprehensive e-recruiting plan and technology architecture in place. We expect that further advances in Web-based technologies and experience with best practices will accelerate the adoption of the holistic e-recruiting system.

Even though stage 5 system is the most advanced and effective one among the five systems, it is the most expensive and complex system. Choosing the e-recruiting system that best fits the company's needs depends on many variables such as company size, IT infrastructure, size of job openings, target job seekers, job categories, location, and so forth. For instance, given the trade-offs between function and cost, stage 5 holistic system may not be the best choice for some small/medium-sized companies with only a few hiring needs a year.

When a company decides to develop a certain e-recruiting system, they should perform a thorough feasibility analysis of alternative system development methods including in-house development and e-recruiting ASPs. E-recruiting ASPs are rapidly growing because of low service costs and a suite of online tools readily available to recruiters. According to IDC research (2001), the top 10 worldwide e-recruiting service providers collectively achieved their revenue growth rate of 232% between 1999 and 2000. As ASPs continue to compete for leading positions in the services market, they create partnerships between them and move toward interoperable component-based systems.

An Architecture of Holistic E-Recruiting System for Corporate Career Web Sites

As discussed in the previous section, a holistic e-recruiting system is an integrated system that will bring a significant payoff to adopting companies. While sound architecture is critical to the successful development of complex systems and seamless integration with other systems, it has not been well established yet for the holistic e-recruiting system because of its infancy stage. The architecture helps recruiters and system developers understand how various components of the e-recruiting system work together to achieve recruiting goals. In this light, this section presents a high-level architecture of the holistic e-recruiting system for corporate career Web sites. Since the architecture is a roadmap to the development of the e-recruiting system that supports the recruiting process, understanding e-recruiting process is required in order to better identify architectural components. In this section, we first focus our discussion on the traditional recruiting process, the e-recruiting process, and their differences. Since companies use many different methods to recruit employees, it would be almost impossible to identify all tasks in the recruiting process across different companies. Therefore, we focus on common tasks that are essential across different companies.

The traditional recruiting process consists of the following iterative phases: (1) identification of hiring needs; (2) submission of job requisition and approval; (3) job posting; (4) submission of job applications; (5) screening of resume/application; (6) interviewing; (7) pre-employment screening; and (8) job offer and employment contract. Both hiring managers and recruiters rely on hard-copy documents and signatures to move things between various phases of the recruiting process. The traditional process has been fraught with task delays and miscommunications, which results in a long hiring process and high hiring costs. Timing is generally viewed as being important in the recruiting process (Barber, 1998). With regard to timing issues in recruitment, Rynes, Bretz, and Gerhart (1991) reported that job applicants frequently drew negative inference about the delays of the recruiting process and delays affected the willingness of individuals to accept job offers.

Computers were used in the traditional recruiting process even before the introduction of e-recruiting. However, computer applications were limited to the automation of internal processes; software packages could not communicate with each other, and the quantity and quality of job applications remained the same. Even with the computer applications, most recruiting processes were still batch processes. E-recruiting systems moved the computer application of the recruiting process to a higher level. It is a Web-enabled, anytime, anyplace, ubiquitous system to job seekers and recruiters.

The e-recruiting process consists of the following iterative steps: (1) identification of hiring needs; (2) submission of job requisition and approval via a job database; (3) job posting on the Internet; (4) online search of the job database by job seekers; (5) online prescreening/online self-assessment; (6) submission of applications by applicants directly into an applicant database; (7) online search of the applicant database for candidate selection; (8) online evaluation of resume/application; (9) interviewing by recruiters/hiring managers; (10) online pre-employment screening; and (11) job offer and employment contract.

While e-recruiting goes through the same phases as the traditional process, the benefits of e-recruiting are accomplished with the extensive use of a central database and an array of Web-enabled integrated applications. Given the complexity of an integrated system, it is essential to create an architecture that will guide the development of interrelated components that support the e-recruiting phases and other human resource processes. Our recent survey of major ASPs indicates that no single vendors provide a comprehensive architecture for the holistic e-recruiting system.

The architecture of the holistic e-recruiting system consists of eight distinct yet interrelated subsystems: (1) applicant tracking management subsystem; (2) job requisition management subsystem; (3) job agent management subsystem; (4) prescreening/self-assessment management subsystem; (5) e-recruiting performance analysis subsystem; (6) candidate relationship management subsystem; (7) workflow management subsystem; and (8) database management subsystem. Figure 1 shows the relationships between e-recruiting processes and the eight components of the holistic e-recruiting system.

Figure 1. Interrelationships between e-recruiting processes and architecture of the holistic e-recruiting system

E- Recruiting Process   **A Component-based Architecture of the Holistic E-Recruiting System**

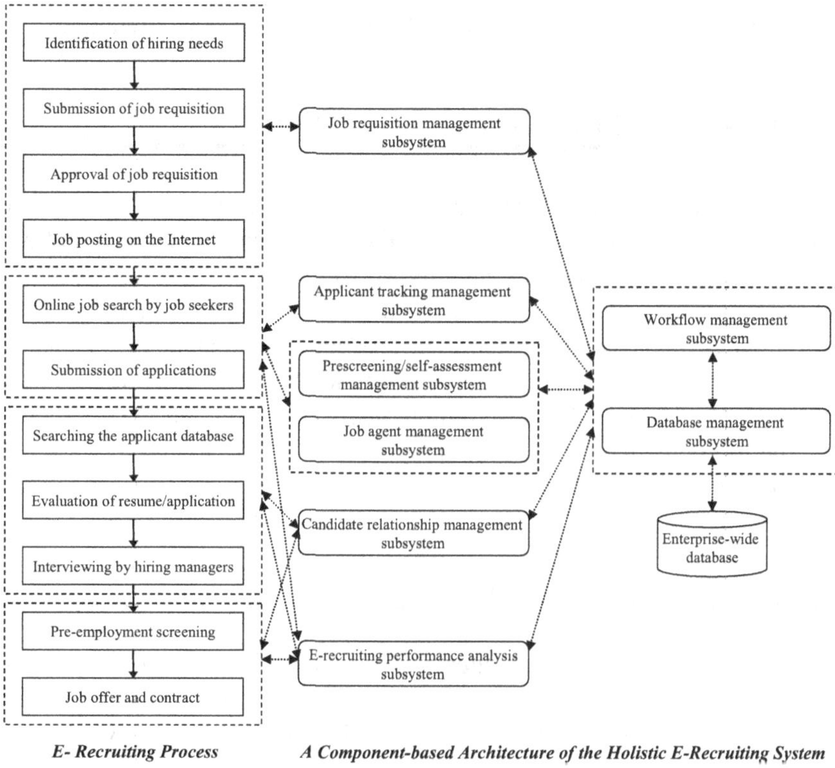

Applicant Tracking Management Subsystem

Finding the right candidates for a particular job is a difficult and costly task for recruiters and hiring managers. Functions of an applicant tracking management subsystem include gathering job applications, storing candidate profile resumes, checking the status of each candidate in the recruiting process, generating requested information for decision makers, and disseminating the information to other human resource management systems. Primary users are job seekers, recruiters, and hiring managers. Job seekers use this system to search for jobs, post a resume, apply for jobs online, and update a resume and profile.

The fundamental technology for applicant tracking is a Web-based search engine, which scans through the applicant database based on keywords, phrases, or natural languages. Once the database search is complete, the requested information, ranked according to the fit between applicants' qualifications and job requirements, is reported to recruiters and hiring managers. The applicant tracking management subsystem, which is an efficiency-oriented technology, enables organizations to evaluate applicants as quickly and precisely as possible against current job openings.

Job Requisition Management Subsystem

The primary function of the job requisition management subsystem is to streamline job requisitions and online postings. Users of the job requisition management system are recruiters and hiring managers. Submission of job requisition and approval can be processed without a manual data entry into a job database when integrated with a human resource management system. The job requisition management subsystem is a single automated job posting point to multiple recruiting sites such as internal career Web sites, external job boards, and industry consortia. During the recruiting process, the job requisition management subsystem allows managers to regularly monitor current job postings and close job postings as they are filled or canceled.

Job Agent Management Subsystem

The purpose of the job agent management subsystem is to promote information exchange between e-recruiting users and e-recruiting systems by using a personalized search agent. Creation of the personalized job agent is interactive, leading to creation of a unique profile. For job seekers, a job agent can perform a particular search based on job search and communication parameters such as job locations, job categories, and the frequency of job search. Based on the job agent's notification, job seekers may apply for jobs online or ignore them. Recruiters specify, to the personalized job agent, the duration of the job postings, frequency of the candidate search, and mode of notification. Then, according to the prespecified profile, the job agent searches for candidates who match the job requirements and notifies the recruiters of the list of candidates, ranked according to the degree of the matches.

Prescreening/Self-Assessment Management Subsystem

The purpose of the prescreening/self-assessment management subsystem is to assess the degree of match between their qualifications and job requirements at the time of online job applications. One of the lingering problems with e-recruiting is the phenomenal growth of job applications by job seekers who can easily submit job applications to multiple companies simultaneously. To improve the overall quality of job applicants, prescreening/self-assessment management system minimizes the submission of job applications from job seekers who do not meet basic job require-ments. For certain job categories, the prescreening helps recruiters sort through a pool of resumes and rank them based on a predefined scoring system.

In addition to administering a variety of questionnaires to job seekers, the prescreen-ing/self-assessment management subsystem provides recruiters with an array of questionnaire development tools. The choice of the questionnaire item is crucial to the success of this subsystem. As a basic requirement, the questionnaire should include question items that are hard to capture from the resume. Commonly used question items include levels of technical skills, personalities, interpersonal skills, work ethics, and aptitude. The process of the prescreening/self-assessment tests is interactive and has an option of "exit any time without completion."

E-Recruiting Performance Analysis Subsystem

The purpose of e-recruiting performance analysis subsystem is to analyze the strategic, financial, and operational performances of an e-recruiting system in order to improve the overall efficiency and effectiveness of the career Web site. Table 3 summarizes major metrics used at leading companies. Performance reports are generated based on a predefined report format and real-time data. As each user has unique reporting requirements, this subsystem should provide recruiters with an easy-to-use report generator equipped with a variety of reporting options. The performance analysis subsystem should be able to alert managers of an exceptional situation when certain performance measure does not meet thresholds defined by managers.

Table 3. Metrics of e-recruiting performance measures

Category	Suggested metrics
Strategic	The number of online applicants; The ratio of qualified applicants; Aggregate profile of online applicants; Time to hire; Quality of online job information; Satisfaction level of job applicants and recruiters with the e-recruiting system; The number of passive job seekers; Compliance on EEO
Operational	Efficiency of various phases of e-recruiting process; Tool utilization rate; The number of page views; Click-through rate; Time to access a company career Web site; Time to search jobs; Quantity of online job information
Financial	Cost per hire; System acquisition cost; Web site operating expense; Cost savings in recruiting

Candidate Relationship Management Subsystem

The purpose of the candidate relationship management subsystem is to provide recruiters with long-term relationship management programs/tools needed to effectively manage applicants. One of the disadvantages of the e-recruiting method is a lack of physical human touch such as face-to-face meeting or conference call. The candidate relationship management is designed to provide applicants with a feeling that they have an ongoing relationship with the company through a "virtual human touch." Delivering a maximum level of virtual human touch will increase the chance of job acceptance by candidates by implicitly indicating how attractive job opportunities at the company might be.

Widely used techniques that enhance virtual human touch include an e-mail reminder on follow-up activities, invitation to company events, personalized e-newsletters, coupons, online chat room, quick response to online inquiry, online seminars on various job-related topics, and so forth. The rationale behind the use of candidate relationship management subsystem is that maintaining the best pool of job applicants at all times is faster and more cost effective than starting to find new job applicants when jobs are available. Given the widespread adoption of the various e-recruiting technologies in the job market, only companies with a positive long-term relationship with job applicants will gain a competitive edge.

Workflow Management Subsystem

While each of the previously mentioned six subsystems support the e-recruiting process partially, the workflow management system integrates these subsystems to support the entire e-recruiting activity. Given the complicated interactions among various phases of the recruiting process and the many people involved, without a proper workflow management in place, companies can easily lose control of the e-recruiting process, resulting in process delays and miscommunications.

The workflow management subsystem enables interrelated subsystems to collaborate around the e-recruiting activities and to integrate with other human resource management systems. For example, once job applicants have entered their resume/profiles in response to a job opening, workflow management system triggers the applicant tracking subsystem for candidate screening, and a job agent sends a list of candidates meeting the desired requirements to hiring managers for further actions. A minimized human intervention in the information exchange improves information quality and decision making. The workflow management subsystem may invoke other subsystems such as a candidate relationship management or prescreening/self-assessment management subsystems to conduct predefined tasks. The potential value of workflow management system is currently regarded as the driving force behind the standardization of e-recruiting processes.

Database Management Subsystem

The holistic e-recruiting system stores all the data on jobs and applicants in a centralized database. During the traditional batch-mode recruiting process, once recruiting is complete, paper-based applications and resumes are kept in the file cabinet for a predefined period of time and thrown away. Later, when a new job is available, another recruiting cycle begins with a new collection of job applications. E-recruiting has changed the recruiting practice from batch mode to ongoing recruiting. Database management subsystem stretches the life of application and resume data almost indefinitely. In addition, the separation of all other subsystems and a database via the database management subsystem leads to the minimization of redundant data in the database.

Many companies encourage job seekers to submit applications and resumes online regardless of the current job availability, store the applications and resumes at the centralized database for a considerable period of time, and evaluate a pool of job applicants stored in the database as soon as a new job is available. Types of data stored in the database include applicant profile, resume, job skill, job requisition data, and various recruiting activities. As the size of the recruiting database increases, the design of database structure becomes more important, because of the rapid increase in the database search time.

A Holistic E-Recruiting:
A Case of DaimlerChrysler

In this section, we illustrate the holistic e-recruiting system with a case study of DaimlerChrysler. We collected data and information on DaimlerChrysler's e-recruiting activities from company press releases and other journal sources. As the e-commerce revolutionized all internal and external processes in the automotive industry, DaimlerChrysler viewed this development as a unique opportunity for the company to improve its competitive position on the international market and undertook decisive measures in this direction. "DaimlerChrysler fully intends to seize and rapidly exploit the enormous competitive advantages of its professionally run e-business," says Jürgen E. Schrempp CEO DaimlerChrysler. Currently, the underpin of DaimlerChrysler's e-business development is DCX NET Initiative, which started in October 2000 for networking of the company across the entire value-added chain.

Background

DaimlerChrysler is one of the world's leading automotive companies. Its passenger car brands include Mercedes-Benz, Chrysler, Jeep®, Dodge, and Smart. Commercial vehicle brands include Mercedes-Benz, Freightliner, Sterling, Western Star, and Setra. It offers financial and other automotive services through DaimlerChrysler Services. With 365,600 employees, DaimlerChrysler achieved revenues of $158.8 billion in 2002. In order to advance the transformation into a comprehensively networked company, DaimlerChrysler consolidated all its existing and future e-business investments and holdings in the newly founded subsidiary DCX NET holding in October 2000. The holding, which was launched with start-up capital of $500 million, formed the framework of the enterprise-wide DCX NET Initiative.

The DCX NET research team is a key player in the development of new e-business strategies at DaimlerChrysler. In order to leapfrog e-business initiatives, they leveraged their resource in technology and acquired shares in companies such as Powerway Inc. (business-to-business [B2B]) and The Cobalt Group (business-to-consumer [B2C]). The DCX NET Initiative covers B2B, B2C, business-to-employee (B2E) activities, and Telematics. Figure 2 shows the relationship between their business processes and DCX NET Initiative. Among them, B2E Workforce Connect is an employee portal which supports the entire value chain of DaimlerChrysler.

ePeople and E-Recruiting at DaimlerChrysler

ePeople project is a part of B2E Workforce Connect that provides both employees and managers with a comprehensive Web-based access to human resource applications.

Figure 2. DaimlerChrysler's networked business systems and business processes

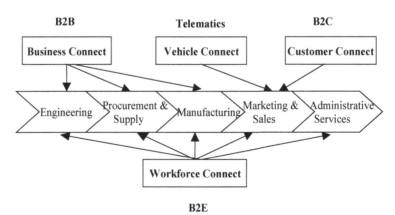

ePeople is a centralized single platform system featuring universally standardized Web-based personnel system processes and automation of human resource workflow. ePeople optimizes human resources work and connects the HR departments around the world via a centralized database and the Internet. With the help of the new Web-based technologies, employees can gain more individual responsibility, decrease administrative cost, and improve quality of work life. The employee job marketplace and the competency management system are the first two modules that have been available since July 2001 via the employee portal. The "Employee job marketplace" offers all of the Group's employees in Germany the opportunity to anonymously advertise their willingness to change jobs on the internal job posting board. The "Competency Management" system is a tool for collecting information about the competencies of all of the company's employees for the purpose of employee development and knowledge transfer.

As a part of ePeople project, DaimlerChrysler created a centralized career Web site in 2000. Our content analysis of the career Web site indicates that it is employing all the necessary features and functions of the holistic e-recruiting system discussed in the previous section. Three unique functions of the e-recruiting system that set DaimlerChrysler's apart from most other companies' career Web sites include job agent management, candidate relationship management, and workflow management. One of the features of the job agent management is the "My Career" world that helps job applicants uniquely design their personal Web interface at the career site. The "Job minder" is an integral part of the "My Career" world, which enables you to compile your own personal "Career" Web page. Applicants can define their own page layout and options to be informed about interesting events. Job applicants can decide how often they are notified of the jobs that match their profile and qualifications.

As a part of the candidate relationship management, the career Web site maintains a virtual-guided tour of the career Web site. Chrysler has offered a 24-hour virtual job fair for graduates. Applicants are able to find out about various entry-level positions and are able to communicate with company executives through a Web-based conferencing. The job fair provided a virtual human touch by company executives who were available in a Web-based conferencing room to answer questions and provide information. It is worth noticing that not only recent graduates but also a large number of professionals used the new medium as a platform for discussion and information.

Employees require skills when working with Web-based applications in order to understand e-business topics and to be able to implement these successfully. DaimlerChrysler has therefore created the qualification program DCePass, which is used by employees to acquire basic knowledge and skills with e-commerce technologies. DCePass is DaimlerChrysler's contribution toward both improving its employees' qualifications and maintaining their competitiveness for the long term. As a part of candidate management program, job applicants are asked to provide input to improve the career Web site. They offer an e-mail forward facility to send job opportunities to friends, and a list of interesting goodies available for download such as screen savers, e-brochures, e-greeting cards, and so forth.

DaimlerChrysler's workflow management is a part of the ePeople project. With the workflow management, human resource tasks are completed more efficiently because human resources processes are standardized and automated. To support automated workflow management, a centralized database is used to ensure end-to-end processes and to minimize redundancy of data. All applications are managed in the centralized database. The workflow management system contains functions to integrate job advertisements, job applications, candidate evaluation, and hiring decisions, as well as candidate correspondence. The benefits of workflow management system at DaimlerChrysler are immense, especially because of the needs of global hiring and interdepartmental collaboration.

Discussion and Conclusion

Given the current technological advances and the pace of environmental change, human resource professionals must proactively embrace technology and integrate their core human resource processes in order to maximize the value of human asset. Conventional recruiting methods have been plagued with high hiring costs and frequent hiring delays. Recently, Web-enabled e-recruiting emerged quickly as a powerful method for both job seekers and recruiters. Many organizations have built their corporate Web site to post job openings along with subscriptions to e-recruiting job boards. As e-recruiting becomes a strategic necessity companies who do not utilize e-recruiting will be at a critical strategic disadvantage. For e-recruiters, the competitive advantages of the e-recruiting systems derive from a balanced combination of state-of-the-art Web technologies and best management practices.

The widespread adoption of corporate career Web sites by companies is driven by the rising cost and inflexibility of using the third-party job boards and traditional media advertisements. Companies use their career Web sites to give detailed job information, to explain the culture and benefits, and to promote long-tem relationships with job seekers. We classified the recruiting systems into five stages of development based on technical components and management practices. The choice of technology and management practices is a managerial decision on the part of the company, as there is a trade-off between technology and cost. Our survey of Fortune 100 companies shows that each of the Fortune 100 companies is in various stages of the e-recruiting system development. The architecture of holistic e-recruiting system for corporate career Web sites consists of eight distinct, but interrelated subsystems: (1) applicant tracking management subsystem; (2) job requisition management subsystem; (3)

job agent management subsystem; (4) prescreening/self-assessment management subsystem; (5) e-recruiting performance analysis subsystem; (6) candidate relationship management subsystem; (7) workflow management subsystem; and (8) database management subsystem. DaimlerChrysler's career Web site was presented as an example of the successful holistic e-recruiting system. DaimlerChrysler launched an e-recruiting project under the DCX NET initiatives. The content analysis of the career Web site shows that two practices such as superior workflow management and candidate relationship management differentiate DaimlerChrysler from other ineffective recruiters.

While e-recruiting has a potential to reduce the hiring cost and hiring time and improve the quantity and quality of job applicants, there are four major challenges that remain to be overcome: (1) organizational, (2) managerial, (3) legal, and (4) technological challenges. The organizational challenges include: (1) business process redesign is needed across the entire human resource management process to realize the benefits of the e-recruiting. Bottleneck and inefficient activities should be identified and redesigned so that the entire recruiting process moves quickly with an exchange of standardized data; (2) most qualified candidates are often passive job seekers who are currently employed but may be interested in new job opportunities. A strategy to identify qualified passive job seekers and encourage them to apply should be developed; and (3) it is difficult to benchmark the best management practice and develop a set of metrics that measure the effectiveness of different recruitment methods. There are no significant statistics available on the effectiveness of various e-recruiting tools and management practices because of a limited experience with e-recruiting.

The managerial challenges include: (1) without a user acceptance of technology, technology would be of little use in the e-recruiting process. Recruiters and hiring managers should be comfortable and knowledgeable about the use of Web-based recruiting methods. A comprehensive training program should be developed for them; (2) the success of e-commerce does not lie in the technical sophistication of the career Web site but the balanced combination of technology and management skills. With so many options available, recruiters must begin to consider ways to integrate technology into the recruitment practices to increase their efficiencies and improve strategies; (3) many job seekers are still not comfortable with using the e-recruiting method. E-recruiting cannot eliminate the use of other recruiting methods such as newspaper advertisements and employees' referrals. Given the limited financial resources, finding the optimal mix of different recruiting methods is a challenge for human resource managers; and (4) e-recruting has helped companies store and retrieve pools of talent quickly, but often fails to screen the pools adequately. Therefore, recruiters or hiring managers have to review each of them manually before interviewing a candidate and conducting an assessment.

The legal challenges include: (1) different reporting requirements for governments such as the EEOC report which can be a problem for centralized recruiting for global companies (Flynn, 2002); (2) there is potential employer liability for violating employment discrimination laws, laws related to applicant background checks, and laws prohibiting false advertising (King, 2000). A comprehensive guideline for applicant data collection should be developed in consultation with legal professionals; (3) the e-recruiting is likely to affect the diversity of the company if conscious efforts are not made. Web users are computer savvy, nonminority, young people who are typically well educated. These biased demographic characteristics can create a serious impact on diversity; certain protected groups have less chance to be hired than others (Flynn, 2002). One way to solve the diversity issue is to maintain a portfolio of recruiting methods that will bring the right level of diversity to the company.

The technological challenges include: (1) integrating the e-recruiting process with existing recruiting processes is difficult due to limited software solutions. Paper-based resumes should be converted into a digitized form and stored in the database; (2) lack of security discourages the online job application. While security is one of the most important issues with job applicants, many leading companies do not explicitly address it on the career Web site; and (3) designing a career database is a complex task. Job databases should be designed to minimize redundant data and optimize the performance of job search and candidate search. The search behavior of the applicants and recruiters should be fully understood.

In our opinion, there are numerous research opportunities in e-recruiting. Research on the perception of job seekers on different e-recruiting methods and job attributes will give a valuable design guideline to recruiters. The longitudinal study of recruiting methods and job performance may provide important results that can be used to optimize the mix of recruiting methods and budget allocations. Many users such as hiring managers, recruiters, senior mangers, and human resource professionals are involved in the recruiting process. An in-depth understanding of what information they ask for, how they use it, and how they interact with each other can be another interesting avenue of research.

References

Barber, A. E. (1998). *Recruiting employees.* Thousand Oaks, CA: Sage.

Barney, J. B. (1991, March). Firm resources and sustained competitive advantage. *Journal of Management, 17,* 99-120.

Cullen, B. (2001). E-recruiting is driving HR systems integration. *Strategic Finance, 83*(1), 22-26.

Flynn, G. (2002). E-recruiting ushers in legal dangers. *Workforce, 81*(4), 70-72.

Gale, S. F. (2001). Internet recruiting: Better, cheaper, faster. *Workforce, 80*(12), 74-77.

Gill, J. (2001, July 18). Now hiring. Apply online. *Businessweek.*

IDC. (2001). Worldwide e-recruiting market forecast and analysis, 2000-2005.

King, N. J. (2000). Is paperless hiring in your future? E-recruiting gets less risky. *Employee Relations Law Journal, 26*(3), 87-116.

Miller, S. M. (2001). Help wanted: Is the online job market working for your business? *Office Solutions, 18*(4), 27-29.

Thomas, S. L., & Ray, K. (2000). Recruiting and the Web: High-tech hiring. *Business Horizons, 43*(3), 43-52.

Tomlinson, A. (2002). Energy firm sharpens recruiting, saves money with in-house job board. *Canadian HR Reporter, 15*(20), 7-8.

Chapter XII

Lessons Learned from EDI and Its Impact on Institutional Trust in Electronic Marketplaces

Pauline Ratnasingam, University of Central Mussouri, USA

David Gefen, Drexel University, USA

Paul A. Pavlou, University of California, Riverside, USA

Abstract

Given the uncertainties of e-business, this chapter examines the role of institutional trust, which has been viewed as a key facilitator of electronic marketplaces (Pavlou, Tan, & Gefen, 2003). In doing so, we draw upon the principles of research on traditional electronic data interchange (EDI) via value-added-networks (VANs) to develop a set of theory-driven, institutional trust-building, facilitating conditions, namely, (1) IT connectivity, (2) standards, (3) security, and (4) uniform product descriptions. This study has implications for (1) the nature and role of institutional trust in e-marketplaces, (2) the strategic design of trust-building mechanisms in e-marketplaces, and (3) an extension of the literature on institutional trust.

Introduction

E-marketplaces have recently received considerable attention in e-business research (Bakos, 1998; Palmer, Bailey, & Faraj, 2000; Sarkar, Butler, & Steinfeld, 1995). E-marketplaces attract a larger pool of trading partners and deal with multiple participants transacting electronically for the best price in order to increase liquidity and have a variety of price mechanisms, such as auctions (Dai & Kauffman, 2001). They have been defined as "e-marketplace or electronic market system is an interorganizational system that allows the participating buyers and sellers in some market to exchange information about prices and product offerings" (Bailey & Bakos, 1997). E-marketplaces may be bringing about one of the most significant structural change in business since the industrial revolution (Rayport & Sviokla, 1994), with a recent increase in interest in e-marketplaces by practitioners and academicians ("Business to business e-boom," 2000; Kaplan & Sawhney, 2000). The emergence of e-marketplaces may substantially contribute to advantages of economies of scale and scope, reduction of search costs (Bakos, 1998), trust building (Pavlou, 2002; Pavlou et al., 2003), and value-added services (El Sawy & Pavlou, 2002).

Despite the technology stock down turn and the cost of 80,000 "minute millionaires," the Internet and other examples of technological innovations are expected to continue to drive wealth creation (Weems, 2001). The evident success of business-to-consumer (B2C) e-marketplaces is still not there for business-to-business (B2B) markets, despite a considerable proportion of IT funds being spent on various B2B marketplaces, such as the GlobalNetXchange (GNX) and WorldWide Retail Exchange (WWRE), and B2B marketplaces are yet to become successful. The main reason for the lack of progress is that, in an electronic world, data must be correct and consistent (Sparks & Wagner, 2003). "B2B exchanges" (2002) claimed that a lack of common product language has reduced the success of B2B marketplaces.

According to Bakos (1998), e-marketplaces serve the following functions: (1) buyer demands seller products to achieve economies of scale and reduce bargaining asymmetry (Williamson, 1975); (2) protecting buyers and sellers from opportunistic behaviors of other participants on the market; (3) facilitating the market by reducing operating costs; (4) matching buyers and sellers (Malone, Yates, & Benjamin, 1987); and (5) providing an institutional infrastructure that enables the efficient functioning of the market. In all five categories, there is less of a legal guaranty than there is in a traditional business environment, and hence a heightened need for trust.

Accordingly, understanding what contributes to the success of these markets is crucial, not only because of their economic impact but also because of the high volatility in these markets. Of the over 1,500 online markets in 2000, only about 150 still exist today (Day, Fein, & Ruppersberger, 2003) and many of these still exist because of the nature of the relationships they have created (Dai & Kauffman, 2004). There are clearly many factors contributing to the success of some B2B e-markets in contrast to others, such as market leadership, being an early entrant, and strategic alliances (Dai & Kauffman, 2004). The focus of this paper is to leverage some of the lessons learned from traditional EDI to guide research on e-marketplaces. In doing so, the chapter provides another potentially contributing aspect, institutional trust. Institutional trust has been shown to be a significant predictor of online activity (i.e., e-marketplace success) in B2C e-marketplaces (Pavlou & Gefen, 2002). This chapter argues for an equivalent effect through reduced social uncertainty in B2B e-marketplaces.

Institutional trust deals with the belief that there are impersonal structures that enable an entity (company or an individual) to act in anticipation of a successful future endeavor (e.g., Shapiro, 1987; Zucker, 1986). More specifically, we examine antecedents of institutional trust, namely, "facilitating conditions" (Pavlou et al., 2003). Following McKnight, Cummings, and Chervany (1998), Shapiro (1987), and Zucker, (1986), this chapter identifies and proposes four facilitating conditions: (1) IT connectivity, (2) standards, (3) security, and (4) uniform product descriptions. The purpose of this study is to analyze the impact of facilitating conditions on institutional trust toward a successful participation in e-marketplaces, drawing upon the literature on traditional EDI via VANs. The study's research question study is: How can the lessons learned from the role of institutional trust in traditional EDI impact the successful design of trust-building mechanisms in e-marketplaces?

Lessons Learned from EDI Adoption

Although trust is a central aspect making EDI possible from a business perspective (Hart & Saunders, 1997), at first glance, issues in EDI relationships seem quite different from the issues in e-marketplaces. EDI typically connects only a few companies and usually those who have close ongoing business relationships. In contrast, B2B e-marketplaces, such as Covisint, Chemconnect, or World Wide Retail Exchange, deal with a broader market. E-marketplace transactions, as compared to the traditional EDI, allow for lower costs and more availability (information is made available 24-7 and no products are moved physically around); convenience (the information is made available for all registered trading parties); and ubiquity (all registered trading parties can log on to the network globally). Moreover, a central part of the B2B e-marketplaces is its ability to be a price discovery method and the ease with which new business alliances can be created through it, whereas, EDI is focused solely on efficient processing among established business alliances, in particular ordering just-in-time delivery between companies using VANs.

Nonetheless, the underlying reason why trust is needed in EDI is actually very much the same as with e-marketplaces: As with other inter-company alliances and joint projects, it is a subjective belief that the expected outcomes will be achieved when there is no explicit guaranty (Gefen, 2002b). Furthermore, the first author conducted a study of EDI security risks and controls via a literature survey of 200 articles from MIS journals and books between the late 1980s to the mid-1990s. A security risk-control framework for EDI was developed and tested via multiple case studies in seven organizations from different industry sectors, namely, automotive (Ford and Toyota), petroleum (Shell), banking, telecommunications (Telecom and Siemens), and a clothing textile firm. The findings revealed that although EDI is traditionally an inward environment, the operating procedures included established industry, document standards, and uniform product descriptions. Still, the underlying reason why trust is needed in EDI is the same. Trust serves as a subjective belief that the expected outcomes will be achieved when there is no explicit guaranty (Gefen, 2002b). Based on this recognition, we identified five lessons learned from EDI (discussed in the next section) that serve as facilitating conditions for successful e-marketplace participation.

The Need for Standards

Standards play an important role in EDI adoption as they contribute to uniform business practices; standard purchase orders and acknowledgements; and invoices. The American National Standards Institute (ANSI X12) standard, the Guidelines for Trade Data Interchange (GTDI) standard in the United Kingdom, and the United Kingdom EDI standard Electronic Data Interchange for Administration, Commerce and Transport (UN/EDIFACT) form the internationally agreed standards that facilitate the smooth flow of EDI transactions, thereby providing a standardized routine set of procedures for transacting EDI documents (Picard, 1992).

Similarly, establishing the right type of standards in e-marketplaces, both message and industry specific can promote trust since institutional trust is not based on personal experience between firms but on more formal impersonal procedures that coordinate standards. Moreover, creating standards promotes a standardized qualification of what is expected, which in turn should create a way of reducing misunderstandings and so promote trust through the reduction of social uncertainty (Gefen, 2002b). We posit that in order to create transparency for e-marketplaces, e-marketplaces need standards for open IT software applications and product description. For example, the Chemical Industry Data Exchange (CIDX) is a global trade association and a standards body whose mission is to improve the ease, speed, and cost of conducting business electronically between chemical firms and their trading partners. The Chem eStandards are "the uniform standards of data exchange developed specifically for buying, selling and delivery of chemicals." Furthermore, the Chem eStandards are open, platform-independent, uniform, and available free of charge as they are based on the universally recognized Extensible Markup Language (XML).

Indeed, certification validating and adherence to standards—as exemplars of institutional trust—have been empirically shown to contribute to creating a more trusting relationship between companies during IT implementation because of the way it reduces social uncertainty (Gefen, in press). By extension of this logic, the same should apply to other instances where companies interact with each other in situations characterized by social uncertainty.

The Importance of IT Infrastructure

EDI demands compatible systems between the buyers and their suppliers because the translation software has to convert an organization's internal transactions into the EDI standard format. For example, Telstra Multimedia's Tradelink software allows the translation of data from the internal format generated by a company's application software to the industry specific format, either using the industry standard (ANSI X12) or the international standard (UN/EDIFACT) formats. The EDI translation software provides this conversion between in-house, application software formats and moves EDI document formats in two directions, thus facilitating EDI transactions.

IT connectivity refers to technological mechanisms that enable firms to be IT connected, in order for them to undertake transaction exchanges. Premkumar, Ramamurthy, and Nilakanta (1994) conducted a study of innovation and diffusion in EDI adoption, and their findings revealed that technical compatibility was found to be a major predictor of EDI adoption. Previous research also supports this view (Chwelos, Benbasat, & Dexter, 2001; Iacovou, Benbasat, & Dexter, 1995; Premkumar, Ramamurthy, & Crum, 1997; Premkumar et al., 1994). Ratnasingam and Tan (2002) identify three dimensions of IT connectivity for e-marketplaces, namely, (1) IT compatibility, (2) IS telecommunication infrastructure, and (3) internal integration. IT compatibility refers to the extent the organizations participating in e-commerce are connected by means of hardware, software, and third party servers. IT telecommunication infrastructure in turn facilitates the medium of exchange over the Internet, and internal integration refers to the extent the organization has integrated their internal IT systems and applications in order to facilitate their in-house business operations and back end business processes. For example, Commerceone is an e-marketplace firm that provides software and IT services through the Global Trading Web. It enables world wide commerce on the Internet by allowing trading partners to create highly efficient e-marketplaces composed of transparent commerce communities that result in improved procurement cycle times and reduced purchasing costs. Similarly, the eStandard document used in the chemical industry supports data exchange in the following areas: customer-company information sharing; product catalogs including data exchanges that support promoting, selling, selecting, and buying of products; orders including support for transmitting data regarding orders for products and services; and envelop and security utilizing Internet protocols to identify and protect computer to computer transaction data shared between trading partners.

The Need for Security Mechanisms

The importance of security mechanisms in traditional EDI is crucial as the system is outsourced to a third-party VAN provider. The trading partners have to be registered in order to transmit transactions via the VAN. VANs were characterized by private messaging networks that paved the way for larger firms who relied on mailbox services and other EDI functions (such as transacting purchase orders and invoices) to operate in a batch mode (Ratnasingam, 1998). EDI security is enforced via user IDs and passwords that contribute to the authenticity of the trading party and provides access to the EDI system thereby mitigating access risks by hackers and unauthorized parties. Some VANs were set up electronically to open and inspect certain parts of the message in order to verify the messages (when checking for the interchange header, group header, and application IDs). Further, functional acknowledgements confirm receipt and transmission of EDI messages transmitted by the trading partners thereby mitigating nonrepudiation and authentication risks. In this manner, security reduces uncertainty by guaranteeing that malicious third parties will not eavesdrop, access, or change information.

Security in e-marketplaces is important because trading partners transact over the Internet, which is globally connected. Security mechanisms in e-marketplaces refer to control safeguards and protection services that provide assurances in the form of security. Previous research relating to Internet security services refers to confidentiality, data integrity, authenticity, availability, and nonrepudiation mechanisms built into e-marketplace systems. These are achieved through security mechanisms such as digital signatures and encryption mechanisms (via public key infrastructure) that enforce confidentiality. Confidentiality mechanisms aim to protect transactions and message content against unauthorized reading, copying, or disclosure using encryption mechanisms. Integrity mechanisms provide transaction accuracy and assurance that e-commerce transactions have not been altered or deleted. Integrity mechanisms apply accounting controls to enforce reference numbers for each e-commerce transaction so that there is accountability. Authentication mechanisms provide transaction quality of being authoritative, valid, true, and genuine, worthy of acceptance or belief by reason of conformity to the fact that reality is present. Authentication mechanisms are enforced by using biometrics, smart cards, and digital signatures that reveal the identity of the trading party. Nonrepudiation mechanisms protect the originator of e-commerce transactions and use acknowledgement procedures applying digital signatures. Nonrepudiation mechanisms are enforced by maintaining paper audit trails and regular audit checks so that backups of electronic transactions are kept. Nonrepudiation services with proof of origin provide the re-cipient of message with proof of origin (Bhimani, 1996; Jamieson, 1996; Marcella, Stone, & Sampias, 1998; Parker, 1995).

The Need for Uniform Coded Product Descriptions

EDI documents include uniform header and footer codes. It is these codes or reference numbers that are identified by the translation software and decoded into a readable format thereby enforcing integrity. An error in the header and footer numbers/codes will contribute to a wrong transaction that will in turn frustrate the receiving trading partner. Hence, the transmitting trading partner has to re-send the same transaction correctly again and may test the tolerance of mistakes of the receiving trading part-ners (Jamieson, 1996). In this manner, uniform coded products reduce uncertainty by making misunderstandings less frequent.

Standardized codes play an important role in e-marketplaces as they create uniform product descriptions and a structure to facilitate large numbers of buyers and sellers to trade with each other. Likewise, having the right codes for product descriptions will create sufficient trust that the trading partner will fulfill their promise to provide better prices. In an e-marketplace, price comparison is only possible if all the market players use uniform product descriptions, again reducing social uncertainty and hence promoting trust. In order to facilitate uniform product descriptions, e-mar-ketplaces provide online catalogs with uniform product descriptions. For example, in the Chemical Industry the eStandard provides 12 business transactions including: (1) qualification request, (2) qualification request update, (3) request for quote, (4) product catalog update, (5) customer specific catalog update, (6) create order, (7) order response, (8) order status, (9) order status inquiry, (10) change order, (11) cancel order, and (12) cancel order response. Each eStandard message is an XML document conforming to a specific Document Type Definition (DTD). Similarly, the quote manager in Covisint.com (an electronic document that manages, analyzes, and supports the automotive sourcing process) creates a standardized environment, thereby providing an environment to enhance the communication between buyers and potential suppliers (Sklar, 2001; Weems, 2001).

An Awareness of Coercive Power and Competitive Pressure in EDI

Past research in EDI supports the claim that trading partners experienced com-petitive pressure (see Chwelos et al., 2001; Hart & Saunders, 1997; Iacovou et al., 1995; Premkumar et al., 1994; 1997). For instance, in the case of Ford, a supplier performance checklist determines whether they should renew the contracts of their suppliers or not. A check on their suppliers' competencies such as; product quality, timeliness of delivery, service quality, and how they resolve disputes were observed. Examples of coercive sources that an automotive manufacturer may exercise include; slow delivery of vehicles, slow payment on warranty work, unfair distribution of vehicles, turndowns on warranty work, threat of termination, and bureaucratic red tape (Ratnasingam, 2000). In all there is considerable evidence of coercion by large manufacturers towards their smaller suppliers.

The impact of coercive power and the competitive pressure was also seen in e-marketplaces (in particular the automotive industry). Despite the limited research to support the impact of power in e-marketplaces, Raisinghani and Hanebeck (2002) suggest that although Covisint's initial goals were to share the costs rather than to force each car builder and supplier to house its own trading software, they have revised their strategy by agreeing to host private exchanges for companies and offer portal services connecting Covisint to purchasing sites fully operated by large manufacturers. Berryman et al (2000) classify B2B e-marketplaces in terms of its control structure positing three types of marketplaces: (1) seller-controlled, (2) buyer-controlled, and (3) neutral. Covisint notes that e-business is not about incremental improvement; it is about redesigning your enterprise. Covisint addresses the entire business, links the trading partner to the entire industry, and provides the energy to accelerate their operations on the Internet. This shift suggests a conflict between creating a self-sustaining business and setting technology standards for the automotive industry. Furthermore, most of the "tier 3" and "tier 4" supplies (i.e., those who make rubber, plastic, aluminum, and other basic car materials), are not using Covisint; and BMW, Honda, Toyota, Volkswagen, and other manufactures have began constructing their own private exchanges (Joachim & Moozakis, 2001). This suggests that coercive power and competitive pressure do exist in e-marketplaces (particularly in the automotive industry), which highlights the need to develop trust among the trading parties.

Although, there is limited empirical research to support the impact of power in e-marketplaces, we assume that the lessons learned on the impact of power in EDI adoption are probably also true for e-marketplaces, because equivalent social uncertainty issues are at play in both cases. The intensity of the problem is somewhat mitigated in e-marketplaces because the dominant trading partners tend to have open standards that serve their purpose for e-marketplaces so that access to a large number of trading partners can enable transparency for price comparisons. Moreover, institutional trust, by limiting the ability of stronger partners to force their agenda and prices on others, should reduce the power plays in e-marketplaces and in doing so facilitate better marketplaces. When effective institutional trust exists in a marketplace in general, its players are both limited in what they can do as far as foul play is concerned and are held responsible for breaching the rules of conduct (Zucker, 1986).

Institutional Trust

Past research has shown the economic advantages of an open marketplace (Williamson, 1975) but has also warned of the necessity of creating trust, especially institutionalized trust (Zucker, 1986), to make these advantages possible. Trust is essential because even when legal regulations do exist, trust is still a necessary ingredient in reducing social uncertainty (Gefen, 2000), that is, the uncertainty created by the uncontrollable behavior of other people (Luhmann, 1979). We need trusted identities and an assurance of who we are dealing with (Cale & McGinnis, 2006). Arguably, since the same applies to other electronic transactions (Gefen, Karahanna, & Straub, 2003), trust should be central to e-marketplaces too. The general principle through which institutional trust is created is by providing ways of reducing social uncertainty (Zucker, 1986). The model developed here discussed some of the ways this can be done based on what has been learned about EDI.

Trust, in general, is necessary when expected outcomes cannot be guaranteed; it is the belief that even without enforcement the trusted party will behave appropriately as it is expected to (Gefen, 2000; 2002a; Luhmann, 1979). Research has shown how trust is central in many types of alliances between business partners (Gefen, 2002b; Kumar 1996). Trust is crucial because legal details cannot always be worked out in the finest of detail, thus, making trust is an essential ingredient of long-term business engagements (Fukuyama, 1995). Since the same underlying limitations apply also to B2B e-marketplaces, trust, and the institutional conditions supporting it should be central also to B2B e-marketplaces. Institutional trust deals with beliefs that an independent third party watches over the transaction, among other things, through safety nets and performance structures (Shapiro, 1987). Indeed, this has been shown to be a central way of building inter-company alliances (Gefen, in press).

When institutional trust is central to a relationship, certification, structural assurances, and situational normality build trust by adding a level of confidence to the expected outcomes from the interaction (Zucker, 1986). Institutional trust may be the most important mode by which trust is created in an impersonal, economic environment where familiarity and similarity (communality) do not exist. There are two dimensions of institutional trust: (1) third party certification, which defines a party's trustworthiness; and (2) escrows, which guarantee the expected outcome of a transaction (Zucker, 1986). Similarly Ba, Stallaret, Whinston, and Zhang (2005) suggest that trusted third parties also include online escrow service providers who provide guidelines in order to establish an optimal pricing strategy. In this study we focus on the former. The importance of the latter has been previously shown in equivalent e-marketplaces (Pavlou & Gefen, 2002).

The institutional view of trust has been widely adopted by e-commerce researchers because e-commerce brings together organizations with no familiarity or similarity (see Gefen et al., 2003; McKnight et al., 1998; McKnight & Chervany, 2002; Pavlou,

2002; Pavlou & Gefen, 2002; Tan & Thoen, 2001; Zucker, 1986). McKnight and Chervany (2002) describe institutional trust as a critical part of Internet transactions and defined it as "the organization's belief that favorable conditions are in place that are beneficial to outcome success." They describe institution-based trust as a critical part of Internet transactions and introduced two dimensions of institutional trust, namely, structural assurances and situational normality. Structural assurances refer to beliefs that favorable outcomes are likely because of contextual structures, such as contracts, regulations, and guarantees. Situational normality refers to beliefs that success is anticipated because the situation is normal. The importance of situational normality in the case of e-commerce has been empirically shown by Gefen et al. (2003).

Facilitating Conditions

Pavlou et al. (2003) examined the role of institutional structures and introduced a third element of institutional trust called facilitating conditions and the subconcepts (IT connectivity, standards, and uniform product descriptions) to engender relationship continuity. Previous research refers to facilitating conditions as dealing with shared standards, relationship values, and common beliefs about behaviors and goals (Heide & John, 1990; Jap & Ganesan, 1999; Morgan & Hunt, 1994). Examples of facilitating conditions include standards that support (1) the use of interoperable IT platforms, (2) business message standards like EDI, or (3) common processes for uniform product descriptions. Industry reports have shown a great need for establishing standards. Since the theoretical contribution of these conditions is to create trust, that is, reduce social uncertainty (Gefen, 2000), these empirical findings should also apply to other circumstances where there is a high degree of social uncertainty and where, consequently, trust is needed (Gefen, 2002b). Such conditions exist also in B2B e-marketplaces. The proposed model is shown in Figure 1.

Ratnasingam and Tan (2002) and Ratnasingam, Pavlou, Tan, and Gefen (2003), adapted the third element—facilitating conditions of institutional trust—and examined its role in the context of the lessons learned from traditional EDI. In addition, they introduced dimensions of measures for each of the subconcepts, namely, IT connectivity, standards, security, and uniform product descriptions.

Facilitating conditions contribute to an orderly manner of transacting electronically and abiding by certain procedures that contribute to best business practices for e-marketplace participation. However, facilitating conditions differ from situational normality, which deals with building trust by assuring the trusting party that everything is customary. That is, situational normality assures the trusting party that there is nothing to indicate social uncertainty (Gefen et al., 2003). Indeed, such assurances as well as situational normality have been shown empirically to have a significant effect in creating institutional trust in B2C markets (Gefen et al., 2003) and in online

Figure 1. Facilitating conditions and institutional trust

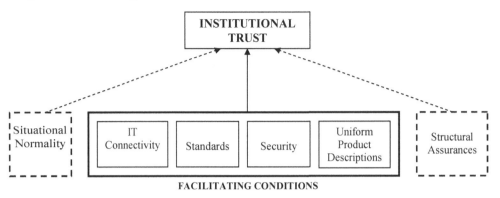

marketplaces (Pavlou & Gefen, 2002). Social uncertainty is the uncertainty added to any interaction with other people by virtue of them being independent agents whose behavior can never be fully accounted for (Gefen, 2000). On the other hand, facilitating conditions build trust by removing nonsocial uncertainty that is the product of the technology. For example, standards of IT connectivity increase trust by creating less uncertainty in the way the technology will behave, while the other human party behaves in a normal way without arousing suspicion about its motives.

Conclusion

Creating trusting relationships is crucial to the success of many business partnerships (Ganesan, 1994; Gefen, 2002b). If this is also true in online B2B relationships, as it is in online B2C relationships (Reichheld & Schefter, 2000), then understanding the impact of institutional trust may help explain the enormous shakeout in the B2B marketplace and the 20-fold decrease in the remaining number of marketplaces in 2003 compared with 2000.

Trust alone of course does not drive a B2B marketplace. Rather it is institutional trust that lubricates the marketplace, supporting the promise of the economic and technical advantages it harbors. Marketplaces, electronic or traditional, exist because of their inherent value, but without trust, and this would be institutional trust in this case, the marketplace will grind to a halt. Judging from related business alliances (e.g., Gefen, 2002b; Kumar, 1996), creating such trust should be crucial in nurturing the appropriate atmosphere within which other factors such as price and technology can take effect. Without creating this trust, companies will just refrain from taking part in any but the simplest of one-time transactions (Luhmann, 1979) and would probably just ignore the advantages the interaction offers because of the social uncertainty involved (Gefen, 2000). Extrapolating from e-commerce research (e.g., Gefen, 2000), it is only through the subjective control of the social uncertainty, made possible primarily through institutional trust when past experience with a particular vendor is nonexistent (Zucker, 1986), that transactions in the marketplace come into being.

In this study, we identified and examined facilitating conditions of institutional trust based on the lessons learned from traditional EDI. This research contributes to practice as we introduced a practical framework based on an elaborated notion of facilitating conditions as one of the elements of institutional trust for successful e-marketplace participation. Because e-marketplaces are linked to a global network, connecting B2B buyers and suppliers around the world should yield benefits beyond e-procurement. E-marketplaces take full advantage of what is known as the network effect. Buyers find supplementary sources for new and existing products, some of which may not have been available in their regional or vertical e-marketplaces. They can leverage services that increase flexibility—for example, enabling auctions for buying and selling goods. The study has implications for the survival of online B2B marketplaces, which have undergone great scrutiny and financial problems given their inability to deliver measurable value to their participating organizations. Similarly, firms that are aiming to initiate long-term online relationships could take advantage of the lessons learned from the EDI literature.

This research contributes to theory by drawing upon institutional trust. This is a unique contribution because past research on B2B success dealt with economic, technical, and other issues, but had basically ignored the need to create trust through institutional methods. By drawing upon related research in EDI, this study highlights the plausible importance of institutional trust and suggests some ways of increasing it. In addition, to the lessons learned from EDI we posit four subconcepts of facilitating conditions, namely, (1) IT connectivity, (2) standards, (3) security, and (4) uniform product descriptions for e-marketplace participation. IT connectivity focuses on the hardware and software requirements that enforce system compatibility for the trading partners to transact. Standards focus on the quality of operations thereby creating uniformity and adaptability for trading partners across the globe to transact using the same system. Security provides mechanisms that enforce the confidentiality, integrity of the transactions, authenticity, and nonrepudiation of the trading parties by applying access controls and availability mechanisms. Finally, uniform product descriptions contribute towards the integrity of the transactions by enforcing a set of codes to describe products in a specified manner thereby ensuring an orderly manner for transacting in e-marketplaces. Facilitating conditions create trust as they provide a framework for trading partners to build verifiable expectations, thereby reducing social uncertainty.

By explicating the lessons learned from EDI for e-marketplace relationships, this chapter stresses the strategic role of e-marketplaces. Not only does this study provide the rationale for e-marketplace relationships success by building institutional trust, but it also prescribes some specific facilitating conditions needed for building trust. This study aims to entice future empirical research to examine how the adoption of EDI affects the dimensions of the model (i.e., whether previous use of EDI positively correlates with the subconcepts and dimensions of facilitating conditions for e-marketplaces). Future research could test the model via multiple case studies comparing organizations that have adopted EDI versus e-marketplaces and organizations that have evolved from EDI to e-marketplaces.

References

B2B exchanges must make strides in supply chain services. (2002, May 18). *The Grocer.* 1-2.

Ba, S., Stallaret, J., Whinston, A. B., & Zhang, H. (2005). Choice of transaction channels: The effects of product characteristics on market evolution. *Journal of Management Information Systems, 21*(4), 173-197.

Bailey, J., & Bakos, J. Y. (1997). Reducing buyer search costs: Implications for electronic marketplaces. *Management Science, 43*(12), 1676-1692.

Bakos, J. Y. (1998). The emerging role of electronic marketplaces on the Internet. *Communications of the ACM, 41*(8), 35-42.

Berryman, K., Harrington, L.F., Layton-Rodin, D., Rerolle, V. (2000). Electronic commerce: three emerging strategies. *The McKinsey Quarterly,* (3), 129-136.

Bhimani, A. (1996). Securing the commercial Internet. *Communications of the ACM, 39*(6), 29-35.

Business to business e-boom. (2000, October 25). *Business Week,* p. 62.

Cale, D., & McGinnis, T. (2006). *Partners share responsibility for marketplace security: B-To-B exchanges must establish security policies and protocols that everyone agrees on.* Retrieved from http://www.informationweek.com/813/prmarketplace.htm

Chwelos, P., Benbasat, I., & Dexter, A. S. (2001). Research report: Empirical test of an EDI adoption model. *Information Systems Research, 12*(3), 304-321.

Dai, Q., & Kauffman, R. J. (2001). Business models for Internet-based e-procurement systems and B2B electronic marketplaces: An exploratory assessment. In *Proceedings of the 34th Hawaii International Conference on System Sciences.*

Dai, Q., & Kauffman, R. J. (2004). Partnering for perfection: An economics perspective on B2B electronic market strategic alliances. In K. Tomak (Ed.), *Advances in the Economics of Information Systems.*

Day, G. S., Fein, A. J., & Ruppersberger, G. (2003). Shakeouts in digital markets: Lessons from B2B exchanges. *California Management Review, 45*(2), 131-151.

El Sawy, O. A., & Pavlou, P. A. (2002). *Using a process-services perspective to the strategic design of B2B exchanges.* (Working Paper). Los Angeles: University of Southern California.

Fukuyama, F. (1995). *Trust: The social virtues & the creation of prosperity.* New York: Free Press.

Ganesan, S. (1994). Determinants of long-term orientation in buyer-seller relationships. *Journal of Marketing, 58,* 1-19.

Gefen, D. (2000). E-commerce: The role of familiarity and trust. *Omega: The International Journal of Management Science, 28*(6), 725-737.

Gefen, D. (2002a). Customer loyalty in e-commerce. *Joural of the Association of Information Systems, 3,* 27-51.

Gefen, D. (2002b). Nurturing clients' trust to encourage engagement success during the customization of ERP systems. *Omega: The International Journal of Management Science, 30,* 287-299.

Gefen, D. (in press). What makes ERP implementation relationships worthwhile: Linking trust mechanisms and ERP usefulness. *Journal of Management Information Systems.*

Gefen, D., Karahanna, E., & Straub, D. W. (2003). Trust and TAM in online shopping: An integrated model. *MIS Quarterly, 27*(1), 51-90.

Hart, P., & Saunders, C. (1997). Power and trust: Critical factors in the adoption and use of electronic data interchange. *Organization Science, 8*(1), 23-42.

Heide, J. B., & John, G. (1990). Alliances in industrial purchasing, The determinants of joint action in buyer supplier relationships. *Journal of Marketing Research, 37*(1), 24-36.

Iacovou, C. L., Benbasat, I., & Dexter, A. S. (1995). Electronic data interchange and small organizations: Adoption and impact of technology. *MIS Quarterly, 19*(4), 465-485.

Jamieson, R. (1996). Auditing and electronic commerce. *EDI Forum,* Perth, Western Australia.

Jap, S. D., & Ganesan, S. (1999). Control mechanisms and the relationship life cycle: Implications for safeguarding specific investments and developing commitment. *Journal of Marketing Research, 37,* 227-245.

Joachim, D., & Moozakis, C. (2001, September 17). Can Covisint find its way? *Internet Week.* Retrieved from http://www.internetweek.com/newslead01/lead091701.htm

Kaplan, S., & Sawhney, M. (2000). E-hubs: The new B2B marketplaces. *Harvard Business Review, 78*(3), 97-104.

Kumar, N. (1996). The power of trust in manufacturer-retailer relationships. *Harvard Business Review, 74*(6), 92-106.

Luhmann, N. (1979). *Trust and power.* UK: John Wiley and Sons.

Malone, T. W., Yates, J., & Benjamin, R. I. (1987). Electronic markets and electronic hierarchies. *Communication of the ACM, 30*(6), 484-497.

Marcella, A. J., Stone, L., & Sampias, W. J. (1998). *Electronic commerce: Control issues for securing virtual enterprises.* The Institute of Internal Auditors.

McKnight, D. H., & Chervany, N. L. (2002). What trust means in e-commerce customer relationships: An interdisciplinary conceptual typology. *International Journal of Electronic Commerce, 6*(2), 35-53.

McKnight, D. H., Cummings, C. C., & Chervany, N. L. (1998). Initial trust formation in new organizational relationships. *Academy of Management Review, 23*(3), 473-490.

Morgan, R. M., & Hunt, S. D. (1994). The commitment-trust theory of relationship marketing. *Journal of Marketing, 58,* 20-38.

Palmer, J. W., Bailey, J. P., & Faraj, S. (2000). The role of intermediaries in the development of trust on the WWW: The use and prominence of trusted third parties and privacy statements. *Journal of Computer Mediated Communication,* 5(3).

Parker, D. B. (1995). A new framework for information security to avoid information anarchy. *IFIP,* 155-164.

Pavlou, P. A. (2002). Institutional trust in interorganizational exchange relationships: The role of electronic B2B marketplaces. *Journal of Strategic Information Systems, 11*(4), 105-143.

Pavlou, P. A., & Gefen, D. (2002). Building effective online auction marketplaces with institution-based trust. *Proceedings of the International Conference on Information Systems (ICIS)*, Barcelona, Spain, December 16-19.

Pavlou, P. A., Tan, Y. H., & Gefen, D. (2003). The transitional role of institutional trust in online inter-organizational relationships. *Hawaii Information Systems Science Conference*, Hawaii, USA.

Picard, G. (1992). *EDI for managers and auditors.* NCC Blackwell.

Premkumar, G., Ramamurthy, K., & Crum, M. (1997). Determinants of EDI adoption in the transportation industry. *European Journal of Information Systems, 6,* 107-121.

Premkumar, G., Ramamurthy, K., & Nilakanta, S. (1994). Implementation of EDI—An innovation diffusion perspective. *Journal of Management Information Systems, 11*(2), 157-186.

Raisinghani, M., & Hanebeck, H. C. (2002). Rethinking B2B e-marketplaces and mobile commerce: From information to execution. *Journal of Electronic Commerce Research, 3*(2), 86-97.

Ratnasingam, P. (1998). Internet-based EDI, trust and security. *Information Management and Computer Security, 6*(1), 33-39.

Ratnasingam, P. (2000). The influence of power among trading partners in business to business electronic commerce. *Internet Research, 1,* 56-62.

Ratnasingam, P., Pavlou, P. A., Tan, Y.-H., & Gefen, D. (2003, May 18-21). Facilitating conditions and institutional trust for electronic marketplace participation. *Information Resources Management Association International Conference,* Philadelphia (pp. 556-559).

Ratnasingam, P., & Tan, Y.-H. (2002). *Institutional trust and related EDI lessons for electronic marketplaces.* (Working Paper). Free University of Amsterdam.

Rayport, J. F., & Sviokla, J. F. (1994). Managing in the marketspace. *Harvard Business Review, 72*(6), 141-151.

Reichheld, F. F., & Schefter, P. (2000). E-loyalty: Your secret weapon on the Web. *Harvard Business Review, 78*(4), 105-113.

Sarkar, M. B., Butler, B., & Steinfeld. (1995). Intermediaries and cybermediaries: A continuing role for mediating players in the electronic marketplace. *Journal of Computer Mediated Communication, 1*(3).

Shapiro, S. P. (1987). The social control of impersonal trust. *American Journal of Sociology, 93*(3), 623-658.

Sklar, D. (2001, April). Building trust in an Internet economy. *Strategic Finance, 82*(10), 22-25.

Sparks, L., & Wagner, B. A. (2003). Retail exchanges: A research agenda. *Supply Chain Management: An International Journal, 8*(1), 17-25.

Tan, Y.-H., & Thoen, W. (2001). Toward a generic model of trust for electronic commerce. *International Journal of Electronic Commerce, 5*(2), 61-74.

Weems, C. (2001). Technology and e-commerce will continue to create wealth. *Trusts and Estates, 140*(7), 10-14.

Williamson, O. E. (1975). Markets and hierarchies, analysis and anti-trust implications. New York: Free Press.

Zucker, L. G. (1986). Production of trust: Institutional sources of economic structure: 1840-1920. In B. Staw & L. Cummings (Eds.), *Research in organizational behavior* (pp. 53-111).

Appendix

Additional Readings

Lee, H. G., Clark, T., & Tam, K. T. (1999). Research report, Can EDI benefit adopters? *Information Systems Research, 10*(2), 186-195.

Moore, S. A. (2001). A foundation for flexible electronic communication. *Information Systems Research, 12*(1), 34-62.

Murkhopadhyay, T., Kekre, S., & Kalatur, S. (1995). Business value of IT: A study of electronic data interchange. *MIS Quarterly, 19*(2), 137-156.

Srinivasan, K., Kekre, S., & Mukhopadhyay, T. (1994). Impact of electronic data interchange technology on JIT shipments. *Management Science, 40*(10), 1291-1304.

Walter, A., Ritter, T., & Gemunden, H. G. (2001)Value creation in buyer-seller relationships: Theoretical considerations and empirical results from a supplier's perspective. *Industrial Marketing Management, 30*(4), 365-377.

Discussion Questions

What is the role of institutional trust in e-marketplaces?

What were the lessons learned from EDI?

How do the lessons learned from EDI facilitate e-marketplaces?

Chapter XIII

Digital Watermarking and Its Impact on Intellectual Property Limitation for the Digital Age

Tino Jahnke, University of Cooperative Education Heidenheim, Germany

Juergen Seitz, University of Cooperative Education Heidenheim, Germany

Abstract

Digital media like audio, video, images, and other multimedia documents can be protected against copyright infringements with invisible, integrated patterns. Such methods are based on steganography and digital watermarking techniques. Most watermarks are inserted as a plain-bit or adjusted digital signal using a key-based embedding algorithm. The embedded information is hidden (in low-value bits or least significant bits of picture pixels, frequency, or other value domains) and linked inseparably with the source data structure. For the optimal watermarking application a trade-off between competing criteria like robustness, nonperceptibility, nondetectability, and security has to be made. Most watermarking algorithms are not resistant against all attacks—even friendly attacks like file and data modifications can destroy the watermark very easily. This chapter gives an overview about the basic ideas of watermarking, applications for e-business, problems, and limitations.

Commercial Relevance of Protection Systems for Digital Media Types

The digital representation of multimedia documents has become very popular in the last decade. This is particularly due to the economical integration of technologies developed in the context of the Internet and the capabilities of efficient transmission, storage, and almost loss-free copying of digital media. Computer games, software, video, audio, and other digital products represent economically significant and expanding markets. E-commerce giants like Amazon or eBay demonstrate the significance of the Internet for advanced business activities and making profits. Besides the increasing popularity and acceptance of Internet distribution channels like online shops, auctions, streaming video and audio stores will promote the Internet to become the most relevant invention ever. Since more people using broadband access methods like DSL, satellite, and T1 the demand for various streaming media products has increased. Streaming media services are set up by most broadband Internet providers. Internet giants like Yahoo, Apple, and Microsoft are enabling the digital distribution of entertainment products like audio and video, steadily establishing new Internet services, and offering DVD-video for one to five euros. Apple has been successfully selling audio tracks via the Internet since 2003, and other companies will soon follow with similar business models. But, as audio, video, and any other digital media can easily be copied and redistributed over networks; a lot of business models (mentioned previously) and devices like DVD recorders were detained on purpose (Cox, Miller, & Bloom, 2002). Particularly, the music and entertainment industry struggles against the illegal distribution over networks, especially peer-to-peer, in recent years. The International Intellectual Property Alliance (IIPA) has estimated the annual world wide trade loss in its country reports due copyright piracy was up to $15.8 billion in 2005, $15.1 billion in 2004 (IIPA, 2006), $13.2 billion in 2003 (IIPA, 2005), and $10.2 billion in 2002 (IIPA, 2004). In 2003 the IIPA estimates the total losses due to piracy between $20-22 billion not counting losses due to Internet piracy (IIPA, 2003). As the copyright industry generates the highest foreign sales for the U.S. economy, the annual loss in 2002 can be estimated up to 15% worldwide by $88 billion in foreign sales (Siwek, 2002).

However, digital media can be straightforwardly copied and illegally redistributed over various channels. Risk and capital loss will prevent further activities and investments until a juristic and technical protection mechanisms are available. These concerns are supported by the facts that digital mass recording devices like MD, CD, MP3 recorder, digital photo devices, and camcorders have impressively entered the market (Anderson & Petitcolas, 1999; Cox, Miller, & Bloom, 2000; Hanjalic, Langelaar, Van Roosmalen, Biemond, & Langendijk, 2000; Hartung & Kutter, 1999; Mintzer, Braudaway, & Yeung, 1997; Petitcolas, Anderson, & Kuhn, 1999; Swanson, Kobayashi, & Tewfik, 1998; Wu & Liu, 2003). The importance and the supposed economical thread for copyright holders can be clarified by initiatives of the entertainment industry, like the Visual Identity Verification Auditor (VIVA) a project of the European Communities (European Communities, 1999b) and Secure Digital Music Initiative (SDMI) (http://www.sdmi.org). Distributors, like Time Warner, Disney, Lucas Film, and various professional companies like T-Systems, SCO, Yahoo, and other Internet service providers have already recognized the advantages of the upcoming digital area and have established on-demand services.

Recapitualing, we would like to refer that the features of the digital world lead to economical chances like cheap distribution of digital information but also to serious risks by simplifying unauthorized copying and distribution (Rosenblatt, Trippe, & Mooney, 2002).

Media Protection and Control Mechanisms

In order to provide protected material from illegal duplication, two typical technologies are being developed. One approach uses key-based cryptographic methods and procedures to control the process of copying, manipulating, and distributing media assets. Cryptographic techniques are enabling the appropriate security during the transmission process, but once the encrypted data is decoded the control of redistribution and its spread falls. To address the mentioned limitations of encryption the main idea is to label a digital material with specific marks. Such a pattern is called a digital watermark. Digital watermarks are often used for copyright and intellectual property protection (Cox et al., 2002; Fridrich, 1998). Watermarking enables the owner to obtain the copyright status of certain documents, and distributors can be made accountable for the content. Additionally, compatible media player technologies, like DivX, DVD player, or DVB set-top boxes can detect distorted marks and refuse to play, display, or execute the media file.

The lack of such technologies has enforced the establishment of research in information science disciplines and the foundation of organizations, like SDMI and The Tracing Authors' Rights by Labelling Image Services and Monitoring Access Network (TALISMAN) (Delaigle, 1996). Such initiatives especially focus on the development and progress of the watermarking technology for different applications. In the future, portable consumer devices may be equipped with specific hardware detectors to protect business models and the rights of the owners. The SDMI portable device specification clarifies such approaches (http://www.sdmi.org).

On the other hand, digital rights management (DRM) concepts are already integrated into the Microsoft Windows Media environment and will be intensively focused in the next generation of operation and hardware systems. The upcoming "palladium operation system" or Next-Generation Secure Computing Base (NGSCB) (Microsoft, 2006) and Trusted Computing Group (TCG) constricts the user rights and only allows users to use certified software and material (Anderson, 2003; http://www.trustedcomputinggroup.org/home/). In this case the duplication of content could be successfully permitted at the technical source. However the implication on society, culture, and market economy is enormous and wide regulations need to be established.

The importance of these techniques for the digital business world has been emphasized by actual introduction of specifically revised copyright legal acts in the American and European legislation and has now been considered in law regulations.

Digital Watermarking: Applications and Domains

Digital watermarking means embedding information into digital material in such way that it is imperceptible to a human observer but easily detected by computer algorithms. A digital watermark is a transparent, invisible, information pattern that is inserted into a suitable component of the data source by using a specific computer algorithm (e.g., Dittmann, 2000; Hartung & Kutter, 1999; Katzenbeisser & Petitcolas, 2000; Petitcolas et al., 1999).

Digital watermarking is described as a viable method for the protection of ownership rights of digital audio, image, video, and other data types. It can be applied to different applications including digital signatures, fingerprinting, broadcast and publication monitoring, authentication, copy control, and secret communication (e.g., Cox, Kilian, Leighton, & Shamoon, 1997; Cox et al., 2000; Cox et al., 2002; Katzenbeisser & Petitcolas, 2000). As a signature the watermark identifies the owner of the content and can be used as a fingerprint to identify content consumers. For example, such a watermarking technique is already used to secure drivers licenses and ID cards against counterfeiting in the United States (Digimarc, 2006). Broadcast and publication monitoring describes the area of computer systems which automatically monitors television and radio broadcasts to track the appearance of distributed material. Several commercial systems already exist that make use of this technology. The MusiCode system provides broadcast audio monitoring (National Association of Broadcasters, 1998), Video Encoded Invisible Light (VEIL) supports broadcast monitoring of video (http://www.veilinteractive.com). In 1997, a European Communities project named Visual Identity Verification Auditor (VIVA) was started that engages the development of watermarking technology for broadcast monitoring (European Communities, 1999b). Watermarking technology can also be used to guarantee authenticity and can be applied as proof that the content has not been altered since the insertion. The watermark is often designed in such a way that any alteration either destroys the watermark or creates a mismatch between the content and the watermark, which can easily be detected (Miller, Cox, Linnart, & Kalker, 1999). Furthermore, watermarking enables applications for copy control. Here the embedded watermark information contains rules of usage and copying (Cox et al., 2002). Digital watermarking is linked to steganography and data hiding. The field of secure and covert communication has been derived from the past as Herodotus, the great Greek storyteller, reports of hidden messages tattooed on skulls of slaves and wax tables for secure communication (Petitcolas et al., 1999). It is the classical application of steganography—the art of hiding pieces of information within another. Digital watermarking can be used to transmit such secret information in images, audio streams, or any type of digital data, and it is reported that some communication activities of people or groups linked to the 9/11 tragedy were based on such data hiding approaches.

Digital Watermarking Procedure

In contrast to common techniques, including copyright information inside data headers or visible areas, digital watermarks are weaved into the core structure of the digital document in an invisible and unrecognizable way (e.g., Wu & Liu, 2003). The main goal of the watermarking research is to develop digital watermarking methods, which survive all known format and conventional transformations, digital to analog (D/A) and analog to digital (A/D) conversions and any other kind of data operations used in image and audio processing. The basic digital watermarking methods integrating information packages in digital data are based on steganography methods. Figure 1 explains this generic and steganographically derived watermarking scheme. Digital watermarks are inserted into pictures, video, and audio with different embedding

Figure 1. Generic digital watermarking scheme

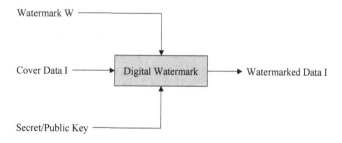

schemes, concepts, and algorithms. Almost all watermarking procedures are based on the use of secret keys, which are applied in the integration and detection process to extract the watermark information properly and enable basic security (Kutter & Hartung, 2000).

In contrast to traditional cryptographic methods the watermark set does not change the main functionality of the file. Therefore the watermark must be inserted into the data structure imperceptibly. Depending on the given data type it should neither be visible, audible, and so forth; nor detectable for strangers or observers. Each watermark method consists of an embedding algorithm and an extracting algorithm. The embedding algorithm inserts the watermark information in the data (e.g., Wu & Liu, 2003).

Digital Watermarking Classification and Requirements

Digital watermarks can be classified and measured on the basis of certain characteristics and properties which depend on the type of application. These characteristics and properties include the difficulties of notice, the surviving of common distortions and resistance of malicious attacks, the capacity of bit information, the coexistence with other watermarks, and the complexity of the watermarking method (Heileman, Pizano, & Abdallah, 1999). In general, they are described as fidelity, robustness, fragility, tamper resistance, data payload, complexity, and other restrictions. Digital watermarks must fulfill the following often contradictory requirements (Kutter & Hartung, 2000):

- **Robustness.** It may not be possible without knowledge of the procedure and the secret key to remove the watermark or to make it illegible. Robustness also means the resistance ability of the watermark information brought in a data material opposite changes and modifications of the original file. As modifications will be particularly considered as resizing, file compression, rotation, and so forth.

- **Nonperceptibility.** It is important to recognize whether the brought bit sample of the watermark produces perceptible changes acoustically or optically. A perfect nonperceptible bit sample is present if it cannot be distinguished between data material marked with watermark and the original.

- **Nondetectable.** The data material with the brought watermark information is not detectable if it is consistent to the origin data. In this case an embedding algorithm could use the noise components of the data of a picture to hide the watermark information.

- **Security.** It is assumed that the attackers have full knowledge about the applied watermark procedure, however, no secret key would be known. Therefore, an attacker will try to manipulate the data material to destroy the watermark, or again print and scan to win the original material without copyright protection note. The complexity is also connected with the security, that is, the algorithm for bringing in and reading of watermark information should work with enough long keys to discourage the search for the appropriate secret key. However, for certain applications and persons the watermark must also be detectable. The problem of secure key exchange emerges.

For the optimal watermarking application a trade-off has to be accepted between the mentioned criteria. Robustness means, for example, that many information of a watermark must be embedded that in case of an attack they will be better visible or detectable. On the other hand, if a watermark consists only of a minimal bit sample, which covers only a small part of the picture, such a watermark is quickly lost as a result of the modifications of the data (Woda & Seitz, 2002). Finally the amount of watermarking information and the robustness could have significant effects on the quality of the data source and influences on any requirements. Therefore a decision has to be made for the right application.

Concepts, Security, and Attack Scenarios on Digital Watermarks

Digital watermarking is a fairly new research sector and combines research work and results of other research areas like digital signal processing, communications, compression, information theory, and cryptography (e.g., Pan, Wang, Jain, & Ichalkaranje, 2003; Yu & Sattar, 2003). Digital watermarking is based on different technical concepts and methods (Katzenbeisser & Petitcolas, 2000). Various watermarking methods have been developed and tested, but they are not reacting uniform on methodical attacks (e.g., Voloshynovskiy, Pereira, Pun, Eggers, & Su, 2001; Le & Desmedt, 2003; Mihcak, Venkatesan, & Kesal, 2003). Primitive watermarking techniques, like least significant bit techniques (Hanjalic et al., 2000) use the existing digital noise pattern in any digital source to bind the watermarking information on its elementary binary structure. Other techniques generate pseudo noise patterns to integrate calculated bit information into different domains of the digital material.

Further methods use fractal, vector, and time variant approaches. Simple watermarking methods described in (Kutter, Jordan, & Bossen, 1997) modulate the blue channel of the images on a specific value. They use the limitation of the human visual system of recognizing minimal changes in the blue color spectrum. Additional methods use spread spectrum modulation and other techniques based on actual compression and multimedia methods, like discrete cosine, fast Fourier, wavelet, and fractal transformations. In general, watermarking techniques can be divided into two main categories. The first category describes correlation-based methods; the second category comprises the noncorrelation-based techniques (Hanjalic et al., 2000). Algorithms of the first category are embedding digital watermarks by adding pseudo-random noise to the image components, which are detected by correlating the image noise with the components of the image. The second category can be sub-divided into least significant bit and geometrical relation techniques. Most common used watermarking methods are based on correlation techniques. The watermarking research area has produced a wide range of watermarking techniques, which can be subdivided into various methodical complexity levels. Each of these methods tries to reduce vulnerability on various attack scenarios. Attacks on digital watermarks can principally be classified into two main groups: friendly and malicious attacks (Hanjalic et al., 2000; Hartung, Su, & Girod 1999). Conventional image or data operations applied in the normal use of computer technology can destroy the watermark information. Different operation of the classical image processing field, like scaling, color, gamma corrections, and so forth can be mentioned at this point. Today compression techniques can also be placed in the field of classical operations, but often separated as a single element in the watermarking research. The friendly attack has two common features. It is generally described as unintentional event, the user has no suppose and/or knowledge of the watermark and its embedded procedure. The second type of attacks—the malicious attacks—on watermarks occur with the intention to eliminate the information (Hanjalic et al., 2000). In order to test the robustness of watermarks some applications have been developed. The powerful StirMark attack has been designed by a research group at University of Cambridge (Anderson & Petitcolas, 1999). The attack simulates image distortions that commonly occur when a picture is printed, photocopied, and rescanned. The image is slightly stretched and compressed by random amounts, a small amount of noise is added (Fridrich, 1998). Comparable applications are the mosaic and histogram attacks. The mosaic attack assembles and reassembles the watermarked image. The histogram attack describes attacks on simple watermark methods. Finally, it is important to consider that a partial knowledge of the watermark or the process of watermarking enables pirates to remove the entire watermark or to disturb it.

Problems of Digital Watermarking

Watermarking techniques are already effectively used in associated copy control applications and broadcast monitoring systems, like VIVA and SDMI. In combination with DRM frameworks they could solve the limitation of the intellectual property dilemma in audio, video, and image-related business areas. However, the main intellectual property problem guaranteeing a worldwide protection cannot be solved by all existing watermarking methods yet. Watermarking techniques behave differently on attack operations or applications. Simple noncomplex methods described in (Kutter et al., 1997) are not very resistant to JPEG and JPEG 2000 compression, but resist against normal image operations. Complex and difficult watermarking techniques based on discrete, fast Fourier, or wavelet transformations are, on the contrary, very robust against compression techniques but have a lack of resistance on normal image operations. Today, most watermarking methods cannot reach the main approach. It is still a wide and attractive field for further research, in which innovative methods and techniques may be established.

Conclusion

As a result, we summarize that the watermarking technology is still at the beginning of its development. Most watermarking algorithms cannot tackle the attacks. Even the friendly attacks in the form of usual file modifications can destroy—very easily—the watermarks or falsify them. Therefore, a desirable watermarking algorithm should not rely on a certain method, but it could insert watermarks repeatedly in different ways (using least significant bits, frequencies, or color and contrast relations) so that at least one of them survives an attack. After editing on the picture has taken place, a watermark should be refreshed automatically. The jurisdiction has to accept a digital watermark as a permissible evidence for copyright infringement. Besides, organizational frameworks are necessary to be able to put through the author's claim. Corresponding to this law and authorization problems, infrastructures are also in demand for the key management and time stamp services.

Meanwhile, several European Communities' projects work on copyright protection and its realization in the digital world: Copyright in Transmitted Electronic Documents (CITED) encloses access and user control (European Union, 1999). The system is put on exceptional flexibility; it accepts all widespread operating systems and can be applied for access over computer networks. COPEARMS provides a uniform standard to guarantee the copyright of digital documents (European Communities, 1998; Scott, 1999). COPEARMS cooperates closely with another European Communities project, named IMPRIMATUR (European Communities, 1999a). The project takes care of the secure transmission and payment of documents including authentification. This year there are a significant increase in these types of activities. Microsoft is planning to develop the Palladium operating system; Apple Computer is successfully operating its music download platform; Yahoo! is trying to complement the same area with audio and video streams; RealNetworks and Microsoft (Windows Media Environment) are establishing digital rights management extension partly based on digital watermarking technology in their products. Such activities clarify the importance of digital watermarking, especially in combination with digital rights management and offers chances for further interesting research activities. However, although the main argument for digital watermarking is linked to enable and secure business activities, like the distribution of goods over networks, in the public and middle class domain, it seems that digital watermarking is primarily supported by mighty, international interest groups. Therefore, we suppose that digital watermarking is dominated by such initiatives and that running applications will be supported by them, before the public domain can use the benefits of such a technology.

References

Anderson, R. J. (2003, August). *Trusted computing. Frequently asked questions.* Retrieved February 16, 2006, from http://www.cl.cam.ac.uk/~rja14/tcpa-faq.html

Anderson, R. J., & Petitcolas, F. A. P. (1999, August). *Information hiding: An annotated bibliography.* Retrieved February 16, 2006, from http://www.petitcolas.net/fabien/steganography/bibliographyAnnotated_Bibliography.pdf

Cox, I. J., Kilian, J., Leighton, F. T., & Shamoon, T. (1997). Secure spread spectrum watermarking for multimedia. *IEEE Transactions on Image Processing, 6*(12), 1673-1678.

Cox, I. J., Miller, M. L., & Bloom, J. A. (2000, March 27-29). Watermarking and their properties. In *Proceedings of the International Conference on Information Technology: Coding and Computing, ITCC 2000.* (p. 6-10). Las Vegas, NV. IEEE Computer Society.

Cox, I. J., Miller, M. L., & Bloom, J. A. (2002). *Digital watermarking.* San Francisco: Morgan Kaufmann.

Delaigle, J.-F. (1996, September 27). TALISMAN. Retrieved February 16, 2006, from http://www.tele.ucl.ac.be/PROJECTS/TALISMAN/

Digimarc. (2006). *Secure ID systems.* Retrieved February 16, 2006, from http://www.digimarc.com/secureid/

Dittmann, J. (2000). *Digitale Wasserzeichen: Grundlagen, Verfahren, Anwendungsgebiete.* Berlin: Springer.

European Communities. (1998, October). *Co-ordinating project for electronic authors right management systems (COPEARMS).* Retrieved February 16, 2006, from http://ica.cordis.lu/search/index.cfm?fuseaction=proj.simpledocument&PJ_RCN=1509473

European Communities. (1999a, February). *Intellectual multimedia property rights model and terminology for universal reference (IMPRIMATUR).* Retrieved February 16, 2006, from http://ica.cordis.lu/ search/index.cfm?fuseaction=proj.simpledocument&PJ_RCN=1510421

European Communities. (1999b, August). *Visual identity verification auditor (VIVA).* Retrieved February 16, 2006, from http://ica.cordis.lu/search/index.cfm?fuseaction=proj.simpledocument &PJ_RCN=2630055

European Union. (1999, May). *CITED (Copyright in Transmitted Electronic Documents).* Retrieved February 16, 2006, from http://europa.eu.int/ISPO/legal/en/lab/lisbon/cited.html

Fridrich, J. (1998, November 4-6). Methods for Detecting Changes in Digital Images. In *Proceedings of the 6th IEEE International Workshop on Intelligent Signal Processing and Communication Systems (ISPACS'98),* 173-177. Melbourne, Australia.

Hanjalic, A., Langelaar, G. C., Van Roosmalen, P. M. G., Biemond, J., & Langendijk, R. L. (2000). *Image and video databases: Restauration, watermarking and retrieval.* Amsterdam: Elsevier.

Hartung, F., & Kutter, M. (1999, July). Multimedia watermarking techniques. *Proceedings of the IEEE, 87*(7), 1079-1107.

Hartung, F., Su, J. K., & Girod, B. (1999, January). Spread spectrum watermarking: Malicious attacks and counterattacks. In *Proceedings of SPIE Electronic Imaging '99, Security and Watermarking of Multimedia Contents,* (pp. 147-158) San Jose, CA.

Heileman, G. L., Pizano, C. E., & Abdallah, C. T. (1999, September). Performance measures for image watermarking schemes. In *Proceedings of the 5th Baiona Workshop on Emerging Technologies in Telecommunications* (pp. 149-152). Baiona, Spain. Retrieved February 16, 2006, from http://www.eece.unm.edu/controls/papers/Hei_Piz_CTA.pdf

Internation Interlectual Property Alliance (IIPA). (2003). *Special 301 coverletter.* Retrieved February 16, 2006, from http://www.iipa.com/pdf/2003SPEC301COVERLETTER.pdf

Internation Interlectual Property Alliance (IIPA). (2004). *Special 301 recommendations.* Retrieved February 16, 2006, from http://www.iipa.com/pdf/2004SPEC301LOSS.pdf

Internation Interlectual Property Alliance (IIPA). (2005). *Special 301 recommendations.* Retrieved February 16, 2006, from http://www.iipa.com/pdf/2005SPEC301LOSS.pdf

Internation Interlectual Property Alliance (IIPA). (2006). *Special 301 recommendations.* Retrieved February 16, 2006, from http://www.iipa.com/pdf/2006SPEC301LOSS.pdf

Katzenbeisser, S., & Petitcolas, F. A. P. (2000). *Information hiding: Techniques for steganography and digital watermarking.* Boston: Artech House.

Kutter, M., & Hartung, F. (2000). Introduction to watermarking techniques. In S. Katzenbeisser & F. A. P. Petitcolas (Eds.), *Information hiding techniques for steganography and digital watermarking.* Boston: Artech House.

Kutter, M., Jordan, F., & Bossen, F. (1997, February 13-14). Digital signature of color images using amplitude modulation. In *Proceedings of SPIE Storage and Retrieval for Image and Video Databases* (pp. 518-526). San Jose, CA.

Le T. V., & Desmedt, Y. (2003). Cryptoanalysis of UCLA Watermarking Schemes for Intellectual Property Proctection. In F. A. P. Petitcolas (Ed.), *Information Hiding. 5th International Workshop, IH 2002,* Noordwijkerhout, The Netherlands (pp. 213-225). Berlin: Springer.

Microsoft. (2006). *NGSCB: Next-generation secure computing base.* Retrieved February 16, 2006, from http://www.microsoft.com/resources/ngscb/default.mspx

Mihcak, M. K., Venkatesan, R., & Kesal, M. (2003). Cryptoanalysis of discrete-sequence spread spectrum watermarks. In F. A. P. Petitcolas (Ed.), *Information Hiding. 5th International Workshop, IH 2002,* Noordwijkerhout, The Netherlands (pp. 226-246). Berlin: Springer.

Miller, M., Cox, I., Linnart, J. P., & Kalker, T. (1999). A review of watermarking principles and practices. In K. K. Parhi & T. Nishitani (Eds.), *Digital signal processing in multimedia systems* (pp. 461-485). New York, NJ. Marcel Dekker Inc.

Mintzer, F., Braudaway, G. W., & Yeung, M. M. (1997). Effective and ineffective digital watermarks. In *Proceedings of the IEEE International Conference on Image Processing (ICIP '97)* (pp. 9-12), Santa Barbara, CA. Piscataway, NJ: IEEE Press.

National Association of Broadcasters. (1998, November 10). *Electronic music copyright in a digital, Web-centric, high-tech universe.* Retrieved February 16, 2006, from http://www.nab.org/Research/topic.asp

Pan, J.-S., Wang, F.-H., Jain, L., & Ichalkaranje, N. (2003). A multistage VQ based watermarking technique with fake watermarks. In F. A. P. Petitcolas & H. J. Kim (Eds.), *Digital Watermarking. First International Workshop, IWDW 2002,* Seoul, Korea (pp. 81-90). Berlin: Springer.

Petitcolas, F. A. P., Anderson, R. J., & Kuhn, M. G. (1999, July). Information hiding—A survey. *Proceedings of IEEE, 87*(7), 1064-1078.

Rosenblatt, B., Trippe, B., & Mooney, S. (2002). *Digital rights management—Business and technology.* New York: M&T Books.

Scott, M. (1999, February). Library-publisher relations in the next millennium: The library perspective. *National Library News, 31*(2). Retrieved February 16, 2006, from http://www.collectionscanada.ca/bulletin/015017-9902-03-e.html

Siwek, S. E. (2002). *Copyright industries in the U. S. economy: The 2002 report.* Retrieved February 16, 2006, from International Intellectual Property Alliance Web site: http://www.iipa.com/pdf/2002_SIWEK_FULL.pdf

Swanson, M. D., Kobayashi, M., & Tewfik, A. H. (1998, June). Multimedia data embedding and watermarking technologies. In *Proceedings of IEEE, 86*(6), 1064-1087.

Voloshynovskiy, S., Pereira, S., Pun, T., Eggers, J. J., & Su, J. K. (2001). Attacks on digital watermarks: Classification, estimation-based attacks and benchmarks. In F. Bartolini, I. J. Cox, J. Hernandez, & F. Pérez-González (Eds.), [Special Issue on Digital Watermarking for Copyright Protection: A Communications Perspective]. *IEEE Communications Magazine, 39*(8), 118-127.

Woda, K., & Seitz, J. (2002, April 24-25). The role of digital watermarking to the protection of rights for digital media assets. In W. Abramowicz (Ed.), *Proceedings of the 5th International Conference Business Information Systems (BIS) 2002* (pp. 107-112). Poznan, Poland.

Wu, M., & Liu, B. (2003). *Multimedia data hiding.* New York: Springer.

Yu, D., & Sattar, F. (2003). A new blind watermarking technique based on independent component analysis. In F. A. P. Petitcolas & H. J. Kim (Eds.), *Digital Watermarking. First International Workshop, IWDW 2002,* Seoul, Korea (pp. 51-63). Berlin: Springer.

Chapter XIV

Framework for User Perception of Effective E-Tail Web Sites

Sang M. Lee, University of Nebraska–Lincoln, USA

Pairin Katerattanakul, Western Michigan University, USA

Soongoo Hong, Dong-A University, Korea

Executive Summary

This study presents the development of an empirically validated framework for users' perception of effective Web sites for retail e-commerce (E-tail). In particular, we attempted to answer the main research questions: What are the major designs determining E-tail Web site effectiveness? How do these designs support Web users' objectives in using the Web? Based on the concept of "fitness for use" and the reasons that consumers use the Web, we proposed that "effective designs for E-tail Web sites should support Web customers for their (a) information search, (b) pleasure and (c) business transactions." Then, data were collected from a survey on 427 potential Web customers. An exploratory analysis was conducted to refine the proposed framework and to provide structure of the constructs in the framework to be validated by a following confirmatory analysis. Results suggest that the major designs determining E-tail Web site effectiveness include 16 factors, with 64 Web designs supporting the three major reasons for customers to use the Web.

Introduction

Despite the demise of many dot-coms, the number of E-tail sales are still promising; that is, the U.S. retail e-commerce sales for the third quarter of 2003 were $13.291 billion, an increase of 6.6% from the second quarter 2003 and 27.0% from the third quarter 2002. Meanwhile, total U.S. retail sales for the third quarter 2003 were estimated at $872.5 billion, an increase of only 6.1% from the same period in 2002 (Census Bureau of the Department of Commerce).

Successful E-tail Web sites must emphasize the importance of their design (Barnes & Vidgen, 2000), as this factor determines the ability of businesses to reap the full benefits of Internet commerce (Schubert & Selz, 2000). Thus, much has been written about effective designs for E-tail Web sites. For instance, Web presentation must be broken down into modules or information units (Conger & Mason, 1998); consistent and sufficient navigation mechanisms must be provided (Lynch & Horton, 1999); any disclaimers that the company will not honor some or all implied liabilities must be stated conspicuously (Schneider & Perry, 2000); and conceptual design guidelines and their related practical contents or features proposed (Katerattanakul, 2002). However, there have been few, if any, empirical attempts to validate these suggested Web design ideas.

As very little is known about the factors that make using the Web a compelling experience for its users (Novak, Hoffman, & Yung, 2000), researchers have conducted many studies to explore the factors affecting online customers. These include customer loyalty (Hoffman & Novak, 2000), customer experience beyond the online shopping navigation experience (Novak et al., 2000), effects of perceived usefulness and satisfaction on online customers' channel preference (Bhattacherjee, 2001), willingness to shop online (Liao & Cheung, 2001), antecedents of online customers' channel satisfaction (Devaraj, Fan, & Kohli, 2002) and factors that influence Internet commerce success (Torkzadeh & Dhillon, 2002). In most of these previous studies, effective Web design was used as one of the constructs. Thus, an empirical attempt to develop and validate a framework of effective designs for E-tail Web sites would provide important value, as metrics are required for Internet commerce to continue to make progress (Devaraj et al., 2002).

This study attempts to develop an empirically validated framework of user perception of effective designs for E-tail Web sites. In particular, this framework will help answer the main research questions: *What are the major designs determining E-tail Web site effectiveness? How do these designs support Web users' objectives in using the Web?* The study particularly focuses on E-tail Web sites that involve *"the buying and selling of goods and the associated and related information provision and gathering between companies and their customers over the Web."* In this study, the terms: "user," "customer," and "consumer" are used interchangeably and as synonyms.

Research Framework

"Fitness for use" is the basic meaning of quality; that is, an essential aspect of products or services is that they be fit for use by consumers (Juran & Gryna, 1970). "Fitness for use" emphasizes the importance of consumers' perception of quality since, ultimately, consumers will judge whether the product is fit for their use. For long-lived or complex products, "fitness for use" is often called "system effectiveness" (Juran et al., 1970). The concept of "fitness for use" has been adopted in information systems research, as well. For example, in conceptualizing the underlying aspects of data quality and information quality, the terms "data quality" and "information quality" were defined as "the data that are fit for use by data consumers" and "the information that is fit for use by information consumers," respectively (Huang, Lee, & Wang, 1999, p. 43; Wang & Strong, 1996, p. 6). Similarly, another formal construct, known as "Task-Technology Fit," focuses on matching the capabilities of the technology to the demands of the task (Goodhue, 1995; Goodhue & Thompson, 1995). The concept of "fitness for use" is consistent with the concept of "Task-Technology Fit" in that technology (e.g., E-tail Web site) will be used if, and only if, the functions available to the users support (i.e., fit) the activities of the user. Thus, we define an "effective E-tail Web site" as *"the E-tail Web site designed to be fit for use by Web users."* That is, an effective E-tail Web site should facilitate Web users to achieve a set of their specific mission requirements.

Additionally, the media "uses-and-gratifications approach" is a traditional research perspective that looks at how individuals consume particular mass media and/or media content to meet their social and psychological needs. This approach looks at consumers who pay attention to a specific medium and then describes why those consumers utilize that particular communication medium and what functions the medium serves for them (Anderson & Meyer, 1975). Researchers have also applied this approach to examine why consumers use the Web. Armstrong (1999) and King (1998) conducted two similar studies to reveal what draws users to this new communication medium. From results of the Factor Analysis conducted in these two studies, the significant reasons that consumers use the Web can be grouped into three main categories: (a) Information search (e.g., to get specific information about products, to learn about what could happen, as a source for general information), (b) Pleasure (e.g., to relax, to have a good time, because browsing is fun) and (c) Business transactions (e.g., to purchase products, to download programs or software).

Based on the definition of effective E-tail Web sites and the reasons that consumers use the Web, we propose a premise that *"effective designs for E-tail Web sites should support Web customers for their: (a) information search, (b) pleasure, and (c) business transactions."* This premise provides a framework (see Figure 1) and helps answer the two main research questions of this study. That is, major Web designs determining E-tail Web site effectiveness are those designs that support Web users

Figure 1. Framework of effective e-tail Web sites

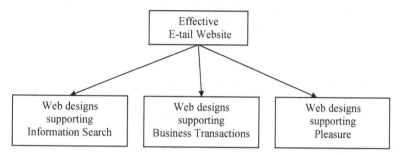

to easily obtain their desired information from the E-tail Web site, to effectively conduct business transactions via the E-tail Web site, and to have pleasure from their browsing activity when visiting the E-tail Web site.

Research Methodology

Research Instrument

Churchill (1979) noted that the development of better measures involves the generation of items that capture the construct. Similarly, to develop the framework of effective E-tail Web sites, we would generate Web design practices supporting each of the three significant reasons that consumers use E-tail Web sites. Thus, we collected 72 preliminary Web design practices suggested by both researchers and practitioners in various literatures (e.g., Gehrke & Turban, 1999; Katerattanakul & Siau, 1999; Rumpradit & Donnell, 1999; Spiliopoulos, 2000; Yoo & Bieber, 2000). Detailed descriptions of these items are in Appendix A.

Then, we developed a questionnaire to measure Web users' perception of how important each preliminary Web design practice is. This questionnaire includes 72 questions corresponding to the preliminary design practices. Each question is an importance-rating question, with a seven-point Likert scale (0 – Not Important at all; 6 – Extremely Important). The questionnaire was adjusted based on responses from the pre-test participants who have experience in research methodology, questionnaire design and Web design. This pre-test focused on content, format, readability, understandability and other potential problems with the preliminary questionnaire.

Additionally, we included instructions on how to answer the questions and the statement for creating a scenario that the respondent was using E-tail Web sites to accomplish the task of finding and/or purchasing appropriate Christmas presents for family members, to ensure that all respondents perceived a similar task while they were answering the questionnaire.

Respondents

Student respondents have been successfully used in many Web-related studies (e.g., D'Ambra 1999; Sukpanich & Chen, 1999; Zhang et al., 2000). Additionally, the HERMES Project (www.personal.umich.edu/~sgupta/hermes/) conducted by the University of Michigan suggested that the majority of Web users are college students or college graduates. Similarly, Jupiter Communications conducted a survey on the profile of online shoppers and found that 57% of the U.S. online shoppers either are college graduates or have some college education (Krantz, 1998). Greenfield Online conducted a survey of 1,400 four-year college students whose ages were between 18 and 24 years. The results showed that online consumer activity among this segment has increased overall—the number of college students making purchases online had jumped from 43% in 1998 to 61% in 1999 (Gaffney, 1999). Thus, college students were used as the respondents in this study.

The questionnaire was distributed to students in several courses for undergraduate and graduate levels at two universities. Totally, 427 students participated in the study. Responses from these students were randomly divided in half. Data in the first half, the "testing" group, consisted of 213 respondents. The other half of data, the "hold-out" group, included 214 respondents.

Analyses and Results

This study consists of two main analyses: exploratory study and confirmatory study. Data in the "testing" group and the "hold-out" group were used in the exploratory study and the confirmatory study, respectively.

Exploratory Study

The exploratory study consists of two analyses: Descriptive Statistics and Exploratory Factor Analysis (EFA). Although some previous studies suggested how preliminary Web design practices could support browsing activity, none of these studies has validated these suggestions. There was no empirically validated foundation to pre-specify the construct structure—which preliminary Web design practices support which reason that consumers use E-tail Web sites. Thus, an EFA was conducted to refine the construct structure for each reason that consumers use E-tail Web sites.

Descriptive Statistics

The exploratory study began with a descriptive statistics analysis to examine: (1) normality of the score distribution for each item and (2) how important the respondents rated each item (see Appendix A). Score distribution for some items (items 7, 13, 38, 41 and 42) may be moderately non-normal, since the absolute values of their skewness and/or kurtosis were ranging from 2.0 to 3.0 and from 7.0 to 21.0, respectively (Curran, West, & Finch, 1996). However, under the condition of moderate non-normality, researchers have held that factor models may be developed appropriately with ordinal measures (e.g., Boomsma, 1987); thus, the following EFA could proceed. Regarding the importance of each item, on average, six items (items 6, 33, 34, 35, 36 and 37) were rated lower than mid-point of the scale (3.0). That is, these six items were perceived as "not-so-important" items; thus, they were dropped from the framework. The remaining 66 items were used in the following EFA.

Exploratory Factor Analysis (EFA)

EFA was conducted by using Maximum Likelihood (ML) as a method for extracting factors. ML was chosen because it is robust to moderate departures from normality in generating appropriate factor solutions (Boomsma, 1987). We specified a minimum factor loading of 0.40, since factors with 10 or more loadings greater than 0.40 are reliable if the sample size is greater than 150 respondents (Guadagnoli & Velicer, 1988).

It was noticed that specifying 16 factors resulted in the most interpretable structure (see Appendix B). This 16-factor solution provides a total explained variance of 69.3%. Coefficient alphas of all emerging factors are higher than the suggested value of 0.70 for exploratory research (Nunnally, 1978). Additionally, all corrected item-total correlations (r) between each item and its corresponding emerging factor are higher than the suggested value of 0.30 used in a previous study (Doll & Torkzadeh, 1988). However, two items, item 7 and item 57, do not have sufficient loadings of 0.40 onto any emerging factor. Thus, these two items were excluded from the framework, and the following confirmatory study analyzed only the remaining 64 items.

In Table 1, we name each emerging factor and hypothesize which reason—(a) information search, (b) pleasure or (c) business transactions—each factor supports when consumers are using the Web.

Confirmatory Study

EFA result provides the construct structure of the proposed research framework, and this structure is ready to be validated by a different data set. Thus, a confirmatory study was conducted to validate the construct structure of the proposed research framework. This confirmatory study employed a model fit test, referred to as "Confirmatory Factor Analysis" (CFA), to validate the emerging structure (with 64 items) that we hypothesized in the previous exploratory study (Table 1). CFA was conducted by using data in the "hold-out" group, with 214 respondents.

Descriptive statistics for data in the "hold-out" group show that none of the 64 items had its mean score lower than mid-point of the scale. Additionally, the maximum absolute skewness and kurtosis values are 2.56 and 7.15 respectively; thus, score distribution for some items may be moderately non-normal but none of them is extremely non-normal (Curran et al., 1996).

In CFA, ML estimation was chosen because: (1) fit indices obtained from this method perform much better than those indices obtained from other estimators (Hu & Bentler, 1998) and (2) ML method was also used in the previous exploratory study. With ML method, Hu and Bentler (1998) recommended a two-index presentation with Standardized Root-Mean-square Residual (SRMR) and Comparative Fit Index (CFI). Results of CFA, including standardized loadings and explained variance (R^2), are presented in Figure 2. Fit indices (SRMR and CFI) for the emerging framework

Table 1. Emerging factors and reasons that consumers use the Web

Emerging Factor	Item	Reason
I Tools supporting navigation	1. Provide clear directions for navigating the Web site	
	2. Provide site map, table of contents, search engine, etc.	
	3. Provide indicator of Web page location	
L Content Customization	4. Adjust contents to match customer's interest	
	5. Refer to customers by their names	
C Complete product information	8. Provide complete detailed product information	
	9. Provide varieties of products	
	10. Provide varieties of brands and models	
	11. Contain availability or "in-stock" information	Information Search
	12. Specify time required for delivery	
	13. Quote current product prices	
	14. Include product pictures	
	ü=ü=üüüüüüüüüüüüüüü=üüüüüü	
E Non-confusing and easy to understand presentation	19. Use non-confusing visual elements	
	20. Arrange well-organized layout of page components	
	21. Consistently use similar visual elements	
	22. Every Web page is of reasonable length	
	23. Logically organize content into various sections	
	27. Not contain any broken hyperlinks	
	28. Hyperlink description is relevant to its destination	
O Hyperlink efficiency	ü=üüüüü=üüüüüüüüüüüüüüüüü	
	25. Provide internal hyperlinks	
	26. Provide similar internal links on every page	

Table 1. continued

üüüüüü	Item	Reason
K Useful information	16. Highlight new products or recent product changes 17. Highlight special offers 18. Specify revision date for each Web page 53. Provide company's contact information 54. Provide Help or Online Customer Service 55. Provide Frequently Asked Questions (FAQs)	Information Search
B Enjoyment	29. Use pleasing colors and background 30. Use pleasing fonts, icons and headings 31. Include attractive images and layout 32. Provide adequate brightness	Pleasure
M Security and trustworthiness	39. Employ user authentication û=ûûû=ûûûûûûûûûûûûûûûûûûûû 46. Include third-party assurance	Business Transactions
H Customers' personal data	43. Inform customers on collecting their personal data 44. State how customers' personal data will be used 45. Ask permission for other uses of customers' data	
F Helpful features	56. Assist customers in completing transactions 58. Provide help for resolving transaction errors 59. Allow customers to review previous transactions 60. Provide transaction acknowledgement 61. Mechanism to track transaction status	
G Company's information	47. Provide company's background 48. Include company's mission statement 49. Include announcements, company news, etc.	
D Transaction rule	50. Employ rules governing the transactions 51. Describe how transaction rules are applied û=ûûûû=ûûûûûûûûûûûûûû=ûûûûû	
A Reliability and flexibility	41. Ensure correct price calculation 42. Ensure correct transaction processing 69. Pending transactions don't need to be re-entered 65. Customers can change their requirements 38. Use secure transaction processing	

Emerging Factors	Item	Reason
P Payment methods	66. Accept payment by credit cards 67. Accept payment by debit or check cards 68. Accept payment by electronic or digital cash	Information Search
J Ease of transaction completion	62. Minimum and simple steps to complete transactions 63. Minimum data required to complete transactions 64. Use pre-registered customer data	
N Response time	70. Provide fast response time 71. Require short time to download each Web page 72. Each Web page is downloaded within 10 seconds	

Table 2. Confirmatory factor analysis—Fit indices

Fit Index	Information Search	Pleasure	Business Transactions
SRMR	0.09	0.05	0.08
CFI	0.86	0.96	0.90

Figure 2. Confirmatory factor analysis

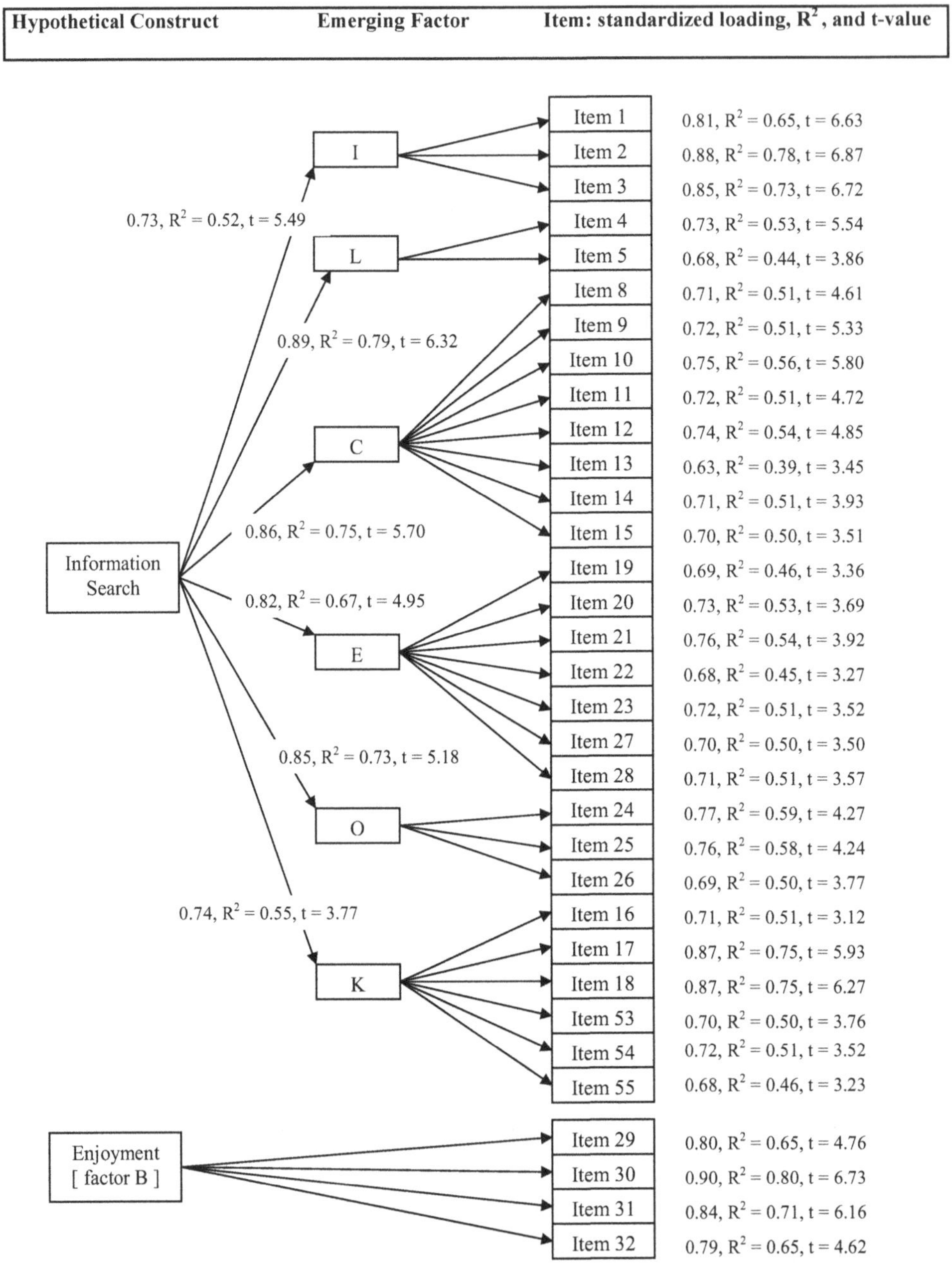

Hypothetical Construct	Emerging Factor	Item: standardized loading, R^2, and t-value

Figure 2. continued

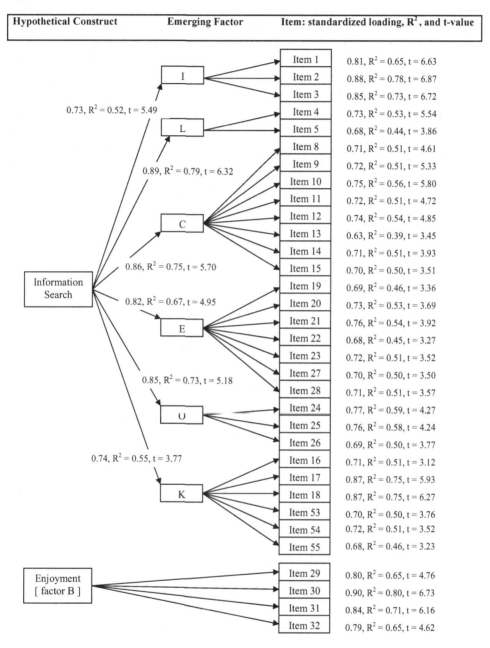

related to each reason that consumers use the Web (i.e., hypothetical construct, see Figure 2) are reported in Table 2.

In CFA, there are 79 standardized loadings (64 loadings from emerging factors to each item and 15 loadings from hypothetical constructs to each emerging factor, see Figure 2). These standardized loadings are in moderate-to-high level, ranging from 0.63 to 0.92. Among these loadings, 74 have their R^2 higher than the rule-of-thumb "50% or more variance extracted" (Bagozzi & Yi, 1988). The R^2 values of all loadings range from 0.39 to 0.84. It is worthy of noting that all five loadings with R^2 lower than 0.50 (loadings for items 5, 13, 19, 22 and 55, see Figure 2) are related to the same hypothetical construct (information search). CFA also reports a t-value for each standardized loading. As the t-value for every standardized loading is greater than 2.58 (see Figure 2), every standardized loading is significant at the p = 0.01 level.

Fit indices reported in Table 2 show that for both pleasure and business transactions constructs, SRMR and CFI values are better than the maximum cutoff value of 0.08 for SRMR and the minimum cutoff value of 0.90 for CFI (Hu & Bentler, 1995). However, for information search construct, both SRMR and CFI do not meet their required cutoff values. Results of fit indices for the information search construct are consistent with the findings that R^2 values for some loadings related to this construct are lower than 0.50.

Discussion

Framework for Effective E-Tail Web Sites

Based on the concept of "fitness for use" and the reasons that consumers use the Web, the proposed framework for effective E-tail Web sites was hypothesized to demonstrate the designs supporting Web customers for their (a) information search, (b) pleasure, and (c) business transactions. The analysis suggested that the emerging framework consisted of 16 factors, with 64 Web design practices supporting the three hypothesized reasons for using the Web (Table 1).

Designs Supporting Information Search

Six emerging factors supporting consumer information search in E-tail Web sites include:

- Tools supporting navigation
- Content customization
- Complete product information
- Non-confusing and easy-to-understand presentation

- Hyperlink efficiency
- Useful information.

Understanding consumer information search is crucial for designing effective marketing communication to provide information and to influence consumers' decisions (Schmidt & Spreng, 1996; Wilkie & Dickson, 1985). Consumer information search processes are mediated by four main determinants: ability, motivation, benefit and cost (Schmidt & Spreng, 1996). We argue that, in the Web context, ability to search is the users' capability to locate particular information included in the Web site. Thus, the emerging factors "Tools supporting navigation" and "Hyperlink efficiency" help increase Web users' ability to search, since these factors emphasize the navigation mechanisms that allow Web users to reach their desired information in the fewest steps.

Motivation to search is influenced by consumers' involvement and need for cognition (Schmidt & Spreng, 1996). Involvement and cognition can be increased by customization of the information provided over E-tail Web sites as shown in the factor "Content customization." Additionally, this customization gives customers a value-added experience and adds to the compelling reasons for revisiting (Turban et al., 1999).

Finally, perceived benefits and costs of information search are affected by the importance of information and its quality since, for example, complete, accurate and easy-to-understand product information can facilitate consumers to perceive lower risks, better justifications for their decisions and ease in reaching their optimal decisions. Therefore, the emerging factors "Complete product information," "Useful information," and "Non-confusing and easy-to-understand presentation," increase Web users' perceived benefit vs. cost advantages in their information search over E-tail Web sites.

Designs Supporting Pleasure

Marketing literature (e.g., Bloch & Richins, 1983) suggests that satisfied consumption activity not only comes from an extrinsic reward of purchasing products, but also gains intrinsic and emotional rewards from purchasing-derived pleasure. Thus, designing the site to facilitate enjoyment is relevant to effective E-tail Web sites.

Since the computer screen functions as the limited stimulus field and users reported being "mesmerized" during their computer interactions (Webster, Trevino, & Ryan, 1993), attractiveness and aesthetic appeal of various visual elements of a Web page can lead users to perceive enjoyment while they are reading or browsing the site. Consequently, the emerging factor "Enjoyment," with its items related to pleasing design, attractive image and brightness of Web page, will support users to perceive pleasure during their visit to e-tail Web sites.

Designs Supporting Business Transactions

Nine emerging factors supporting business transactions conducted over e-tail Web sites include:

- Security and trustworthiness
- Customers' personal data
- Helpful features
- Company's information
- Transaction rule
- Reliability and flexibility
- Payment methods
- Ease of transaction completion
- Response time.

Maximizing trusts and minimizing perceived risks of online transactions is necessary for effective e-tail Web sites. The emerging factor "Security and trustworthiness" consists of the items that directly interact with users and increases their trust in transactions conducted over E-tail Web sites (the items include user authentication, information on secure transaction systems and trusted third-party assurance). Similarly, the factor "Customers' personal data" also helps improve users' trust in online transactions, since this factor directly addresses users' concern about the secondary uses (other than for shipping and billing) of their personal information (Culman, 1995). Furthermore, customers trust a seller because of the seller's reputation, contractual statements and regulation of transactions (Milne & Boza, 1998); thus, two emerging factors, "Company's information" and "Transaction rule," help increase customers' trust in E-tail Web sites.

Perceived system quality also affects users' trust in e-tail Web sites. A number of distinct measures for IS quality includes system reliability and flexibility (Srinivasan, 1985). Thus, the emerging factors "Reliability and flexibility" and "Response time" include the items that lead users to perceive system quality and eventually increase their trust in E-tail Web sites.

Similarly, perceived ease of use is one of the measures for user satisfaction, system adoption and IS success (e.g., Davis, 1989; Moore & Benbasat, 1991). Additionally, useful and helpful information provided is a significant factor for successful retailing (Clodfelter & Overstreet, 1996). Thus, transactions conducted over E-tail Web sites should be simple and short, and should provide customers their convenience and the help that they may need. Ease of use, convenience and help are the issues emphasized by three emerging factors: "Ease of transaction completion," "Payment methods" and "Helpful features."

Implications

The empirically validated framework for user perception of effective e-tail Web sites developed in this study provides the participants in E-tail Web site development a preliminary checklist of anticipated effective designs. This framework is a useful tool in recognizing and understanding customer requirements and should serve as a starting point for designing effective e-tail Web sites.

In addition, this study offers contributions and implications for research. First, the empirically validated framework could be used as the conceptual basis for classifying groups of e-tail Web sites that are designed by emphasizing different specific requirements. Then, researchers would be able to study these different categories of E-tail Web sites in a heterogeneous manner. Second, this framework could also be used to provide variables related to an effective Web design construct in any Web-related studies. Third, while further testing of the framework with other data sets is warranted, the extensive framework development process employed in this study makes a methodological contribution to e-business literature.

Fourth, it was noted that items 36 and 37 were dropped from the framework since they were perceived as the "not-so-important" items (Appendix A). The deletion of these items is inconsistent with the concept of information sharing on a virtual community (Armstrong & Hagel, 1996; Peppers & Rogers, 1997; Schubert & Ginsburg, 1999) that emphasizes the importance of knowledge shared by community members. Thus, further investigations are needed to draw any specific conclusions regarding the deletion of these items. Fifth, although the EFA conducted in this study provides all satisfactory results, the CFA shows some results, related to the information search construct, that do not meet the recommended standards (i.e., some R^2 values are lower than 0.50 and the fit indices do not pass the suggested cutoff values). These results suggest that further studies are needed to improve the structure of the information search construct (e.g., additional design practices for this construct).

Sixth, this study does not investigate any reciprocal influences among the three reasons that consumers use the Web. Thus, further studies to hypothesize and test these reciprocal influences would help researchers better understand the effects of the three reasons that consumers use the Web on their online experience. Finally, since this study is cross-sectional, the framework tested in this study represents a "snap-shot" in time. Because Internet commerce is a new, rapidly growing and fast-changing area, Web user requirements may not always remain the same. Thus, a longitudinal study to monitor this change and its effects on the framework would be of important value.

Limitations

Similar to other empirical studies, this study has certain limitations. First, as with all other studies conducted in academic settings with student respondents, results of this study represent the perceptions and particular characteristics of this specific group. Second, some results from the CFA do not meet recommended values. Thus, researchers should exercise caution and judgment in extrapolating results of this study from the responding sample to the broader population.

As the first part of the analysis (i.e., the exploratory study) takes an exploratory approach to refine the construct structure for each reason that consumers use e-tail Web sites, some Web design practices were dropped from the framework. Researchers should be aware that dropping these Web design practices may result in an incomplete framework, unfavorable fit indices in the CFA and inconsistent results with marketing literature. Nevertheless, only further studies suggested in the aforementioned implications would provide more explanations.

Conclusion

The empirically validated framework for effective e-tail Web sites developed in this study helps answer two main research questions: *What are the major designs determining E-tail Web site effectiveness?* and *How do these designs support Web users' objectives in using the Web?* From the emerging framework, the major designs determining E-tail Web site effectiveness consist of 16 factors, with 64 Web design practices. These 16 factors support the three main reasons that consumers use the Web: (a) Information search, (b) pleasure, and (c) business transactions.

In the emerging framework, there are six factors supporting consumer information search. How these six factors support consumer information search can be explained by main determinants of the consumer information search process. Similarly, one emerging factor supporting pleasure is explained by results of previous research on effects of the computer display on its users. Finally, nine factors supporting business transactions are based on the issues of trust and security, system quality and perceived ease of use.

References

Anderson, J.A., & Meyer, T.P. (1975). Functionalism and mass media. *Journal of Broadcasting, 9*(1), 11-22.

Armstrong, A., & Hagel, J. (1996). The real value of on-line communities. *Harvard Business Review, 74*(May/June), 134-141.

Armstrong, M.H. (1999). *The gratification dimensions of the Internet's World Wide Web: An exploratory study.* Unpublished doctoral dissertation, Florida State University.

Bagozzi, R.P., & Yi, Y. (1988). On the evaluation of structural equation models. *Journal of the Academy of Marketing Science, 16*(1), 74-94.

Barnes, S.J., & Vidgen, R. (2000). Information and interaction quality: Evaluating Internet bookshop Web site with Webqual. *Proceedings of the 13th International Bled Electronic Commerce Conference*, 426-444.

Bhattacherjee, A. (2001) An empirical analysis of the antecedents of electronic commerce service continuance. *Decision Support Systems, 32*(2), 201-214.

Bloch, P.H., & Richins, L. (1983). Shopping without purchase: An investigation of consumer browsing behavior. In R.P. Bagozzi & A.M. Tybout (Eds.), *Advances in consumer research* (pp. 389-393). Ann Arbor, Michigan: Association of Consumer Research.

Boomsma, A. (1987). The robustness of maximum likelihood estimation in structural equation models. In P. Cuttance & R. Ecob (Eds.), *Structural equation modeling by example: Applications in educational, sociological, and behavioral research* (pp. 160-188). Cambridge: Cambridge University Press.

Churchill Jr., G.A. (1979). A paradigm for developing better measures of marketing constructs. *Journal of Marketing Research, 16*(February), 64-73.

Clodfelter, R., & Overstreet, J. (1996). Technological profiles of shopping centers: Present and future use. *Journal of Shopping Center Research*, (Spring/Summer), 59-94.

Conger, S., & Mason, R. (1998). *Planning and designing effective Web sites.* Cambridge: Course Technology.

Culman, M.J. (1995). Consumer awareness of name removal procedures: Implications for direct marketing. *Journal of Direct Marketing, 9*(2), 10-19.

Curran, P.J., West, S.G., & Finch, J.F. (1996). The robustness of test statistics to non-normality and specification error in confirmatory factor analysis. *Psychological Methods, 1*(1), 16-29.

D'Ambra, J. (1999). Preliminary investigations of user evaluation of the WWW. *Proceedings of the Fifth Americas Conference on Information Systems.*

Davis, F.D. (1989). Perceived usefulness, perceived ease of use, and user acceptance of information technology. *MIS Quarterly, 13*(3), 319-340.

Devaraj, S., Fan, M., & Kohli, R. (2002). Antecedents of B2C channel satisfaction and preference: Validating e-commerce metrics. *Information Systems Research, 13*(3), 316-333.

Doll, W.J., & Torkzadeh, G. (1988). The measurement of end-user computing satisfaction. *MIS Quarterly, 12*(2), 259-274.

Gaffney, J. (1999). College students are ready to buy online. Retrieved January 27, 2003 from www.channelseven.com/adinsight/surveys_research/#1999

Gehrke, D., & Turban, E. (1999). Determinants of successful Web site design: Relative importance and recommendations for effectiveness. *Proceedings of the 32nd Hawaii International Conference on System Sciences.*

Goodhue, D. (1995). Understanding user evaluations of Information Systems. *Management Science, 41*(12), 1827-1844.

Goodhue, D., & Thompson, R. (1995). Task-technology fit and individual performance. *MIS Quarterly, 19*(2), 213-236.

Guadagnoli, E., & Velicer, W. (1988). Relation of sample size to the stability of component patterns. *Psychological Bulletin, 103*(2), 265-275.

Hoffman, D., & Novak, T. (2000) How to acquire customers on the Web. *Harvard Business Review, 78*(3), 179.

Hu, L., & Bentler, P.M. (1998). Fit indices in covariance structure modeling: Sensitivity to underparameterized model misspecification. *Psychological Methods, 3*(4), 424-453.

Hu, L., & Bentler, P.M. (1995). Evaluating model fit. In R.H. Hoyle (Ed.), *Structural equation modeling: Concepts, issues, and applications* (pp. 76-99). Newbury Park: Sage.

Huang, K., Lee, Y.W., & Wang, R.Y. (1999). *Quality information and knowledge.* Upper Saddle River, NJ: Prentice Hall.

Juran, J.M., & Gryna, F.M. (1970). *Quality planning and analysis: From product development through usage.* New York: McGraw-Hill.

Katerattanakul, P. (2002). Framework of effective Web site design for business-to-consumer Internet commerce. *INFOR, 40*(1), 57-70.

Katerattanakul, P., & Siau, K. (1999). Measuring information quality of Web sites: Development of an instrument. *Proceedings of the 19th International Conference on Information Systems.*

King, R.E. (1998). *The uses and gratifications of the World Wide Web: An audience analysis for local television broadcasters.* Unpublished doctoral dissertation, University of Tennessee.

Krantz, M. (1998). Click till you drop. *Time Magazine*, (July 20), 34-41.

Liao, Z., & Cheung, M. (2001). Internet-based e-shopping and consumer attitudes: An empirical study. *Information & Management, 38*(5), 299-306.

Lynch, P., & Horton, S. (1999). *Web style guide: Basic design principles for creating Web sites.* Yale University Press.

Milne, G.R., & Boza, M. (1998). Trust and concern in consumers' perceptions of marketing information management practices. *MSI Working Paper*, Report No. 98-117, September.

Moore, G.C., & Benbasat, I. (1991). Development of an instrument to measure the perceptions of adopting an information technology innovation. *Information Systems Research, 2*(3), 192-222.

Novak, T., Hoffman, D., & Yung, Y. (2000). Measuring the customer experience in online environments: A structural modeling approach. *Marketing Science, 19*(1), 22-42.

Nunnally, J.C. (1978). *Psychometric theory.* New York: McGraw Hill.

Peppers, D., & Rogers, M. (1997). *Enterprise one to one: Tools for competing in the interactive age.* New York: Bantam Doubleday Dell.

Rumpardit, C., & Donnell, L. (1999). Navigational cues on user interface design to produce better information seeking on the World Wide Web. *Proceedings of the 32nd Hawaii International Conference on System Sciences.*

Schmidt, J.B., & Spreng, R.A. (1996). A proposed model of external consumer information search. *Journal of the Academy of Marketing Science, 24*(3), 246-256.

Schneider, G., & Perry, J. (2000). *Electronic commerce.* Cambridge: Course Technology.

Schubert, P., & Ginsburg, M. (1999). Virtual communities of transaction: The role of personalization in electronic commerce. *Proceedings of the 12th Bled Electronic Commerce Conference*, 647-663.

Schubert, P., & Selz, D. (2000). Measuring effectiveness of e-commerce Web site. In S.J. Barnes & B. Hunt (Eds.), *Electronic commerce and virtual business.* Oxford: Butterworth-Heinemann.

Spiliopoulos, M. (2000). Web usage mining for Web site evaluation. *Communications of the ACM, 43*(8), 127-134.

Srinivasan, A. (1985). Alternative measures of system effectiveness: Associations and implications. *MIS Quarterly, 9*(3), 243-253.

Sukpanich, N., & Chen, L. (1999). Antecedents of desirable consumer behaviors in electronic commerce. *Proceedings of the Fifth Americas Conference on Information Systems.*

Torkzadeh, G., & Dhillon, G. (2002). Measuring factors that influence the success of Internet commerce. *Information Systems Research, 13*(2), 187-204.

Turban, E., Lee, J., King, D., & Chung, H.M. (1999). *Electronic commerce: A managerial perspective.* Upper Saddle River, NJ: Prentice Hall.

Wang, R.Y., & Strong, D.M. (1996). Beyond accuracy: What data quality means to data consumers. *Journal of Management Information Systems, 12*(4), 5-34.

Webster, J., Trevino, L.K., & Ryan, L. (1993). The dimensionality and correlates in human computer interactions. *Computers in Human Behavior, 9*(4), 411-426.

Wilkie, W.L., & Dickson, P.R. (1985). Shopping for appliances: Consumers' strategies and patterns of information search. *MSI Working Paper*, Report No.85-108, November.

Yoo, J., & Bieber, M. (2000). Towards a relationship navigation analysis. *Proceedings of the 33rd Hawaii International Conference on System Sciences.*

Zhang, P., Dran, G.M.V., Small, R.V., & Barcellos, S. (2000). A two factor theory for Web site design. *Proceedings of the 33rd Hawaii International Conference on System Sciences.*

Appendix A

Preliminary Items and Their Descriptive Statistics

For each of the following items, please rate *its degree of importance for effective COMMERCIAL WEB SITES.* The more important the item is, the higher the number that should be circled.

Assume that you are facing the following scenario:

Christmas eve is around the corner. You are too busy to go shopping so you decide to try purchasing Christmas presents online. You begin to visit some Web sites, hoping to find appropriate Christmas presents for your loved ones. You remember that your mother loves to listen to Elton John and you wish you could get some Elton John CDs to surprise her. Furthermore, you are thinking of getting a Barbie doll or a children's storybook for your daughter, but you are not sure which presents will be suitable for your sister and for your nephew. Traveling from one Web site to another, you visit the "All-Presents.com." You see some products and hope to find and purchase the appropriate presents from this Web site.

What are the characteristics of the "All-Presents.com" Web site that are important to help you to find the appropriate Christmas presents and what are the features of the "All-presents.com" that will influence your purchasing decisions from the Web site?

Web design practices	from scale 0 - 6					
	Mean	Max.	Min.	SD	Skewness	Kurtosis
1. Provide clear directions for navigating the Web site	4.362	6	0	1.27	-0.484	-0.301
2. Provide site map, table of contents, search engine, etc.	4.554	6	0	1.19	-0.705	0.514
3. Provide indicator of Web page location within the site	4.254	6	0	1.30	-0.559	-0.042
4. Automatically adjust contents to match customer's interest	3.474	6	0	1.47	-0.373	-0.075
5. Refer to customers by their names	3.094	6	0	1.69	-0.025	-0.708
6. Suggest products related to previous purchase(s)	2.755[a]	6	0	1.28	-0.265	-0.705
7. Web site provides reliable information	5.615	6	2	0.73	-2.422[b]	6.833
8. Provide complete detailed product information	5.085	6	2	1.00	-1.037	0.560
9. Offer varieties of products	4.592	6	0	1.17	-0.985	1.457
10. Offer varieties of brands and models	4.620	6	1	1.10	-0.636	-0.095
11. Contain availability or "in-stock" information	5.042	6	3	0.95	-0.621	-0.644
12. Specify time required for delivery	5.244	6	2	0.90	-1.121	0.655
13. Quote current product prices	5.535	6	1	0.78	-2.105[b]	5.974
14. Include product pictures	5.315	6	2	0.88	-1.333	1.543
15. Provide detailed product differentiation and comparability	4.150	6	1	1.20	-0.343	-0.384

Web design practices	from scale 0 - 6					
	Mean	Max.	Min.	SD	Skewness	Kurtosis
16. Highlight new products or recent product changes	4.113	6	0	1.26	-0.459	-0.011
17. Highlight special offers	4.573	6	0	1.23	-0.785	0.418
18. Specify revision date for each Web page	4.066	6	0	1.56	-0.540	-0.436
19. Use non-confusing visual elements	4.639	6	2	1.04	-0.425	-0.499
20. Arrange well-organized layout of page components	4.643	6	2	1.00	-0.387	-0.422
21. Consistently use similar visual elements on each page	3.887	6	0	1.43	-0.361	-0.311
22. Every Web page is of reasonable length	4.005	6	0	1.46	-0.620	0.203
23. Logically organize site's content into various sections	4.714	6	1	1.14	-0.660	-0.248
24. Users will obtain desired information in fewest steps	4.296	6	0	1.24	-0.681	0.176
25. Provide internal hyperlinks to navigate within the site	4.441	6	0	1.16	-0.812	1.152
26. Consistently provide similar internal links on every page	4.296	6	1	1.13	-0.263	-0.398
27. Not contain any broken hyperlinks	4.789	6	1	1.26	-0.861	-0.130
28. Hyperlink description is relevant to its destination	4.648	6	1	1.15	-0.719	0.166
29. Use pleasing colors and background	3.502	6	0	1.27	-0.139	-0.303
30. Use pleasing fonts, icons and headings	3.643	6	0	1.30	-0.195	-0.476
31. Include attractive images and layout	3.941	6	1	1.15	0.067	-0.836
32. Provide adequate brightness	3.831	6	0	1.28	-0.227	-0.270
33. Include background sound or music	2.211 [a]	6	0	1.72	0.389	-0.793
34. Use animation	2.498 [a]	6	0	1.73	0.240	-0.742
35. Include senses of humor	2.775 [a]	6	0	1.65	0.036	-0.695
36. Create online community (e.g., bulletin, discussion group)	2.386 [a]	6	0	1.60	0.219	-0.729
37. Accept/provide customers' recommendations	2.895 [a]	6	0	1.48	-0.147	-0.269
38. Use secure transaction processing	5.700	6	1	0.73	-3.000 [b]	10.800 [b]
39. Employ user authentication to prove customer identity	5.319	6	0	0.99	-1.792	4.157
40. Inform customers about use of secure transaction systems	5.197	6	0	1.07	-1.598	3.137
41. Ensure correct price calculation	5.526	6	0	0.95	-2.605 [b]	7.926 [b]
42. Ensure correct transaction processing	5.592	6	1	0.78	-2.433 [b]	7.302 [b]
43. Inform customers on collecting their personal data	4.563	6	0	1.32	-0.650	-0.173
44. Clearly state how customers' personal data will be used	4.920	6	0	1.32	-1.157	0.612
45. Ask permission for other uses of customers' personal data	5.385	6	2	1.05	-1.769	2.340
46. Include third-party assurance	5.075	6	0	1.08	-1.184	1.525

Web design practices	from scale 0 - 6					
	Mean	Max.	Min.	SD	Skewness	Kurtosis
47. Provide company's background	3.728	6	0	1.33	0.012	-0.612
48. Include company's mission statement	3.000	6	0	1.47	-0.054	-0.541
49. Include announcements, company news, etc.	3.193	6	0	1.42	0.125	-0.654
50. Employ rules governing the transactions	4.897	6	2	1.08	-0.754	-0.245
51. Describe how transaction rules are applied ü=üüüüü=üüüüüü	5.061	6	2	1.00	-0.962	0.289
ü=üüüüü=üüüüüüüüüüüü=üüüüü	5.197	6	2	0.95	-1.147	0.751
53. Provide company's contact information	4.991	6	2	1.02	-0.792	-0.135
54. Provide Help or Online Customer Service	4.934	6	1	0.97	-0.841	0.768
55. Provide Frequently Asked Questions (FAQs)	3.817	6	0	1.32	-0.358	0.256
56. Assist customers in completing steps of the transactions	4.840	6	0	1.10	-1.016	1.357
57. Assist customers in product selections	3.798	6	0	1.24	-0.456	0.112
58. Provide help for resolving transaction errors	4.925	6	3	0.96	-0.424	-0.884
59. Allow customers to review their previous transactions	4.690	6	0	1.08	-0.800	1.106
60. Provide transaction acknowledgement	5.343	6	1	0.90	-1.448	2.298
61. Include/provide mechanism to track transaction status	5.085	6	0	1.10	-1.357	2.188
62. Minimum and simple steps required to complete transaction	5.099	6	0	0.94	-1.319	3.384
63. Minimum customer data required to complete transaction	4.826	6	0	1.11	-0.867	0.809
64. Use pre-registered customer data to shorten time to complete transaction	4.676	6	0	1.38	-1.180	1.333
65. Customers can change their requirements anytime before submitting the transactions	5.155	6	0	1.07	-1.532	2.947
66. Accept payment by credit cards	5.423	6	2	0.86	-1.557	1.916
67. Accept payment by debit or check cards	4.977	6	0	1.32	-1.687	3.136
68. Accept payment by electronic or digital cash	3.850	6	0	1.71	-0.695	-0.167
69. Pending transactions can be submitted without re-entering	4.535	6	0	1.33	-0.993	1.121
70. Provide fast response time	5.465	6	3	0.81	-1.473	1.430
71. Require short time to download each Web page	5.549	6	2	0.72	-1.808	3.805
72. Each Web page is downloaded within 10 seconds	5.132	6	1	1.08	-1.121	0.519

a. These items received the average rating lower than mid-point of the scale (3.0)

b. Score distribution for these items may be moderately non-normal since the absolute values of their skewness and/or kurtosis were ranging from 2.0 to 3.0 and from 7.0 to 21.0, respectively (Curran et al., 1996)

Appendix B

Exploratory Factor Analysis

Emerging Factors

Items	r	A 0.80[b]	B 0.92[b]	C 0.80[b]	D 0.90[b]	E 0.84[b]	F 0.78[b]	G 0.83[b]	H 0.82[b]	I 0.81[b]	J 0.79[b]	K 0.75[b]	L 0.75[b]	M 0.78[b]	N 0.79[b]	O 0.75[b]	P 0.70[b]
41	0.71	.734															
42	0.72	.731															
65	0.67	.696															
69	0.46	.539															
38	0.48	.537															
30	0.87		.887														
29	0.85		.866														
31	0.82		.830														
32	0.69		.764														
10	0.63			.774													
9	0.57			.732													
11	0.50			.580													
13	0.54	.475		.556													
15	0.46			.473													
12	0.52			.443													
14	0.52			.409													
8	0.43			.402													
51	0.86				.828												
52	0.75				.775												
50	0.78				.746												
21	0.61					.691											
22	0.57					.689											
23	0.64					.567											
27	0.50					.548											
19	0.66					.528											
20	0.70		.424			.506											
28	0.53					.458											

Items	r	A 0.80[b]	B 0.92[b]	C 0.80[b]	D 0.90[b]	E 0.84[b]	F 0.78[b]	G 0.83[b]	H 0.82[b]	I 0.81[b]	J 0.79[b]	K 0.75[b]	L 0.75[b]	M 0.78[b]	N 0.79[b]	O 0.75[b]	P 0.70[b]
60	0.63						.753										
59	0.57						.507										
56	0.48						.573										
61	0.52						.571										
58	0.57						.426										
48	0.72							.779									
49	0.72							.753									
47	0.65							.729									
43	0.67								.792								
44	0.73								.787								
45	0.64								.738								
2	0.70									.779							
1	0.62									.764							
3	0.64									.726							
63	0.63										.734						
62	0.63										.723						
64	0.50										.677						
54	0.52							.410				.630					
18	0.55											.548					
53	0.45											.545					
16	0.55											.452	.439				
17	0.52											.424					
55	0.38											.404					

Emerging Factors

Emerging Factors

Items	r	A 0.80[b]	B 0.92[b]	C 0.80[b]	D 0.90[b]	E 0.84[b]	F 0.78[b]	G 0.83[b]	H 0.82[b]	I 0.81[b]	J 0.79[b]	K 0.75[b]	L 0.75[b]	M 0.78[b]	N 0.79[b]	O 0.75[b]	P 0.70[b]
5	0.61												.728				
4	0.61												.720				
40	0.69													.790			
46	0.73													.783			
39	0.46													.502			
71	0.78														.701		
70	0.65														.643		
72	0.55														.606		
25	0.72															.780	
26	0.53															.715	
24	0.49															.496	
67	0.53																.768
68	0.45																.553
66	0.42	.447															.506
7[a]																	
57[a]																	

a. These items did not load onto any emerging factor based on the required factor loading of 0.40
b. Coefficient alpha for each emerging factor
r: Corrected item-total correlation between the item and its corresponding emerging factor

The chapter was previously published in the Journal of Electronic Commerce in Organizations, 3(1), 13-34, 2005.

Chapter XV

E-Commerce Education in China: Driving Forces, Status, and Strategies

Xianfeng Zhang, Xi'an Jiaotong University, China

Qi Li, Xi'an Jiaotong University, China

Zhangxi Lin, Texas Tech University, USA

Executive Summary

With an explosive growth of e-businesses worldwide, e-commerce in China is booming, leading to the development of e-commerce education. This paper is intended to investigate whether the education system in China accords well with the market demand and the status of e-commerce programs in China in order to seek strategies for China to cope with the challenges of global e-commerce empowered by fast updated information technologies. First, we construct a four-layer conceptual model to describe the relevant factors influencing e-commerce and e-commerce education. We then present the status of China's e-commerce education in different educational categories. Although we find that current problems in China's e-commerce education can be resorted in quantity and quality aspects, it generally is on the right track. Finally, we propose several main strategies for promoting the development of e-commerce education, in which the education system reformation is top priority and in which the government will play a critical role.

Introduction

The rapid growth of e-commerce imposes an increasing demand for professionals who possess the knowledge of conducting businesses in this fast-evolving electronic marketplace (Brin, 1999). In order to cope with the ever-increasing demand in e-commerce education in the last decade, the education system has undergone a structural evolution in many countries. Taking the U.S. as an example, by February 2001, 15 schools offered master programs in e-business related majors, 39 schools issued master's degrees with a concentration in e-business, 17 schools had certificate programs in e-commerce, and seven schools furnished undergraduate programs in e-business (Krovi & Vijayaraman, 2001). In fact, e-commerce courses or the courses covering issues in e-commerce are common in colleges in the U.S. and Europe.

E-commerce education also has developed rapidly in China during the recent years, owing to the booming e-businesses with an explosively growing participant population connected by constantly expanding Internet capacity. By July 2003, the number of Internet users in China reached 68 million, ranked as the second largest in the world next to the U.S. (UNCTAD, 2002). The popularization of the Internet in China, which is reinforced by the ubiquitous wireless network, provides huge e-commerce opportunities for China as well as the world. To further promote e-commerce, China has drawn an ambitious e-commerce education plan for its 1.3 billion people. Since 2000, various e-commerce programs have been established in many Chinese universities.[1]

According to a citation in *People's Daily* (2003), the official Chinese medium, there will be more than 2,000,000 e-commerce related positions to be filled in the next 10 years, while currently there are only about 100,000 staff members working in e-businesses. Specifically, the impacts of e-commerce on the education in China are not only in the aggregate demand for e-commerce professionals, but also in the content of the educational programs. Underpinned by Internet technology, e-commerce has actually made the marketplace more globally accessible. This, in turn, stimulates the need for the education of e-commerce in all areas of business administration information systems and technology, management, marketing, finance, organizational design, and so forth with the increasing requests for the knowledge of different political, economic, and cultural systems (Hromadka, 2000).

Currently, China's education system is confronted with increasing pressures from internationalized e-businesses. Consequently, issues arise: could the current education system and e-commerce programs accord well with what schools have committed? What are the key strategies for coping with the challenges from global e-commerce empowered by fast updated information technologies? This paper is intended to tackle these two questions based on the investigation of the factors driving e-commerce education in China. The organization of this paper is as follows: section 2 discusses the driving forces of e-commerce education in China; section 3 presents an overall picture of China's e-commerce education; section 4 analyzes the internal problems; finally, a number of strategic suggestions are proposed in section 5 as the concluding remarks.

Driving Forces of E-Commerce Education in China

E-Commerce Education Research

So far, e-commerce education research has been mostly case-oriented and commonly stressed curriculum design. A typical curriculum proposal for the graduate program in e-commerce is based on an e-commerce reference model composed of business level, customer-behavior level, and IT-resource level (Menascé, 2000). In general, e-commerce education is the extension of existing programs by adding extra courses. For example, Jenkins (2000) proposed that four courses with e-commerce concentration were needed in the program –(two required courses and two electives), whereas Cloete (2002) suggested that the course settings should conform to the nation's development. Therefore, it is understandable that e-commerce has been a specific program in many universities in China and provides curricula at different levels (Yang, 2003).

In comparison, relatively less research has been conducted regarding the impacts of social, economic and cultural factors on the curriculum of e-commerce. Words on the driving forces of e-commerce education are sporadic and non-methodical. They mostly ascribe the impetus for rapid growth of e-commerce. In an early explanation of changing diverse in education, Williams (1999) classified e-commerce as the technology pull. Jenkins (2000) broadened the meaning of e-commerce and deemed the growing demand for employees with knowledge in e-commerce derived by the expanding e-commerce as the main cause of e-commerce education. Cloete (2002) added the complexity of the multi-disciplinary nature of e-commerce. Fortunately, in the context of China there is a richer literature in discussing the influential factors of e-commerce, which may explain the fast-growing demand for e-commerce education (Foster, 2001; Tan & Oyang, 2002; Turban, 1999). Turban (1999) classified these influential factors into three levels of pressure: market and economic, societal and environmental, and technological. Forster (2001) put the factors affecting the adoption of e-commerce in China into four dimensions: top-down, bottom-up, globalization and cultural. Tan and Oyang (2002) explored multifold environmental factors that could facilitate or retard e-commerce diffusion in China from the aspects of national environment and national policy. However, how these factors will affect e-commerce education still remains untouched.

A Four-Layer Conceptual Model for E-Commerce Education

In light of these research outcomes, we sketch a four-layer conceptual model to illustrate what affects the evolution of e-commerce education and how this mechanism works (Figure 1). Within the surrounding social, economic, and cultural environment, we identify the relevant factors influencing the adoption and growth of e-commerce, which further pushes forward e-commerce education (Figure 1). There are four main factors in the model: economic globalization, domestic economic growth, IT advancement, and government promotional interventions. These factors influence the growth of e-commerce, which can further push forward e-commerce education. The four angles are applicable to both e-commerce and e-commerce education.

Economic Globalization

Since China started its economic reformation a quarter of a century ago, its economic system has been progressively migrated to suit the globalizing world economy. Inevitably, the booming e-commerce worldwide exerts critical influence on China's domestic market evolution. Gartner Group (ECTSC, 2001) reported that worldwide e-commerce sales were U.S. $953 billion in 2000, and that the figure was predicted to be U.S. $5.95 trillion in 2004. According to a survey conducted by the U.S. Department of Commerce (2003), retail e-commerce sales (B-to-C) in America increased to $12.5 billion in the second quarter of 2003, up 27.8% from the previous year. E-commerce development in China appears to be highly correlated with a sales

Figure 1. A conceptual model of driving forces for e-commerce education

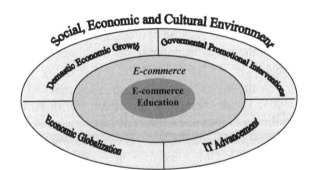

Figure 2. E-commerce growth in China (Source: China E-Commerce Year Book, 2002 & 2003)

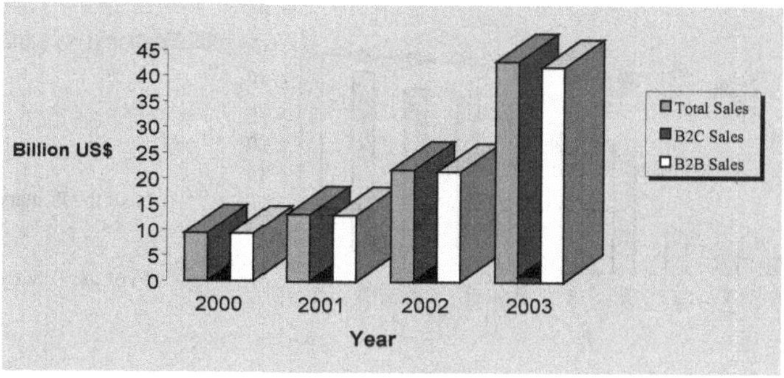

value of U.S. $9.33 billion[2] in 2000 and a prospected target of U.S. $43 billion in 2003 (Figure 2). Meanwhile, being a member of WTO also leads to a more rapid growth of e-commerce, especially when China dedicated itself to lowering tariff rates, deregulating previously protected industries, and enhancing overall market competition during these years.

Accordingly, more and more Chinese enterprises involved in e-businesses are facing challenges in complying with international business laws and conventions. They need to compete with those experienced rivals in the worldwide marketplace. So, the demand for e-commerce professionals is increasing rapidly with the qualification requirements in international businesses, particularly the advanced concepts in e-commerce due to the globalization trend of China's economy.

Domestic Economic Growth

The development of e-commerce in China has been accelerated by its booming economy. In recent years, China has been enjoying an average rate of 8% in economic growth. At the end of 2001, China's GDP reached U.S. $1,160 billion, which is U.S. $912.1 per capita (Figure 3). Meanwhile, the structure of GDP regarding different industries has changed greatly, with the primary industry declining and the tertiary industry increasing significantly[3] (China National Bureau of Statistics, 2002a). Undoubtedly, Chinese enterprises have to speed up their pace by adopting the cutting-edge information technologies and the advanced managerial ideas in e-businesses in order to be more competitive in the market. The reported consecutive investment of U.S. $3.26 billion each year in IT applications since 1996 by China's banking industry is strong evidence (CCID, 2003). Therefore, the demand of e-commerce education driven by China's domestic economy comes from Chinese enterprises in two aspects: to participate in the e-commerce in maintaining sustained business growth and to survive the more competitive marketplace.

Figure 3. China's economy growth

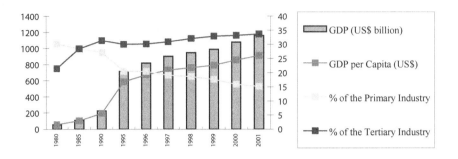

IT Advancement

The increasing capacity of telecommunication infrastructures and the popularization of IT applications in China, particularly in the last decade, have refueled the growth of e-commerce. In 1995, long-distance, local and mobile phone systems totaled an exchange capacity of 3.52 million routes, 72.04 million units and 7.97 million users. With an average year growth rate of 12.53%, 19.24% and 60.20% respectively, the capacity of telephone services increased to 7.04 million routes, 205.70 million units, and 219.26 million users by the end of 2001 (China National Bureau of Statistics, 2002b). In 2000, with its two-digit growth rate, China's IT industry revenue reached almost U.S. $56.38 billion with attributions of U.S. $22.7 billion from hardware, U.S. $2.87 billion from software, and U.S. $3.88 billion from services (ITU, 2001). By the end of 2000, computer holders per 100 capita had improved to 2.32. Telephone and mobile phone holders also reached a level of 20.10 and 6.77 (China National Bureau of Statistics, 2002c). Figure 4 shows the upward changing curves of these indicators.

Figure 4. IT adoption in China

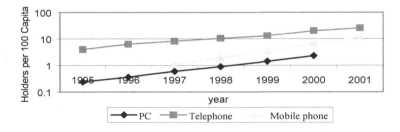

IT factors promoting e-commerce education generally can be summarized into two aspects: the improved public information infrastructures and the increasing investment in e-commerce education. In 1995, CERNET (China Education and Research Network), the Chinese government-sponsored Internet for academic services was put into use. By the end of 2001, a 20,000-kilometer DWDM/SDH communication network covering more than 30 central cities were in operation. Currently, the backbone capacity of CERNET reaches 40Gbps, and the internal user population is more than 8,000,000. CERNET provides free access to the Internet for colleges in China and has become an important facility for e-commerce education. Since the late 1990s, most colleges in China have connected their campus network to the Internet via CERNET (CERNET, 2001).

Government's Promotional Interventions

In order to improve the institutional infrastructures of e-commerce and e-commerce education, the Chinese central government and local governments have been issuing laws and regulations successively. They also sponsored financially some key academic projects, which greatly benefited e-commerce education. For example, in the first stage of the "211" Project, a core project to cultivate 100 top Chinese universities in the 21st century and carried out _from 1995 to 2000, the central government devoted U.S. $443.37 million in public service system constructions and U.S. $120.48 million in basic infrastructures for selected Chinese universities (China Ministry of Education, 2001b). In the "985" Project, another academic project started in May 1998, a total of U.S. $2,656.59 was invested jointly by central and local governments in China to support the efforts of some key Chinese universities in entering the top tier in the world (Yang, 2003).

In addition, the adoption of e-government in China has further strengthened the demand for e-commerce education. Launched in January 1999, China's "Government Online Project" involves most government agencies in a countrywide Internet-based application system. At the end of 2002, more than 7,200 governmental departments had set up Web sites and deployed some of their public services on the Internet (*http://www.gov.cn*). Because government employees with the required Internet application skills share the similar qualifications as those for e-commerce, the adoption of e-government in China will fuel the demand for e-commerce education.

Current Status of
E-Commerce Education in China

E-commerce education in China is carried out in three categories: regular collegiate education, continuing education and professional education. Usually, students of regular college education are those who have access to colleges after entrance examinations and intend to pursue academic degrees. The main form of continuing education programs is the Self-Taught with Certifying-Examination (STCE) program, available to those who have no means to study in colleges but have a desire for academic degrees. They either take classes in colleges or are self-taught and participate biannually in certification examinations for each course required for the enrolled program. An STCE student must pass all exams of certified courses to receive an associate or bachelor degree. Provincial governments normally administrate STCE programs, because most students in STCE programs are from the local or nearby area. Professional education mainly offers those who want to learn more practical skills for better job opportunities. It includes those professional retraining programs offered by all kinds of educational institutions in China. A qualified trainee will receive the certificate of the specific course that he or she has taken.

E-Commerce Education in Regular Colleges

E-commerce education in regular colleges in China has undergone four stages in the last eight years in accordance with the pace of Internet popularization since 1995.

Stage 1: Exploratory Stage

Inspired by the early claim of "making money on the Internet" in 1995, the exploration of e-commerce education in China was started mainly in universities. Since 1997, some universities have accordingly established e-commerce concentrations for Master's or PhD students.

Stage 2: Piloting Stage

As early as 1998, a number of electives or required e-commerce-related courses were developed in some universities. Before China's Ministry of Education formally issued the regulations for e-commerce program administration, some universities allowed students to choose e-commerce as a minor or second major based on these courses. A few leading universities even offered e-commerce concentration in MIS, economics, management, or computer science programs. E-commerce courses in different colleges also diversified concentrations at that time. Some emphasized business administration, while others focused more on technologies.

Stage 3: Formalizing Stage

The Ministry of Education approved 152 colleges to offer the e-commerce programs by the end of 2002. In the meantime, the Association of E-Commerce Curriculum for Chinese Colleges (AECCC), affiliated with the Ministry of Education, was founded to coordinate the e-commerce programs. In the First Workshop of AECCC held in Xi'an, Shaanxi, April 23-25, 2002, a goal was set to foster 100,000 college students and professionals in e-commerce during the next few years. The 1st and 2nd AECCC council meeting held recently proposed guidelines for e-commerce programs in nine topics[4]. In addition, the council suggested an annual training program for senior faculties and a biannual training for junior faculties in e-commerce education to further enhance the quality of e-commerce programs. Two such training sections were already held in 2002 and 2003.

Stage 4: Popularizing Stage

Currently, e-commerce education has been a hotspot in China, and many colleges are actively recruiting students. It is reported that over 10,000 bachelor and associate level students in the e-commerce major have graduated so far with 30,000 more in the school. As for master and doctoral graduates, the total number is no more than 1,000 (Li & Zhang, 2003). The replacement of these graduates has been in a wide spectrum, including government agencies, industries, colleges, or research institutes (Wang, 2002).

E-Commerce Continuing Education

STCE programs are the main form in China's continuing education. Since the commencement of the STCE program in 1983, the participating schools and students increased dramatically. At the very beginning, only a few public colleges offered the STCE education programs. However, STCE programs evolved significantly after years with the dominant involvements of private colleges because of their improved educational facilities and flexible curricula. In 1988, there were 40 private colleges nationwide, and the number rose to 880 in 1994 (China National Bureau of Statistics, 2001). The China Ministry of Education (2003) recently reported that there are now 1,202 private colleges in China. In 1983, there were only 64,757 registered students in the private colleges. The number rocketed to 6.89 million in 2000. By the end of 2001, the number of STCE students totaled 103.97 million, with 3.31 million graduates during the last 17 years. According to Yan (2002), there were 6.4 million STCE students registered for examinations in the first half of 2002, of which 41% were bachelor degree students and 59% were enrolled in the associate diploma program.

The pilot e-commerce programs for STCE students were established before any official regulations availed. The first regulation for e-commerce continuing education was issued on August 31, 2000. It was amended to define the assessments of student qualifications, including program contents, credit allocations and examination formats. By January 2003, more than 16 provinces, cities or autonomous regions out of 31 in China had established e-commerce programs of the associate level for STCE students, of which five co-offered bachelor programs. Currently, the e-commerce program of STCE offers curricula covering e-commerce basics (i.e., e-commerce overview, business laws for e-commerce), e-commerce-related technologies (i.e., computer and network technologies, Internet-based software application and planning, Web page designing), and e-commerce applications (i.e., e-commerce case study, online finance, e-commerce logistics, Internet marketing) (STCEC, 2000).

E-Commerce Professional Education

As e-commerce education is becoming popular in China, an increasing number of Chinese organizations have launched training programs in e-commerce with certificates for trainees in different concentrations. In order to standardize retraining programs with required quality, the Occupational Appraisal Center (OAC), affiliated with the Ministry of Labor & Social Security (MLSS), has recently issued several important regulations for e-commerce education, defining the qualifications of e-commerce professionals on different levels, the formalities to apply the certificates for training centers, and the examination procedures. The regulations further urged ratification of professional training organizations and strict regulation of examinations in order to guarantee the quality of training programs. According to OAC (OAC, 2002), there are core courses: Fundamentals of E-Commerce, the Application of IT, Online Marketing and Electronic Market. Each course has a final test. Students must pass all four tests before they can take a national-level comprehensive exam in order to receive the certificate.

There are two forms of e-commerce professional training programs: on-site training and distance learning. On-site training is conducted by training centers and targeted at non-e-commerce professionals, who intend to gain the latest knowledge in e-commerce for businesses. The program is available to both full-time and part-time trainees. Distance learning e-commerce programs are specially designed for those who are practically involved in e-commerce activities. By visiting designated training Web sites, they can join learning procedures in virtual classrooms and take online tests. By the end of September 2003, more than 140 institutes in China were authorized to issue primary and assistant e-commerce professional certificates, and more are under the approval process (*http://www.chinact.org.cn*).

Problems and Challenges in China's E-commerce Education

Although great success has been achieved in e-commerce education in China, problems still exist in different categories. These problems can be generally classified in either quantity or quality aspects. Understanding the inner causes will help China further draw strategies in e-commerce education to achieve the long-term social and economic development goals.

Unfulfilled Demand for E-Commerce Education

According to previous discussions, we can see a big gap between the demand and supply of e-commerce professionals: the expected demand for e-commerce professionals in the next decade is 2,000,000 (i.e., an average 200,000 per year), while the number of students enrolled in different e-commerce programs is 50,000. If taking into account the number of students in other relevant programs that can be enhanced to meet the demand from the e-commerce job market, the total number of professionals from different e-commerce programs each year in China is about 130,000. It is obvious that the supply of e-commerce professionals is far below the demand. An evident cause for this deficiency is that the majority of Chinese colleges either does not have e-commerce programs or does not offer proper e-commerce courses to complement other relevant programs.

Presently, there are more than 2,598 public and private colleges in China (China Ministry of Education, 2002). However, no more than 400 colleges, 15.4% of the total, have established e-commerce-related programs. After adding those who have opened e-commerce-related courses or set special focus on e-business, the total number is still fewer than 800. Presumably, we could ascribe the solution to the active participation of more colleges in offering e-commerce programs. However, in depth, the main cause in supply side is that many colleges do not have sufficient teaching facilities for e-commerce programs, even though they are responsive to the structural changes of the job market.

E-commerce education is interdisciplinary and requires both theoretic study and practical skills training. One indispensable facility for e-commerce education is computer labs with Internet access. For a long time, China has emphasized the provision of experimental environment for science subjects and long overlooked that for business schools. Currently, there are no more than 20 computer labs for e-commerce programs in China with consecutive inputs surmounting U.S. $12 million. For small- and medium-sized colleges, including many private educational institutions, building a computer lab is to too much to be realistic. Although CERNET has greatly improved Internet access for many colleges in China, due to the limited budget, the small- and medium-sized educational institutions have to cooperate with off-campus Internet cafes, which are open to the public for profit-making purposes. Therefore, the insufficient network computing resources and the limited in-campus Internet access have become the major obstacles for many Chinese colleges to operate their e-commerce programs.

Inconsistent Quality Among E-Commerce Programs in Different Educational Institutions

Quality is another vital problem in China's e-commerce education. According to a survey based on the students in e-commerce-related programs, among the 575 undergraduate student respondents, 39.5% did not know what e-commerce is, and 68% could not tell how an e-business works; among the 38 postgraduate student respondents, 20% could not explain the process of any e-business (Zhang, 2000). It is still common that many graduates of e-commerce programs cannot fulfill employers' requirements in practical work, and many certified trainees from e-commerce retraining programs normally do not catch the essence of e-commerce due to the lack of systematic study (Song, 2002). E-commerce professionals familiar with international business laws and regulations are even fewer, as the report (Beijing Youth, 2003) indicated. Consequently, the existing e-commerce programs in China still do not suit what the market demands. Here are several causes for the undesirable quality problems in e-commerce education.

Lacking Enough Qualified Faculties

Many e-commerce institutions do not have enough qualified faculties for their newly established e-commerce programs. Most faculties involved in e-commerce programs were transferred from other programs and prepared their own e-commerce courses (Liang, 2002). Lacking the working experience in e-businesses and the understanding of the course contents, their teaching is normally ineffective. In order to save costs, continuing or professional education institutions even hired unqualified short-term lecturers; some of them were unqualified to teach the classes they were teaching. Although AECCC has started the training programs for e-commerce faculties, it may take several years to gradually improve the teaching quality.

Lacking Quality Textbooks

On the other hand, the overflow of low-quality textbooks for e-commerce courses worsens the problem. According to Chen (2003), there were more than 12 series of e-commerce textbooks, each of which contains, on average, six books for college students during 2000-2002. Since many textbooks were translated and edited from English versions, their contents could be quite obsolete due to the time lag. The situation of STCE or professional education is even worse, because some colleges may have adopted the same set of textbooks for several years to cope with the certificate examinations.

Lacking Advanced Research to Refuel E-Commerce Education

A good research in e-commerce will reinforce teaching with the latest e-business ideas. Realizing this, the Chinese government has increased the budget of Social Science Foundation to support more e-commerce research in Chinese colleges[5] (NPOPSS of China, 2003) and has highlighted Internet-based business administration as a preferential research area sponsored by China's National Natural Science Foundation (NNSFC, 2001). However, current e-commerce-related research in China (e.g., applied economic research) is still far behind that in developed countries[6]. In general, China has lagged behind the world in information systems (IS) research, the upper level of e-commerce research. For example, in the last five years, there has been no research paper from researchers in China accepted by the International Conference on Information Systems (ICIS), the top conference in information systems research, and no participants from any Chinese colleges in the conference during the same period (AIS, 2003).

In-Depth Analysis of the Problems

In general, the problems of e-commerce education can be attributed to systematic causations with an in-depth analysis.

Unfitness of Higher Education System to Advocated Market Economy

Although China has embraced the market economy for many years, the higher education system still does not suit the prospected market economy well. Among the three e-commerce education categories, professional education programs adapt to the job market demand the best, since the training programs usually last only several months and can frequently adjust in accordance with the training demands reflecting the status of the job market. In the other extreme, national higher education, the last fortress of the planned economy, is the most sluggish. Since 1995, the graduate replacement system has been transformed from government-planned uniform replacement to a market-oriented replacement mechanism. However, all matters regarding student enrollments, major establishments, and guideline settings are still planned by the government.

In China, the average higher education admission rate is still fairly low, wavering between 7% and 12% (Yang, 2003). The Ministry of Education prospected in its "Tenth Five Year Plan of National Education" that the admission rate was to be raised to 15% in 2005, and increased to 20% in 2010 (China Ministry of Education, 2001a). The excessive education demand makes the education system never in shortage of student candidates. Thus, colleges in China, whether public or private, seldom worry about student sources, accordingly overlooking the improvements of educational programs. For instance, graduates of STCE programs are normally less competitive in the job market because of their lower qualifications, compared to those who graduate from regular colleges, whereas the STCE programs are seldom adjusted_accordingly, since they always have enough applicants.

So far, there is still plenty of incompleteness and inconsistency in China's education system with the ongoing reformation. Course selection is a typical example. In China, the majority of the schools restrict students from taking courses offered on their own, discouraging students from acquiring more comprehensive knowledge from other sources. Typically, students in e-commerce programs in the college of business administration are not allowed to take courses in computer science in the college of natural science, even though the latter might cover more advanced contents in technology.

Insufficient Budget in Education

Generally speaking, the quality of education and research in colleges is positively related to the available financial resources. In China, the general education outlay is rather small. Although in 2000, the national fiscal budget of education increased from U.S. $22.52 billion in 1997 to U.S. $30.99 billion, its percentage in GDP and fiscal expenditure stood only at 2.87% and 13.8%, respectively (China Ministry of Education, 2002). In 2000, the overall higher education outlay was U.S. $11.89 billion, 6.18% of the national fiscal expenditure (China National Bureau of Statistics, 2002d). Taking into account the population, the input to higher education in China is far lower than that in developed countries. For example, in the U.S., the total expenditure of higher education was U.S. $42.6 billion in 1960, which is four times that of China 40 years later. The U.S. $277 billion for higher education in the U.S. in 2001 is certainly an astronomical figure compared to China (U.S. Census Bureau, 2003). Thus, the available funds for Chinese colleges to develop new programs, construct labs, and train faculties are rather small.

Concluding Remarks

In this paper we analyzed the driving forces of e-commerce education in China, presented its current status, and discussed the major problems regarding the quantity and quality of e-commerce education in meeting the job market requirements. The proposed four-layer model indicated that the demand of e-commerce education was the consequence of fast growing e-commerce, which was driven by four factors: government intervention, economy globalization, domestic economy growth, and IT advancement. From the system point of view, government promotional intervention is a controllable factor when contrasted to the other three. Hence, the Chinese government should take into account the other three factors in order to choose proper actions to promote e-commerce education and, in turn, benefit the e-commerce industry as well as the whole economy. In another aspect, to maintain an innovative e-commerce program, an educational institution must investigate the trend of four driving forces and their effects on e-commerce evolution and, thereafter, make proper decisions.

In order to help e-commerce education in China keep pace with the economy growth, we need to clarify several strategic issues with the guidance of the four-layer model. Although the following three perspectives are based on China's case, we claim that the main ideas are applicable for other developing countries.

Intervention of Government: A Necessity in Driving E-Commerce Education in China

Government interventions, such as issuing legislative regulations, drawing promotional policies, and providing subsidies in research and educational projects, are critical to e-commerce education in China. First, the government plays a key role in education reformation that will guarantee the sustainable and healthy growth of e-commerce education. Although China has achieved great success in education system reformation, the problems in current e-commerce education indicate that China's education system still needs major improvements in order to adapt to the market economy. The top priority issue in the reformation agenda is to resolve the inconsistency between the college admission system and the replacement system. As the Chinese government has transformed the graduate replacement from a planned system into a market-oriented system, the government needs to step forward to de-regulate the centralized control of education program planning and allow all colleges to face the market. Second, the government needs to sponsor some non-governmental administrative facilities for the education system, which are particularly important in the process of the education system becoming market-oriented. For example, the government may encourage the establishment of non-profit organizations for educational programs that should be rather independent, but take over previous roles of the government in servicing educational program standardization and edu-cational institution accreditation in China. This semi-official form of organization will match better the further transformations of the education system and reduce excessive governmental interventions.

Structure of E-Commerce Education System: Dedicated Programs vs. Add-Ons Programs

It is reasonable that China's e-commerce education has adopted an educational system with the coexistence of the dedicated e-commerce major and the exten-sions of e-commerce to relevant programs (i.e., add-on programs). E-commerce is considered an interdisciplinary and applied subject (China E-commerce Year Book, 2003). With a combination of economic, administrative, technological, and legal knowledge, those prospective graduates in e-commerce programs should have a solid theoretical background, a comprehensive understanding of administrative context of organizations in e-business, certain technical skills, and the ability to cope with the major demands off e-commerce professionals in the market. Mean-while, retraining in e-commerce is a necessity for both employers and employees. Though now in China, only a small percentage of working staff has participated in e-commerce professional retraining programs accredited by the Ministry of Labor and Social Security, the potential trainee population is still large. With the growing trend of high flexibility in the labor market, it is more the individuals responsibility to improve themselves than a company's responsibility to train their employees. Consequently, the demand for e-commerce retraining will be sustainable. Based on the above e-commerce education system structure, both the government and the involved institutions in different educational categories might conduct proper actions to take their piece of the pie.

The Effort by Educational Institutions: Original Impetus

Whatever the external environment, the most essential point for the healthy and effective evolution of e-commerce education is the persistent efforts by all kinds of educational practitioners: public and private colleges, STCE program operators, and professional training centers. When the market mechanism is becoming more coherent and complete, educational institutions of China, especially those public colleges that may have many legacy problems, must take proper strategies to adapt to the changing environment. First, they must keep pace with the education system reformation and become more market-oriented. With the improved market mechanism, keen insights and fast responses with regard to environmental changes are of vital importance to educational institutions to be successful in the more competitive education market. Second, they consequently must transform their internal administrative system to adapt to the changing external environment. This includes student's academic credit systems, public relations with the industry, the adjustments of educational programs, and so forth. The third is that faculty training must be a high priority. A good faculty team is the determining factor in quality education for e-commerce programs. Finally, we suggest that educational institutions must pay attention to the academic research relative to their long-term goals. Although colleges have different research agendas and interests, there is no doubt that e-commerce research will increase significantly in the future (Ngai & Wat, 2002). More effort in e-commerce research will certainly reinforce e-commerce education with good quality.

References

Association for Information Systems (AIS). (2003). *Future and past ICIS conferences*. Retrieved September 1, 2003, from http://www.aisnet.org/icisnet/conf.shtml

Beijing Youth. (2003). *Professionals knowledgeable of e-commerce as well as business laws are in a scarcity in China* [in Chinese]. Retrieved August 20, 2003, from http://www.chinaeclaw.com/readArticle.asp?id=889

Brin, D.W. (1999). More b-schools offer e-commerce programs. *Wall Street Journal Interactive Edition*. Retrieved May 12, 2002, from http://public.wsj.com/careers/resources/documents/19990816-brin.htm

CCID. (2003). *Banking informationization investment remains balanced*. Retrieved September 2, 2003, from http://industry.ccidnet.com/pub/disp/Article?columnID=5&articleID =46006&pageNO=1

CERNET. (2001). *CERNET development survey.* Retrieved August 20, 2003, from http://www.edu.cn/20010101/21582.shtml

Chen, D. (2003). E-commerce program construction [in Chinese]. In *China e-commerce yearbook* (p. 400). Beijing: China E-commerce Year Book Editing House.

China e-commerce yearbook. (2002, 2003). Beijing: China E-commerce Year Book Editing House.

China Ministry of Education. (2001a). *The 10th five year plan in national education.* Retrieved September 4, 2003, from http://info.edu.sinobnet.com/HTML/001/196.htm

China Ministry of Education. (2001b). *211 project achievements overview.* Retrieved August 4, 2003, from http://www.moe.gov.cn/gc/211/7.htm

China Ministry of Education. (2002). *Statistics of national education expenditure and budget: 1997-2000.* Retrieved July 4, 2003, from http://www.moe.edu.cn/jytouru/zlwenxian/

China Ministry of Education. (2003). *Basic education statistics of China in 2002.* Retrieved July 10, 2003, from http://www.moe.edu.cn/stat/tjgongbao/report_2002.doc

China National Bureau of Statistics. (2001). *China STCE education statistics 2000.* Beijing: China Statistics Press.

China National Bureau of Statistics. (2002a). *China industrial economic statistics 2002.* Beijing: China Statistics Press.

China National Bureau of Statistics. (2002b). *China's telecom capacity statistics: 1978-2001.* Beijing: China Statistics Press.

China National Bureau of Statistics. (2002c). *China telecom level statistics: 1995-2001.* Beijing: China Statistics Press.

China National Bureau of Statistics. (2002d). *Education finance statistics in China 2000.* Beijing: China Statistics Press.

Cloete, E. (2002). *The design of an e-commerce course for final year information systems students* [working paper]. Retrieved March 10, 2004, from general.rau.ac.za/infosci/www2002/Full_Papers/ Cloete%20E/Cloete_ eCommerce-Course.pdf

Electronic Commerce Task Force of Canada (ECTFC). (2001). *Worldwide b2b revenues 1998-2003.* Retrieved June 4, 2003, from http://www.e-com.ic.gc.ca/english/research/inter/interb2b/sld002.htm a slide

Foster, W.A. (2001). The diffusion of the Internet in China. *Dissertation Abstracts Ondisc* (UMI microform 3010214).

Gong, L. (2001). Research methodology and focus of economics in China [in Chinese]. *Economic Research, 8,* 26-29.

Hromadka, E. (2000). E-curriculum? How are Indiana business schools teaching e-business? *Indiana Business Magazine, 44*(2), 55-61.

International Telecommunication Union. (2001). *Yearbook of statistics 1991-2000.* Geneva: ITU.

Jenkins, A. (2000). Meeting the need for e-commerce and e-business education: Creating a global electronic commerce concentration in the masters of business administration (MBA) program. *Communications for the Association of Information Systems.*

Krovi, R., & Vijayaraman, B.S. (2001). E-commerce content in business school curriculum: Opportunities and challenges. *Internet and Higher Education, 3,* 153-160.

Li, Q., & Zhang, X. (2003). An overview of e-commerce major programs in higher education of China [in Chinese]. *Computer Education,* 31-33.

Liang, C. (2002). *Concerns on e-commerce professionals* [in Chinese]. Retrieved June 26, 2003, from http://www. blogchina.com/new/display/1775.html

Menascé, D.A. (2000). A reference model for designing a curriculum for e-commerce. *IEEE Concurrency.*

National Natural Science Foundation of China. (2001). *The preferential support sphere of administration science* [in Chinese]. Retrieved August 4, 2003, from http://www.nsfc.gov.cn/nsfc/cen/00/kxb/gl/glkx-105content.html

National Planning Office of Philosophy and Social Sciences. (2003). *The state social sciences fund support project 1999-2003* [in Chinese]. Retrieved August 4, 2003, from http://www.npopss-cn.gov.cn/planning/index.html

National Natural Science Foundation of China. (2001). *The Preferential Support Sphere of Administration Science.* Retrieved August 4, 2003 from http://www. nsfc.gov.cn/nsfc/cen/00/kxb/gl/glkx-105content.html. (in Chinese)

Ngai, E.W.T., & Wat, F.K.T. (2002). A literature review and classification of electronic commerce . *Information & Management, 39,* 415-429.

Occupational Appraisal Center (OAC). (2002). Memorandums on e-commerce professional training. Doc#: [2002]-18, approved by Ministry of Labor & Social Security Ministry on September 24, 2002. Retrieved from http://www. chinact.org.cn/jxzy/index.html

People's Daily. (2003). The passport for golden bowls [in Chinese]. Retrieved July 16, 2003, from http://www.people. com.cn/GB/paper447/10148/929507.html

Self-Taught Certifying-Examination Committee (STCEC). (2000). *Examination plan for self-taught students in the e-commerce program of higher-education.*

Doc#: [2000]-6, approved by Ministry of Education and issued on August 31, 2000. Retrieved from http://www.moe.edu.cn/wreports/

Song, L. (2002). *E-commerce and professionals training* [in Chinese]. *Internet World*. Retrieved September 2, 2003, from http://www.e-works.net.cn/ewkArticles/Category76/Article10619.htm

Tan, Z., & Oyang, W. (2002). Globalization and e-commerce I: Factors affecting e-commerce diffusion in China. *Communications of the Association for Information Systems, 10*, 4-32.

Turban. (1999). Ecommerce driving forces. In M. Greenstein, & T.M. Feinman, (Eds.), *Electronic commerce: Security, risk management and control*. Beijing: Mechanical Industry Publishing House.

UNCTAD. (2002). *E-commerce and development report: New York and Geneva*. Retrieved May 4, 2003, from http://www.unctad.org/en/docs/ecdr2002summary_en.pdf

U.S. Census Bureau. (2003). *Section 4: Education. Statistical abstract of the United States 2002*. Retrieved August 15, 2003, from http://www.census.gov/prod/www/statistical-abstract-02.html

U.S. Department of Commerce. (2003). *Retail e-commerce sales in second quarter 2003 were $12.5 billion, up 27.8 percent from second quarter 2002*. Retrieved September 24, 2003, from http://www.census.gov/mrts/www/current.html

Wang, X. (2002). Research on e-commerce intellectuals training system in China [in Chinese]. *Books Information & Knowledge 3*, 36-42.

Williams, J.R. (1999). *E-commerce and e-education*. Retrieved March 10, 2004, from http://www.webecon.bris.ac.uk/toolbook/ download/tb99/JWKeynote. PDF

Yan, J.L. (2002). *STCE students: Associate level lowers and bachelor degree uprises* [in Chinese]. Retrieved June 1, 2003, from http://www.edu.cn/20020527/3057295.shtml

Yang, C. (2003). Curriculum designing in e-commerce program [in Chinese]. *Journal of China Women's College, 15*, 70-72.

Yang, X. (2003). The development of higher education in China [in Chinese]. *World Education Outlook 12*, 21-26.

Zhang, D. (2000). How students See see e-commerce: A survey in colleges [in Chinese]. *China Computer and Communication, 2*,41.

Endnotes

[1]   In China, there are comprehensive universities as well as colleges emphasizing a specific field. Here in this paper, we normally call them colleges for convenience, excluding a few exceptions with peculiar meaning.

[2]   Throughout the paper, the exchange rate of U.S. dollar and Chinese RMB is 1: 8.27.

[3]   The primary industry refers to extraction of natural resources; the secondary industry involves processing of primary products; and the tertiary industry provides services of various kinds for production and consumption. This classification is universal, although it varies to some extent form country to country.

[4]   They are E-Commerce Overview and Projects Designing, E-Commerce Economics, Internet Marketing, E-Commerce Management, Online Payment and Settlement, E-Commerce Logistics, E-Commerce System Construction and Administration, E-Commerce Technology, and Business Laws for E-Commerce.

[5]   Referring to the facts in the College of Economic and Financial, Xi'an Jiaotong University, the figure is estimated from the approximate capacity of educational institutions offering e-commerce education programs. On average, every year, 60 e-commerce students will graduate from each of the 152 Chinese universities that are offering different levels of degrees in e-commerce, and each of the 140 professional educational institutions may issue 200 e-commerce professional certificates in the same period. We further assume that 10 e-commerce students will graduate from each of the 1,202 private colleges. Then, the total number of e-commerce professionals entering the job market from the three sources is 152*60+140*200+1202 *10=49,140. The figure can be approximated at 50,000.

[6]   Two projects in e-commerce were granted in 1999, and more than twenties 20 in the same category were granted in 2003.

[7]   In a high level forum of Chinese economists held in June 2001, many economists addressed the great deficiency in economic research methodologies (Gong, 2001).

The chapter was previously published in the Journal of Electronic Commerce in Organizations, 3(3), 1-17, 2005.

About the Editor

Mehdi Khosrow-Pour, DBA, is the executive director of the Information Resources Management Association (IRMA) and senior academic editor for Idea Group Reference. He previously served on the faculty of The Pennsylvania State University as an associate professor of information systems for 20 years. He has written or edited over 20 books in information technology management, and he is also the editor of the *Information Resources Management Journal, Journal of Electronic Commerce in Organizations, Journal of Cases on Information Technology*, and *International Journal of Cases on Electronic Commerce.*

About the Authors

Noushin Ashrafi is a professor of information systems and chair of the executive committee of the Faculty Council at the University of Massachusetts Boston. Dr. Ashrafi received her PhD from the University of Texas at Arlington. Her area of research includes software process improvement, application of mathematical models to assess fault tolerance in software, and privacy issues in electronic commerce. Her publications have appeared in journals such as *IEEE Transactions, Information and Management, Journal of Electronic Commerce in Organizations*, and *Journal of Database Management*. Dr. Ashrafi has made presentations on various topics of information systems at national and international conferences.

David Barnes is a senior lecturer in operations and strategic management at Royal Holloway University of London. His research interests centre on the strategic management of operations and the impact of e-business on operations. Prior to his academic career he worked in the process plant contracting and building products manufacturing industries, in engineering and line management positions for a number of organizations ranging from blue chip to small family owned businesses. He holds a BSc (English) from Imperial College London, an MBA from the Open University and a PhD from Staffordshire University.

Raquel Benbunan-Fich is an associate professor in the Computer Information Systems Department at the Zicklin School of Business, Baruch College, CUNY. She received her PhD in MIS from Rutgers University (1997). Her research interests include issues on e-commerce, evaluation of Web-based systems, group collaboration and computer-mediated communication systems. She has published articles on related topics in *Communications of the ACM, Decision Support Systems, Group Decision and Negotiation, IEEE Transactions on Professional Communication, Information & Management, International Journal of Electronic Commerce, Journal of Electronic Commerce in Organizations* and other journals.

Ong Chin Eang is a lecturer at Monash University, Malaysia, with a specialty in e-commerce. He has a bachelor's degree in logistics and transportation management, a postgraduate diploma in business systems and a master's degree in business information technology from RMIT (Royal Melbourne Institute of Technology) University, Melbourne, Australia. He obtained his postgraduate certificate in higher education and is currently conducting doctoral research on trust and redress mechanism in B2C e-commerce context with Monash University. His doctoral research examines methods that enables the used of these redress mechanisms to its jurisdictions in cross border disputes without compromising the benefits and trust between businesses and consumers.

Nikhilesh Dholakia is professor in the Marketing, E-Commerce, and International Business areas at the College of Business Administration, University of Rhode Island, USA. He has published extensively in various international journals in the fields of marketing and technology, telecommunications, e-commerce, and m-commerce. His latest edited book is *M-Commerce: Global Experiences and Perspectives* (Idea Group Publishing, 2006).

Henry H. Emurian is an associate professor of IS at UMBC. He is a licensed psychologist in Maryland, and he is interested in exploring the applications of information technology to education, health, and public service. He has published in *The Journal of the Experimental Analysis of Behavior, Journal of E-Commerce in Organizations, Computers in Human Behavior, International Journal of Distance Education Technology*, and *The International Journal of Information Technology and Communication Education*. His editorials have appeared in the *Information Resources Management Journal*. He is a member of the American Psychological Association, IRMA, and the Association for Behavior Analysis.

Eliezer M. Fich is in the Department of Finance at the LeBow College of Business, Drexel University. He received his PhD (Hons.) from the NYU Stern School of Business in 2000. His research interests include corporate governance, merger and acquisitions and electronic commerce. His research has been published in the *Journal of Finance, Journal of Business, Journal of Corporate Finance, Journal of*

Electronic Commerce in Organizations, International Journal of Electronic Commerce and other journals.

Jing Gao is currently working as a full-time research fellow/lecturer for the school of computer and information science at the University of South Australia. He has also been working as a professional trainer/consultant for many Australian leading organizations including the Defence Science and Technology Organisation (DSTO) of Australia, SA water, etc. His research interest is about how to obtain an alternative view to appreciate complex social and technical problems.

David Gefen is an associate professor of MIS at Drexel, where he teaches strategic management of IT, database analysis and design, and VB.NET. He received his PhD from GSU and a master's degree from Tel-Aviv. His research focuses on psychological and rational processes in IT implementation which stem from 12 years developing and managing large IT projects. His research findings are published in *MISQ, ISR, IEEE TEM, JMIS,* among others. David is SE at *DATABASE* and a VB.NET textbook author.

Matthew Hinton is a senior lecturer in information and knowledge management at the Open University Business School. His research interests include the impact of electronic commerce on operations and information technology evaluation, especially the performance management of e-business applications. In addition he is interested in the system implementation dynamics of customer relationship management (CRM) systems. He holds a PhD in innovation and technology assessment from Cranfield University and a BSc (Hons.) in business information technology from Kingston University. Prior to his academic role he worked in the petrochemicals industry providing computer support and IT training.

Soongoo Hong is an assistant professor at the Department of Management Information Systems at Dong-A University, Korea. He received his PhD in MIS in 2000 and a Mater of Arts in management in 1996 from the University of Nebraska–Lincoln. Prior to joining Dong-A University he was an assistant professor at Texas A&M International University. His research interests include electronic commerce, knowledge management, data warehousing, and IT impacts on organizations.

Tino Jahnke received his diploma in business information systems from the University of Cooperative Heidenheim, Germany, and his bachelor's degree from Open University, London (2001). He received his master's degree in advanced software technology from University Lueneburg, Germany and the University of Wolverhampton, UK (2005). Apart from his teaching experience in universities and different companies, Jahnke has been appointed to examine students in their diploma exams. Since 2001 he has been done research in digital watermarking technology, motion pictures and audio signals. Furthermore he has developed the knowledgebay e-learning framework and manages his own software company. Since 2005, he has been CEO of two companies specialized on the development of tools and products for the tourism industry in Germany, Poland and The Netherlands.

Salim Jiwa is a senior lecturer in international fashion marketing at the Department of Clothing Design and Technology, Manchester Metropolitan University. He is also project manager at the Retail Enterprise Network and quality and learning manager for the Retail Academy. Jiwa has an ongoing interest in the design development of management simulation games and virtual world contexts, and has previously presented and published papers on various aspects of simulation gaming design, student experience and pedagogy.

Pairin Katerattanakul is an assistant professor in the Department of Business Information Systems, Western Michigan University. He received his PhD in MIS in 2000 and Master of Arts in marketing in 1996 from the University of Nebraska–Lincoln. His research, focused on electronic business, marketing aspects of electronic commerce, enterprise systems, and management information systems, has been published in such journals as *Communications of the ACM, European Journal of Information Systems, Communications of the AIS*, and *INFOR.*

Jean-Pierre Kuilboer is an associate professor in information systems and chairman of the Management Science and Information Systems Department at the University of Massachusetts Boston. Dr. Kuilboer's current interests are in the area of business agility, electronic business, information security and privacy, and database management. He has published a book on e-business and e-commerce infrastructure and articles in such journals as the *Database for Advances in Information Systems, Journal of Database Management, Information & Management, Annals of Cases on Information Technology, Information and Software Technology, International Journal of E-business Research*, and *ACM – Computers and Society.*

Wing Lam is an associate professor at U21Global and MISM program director. He was previously at the National University of Singapore where he was a faculty member at the Institute of Systems Science. In addition to holding other academic positions in the UK, Dr. Lam has held consultancy positions with Logica-CMG, Fujitsu (formerly ICL) and Accenture (formerly Andersen Consulting). He has over 75 publications in peer-reviewed journals and conference proceedings. His work appears in the *European Journal of Information Systems, Journal of Knowl-*

edge Management and *Communications of the Association of Information Systems,* among others. Dr. Lam's current research interests include enterprise integration, knowledge management and software engineering management. Dr. Lam currently serves on the editorial review boards of the *Journal of E-Government* and *Online Information Review*. He has a PhD in computer science from Kings College, University of London.

Dawn Lavelle is a principle lecturer in retail management at the University of the Arts, London. She is also manager of the Centre of Vocational Excellence (COVE) in retailing. Lavelle has an ongoing interest in the design development of management simulation games and virtual world contexts, and has previously presented and published papers on various aspects of simulation gaming design, student experience and pedagogy.

In Lee is an associate professor in the Department of Information Management and Decision Sciences in the College of Business and Technology at Western Illinois University, USA. He received his MBA from the University of Texas at Austin and Ph.D. from University of Illinois at Urbana-Champaign. He is a founding editor-in-chief of the *International Journal of E-Business Research*, the primary objective of which is to provide an international forum for researchers and practitioners to advance the knowledge and practice of all facets of electronic business. He has been serving on the Executive Council of the Information Resources Management Association since 2003. He has published his research in such journals as *Communications of the ACM, IEEE Transactions on Systems, Man, and Cybernetics, IEEE Transactions on Engineering Management, Computers and Operations Research, Computers and Industrial Engineering, Business Process Management Journal, Journal of E-Commerce in Organizations*, and *International Journal of Simulation and Process Modeling*. His current research interests include e-commerce technology development and management, agent-oriented enterprise modeling, and intelligent simulation systems.

Sang M. Lee is the university eminent scholar, Regents distinguished university professor, and chair of the Management Department at the University of Nebraska–Lincoln. He has authored or co-authored 55 books, more than 200 journal articles, and has presented over 2,000 speeches. His current research interests include value networked organizations, interorganizational information systems, and new enterprise models. He is a fellow of the Academy of Management, Decision Sciences Institute, and Pan-Pacific Business Association. He has organized 27 international conferences as the program chair, is on the editorial board of 23 journals, and has received numerous honors including three honorary degrees.

Qi Li has a PhD in economics, is a professor of electronic commerce, and published *China Electronic Commerce* which was the first e-commerce book in China in 1997. Until now, more than 50 papers and over 10 books have been published, 20 projects accomplished, and one patent certified. There are 13 doctoral students and 22 postgraduates under his instruction. He is also the director or dean of the following organizations: vice-president of School of Economics and Finance, Xi'an Jiaotong University; E-Commerce Research Institute of Xi'an Jiaotong Uni (the first e-commerce research center in China); E-Commerce Commission of Chinese Information and Economics Association; The Coordination Group for the Establishment and Development of Electronic Business Specialty of China's Higher Education Institutes.

Zhangxi Lin, PhD, is an assistant professor with the Department of ISQS, Texas Tech University. Lin's research interests include online reputation, electronic commerce, IT strategy for China, and information economics. Lin acted as the member of Advisory Board for Digital Fujian since 2002, was a guest professor of Fujian Institute of Technology, has been affiliated as a senior researcher of the Network Research Center for CERNET since 1998, has been affiliated as an associate professor of the Computation Center of Tongji University since 1995and has published a large number of papers in international journals and conference proceedings.

Anil M. Pandya is an associate professor of marketing in the College of Business and Management, Northeastern Illinois University in Chicago, USA, and an adjunct professor of marketing in the College of Industrial Engineering and Management Science, Northwestern University in Evanston, Illinois. His scholarly research has appeared in the *Journal of Electronic Commerce and Organizations, European Journal of Marketing, Journal of Finance and Strategy, Research in Marketing*, and *Journal of Macromarketing*.

Paul A. Pavlou is an assistant professor of IS at the University of California at Riverside. He received his PhD from the University of Southern California in 2004. His research focuses on information systems strategy in turbulent environments and institutional trust building in electronic commerce and online marketplaces. His research has appeared in *MIS Quarterly, Information Systems Research, Journal of the Academy of Marketing Science, Journal of the Association of Information Systems, International Journal of Electronic Commerce,* and *Journal of Strategic Information Systems*, among others. His research has been cited over 400 times in Google Scholar and over 150 times in the Institute of Scientific Information (ISI). Pavlou received the 2003 *MIS Quarterly* 'Reviewer of the Year' award, and the 'Best Reviewer' award of the 2005 Academy of Management Conference (OCIS Division). He also won the 'Best Doctoral Dissertation Award' of the 2004 International Conference on Information Systems (ICIS).

Pauline Ratnasingam is an associate professor of MIS, Department of Computer Information Systems, Harmon School of Business Administration, Central Missouri State University (CMSU). Before joining CMSU, she was an assistant professor at the School of Business Administration, University of Vermont. She received her PhD titled "Inter-organizational Trust in Business to Business Electronic Commerce" from Erasmus University, Rotterdam School of Management, The Netherlands(2001). She lectured on topics such as project management, MIS, and e-Commerce in Australia, New Zealand, Europe and America. She is an associate member of the Association of Information Systems, and is a member of the Information Resources Management Association and Academy of Management. Her research interests include business risk management, Internet-based B2B e-Commerce, small business e-commerce adoption, security in knowledge management, and organizational behavior and trust. She is a recipient of a National Science Foundation Grant and has published several articles related to this area in national and international conferences, refereed journals and chapters in books. Her biography is also published in the 58th Edition of Marquis Who's Who – Who's Who in America.

Juergen Seitz received his diploma in business information systems from the University of Cooperative Education Stuttgart, Germany, and in economics from the University of Stuttgart-Hohenheim. He received his PhD from Viadrina European University, Frankfurt (Oder), Germany. He is a professor for business information systems and finance, and chair of business information systems, especially e-commerce/e-business and m-business/telematics, at the University of Cooperative Education Heidenheim, Germany.

Ye Diana Wang is a doctoral student of IS at the University of Maryland, Baltimore County (UMBC). In addition to research in online trust, her research interests include electronic commerce, information retrieval, and decision support. She has published in various journals including *Information Processing & Management*, *Computers in Human Behavior*, *Journal of Electronic Commerce in Organization*, and *International Journal of Healthcare Technology and Management*. She is a member of the American Society for Information Science and Technology, the Association for Information System, and the Information Resources Management Association.

Xianfeng Zhang is a PhD student in the School of Economics and Finances, Xi'an Jiaotong University. Zhang's research interests focus on trust building mechanism in the Internet environment, electronic commerce theories, and e-commerce education. In addition to those published in China, Zhang's papers have also been issued in such international conference proceedings as ICEC 2000, PACIS 2001, IRMA 2002, ECIS2003 and so on.

Index

A

absence of "touch and feel" 114
absence of leading discussions 127
access 3, 4, 192
access to markets 65
action learning 141
adaptation 165
adapted presence questionnaire (PQ) 165
add-ons programs 329
administration panel 152
adopting e-commerce 103
adoption of e-business 8
American National Standards Institute
      (ANSI X12) standard 262
analysis 195
applicant tracking management subsystem
      235, 248
applications for e-business 276
application of netrepreneur 154
application of new knowledge 217
architecture of the Internet 210
ATM banking 65
attack scenarios on digital watermarks 282
Australian manufacturing 103
Australian manufacturing industry 106
Australian newspapers 102

authentication mechanisms 264
automated response systems 5

B

"B2B exchanges" 260
"brick-and-mortars" 189
B2B commerce 211
B2B e-commerce 127
B2B interactions 201
B2B marketplaces 260
B2C-commerce 211
B2C businesses 61
B2C dot-coms 169
B2C e-commerce 42, 62, 170
B2C e-commerce failure 171
B2C failures 172
B2C interactions 201
B2C market crash 171
B2C problem 171
B2C retailing 61, 65, 69
B2C retailing services 64
B2C retail methods 183
B2C retail service quality 67
B2C settings 170
B2C start-ups 178
B2C Systemic Connections 70

customer need 179
customer relationship management (CRM)
    systems 5, 189, 209
customer services 6, 10, 89
customer service encounter 2
customer service operations 1, 2, 15
cyber-trust 209
cybernetic service encounters or e-encoun-
    ters 65

D

"discordant" perceptions 169
DaimlerChrysler 252
database management subsystem 236, 252
Data Collection 116, 195
Data gathering 6
debt collection 12
Decision Support E-Recruiting System
    244
Dedicated Programs 329
Delivery 214
Demographic Characteristics 85
Demographic subgroups 85
demonstrations, 89
Descriptive Statistics 293, 294
Designs Supporting Business Transactions
    301
Designs Supporting Pleasure 300
Design Issues 225
Design of MBA650 E-Business 209
Development of an Online Course 206
development of e-commerce 49
Development of Realism 137
Digital Age 276
Digital Media Types 277
digital representation of multimedia docu-
    ments 277
digital rights management (DRM) 278
digital signal 276
Digital Watermarking 276, 279
Digital Watermarking Classification 281
Digital Watermarking Procedure 280
Digital Watermarking requirements 281
digital watermarking techniques 276
dis-embedding 87
Domestic Economic Growth 318

Dominant Thinking 126
dot-com 10
dot-com B2C ventures 169
dot-com bust 169
dot-com crash 62
Dot-Com Failures 61
Driving Forces 314
driving forces for e-commerce education
    317
Driving Forces of E-Commerce Education
    in China 316
DVD-video 277

E

e-Accounting 10, 13
e-business 2, 15, 206, 207, 259, 314
E-Business Course Design 225
e-business in customer service 13
E-business in industry 210
E-business leadership 211
e-business models 209
E-business outsourcing 210
E-business strategy 209
E-business transactions 3
e-commerce 43, 75, 103, 211, 235
e-commerce announcements 20
e-commerce applications 236
E-Commerce Continuing Education 322
E-Commerce Directive 50, 53
E-Commerce Education 314, 317, 326
E-Commerce Education in China 321, 328
E-Commerce Education in Regular Col-
    leges 321
E-Commerce Education Research 316
E-Commerce Environment 146
E-commerce growth in China 318
e-commerce initiative 20
e-commerce initiatives in Australia 102
E-Commerce in Australian Manufacturing
    102, 107
e-commerce in functional areas 107
E-Commerce in Manufacturing 107, 108
E-commerce jurisdiction 42
E-Commerce Professional Education 323
e-commerce programs 315
e-commerce revolution 236

K

L

M

N

O